DEFENSE AND RESISTANCE

Historical Perspectives and Current Concepts

EDITED BY

Harold P. Blum, M.D.

INTERNATIONAL UNIVERSITIES PRESS, INC.

New York

Library of Congress Cataloging-in-Publication Data
Main entry under title:

Defense and Resistance.

  Includes bibliographies and index.
  1. Defense mechanisms (Psychology) 2. Resistance
(Psychoanalysis) 3. Ego (Psychology) 4. Psychoanalysis.
5. Freud, Anna, 1895-   . Ich und die Abwehrmechanis-
men. I. Blum, Harold P., 1929   . [DNLM: 1. Defense
Mechanisms. WM 193 D313]
BF175.5.D44D44 1985   150.19′5   85-18028
ISBN 0-8236-1157-4

Manufactured in the United States of America

CONTENTS

DEFENSE AND RESISTANCE

*Historical Perspectives
and Current Concepts*

FOREWORD   Harold P. Blum, m.d.

T HE CONCEPT OF DEFENSE IS PART OF THE CORE of psychoanalysis. As early as 1896, Freud alluded to the psychical
process of "defense" or "repression." The use of the term defense was soon temporarily suspended and replaced by repression, which was a specific and central defense mechanism and,
at the same time, a rather general synonym for defense. So
important was the concept of defense that even during the so-
called id phase of psychoanalysis, Freud (1914) had actually
declared, "The theory of repression is the corner-stone on
which the whole structure of psycho-analysis rests. It is the most
essential part of it . . ." (p. 16). The relation of repression to
analytic resistance followed immediately thereafter, in the same
paragraph, culminating in the characterization of psychoanalysis in terms of the phenomena of transference and resistance.
The concept of defense and the parallel concept of resistance
are fundamental to the evolution of psychoanalytic thought and
intrinsic to the theory of technique. The importance of defense
was elucidated in numerous theoretical papers, derived afresh
and clinically illustrated in the case histories and other clinical
examples. Gradually distinguished from related formulations
of censorship and distortion, defense was differentiated from
a global concept to include a number of different defense mechanisms. Freud (1926) then noted the advantages of the old
concept of defense, "provided we employ it explicitly as a general designation for all the techniques which the ego makes use
of in conflicts which may lead to a neurosis, while we retain the
word 'repression' for the special method of defence which the

5

line of approach taken by our investigations made us better acquainted with in the first instance" (p. 163). In addition to differentiating the defenses, Freud (1926) simultaneously reformulated conflict and anxiety, describing the danger situations and the efforts of the ego to cope with the danger.

This became a starting point for Anna Freud's (1936) classic contribution, *The Ego and the Mechanisms of Defense*. She chose to investigate the specific defenses, their modes of operation, their role in normal and pathological development, their relation to specific forms of illness, their hierarchical organization, and their relation to developmental phases along with their infuence on development. Beyond quantitative factors and the balance of forces, there was new interest in the choice of defense and the nature of conflict and compromise formation, the interaction and influence of defense on other ego functions. Her work on defense was an original and far-reaching study which transcended the concept of defense and had a major influence on the subsequent evolution of psychoanalytic theory and technique. Her work was crucial to the larger study of ego functioning and to ego analysis. The ego integrated the demands of the id, superego, and external reality, and the analyst was to take a neutral position equidistant from the tripartite structures in interpreting the patient's material. Structural and developmental theory were correlated with dynamics.

To the nine familiar mechanisms of defense Anna Freud modestly stated had been exhaustively described in the theoretical writings of psychoanalysis (regression, repression, reaction formation, isolation, undoing, projection, introjection, turning against the self, and reversal), she added a normal tenth mechanism—sublimation. The introduction of sublimation was a bridge to studies of the nondefensive functions of the ego and to developmental achievement. Sublimation followed from defensive transformation of instinctual aims and goals, but ego and superego goals were attained. At the same time, the focus on ego defense and on sublimation as defense competed and conflicted with studies of nondefensive ego functions. Defense

was not static or necessarily pathogenic, but also served adaptive, protective functions. Anna Freud's investigations of ego defenses and Hartmann's investigations of autonomous ego functions were confluent, complementary, and in conflict. The concept of ego autonomy was regarded by many analysts as a theoretical advance, but others considered it a resistance to the centrality of conflict and defense in psychoanalysis. Sublimation and secondary autonomy were interrelated terms, but they also had different meanings and applications.

Anna Freud traced the path from precursors of defense to sublimation, with a change of function. She noted the special importance of repression in normal development, pathology, and defense organization. Repression was assigned a unique position among the defense mechanisms. She followed Freud in regarding repression as the central defense mechanism for coping with internal danger situations, with other defenses rather allied, subordinate, and supplementary once repression was available. Repression was largely responsible for infantile amnesia, and a potential danger to other ego functions when it was over- or underutilized. Repressions were essentially made in early childhood, and analytic treatment corrects the original repression. Much of the repressed was never in conscious awareness, and there was a core of primal infantile repression.

The level of ego development necessary for active ego use of defense has not been precisely defined. While lifting repression and making the unconscious conscious are still analytic goals, currently the recovery of childhood memories is subsumed in a wider context of transference analysis, reconstruction, and reintegration. The analysis of repression resistance and the diverse derivatives of unconscious conflict in contemporary psychoanalysis is quite different from the analysis of the return of the repressed and prestructural notions of overcoming resistance and uncovering infantile amnesia.

Anna Freud actually added profound original studies of defense, which greatly influenced the psychoanalytic theory of technique, indeed all psychotherapeutic endeavor, and which

entered the general realm of intellectual discourse. She presented a clarifying exposition of denial in fantasy, play, word, and action. Her exposition of denial had been convergent, through attention to what was denied, to the increased interest given to reality and the object world in ego psychology. Denial of painful perceptions of external reality was different from defense against the internal instinctual drives, though denial operated with other interrelated defenses in a given defensive configuration. The sharp distinctions then drawn between externally and internally directed defense are still relatively valid but less clearly demarcated today. External reality has subjective and intersubjective attributes, and sociocultural modes influence the choice of defense (Erikson, 1950). Anna Freud's "objective anxiety" should not be shorn of subjective danger with id and superego as well as reality components in the evaluation of and response to danger. Her own exposition of denial included connections to intrapsychic conflict and danger and ranged from clinical discourse to folklore and literature. Today we are more inclined to distinguish among denying as not noting or perceiving, withdrawing attention and signification, disavowing what has been perceived, distorting and misperceiving, and isolating a percept from affective or contextual meaning, as in minimizing danger or anticipated adversity (also partial denial). This is not the same as, though often linked to, having conscious knowledge one chooses not to think about. Denial is sometimes used in relation to affective experience, but this is more likely to confuse definition than to extend explanation or application. Anna Freud (1936) noted that from a developmental viewpoint denial was a primitive mechanism, a prestage of defense, which itself develops in denial in word and fantasy. Denial may be pathological, adaptive (as other defenses), or both, depending on multiple functions, as in the denial of illness or death.

She first described and illustrated the complex defenses of identification with the aggressor and altruistic surrender, which have become familiar analytic concepts. Identification with the

aggressor, like repression, denial, and projection has become part of the terminology of psychiatry and psychology and has appeared in general discussions of such diverse topics as brainwashing, child abuse, and power politics. Identification with the aggressor is ubiquitous and universal in personality development and is important in mastery of trauma and superego formation. Defense contributes to superego development, then operates at the behest of the superego and may be turned against it.

Very recently, Anna Freud and Joseph Sandler undertook a review of *The Ego and the Mechanisms of Defense*, providing the rare opportunity for the author of a psychoanalytic classic to review her own work forty-five years later. Through their gracious permission, a representative distillate of their dialogue is presented to open the general discussion of contemporary views of defense and resistance. It was hoped that Anna Freud would also write a specific commentary for this publication. Alas, she was prevented from doing so by her serious illness, culminating in her death on October 9, 1982. Impoverished by her loss, we have, nevertheless, been left a monumental analytic legacy. The following papers, which were to have sampled the development of her ideas in later years and the current formulations of many other psychoanalytic investigators, now also serve as a scientific tribute to her pioneering contributions. Her work will doubtless be evaluated, extended, amplified, and modified in various directions. This publication serves not as a scientific summary or assessment of her lifelong work which so enormously stimulated and enriched child and adult analysis and which embraced child care, preventive care, and many related fields, but as a representation of her thought and vision and its interrelation with ongoing scientific activity and research.

The Ego and the Mechanisms of Defense is an exposition of intrapsychic defense mechanisms which are theoretical abstractions. These defense mechanisms are a special group of ego functions which operate automatically outside of awareness and are intrapsychic. They are inferred from defensive maneuvers,

strategies, or constellations employed by the patient as observable and describable phenomena. A defense mechanism serves
a protective function against an inner or outer danger situation.
The defense mechanisms employed in the defensive maneuver
or strategy are mobilized by anxiety (and it is now recognized,
also by other unpleasurable affects) and, in structural terms,
are used at the behest of the superego. A defensive mechanism
primarily serves opposing, restricting, or warding-off functions
and may be directed against drives, the superego, reality, or
other ego functions; defense is not static and may continue
against various derivatives of unconscious conflicts; defense
against symptoms and defense against defense have also been
recognized. Freud (1937) referred to "resistance against uncovering resistance"; similarly, what has been uncovered may
succumb again to repression.

The Defenses have been understood in terms of their relation
to consciousness from a topographic viewpoint and, indeed,
from all of the metapsychological frames of reference. While
a complex defensive configuration or method may represent
a compromise formation in structural terms, it is the role of the
defense mechanism and conflict that have primarily determined
their conceptualization and their dynamic centrality. Defenses
have also been classified according to their primary and preferred use; their complex interaction in a defensive configuration; simple versus complex, such as altruistic surrender;
precursors and precocious; developmental sequence with considerations of a defense mechanism as being more primitive or
more mature; likelihood of use against aggressive drive derivatives, e.g., undoing and reaction formation; strength and
power *vis-à-vis* opposing forces; developmental and reality-ap-
propriateness, e.g., extensive denial in fantasy and action has
a quite different significance in early childhood than in adulthood.

As is so often the case in psychoanalysis, problems abound
even where concepts such as defense seem to be taken for
granted. Analytic concepts themselves often go through an evo-

lution in which definitions expand and contract, new relations are established between concepts, new concepts are introduced, older concepts acquire new and additional meanings, and some obsolete concepts coexist within expanded theory. Theoretical or technical change has always been associated with recurring questions and controversies. Serious questions have arisen as to whether there are specific mechanisms of defense; whether "defense mechanism" is not too mechanistic, arbitrary, and restricted in its implications; whether defense mechanisms are not better understood as compromise formations or as nonspecific mechanisms having multiple functions (in addition to defense); whether a defense always has content; and whether other mental functions and attributes may not just as readily be used for purposes of defense. That defense mechanisms may also be put to other use and that other psychic phenomena such as drives and affects, memories and symptoms, humor and hubris may serve defensive purposes, does not *per se* invalidate the concept of specific defense mechanisms. The defense mechanisms elaborated by Anna Freud have primary defensive functions, both qualitative and quantitative, and are given developmental, diagnostic, and special dynamic explanatory significance not shared by other defense methods. The defenses are always linked to the activity of the ego and to what is defended against. It should be noted that Freud emphatically distinguished between repression and compromise formation as well as libidinal regression. He stated (1917), ". . . the concept of repression involves no relation to sexuality. . . . It indicates a purely psychological process, which we can characterize still better if we call it a 'topographical' one. . . . What we have hitherto spoken of as regression, however, and have related to fixation, has meant exclusively a return of the libido to earlier stopping-places in its development—something, that is, entirely different in its nature from repression and entirely independent of it" (p. 342).

The many different theoretical expositions of defense mechanisms and defensive attitudes, maneuvers, methods, con-

figurations, styles, and organizations continue to influence and stimulate psychoanalytic discourse. The work of Anna Freud, especially her contributions to defense analysis and to developmental considerations, represents and remains a powerful and important trend in psychoanalytic thought.[1]

The means of defense may change in different developmental phases in different situations, and defense itself may undergo a change of function. Hartmann's formulations converge with Anna Freud's observations. What is defended against may be not only the drives and superego, but other areas of ego function which then have to be reclaimed and reintegrated. Both intersystemic and intrasystemic conflicts and dysharmony would require analysis in order to restore personality continuity.

While defense, in the long run, serves to ward off full conscious awareness and verbalization of warded off thoughts and feelings, the analysis of defense and of defended content also permits restoration of old connections and the establishment of new links between different facets of the personality and between past and present, reality and fantasy. The awareness of defense and resistance is inextricably linked to the analysis of conflict. Freud's (1926) consideration of the danger situation led to the how, why, and when of danger situations. The delineation of danger and of the ego reaction to danger made possible the understanding of the cause and effect of the defensive maneuver. The defense mechanisms, which are powerful, protective, and adaptive tools, can injure the nondefensive personality functions and interfere with personality development. The excessive utilization of defense will lead to ego constriction or, in some more severe forms, to pathological alteration of the ego, although it is probable that there are other causes and reasons for ego alteration.

---

[1] The reader is additionally referred to the work of Arlow, Brenner, Fenichel, Greenson, Kanzer, Kris, Loewenstein, Mahler, Nunberg, Rangell, Schafer, Stone, Valenstein, and panels on defense reported in the *Journal of the American Psychoanalytic Association*, 1954, 1967, 1970, 1978.

The concept of defense is broader than that of resistance since resistance is a treatment function that takes its meaning from the analytic process. Resistance may usually be seen in its influence on free association and the patient's cooperation with the analytic effort in the therapeutic alliance, but resistance may also be defined and described from many other points of view, e.g., transference resistance, superego resistance, id resistance, negative therapeutic reaction, repetition and regression tendencies, etc. In a broad sense, defense impedes insight, and insight permits the awareness and lifting of defensive operations serving as resistance within the analytic process.

While Freud (1900) recognized that his dictum, "whatever interrupts the progress of analytic work is a resistance" was easily open to misunderstanding, he also noted the truth within the proposition. Even if an interruption were independent of the patient, "Resistance shows itself unmistakably in the readiness with which he accepts an occurrence of this kind or the exaggerated use which he makes of it" (p. 517n). The source and nature of the resistance has to be brought into relation with the unconscious danger situation and with the participation of the total personality in the attempt to cope with the danger.

Analytic transference was initially recognized both as resistance and the vehicle of treatment. It is a recapitulation of what is not consciously remembered, a return of the repressed with the analyst unconsciously represented in the transference fantasy and conflicts. The transference became the pivotal area for interpretation, although other sources of analytic understanding and resistance remain important. We know now that there are no royal roads to the unconscious without resistance and that the nature of the resistance and its resolution are an informative and regular part of the analytic work that leads to structural change. The patient comes to understand his own inhibition of curiosity, resistance to revealing, touching, looking, understanding, etc. Character is not simply resistance nor necessarily the primary focus of resistance, and resistance is flexibly interpreted at the surface where it can be clearly under-

stood by the patient. Of particular interest today are studies of resistance connected with problems of structural regression; character; archaic forms of defense, including the splitting of the ego and of its self and object representations; the relation of defense and resistance to object relations, identifications, external adaptation, and secondary gain; defense against affect and affect as defense and communication. Anna Freud proposed defense against affects as well as a basic, innate antagonism between the ego and instinctual drives. Affects were the objects of defense, since they were linked to the instinctual drives, a proposition that harked back to the first anxiety theory. However, defense against affect was an important reemphasis, with roots in the preanalytic theory of catharsis according to which strangulated affect requires therapeutic abreaction. Her observations stressed defense against unpleasurable affect while already indicating defense could also be employed against pleasurable affects. The appealing assumption of the innate antagonism between ego and id has never been clarified since the ego simultaneously serves as the executive agent of drive gratification and of coordination between drive and object. There is greater awareness of the subversion of free association, the "use" of the analyst, and analysis for defensive purposes. What was called ego alteration or modification and looked at from the point of view of defense at the time of Freud's *Analysis Terminable and Interminable,* and Anna Freud's *Ego and the Mechanisms of Defense,* today involves studies of ego deficits and of developmental arrest and deviation.

Analytic considerations of defense inevitably lead also to the theory of therapeutic change and the effects of the analytic processes on the defense organization and the defense mechanisms. Analysis effects structural change which includes change in the choice, flexibility, and quantitative intensity of defense. More mature defenses may be used, but it is highly questionable whether the defense mechanisms are qualitatively altered or whether it is far more accurate to infer that conflicts are mastered with new solutions and different compromise formations.

Previously unconscious conflicts and fantasies can be admitted to consciousness and reevaluation. The ego is modified so that other ego functions can operate with greater strength, freedom, harmony, with reduced reliance on and interference from defense. New integration leads to personality reorganization with taming of infantile drives and affects, and defense becomes subordinate to mature ego-superego regulation. Further alternative formulations of alterations of defense in the analytic process may be found in the literature. What is no longer at issue, as it was in past decades, is the notion that defenses are analyzed away, i.e., that defenses disappear or are obliterated, or that pathological defenses are removed leaving normal defenses after analysis.

Anna Freud, with her elegant lucidity and logic which made analytic ideas appear deceptively simple, was also aware of the twin problems of resistance to hard-won analytic discoveries and resistance to the integration of new ideas. Her own attention shifted increasingly from the ego's defensive operations and defense analysis to studies of development which encompassed normality and pathology. The "developmental line" of a fantasy and its evolution through personality development can be discerned as incipient in her first paper, "Beating Fantasies and Daydreams" (1922) in which she continued Freud's study of the evolution of a beating fantasy. Anna Freud traced the development of the fantasy beyond early childhood through latency and into adolescence, further showing its alteration from crude, thinly disguised drive derivatives to highly organized sublimated stories. The sword was beaten into the plowshare; sublimation was added to the list of defenses, and the defenses themselves were examined from a developmental point of view. Her relatively recent metapsychological profile and the concept of developmental lines showed many points of contact with ego-psychological concepts of the conflict-free sphere, secondary autonomy, and developmental mastery (A. Freud, 1965). The study of defense and resistance and the parallel study of nondefensive ego functions and ego psychol-

ogy in the problem of adaptation (Hartmann, 1939) became the entwined roots and separate, interweaving developmental lines of much of contemporary psychoanalysis.

The developmental line of Anna Freud's own work followed from her father with all the advantages, pressures, and problems to which a brilliant child of a genius is subjected. Building upon the analytic foundation created by Freud, she carefully correlated theory and therapy, observation and inference. She was willing to learn from experiments of nature, devise rigorous experimental studies and standards. She applied psychoanalysis to child analysis and therapy development, and care, and to many other mental health and humanitarian endeavors. Beginning with education and moving freely from psychoanalysis to other disciplines and modes of discourse, she always maintained and illuminated analytic principles and enlarged analytic knowledge. Child analysis itself became a source of analytic growth.

With her passing, the direct line of brilliant, professional, and personal succession from Freud passes into history. But the development of psychoanalysis goes on inspired and permanently enriched by Anna Freud's pioneering work. The following papers continue the effort to question and challenge our own assumptions and propositions, to correlate the clinical and theoretical, and to further expand our explanatory reach and develop our formulations and models. The concept of developmental lines, as in the line from play to work, is a valuable formulation that links developmental change with increasingly complex function and achievements. Yet the concept should not be understood in a literal or concrete sense. We can too readily isolate simple, discrete, developmental sequences. Developments in different areas and in different phases overlap and interweave, and there probably is no simple, linear developmental sequence. Developmental transformations influence and, at the same time, become part of a reorganization as occurs with libidinal phase development and infantile neurosis. If in time we should opt for a hierarchical organization that inte-

grates, supplements, and supercedes discrete developmental lines, we shall still want to trace regressive and progressive pathways within the personality and the body of psychoanalysis. Analytic developmental advance proceeds with an analytic attitude, analyzing our defenses and our wishful preferences, pursuing analytic understanding, and posing significant questions in a field that is rife with conflict, defense, and efforts toward mastery.

REFERENCES

Erikson, E. (1950). *Childhood and Society.* New York: Norton.
Freud, A. (1922). Beating fantasies and daydreams. *Writings*, 1:137-157. New York: Int. Univ. Press.
———— (1936). *The Ego and the Mechanisms of Defense. Writings*, 2. New York: Int. Univ. Press.
———— (1965). *Normality and Pathology in Childhood. Writings*, 6. New York: Int. Univ. Press.
Freud, S. (1896). Further remarks on the neuropsychoses of defence. *S. E.*, 3.
———— (1900). The interpretation of dreams. *S. E.*, 5.
———— (1914). On the history of the psychoanalytic movement. *S. E.*, 14.
———— (1917). Introductory lectures on psychoanalysis. *S. E.*, 16.
———— (1926). Inhibitions, symptoms and anxiety. *S. E.*, 20.
———— (1937). Analysis terminable and interminable. *S. E.*, 22.
Hartmann, H. (1939). *Ego Psychology and the Problem of Adaptation.* New York: Int. Univ. Press, 1958.

23 The Hemlocks
Roslyn Estates, New York 11576

DISCUSSIONS IN THE HAMPSTEAD INDEX OF *THE EGO AND THE MECHANISMS OF DEFENSE*

JOSEPH SANDLER, PH.D. M.D.
ANNA FREUD, C.B.E., LL.D.,
SC. D., M.D. (HON.)

The Ego's Defensive Operations as an Object of Analysis

CHAPTER 3 OF ANNA FREUD'S BOOK begins with a recapitulation of the view that it is the analyst's work "to bring into consciousness that which is unconscious, no matter to which psychic institution it belongs." And, as she puts it, "when he sets about the work of enlightenment, he takes his stand at a point equidistant from the id, the ego, and the superego" (p. 28).

As far as the id is concerned, the work of analysis reinforces

Participants: A. Berger, L. Biven, D. Campbell, R. Edgecumbe, I. Elkan, R. Evans, W.E. Freud, I. Hellman, A. Holder, H. Kennedy, T. Lopez, S. Rosenfeld, M. Sanai, L. Schacht, M. Sprince, V. Spruiell, R.L. Tyson, C. Yorke.

This is an abridged version of discussions (during 1972-1973) of Chapters 3 and 4, first published in the *Bulletin of the Hampstead Clinic*, 4:119-277, 1981. These and the remainder of the discussions will be published in a book titled *The Analysis of Defense: The Ego and the Mechanisms of Defense Revisited,* by Joseph Sandler with Anna Freud. New York: International Universities Press (in press).

Page numbers in parentheses refer to the 1966 edition of *The Ego and the Mechanisms of Defense. Writings*, 2. New York: International Universities Press.

the id's tendency to express itself on the surface. But the situation is different with the ego and the superego. The aim of the analyst and of the patient's ego are at variance with one another. Although the analyst and the patient's ego work together during the analysis in the process of self-observation, the ego is biased, distorting and rejecting certain facts. Moreover, the ego's unconscious operations are themselves the object of analysis, and naturally it resists the process of making them conscious.

The Ego's Defensive Operations as an Object of Analysis

Anna Freud points out (p. 30) that "in analysis all the material which assists us to analyse the ego makes its appearance in the form of resistance to the analysis of the id." While there are other sources of resistance (transference resistance and the working of the repetition compulsion) it is important to analyse the ego resistances in order to make conscious the unconscious defenses of the ego, which show themselves as a strengthening of defensive measures and as hostility to the analyst.

The ego not only defends itself against instinctual impulses and their derivatives, but also against the affects associated with such impulses (e.g., love, longing, jealousy, mortification, pain, and mourning). The fate of an affect is not necessarily the same as that of the ideational content of the instinctual demand, but a knowledge of the way the patient defends himself against his instinctual impulses will tell us about the defenses he will probably use toward his own unwelcome affects.

Anna Freud now refers to Wilhelm Reich's idea of character "armor-plating" (Charakterpanzerung). This reflects attitudes (in particular bodily attitudes and character traits) which are residues of past defenses, which have become, in the course of time, separated from the original conflict situation. The analysis of character armor is difficult, and such traits should only be concentrated on in the analysis when the analyst cannot detect a current conflict involving ego, drive, and affect. In

general, the analysis of resistance should be applied to all resistances and not only to character resistances. Analysis shows that the neurotic symptoms involve defense mechanisms and compromises in which specific methods of defense are used unvaryingly. There is a special relation between particular neuroses and certain mechanisms of defense. We can see the operation of such defenses on the patient's free associations, and can therefore gain an understanding of his symptoms from the form of his resistances. Thus the resistances of the hysteric and of the obsessional patient are quite different.

Anna Freud goes on to describe the case of a young girl who had symptoms of acute anxiety, but who avoided making reference to her symptoms during the analysis. When the analyst commented on this the patient became contemptuous, and the analyst felt at a loss. Later it was seen that the resistance was not a transference reaction in the true sense, but reflected rather the patient's vehemently critical attitude toward herself whenever she experienced affects of tenderness, longing, or anxiety. The interpretation of the content of the anxiety had no result until the patient's method of defending herself (based on identification with her critical father) had been analyzed.

The parallel between a patient's defense against his instincts and against his affects, and that between his symptom formation and his resistance, is of great technical relevance. This is especially so in child analysis, where the analyst cannot use free association, and has to resort to other methods. However, the child's play is not completely equivalent to free association, and it is by turning to the analysis of the way in which the child's affects have been transformed that we may learn more of the ego's activities. Thus, in child analysis, the analysis of defenses against affects is of particular importance. It gives the analyst clues to the child's attitude toward his instincts and to the nature of his symptom formation. Anna Freud illustrates this by reference to a little boy who defended himself against castration anxiety by dressing up as a soldier and being aggressive. He reversed the affect of anxiety by turning it into its

opposite. He was also obsessional, indicating that he did the same sort of "turning around" in his instinctual life. Anna Freud then gives two further examples to illustrate the parallel between defenses against affects and those against instinctual impulses. She concludes the chapter by pointing out that the analysis of defensive changes in regard to affects corresponds to the resolution of ego resistances (as they are found in free association). The more we can bring ego resistances and defenses against affects into consciousness, the nearer we shall get to an understanding of the id of the patient.

Discussions

J. Sandler: I should like to refer to the question of unconsciousness. You say (p. 28), "It is the task of the analyst to bring into consciousness that which is unconscious, no matter to which psychic institution it belongs. He directs his attention equally and objectively to the unconscious elements in all three institutions."

We have a problem, I think, of different sorts of unconsciousness, and of what it is that one makes conscious through one's interpretations. It seems to me that we should really spell out a distinction between, for example, making conscious again a memory or an image which has been repressed, and making the patient aware of a mechanism which he is using. He may never have been conscious of that mechanism. One could compare it to the engine of a motor car. The driver may never have seen that piece of machinery, but in order to understand the functioning of the car—particularly if something has gone wrong—one might give him a representation of it. This is very different from releasing a repressed memory. Would you go along with such a distinction, Miss Freud? I suppose that we could also say in this context that there are two sorts of interpretation which can be given.

Anna Freud: There are. There are also two sorts of uncon-

sciousness, and, descriptively speaking, both things you have described are unconscious, but one is repressed content, and the other is an automatic process which we try to lift into consciousness. Naturally there is a great difference between the two, and the analytic work is different. It is received in a different way by the patient.

J. Sandler: The analyst verbalizes and brings to the surface something the individual has not been conscious of before. Phrases like "brought to the surface" and "lift into consciousness" refer, of course, to both processes you mentioned. However, in this chapter you put stress on something which involves spelling out for the patient what he is actually doing, so that he becomes aware of it perhaps for the first time. Although people do not like the word, in a sense one "educates" the patient about his defense mechanisms.

Anna Freud: One demonstrates his defense mechanisms to him. To educate him would be to suggest a better defense mechanism to him.

J. Sandler: No, that isn't what I meant.

Anna Freud: It really is a demonstration. The analyst shows him something he knows in his unconscious (in the descriptive sense of the word).

J. Sandler: I am not at all sure one can say the patient is unconsciously aware of the defense mechanisms he uses.

Anna Freud: There is one important similarity between the two processes of interpreting defense mechanisms and of bringing content to the surface. Both are resisted by the ego for the same reasons. The one because the defense is undone and anxiety aroused when the analyst lifts a repressed content to the surface, and the second because an anxiety or other affect which has been warded off now has to be experienced. That is where the similarity lies.

J. Sandler: I am sure that we would agree that the defended

content and the defense mechanisms are, descriptively speaking, unconscious, but that there are different sorts of unconsciousness.

Anna Freud: Yes.

J. Sandler: There is a question I have been wanting to ask you. You say that "the id impulses have of themselves no inclination to remain unconscious. They naturally tend upward and are perpetually striving to make their way into consciousness" (p. 29). You go on to say that the analyst's work follows the same direction as the upward tendency and reinforces it. From the point of view of the repressed elements in the id the analyst is helping them in their move toward the surface. There is something about this which is a puzzle to me and I wonder if you would say something about it, Miss Freud. Why is it that a repressed wish, or perhaps an instinctual wish in general, obtains gratifications if it can find its way to consciousness?

Anna Freud: It doesn't find it, but it looks for it. This is really the way in which the id is deceived during analysis. The upward move to the surface is a striving toward gratification. The analytic work attempts to catch it before gratification is achieved. Of course the mere fact of the impulse being verbalized gives a slight amount of satisfaction, but this is certainly not what the id intended. I think this is what the psychoanalytic method is based on.

J. Sandler: Could you elaborate on this a little, Miss Freud? We speak of the wish reaching consciousness, and sometimes of gaining access to motility. In the analytic situation, of course, motility is hindered. The patient lies on the couch and, like the person who is asleep, cannot discharge the wish in a physical way. If I understand it correctly, you would say that at the moment of the person becoming conscious of the wish he would experience some slight gratification, some wish fulfilment. Do you mean that he would, for example, experience a wish-fulfilling fantasy?

Anna Freud: We know that the most effective discharge of an impulse is through the action which leads to gratification. But there are, after all, lesser modes of discharge with reduced amounts of gratification, for example, discharge into words. Discharge into fantasy which can be put into words is what we analysts prefer, but as analysts we also see discharge through acting out. Acting out really means that what has come to the surface has escaped the analyst's grasp, has gone into action, whether the analyst wanted it to go there or not. If we can catch it before it goes into action, then we have really done what we wanted to do.

J. Sandler: If we think for the moment not of an instinctual impulse, but of a need like hunger, the person who becomes aware that he is hungry will often feel more hungry as a result of that awareness. Would that not also apply, say, to a sexual wish? If a person has a sexual impulse and becomes aware of it can we really say that discharge takes place at that moment? Are you not in fact referring here to a derivative of the impulse, to a wishful fantasy, into which a modicum of satisfaction has already been embroidered? I refer to something which is not quite the wish, but a wish fulfilment in a partial form, which might be a compromise formation or something of that sort. If we use the phrase "id impulse reaching the surface," are we not speaking too broadly?

Anna Freud: What I have written refers to the impulse or its derivative, but I have certain examples in mind. I remember hearing an analyst describe his work with a case of latent homosexuality, and he could show that he had been successful in reaching the wish behind the attitude that made for the latent homosexuality. But his patient actually became homosexual. The analyst didn't seem to mind, but he should have minded, because he should have caught the homosexual wish before it went into action. Otherwise the patient may like it so much that the analyst may never catch it again.

J. Sandler: What happens if this patient really had a strong homosexual disposition and the heterosexuality was a defensive facade? What right have we to bring our morality and sexual preferences into the situation? May not the satisfactory progress of the analysis result in the person becoming an overt homosexual, following analysis of the defenses?

Anna Freud: It is not our morality that made him defend against the homosexual wish. It is *his* morality. It is *his* conflict about his wish to be homosexual. It is only at the moment that the impulse he has repressed becomes conscious again that he is swamped by it, because the conscious impulse now has more force. One could ask "what about a murderous wish?" Think of the patient who has only displayed a very loving attitude toward his mother, but behind it is the wish to kill her. Naturally, you as his analyst would want to uncover that, but is it an analytic success if he then kills his mother? You might say, "well, if he wants to be a murderer it is his affair," only he doesn't want to be a murderer, otherwise he would never have developed his neurosis.

J. Sandler: If one has a patient one suspects might be dangerous, who might actually murder his mother, I think one would tread very warily and perhaps abandon strict analytic work. In fact, I don't know of any instance in which the analyst has gone on with a patient in such circumstances. I don't imagine you would have gone on analyzing a patient in whom you felt there was risk that he might discharge his aggressive wishes in action as violent as this. We must all have experience of cases in which we felt that analysis was not really indicated any more, and have then taken it easy, soft-pedaled, been supportive, and interpreted only selectively because of the fear of the wish being turned into action. I suppose this relates to the question of selection of cases for analysis. I don't know if you agree.

Anna Freud: I agree in one way, because the ordinary sort of patient, the neurotic patient, has actually built up his whole character on the basis of repressed wishes. The analysis puts pressure on that character and usually the patient will be able to deal with what is coming up again. Perhaps I should not have chosen the example of the murderer, but if such an aggressive impulse does come up, and you do not catch it in the analysis, it can go into action. While the patient may not murder his mother or his wife, he may wound them or offend them, to an extent that through acting out he destroys a relationship which he never meant to destroy.

J. Sandler: Are we not speaking of two completely different things here? First there is the failure of the analyst to interpret and to verbalize something, so that instead of this being contained as a thought or idea, the patient acts out or enacts the impulse. This puts the patient and the environment at risk in some way. But the other case is that of the patient who has tendencies which are truly related to fixation points to which he may have regressively retreated during development. So he has tendencies which we would call perverse, and has then built up a layer of defenses against these. When he becomes able to tolerate such impulses in his awareness, he might say "why should I not enjoy myself in this perverse way instead of being completely asexual?" I have a patient who was completely sexually inhibited before he started analysis but regarded himself as heterosexual. He had no heterosexual relations during analysis but has now had some homosexual experiences which he accepts and enjoys. He feels that this is an improvement, and I also think it is. Perhaps one day he will get round to heterosexuality, because possibly he has a basically heterosexual disposition, but I doubt it, even though it is certainly true that his homosexuality has only taken the form of cuddling and mutual masturbation, and there is some evidence that there are heterosexual fantasies

behind this. This could all be considered to be acting out, but I do not see it as acting out in my patient.

Anna Freud: You know, it depends very much on external circumstances, because the whole idea of acting out an impulse which has come up from the unconscious is connected with our view of the potential harm that the patient can do to himself if he decides to act on the impulse. If he acts out, and that lands him in prison, or smashes his career, then we certainly haven't done him any good, and he has not done himself any good. If it is harmless, and (as we hope) transitory, then that is another matter. This may be true for the homosexual. Under certain conditions he could harm himself very much, and under other conditions not at all. But I really speak here from the point of view of the impulse itself. If it could speak it would say "I would never have come up if I hadn't hoped that I could break into action." And what I wanted to point out in this chapter, and nothing else, is that there is nothing in the unconscious defense mechanism (perhaps I should say "not-conscious" defense mechanism) similar to this. The "not-conscious" mechanism has no reason to become conscious.

J. Sandler: Yes, it has no urge to force itself to the surface. Isn't what you are describing, a mode of functioning?

Anna Freud: Yes.

J. Sandler: When you say that the analyst's attitude to the impulse depends on the way he sees it in terms of danger to the patient, how would this affect the analyst's work?

Anna Freud: It would make him more eager to catch the material before it goes over into action.

J. Sandler: So with certain material one is much more on the alert in regard to acting out than with other impulses.

Anna Freud: Yes. After all, what comes up may be a suicide

wish. If this goes into action, you have lost the patient, and the patient has lost his life or his health. If you catch it in time, it is extremely useful. I think that much of analytic technique of the past was built on the analyst's skill in this regard.

J. Sandler: I am reminded of the way in which one may warn the patient about a tendency to act in some particular way, after a bit of analytic work has been done. I am not thinking here so much of acting out an instinctual wish, but more of negative therapeutic reactions based on guilt. One might say to the patient, "now you feel very pleased with yourself, but you know what has happened in the past," warning the patient that he might be tempted to do something self-damaging because of guilt feelings following his pleasure in gaining a piece of insight. This can be a very convincing confirmation for the patient if he actually does something one has predicted he might do. The next time he might not because he is on his guard.

Often we hear public statements about the "purity" of the analytic process, with the analyst seeming to function almost as an interpreting machine. Of course, it isn't like that at all. If the homosexual patient we have been discussing was tempted, say, to seduce little children, one might say to him, "Look, you had better be careful, because people are caught doing this. You involve someone else, and can do that person harm. I think we should talk more about it." We might not say that in regard to another wish. There is a certain responsibility felt by the analyst in regard to what the patient does, although this raises many difficulties. The analyst would be less than human if he didn't feel such a responsibility. To think that our job is only to translate what the patient says in an automatic or "objective" way, without being concerned at all about what the patient does, is a big mistake.

Anna Freud: Yes. One has only to try out these thoughts

in regard to the suicidal impulse of a patient. If you feel that what is coming up might easily lead to his carrying out his suicidal impulse, you certainly would not interpret it with the same quiet attitude as you would another impulse.

J. Sandler: We come now to the question of the distinction between defense against drives and defense against affect. I wonder if you have any comments to make on this, or if you would like to sharpen the distinction. In my own mind I always see defense as against affect, as implying that, if it were not for the unpleasant affect, one would not defend. But the distinction to which you refer lies in regard to what is worked on in the defense, that is, the ideational content that is transformed on the one hand, and the affect that is avoided or reduced on the other. It isn't altogether clear whether there are two sorts of defense, or two motives for defense, or some other difference.

Anna Freud: If I think back to the climate in which this was written, I remember well that at the time defense against affect was not really talked about. As you have said before, affect was considered as an accompaniment to the drive or as a drive derivative, and it was more or less taken for granted that the defense was directed against the drive and not the affect. What I had in mind here was something slightly different. I meant that every individual has a limited number of defenses at his disposal, and that he may use them against the drive or against the affect, but (and this takes us over to child analysis) the defense against the affect is much easier to demonstrate to the patient. If we start from the defense against the affect, we get an inkling of what defenses the patient uses against the drive. Then we may find out what impulse or drive is defended against. We usually have a fairly good knowledge of what the patient should feel at a certain moment, of what is appropriate for him. I mean that when something bad happens, the patient should not begin to giggle, as so many patients

DEFENSE AND RESISTANCE

*Historical Perspectives
and Current Concepts*

ANNA FREUD
1895-1982

Portrait by Allan Chappelow

do, or have a sudden feeling of elation when he is deeply disappointed. I think of a patient who, whenever a girl he loved told him the affair was over, became elated when he should have been depressed. It wasn't that he was glad to be rid of her; it simply was not the affect that one would have expected. We all know from child analysis that if the child shows the wrong affect at the wrong moment, this is a very helpful thing, a useful guide to the defenses. This then leads one to the defenses against the drive derivative. When I wrote what I did, I took it much more from that point of view.

J. Sandler: It is very clear how you have used this point as a bridge from adult to child analysis. In this connection, you are saying that we can see defensive operations working on the child's mood and on his feelings in the same way we see them working on ideational content. But there is another level in which all defense is ultimately defense against the signal of trauma, against anxiety, or against any other unpleasant affect or the affect signal.

Anna Freud: I agree, but I also took it from another point of view. If one notices that the appropriate affect isn't there, and one starts with the defense against the affect, which has nothing to do with the drive, it still leads one to the battle against the drive.

J. Sandler: I cannot tell you how delighted I am to hear you make these points, Miss Freud. So many analysts have been hindered for a very long time in trying to deal with the psychoanalytic theory of affect because they have assumed that all affects were to be considered as drive derivatives. But is it not obvious that some affects arise because of the influence of the external world? We have really been speaking about defenses which involve the manipulation of affect, as opposed to defenses involving manipulations of ideational content and ideational re-resentation. Knowledge of one context in which defenses are

used gives us clues to the defenses used in another context, but this doesn't mean that the first context is a derivative of the second.

Anna Freud: Yes ... I tried to establish a unity between defense against the drive, defense against the affects (wherever they come from), and resistance in analysis. Resistance in analysis is, of course, resistance against the unpleasure that is aroused by the analytic process. And if it is true that the three can all reflect the same defensive process, one can start from any one of the three and throw light on the other two.

J. Sandler: Perhaps with adults one can add another area in which we see defense. I mean the area of dreams, where the defenses used tend to be those generally used by the patient. If he tends to project his feelings onto others in his general life, he will tend to externalize aspects of his own self onto other figures in dreams. If he tends to use displacement, he will show more displacement in his dreams. I think that one can pick up an indication of the patient's repertoire of defenses from the way in which the dream work has gone on. Perhaps with adults there are a number of paths one can take toward an understanding of the defenses, whereas with children we are much more limited.

Anna Freud: With the dreams there is an added complication. What we see in the dreams are those defense mechanisms that have a very strong relation to the primary process. And that makes it not quite the same.

J. Sandler: I am sure one has more condensation, displacement, reversal, and equation of opposites in dreams. But I do have the impression that one can also see, perhaps particularly in the revision of the dream and in the recounting of the dream, the defense mechanisms that are characteristic of the patient.

Anna Freud: I think you are right about the recounting of the dream, which means producing the last version, but I am not so sure about the dream itself.

J. Sandler: To move on to the discussion of the permanent defense phenomena, Miss Freud, you have drawn attention to Wilhelm Reich's views. What I understand from what you say is that certain modes of functioning which were originally defensive have, in a sense, become autonomous. They don't depend any longer on the particular impulse defended against in the present, and have become part of what we would call the person's "style." Incidentally, when Heinz Hartmann developed his idea of secondary autonomy and change of function in relation to such things as skills (he spoke of "apparatuses") he did not take the step of speaking of the secondary autonomy of symptoms and of character traits. We know there are symptoms which are not necessarily solutions of conflict at the moment, but have crystallized, just as Reich's character traits have become "fixed." I suppose one could speak of a secondary autonomy both of symptoms and character traits, and in analysis we would have to look at symptoms of this sort differently from the way in which we look at recent symptoms or those which develop during the analysis, which may be compromises of a neurotic sort. It seems to me you have drawn attention to something which has not yet been sufficiently studied. I wonder if you could say something about the question of character analysis.

Anna Freud: I would like to add to this that there was quite a battle at the time over this idea of Wilhelm Reich, who was then a very good analyst. His ideas had caught on, and although I agreed with Reich in many instances, I fought against his maintaining over and over again that the "fixed" defensive attitude in a patient was really transference. If it was it would mean that the attitude was aroused at that particular moment by the analytic situation. I used to say,

"but the patient does that wherever he is, outside the home, with his children, with his parents, with his colleagues. It has nothing to do with what is aroused in the analytic situation." And therefore I felt that the character trait had to be reached in a completely different way. It is not material for the analysis, unless something happens which revives it. I probably would not have discussed things in this particular way in the book if there hadn't been such a lively battle at the time.

I remember Reich used as an example the submissive patient, the patient who agreed with whatever the analyst said. Well, Reich said that there is a passive feminine transference to the analyst, and he analyzed it as such, but it is not a passive feminine transference. It's a passive feminine character attitude which has been built up over a long time, and which is now displayed, not only toward the people who aroused it in the first place, but to everybody. It seemed to me that there was an enormously important difference here.

J. Sandler: We have, of course, the question of what we choose to take up in the analysis. Is there a case for interpreting a character attitude as transference, when it comes up in the analysis, even though we know that it also comes up everywhere else, as you described? The patient also brings his character to the analysis. Or should we interpret it in some other way? Some people might argue that the only effective analytic way is to take the transference aspects as if the attitude involved the analyst only.

Anna Freud: I would call this "forcing it into the transference," because the way to reach it in the transference is to show how it is inappropriate in all situations.

J. Sandler: There are big differences between individual analysts in this regard. For example, there is the difference between those who will say to a child, "you are angry" and those who will say, "you are angry with me," if something

has happened to annoy the child in the session. It has become almost automatic for some analysts to add the "with me," to pull the material into the transference. And I think they would say that they are "leading" rather than "forcing" it into the transference. There is perhaps something to be discussed here in terms of technique. We know there are certain patients, particularly those with narcissistic character disorders, where the material they report has very much to do with their character and does not appear to have much to do with the transference, at least not at the beginning. The analyst may be set up as a good, listening figure, and one has to do one's interpretative work about the way the patient interacts with other people. If one waits for a transference neurosis, it may never come, because the patient may like coming to the analysis, may keep the analyst as a "good" figure. He may defend successfully against the development of other sorts of transference. I think that sometimes one has to go along with the patient for quite a long time, showing him the mechanisms he has been using, leaving oneself out until the patient is well and truly in analysis. My experience is that taking up all the material in terms of transference early in the analysis may put certain patients into resistance and may lead to a breakdown of the analysis.

Anna Freud: Because it extends the transference to a phenomenon the patient doesn't need to feel. The original idea about transference is that it is something the patient feels is going on in him, not something dragged in by the analyst.

J. Sandler: Perhaps the point you are making, Miss Freud, is that one would not refrain from interpreting the attitude in regard to oneself even though it is a fixed character trait, although one would also show how general it is. So for the patient who is overly submissive one might say, "I am very struck by the fact that you have agreed with

everything I have said since the beginning of this analysis." This might be better than saying, "I am struck by the fact that you agree with what everybody says to you."

Anna Freud: I would say, "How curious that you agree even when it is quite obvious that you disagree, when I would expect you to disagree." There is a different technique of interpretation here.

J. Sandler: Of course, showing the patient that he has taken up a particular attitude in the analysis does not mean that it is transference in the original sense.

Anna Freud: The whole question is whether transference is in the patient's mind or in the analyst's mind. And one should interpret what is in the patient's mind. That is the great difference.

J. Sandler: There are some points about symptom formation which are intriguing. You say (p. 34), ". . . the part played by the ego in the formation of those compromises which we call symptoms consists in the unvarying use of a special method of defense, when confronted with a particular instinctual demand, and the repetition of exactly the same procedure every time that demand recurs in its stereotyped form." Presumably the procedure you refer to is the use of the defense mechanism. You go on to point to the connection between particular modes of defense and types of illness. Perhaps it is worth commenting that we also traditionally link the different neuroses to the fixation points to which the individual has returned. Certainly we emphasize this less nowadays in regard to psychotics, but it is still an important part of our clinical theory that the obsessional, for example, regresses to anal fixation points. But linked with these fixation points are also particular types of defense. We can ask whether the person had persisted in the use of these specific defense mechanisms (like doing and undoing) before the regressive revival on the

side of the drives, which then had to be dealt with by the symptoms of the neurosis; or is there also a regressive revival of the particular defense mechanisms involved in the neurosis. I have the impression that such mechanisms as reaction formation and undoing may be built into the character of the person who has the predisposition to develop an obsessional neurosis at a later time. In this connection one has to think of the patient who may show drive regression to the anal phase but does not develop an obsessional neurosis. Instead he may develop some other "anal" symptom. From what you say it is the defense mechanisms which turn the regressively revived instinctual wishes into the obsessional neurosis.

Anna Freud: Yes. But you introduce another subject into the discussion, which is not really touched on in the chapter. What you ask about is a very much later consideration concerning regression within the ego. At the time I wrote the book it played no part at all in our thinking, because the whole concept of regression was limited to the side of the drives. And with ego regression we get regression in the use of defense mechanisms.

J. Sandler: You give the example of the young girl who came to see you because of states of acute anxiety. At one point (p. 36) you say, "The more powerfully the affect forced itself upon her, the more vehemently and scathingly did she ridicule herself. The analyst became the recipient of these defensive reactions only secondarily, because she was encouraging the demands of the patient's anxiety to be worked over in consciousness."

You go on to say that it was then impossible to bring the unconscious content into consciousness until you had made the patient aware of the way she defended herself against her feelings by contemptuously disparaging herself. Later you show how you elucidated her resistance in the transference. I would like to ask whether in this case the method the patient used to defend herself was taken

up and shown to her in relation to you as a person, as the analyst who was present, even though this mechanism was used in the patient's customary attitude to herself. This relates to something we discussed earlier, but I want to take it up because you mentioned it so specifically.

Anna Freud: Well, it comes to the analyst's notice because suddenly the analyst becomes the innocent victim of the patient's attacks. But it isn't the transference of an object relationship. What she displays toward the analyst is an attitude toward herself, and it reveals itself in what we might call a form of transference. But if it did not reveal itself in the transference, the analyst would notice after some acquaintance with the patient that this particular attitude appears at inappropriate moments. One could say to the patient, "Why are you so angry with yourself?" Just as later on one could say, "Why are you so angry with me?" Then we could show the patient her way of warding off unwelcome feelings. I have a patient now where I see something like this. Whenever she has feelings of guilt or tenderness, which also make her unhappy, she becomes extremely tough in her feelings. And she does exactly the same thing in relation to me. If I side with her feelings, she becomes tough with me. But that is secondary. It isn't her anger with me, it is her anger with her feelings. This brings us to a useful distinction, because here what we have is a pseudo transference.

J. Sandler: I think that you have made a very useful distinction for us. Again, we see that the patient can be involved with the analyst without it being a real transference. We have a reflection of a habitual mode of reacting, which at a particular time involves the analyst. I suppose that the question which nags at me is whether one would take this up in relation to oneself as analyst, or whether one would put it in general terms to the patient. What you call pseudo transference may perhaps be dealt with in a useful way by

saying to the patient, "you know, when you feel tender toward me, you have to be tough" or, the other way round, "when you disparage yourself now, I think you do so in reaction to a tender feeling toward me," rather than, "this is what you do whenever you feel tender."

Anna Freud: I know that it is a current idea that only material which comes into the transference, and is shown as a transference phenomenon, can be helpful to the patient. I don't quite believe it.

J. Sandler: But you need not call that transference, Miss Freud.

Anna Freud: Yes, but I don't see that there is a great difference between putting it in terms of the patient's relation to herself or in terms of the patient and the analyst. So long as you get hold of it the impression on the patient is very much the same. It does not matter whether you say, "Now I know whenever you are angry with me such and such is really the case," or whether you say, "I know whenever you are so self-abusive it is because of so and so." I do not see the difference as being so glaring as people do nowadays.

J. Sandler: I think we have here again a multiple use of the term transference which is very confusing. When we use it in a general sense, we use it as a synonym for "relationship," something which is quite different from the intensification of feeling focusing on the person of the analyst, a revival of the past in the analytic situation. In transference, the patient sees it as something new in the present, but it is something specific to the analytic situation. I suppose that we often use the term "transference" instead of "relationship," and when we speak of interpreting in the transference, we often mean interpreting in the relationship, opposing this to interpreting the defense. I am not sure that such an opposition is a valid one, because the

analyst can be drawn into the working of the defense without it being transference, in the narrower sense of the term. I think that here too there is a significant difference between analysts in their approach to this particular problem. Some more than others want to draw the patient into a heightened awareness of feelings toward the analyst in the analytic situation, even though the patient may be reacting toward the analyst with his habitual modes of reacting, particularly at the beginning of the analysis. The implicit idea is, I think, that the threshold for perception and awareness of later "truer" transference phenomena would be heightened. At least, I think this would be the argument.

Anna Freud: It would probably be the argument, but I think that it would be much the same whether you start with the attitude of the patient toward herself, and then seeing the same happening to the analyst, or whether you start with the analyst and then show her that she does the same to herself. I think that one has to do both.

J. Sandler: With this we get into the area of the so-called "mutative" interpretations, which led to the tendency (in England certainly) to put everything in transference terms. It led to the idea that no comment should be made to the patient without bringing in the analyst.

Anna Freud: It reminds me of the joke of the patient who says to the analyst "You can never say anything without bringing yourself into it."

J. Sandler: That's no joke, Miss Freud. I think that we have all heard it as a complaint from patients. And of course, the patient may have a real cause for grievance.

Anna Freud: That's right.

J. Sandler: Toward the end of the chapter you speak, Miss Freud, of the defense mechanism of reversal, which you call "a kind of reaction formation against the affect." It

sounds as if one takes the affect itself and stands it on its head. If I understand you correctly, what you are saying is that one replaces the affect with its opposite, which is, of course, like the reaction formation. But it is not the affect that is being reversed, but a new and opposite experience which is being created. I don't know if this makes sense.

Anna Freud: Well, if someone says to you that whenever he feels sad he laughs it off, would you say he created a new experience?

J. Sandler: Yes, I would. Otherwise it would sound as if he were taking the sadness and transmuting it into laughter.

Anna Freud: It's a very fine theoretical distinction. We speak about transforming anxiety, but it is not strictly meant that way. What is meant is that the opposite appears on the surface.

J. Sandler: Now we come closer to the actual mechanisms of defense. We found it practically impossible, in the [Hampstead] Index group, to give an unambiguous definition of defense. Of course we distinguish between defense mechanisms and defensive measures (or defense maneuvers) which, on the whole, seem to be more complicated processes. But we felt that the mechanisms we call defenses were not necessarily simple units. Some of them are quite complicated, involving several steps. On the other hand, it seems that from a historical point of view the defenses have emerged in the course of clinical work as mechanisms of particular clinical significance which could be identified by particular characteristics. This seems to have been sufficient for them to be singled out as mechanisms of defense. Where we had difficulty in our discussions was in deciding how one could say, for other than historical reasons, that something should be called a defense mechanism as opposed to a defensive maneuver. For

example, it is clear that a reaction formation is a particular constellation which has a certain coherence, and we can identify it. At the same time we know there is no reaction formation without there being simultaneously an identification with an attitude of the parent or of some other authority figure. This would be an attitude which is opposed to the impulse or the affect concerned. So identification is one component of the reaction formation, but the reaction formation is nevertheless identifiable as something which has its own characteristics. Why do we label that compound reaction as a mechanism of defense, whereas such things as clowning or joking might be categorized as defensive maneuvers or as defensive measures and not be called defense mechanisms proper?

Anna Freud: I suppose you are right that the reason is historical. But there is a close connection between the defense mechanism and the neurosis proper, whereas what we call defensive maneuvers are nearer to the normal and nearer also to character formation. We cannot really link them specifically with any of the major neuroses. I think that the distinction is made from the side of pathology.

J. Sandler: You mean that if we are to distinguish neuroses in terms of particular patterns of defenses used, as we discussed earlier, the units involved would be the defense mechanisms, whereas the defensive measures would not be consistent parts of the neurosis, say of an obsessional neurosis or hysteria.

Anna Freud: I don't remember when the distinction between defense mechanisms and defensive maneuvers was introduced. I don't think it existed in German at all.

M. Berger: You introduced it, Miss Freud, when we were first preparing the manual on defenses for the Index.

Anna Freud: I think that it is the defense mechanisms that have clinical importance.

J. Sandler: I remember that we came to the conclusion that in teaching technique one needs to demonstrate the major defense mechanisms very carefully, because they are consistently used by patients and we can identify them. We had a certain amount of difficulty in the Index when we came to what one could call the minor defenses because we found that we had increased our list of mechanisms of defense to a point where we really had far too many, and differences became difficult to see. You know how subtle the distinction is between reversal of roles, identification with the aggressor, turning passive into active, and so on. Identification with the aggressor is clear, but reversal of roles comes close to it, yet isn't quite the same.

Anna Freud: It is only identification with the aggressor which is a newcomer to the aristocracy.

J. Sandler: To Freud's list.

Anna Freud: Yes.

J. Sandler: One wonders then whether it is appropriate to keep on adding to the list.

Anna Freud: It is good to know them all, list or not.

J. Sandler: Of course we know now that practically everything can be used for the purposes of defense, and this makes the situation even more difficult for us.

Anna Freud: Take, for example, falling asleep. Falling asleep is certainly not a defense mechanism, but it can be used to defend against aggression, to ward it off. For the person who is using it at a particular time it is defensive, but it's not a general defensive measure, let alone a defense mechanism.

J. Sandler: We still have the problem of where to draw the line between the mechanism and the measure, and I think we can't do this except on a historical basis and a clinical

basis. The major defenses were, of course, first described by Freud, and some were added by you, Miss Freud, in your book. Since then we have had the difficult task of trying to decide whether to include certain new ones which were not mentioned by you in the book, or whether we should consider them automatically as defense measures. As you point out, we can have an infinite number of defensive measures.

Anna Freud: I would say that whatever serves a particular individual for the purpose of warding off either id content or affect (or whatever the ego doesn't want to accept) would be defensive. If it is personal to the individual, or to a few selected individuals, we can call it a defensive measure. If it is general in the sense that it is always tied to specific clinical states, which could not exist without it, we put it in another more important category. You have mentioned clowning, which is certainly important as a defensive measure, and you could name character types that are based on it, but can you name illnesses that are based on it?

J. Sandler: Now that we recognize so much more the existence of narcissistic disorders, it seems to me that something like clowning could be considered to be specifically defensive, directed toward restoring self-esteem. Would we still consider it to be something which is part of a person's character or would we have to give it the status of a defense mechanism?

Anna Freud: It is important to know where these things belong, and you are quite right that probably the narcissistic states and the disturbances of narcissism are linked to this quite specific defense. But whether you want to call it a mechanism or a measure doesn't really matter.

J. Sandler: Perhaps it is more a question for us as teachers or conceptualizers.

Anna Freud: When I explain the difference between de-

fense mechanism and defensive measures, I compare the defenses to weapons which only exist as weapons, things such as guns and spears and clasp-knives, and so on. There are other things which you only use for a weapon at a certain moment. There is a young man before the courts at present, accused of killing his mother with a frying pan. Now is the frying pan a weapon or a measure? It's something which is really there for another purpose and used for the moment as a weapon. Isn't that the best way of making the distinction? This means that repression or projection would always be defense mechanisms, but clowning or many other activities would only be picked up for momentary use and would be defensive measures.

J. Sandler: I think that this is very convincing, Miss Freud. Earlier, when we were speaking of the clinical units of defense, you said that the mechanisms used were what characterized each type of neurosis. But isn't repression, for example, something we need to use normally? If we didn't we would be overwhelmed by the return of what is normally unconscious, and become quite psychotic.

Anna Freud: That wouldn't alter the fact that repression always serves the purpose of keeping something out of the ego, or rather out of consciousness.

J. Sandler: A protective device.

Anna Freud: Yes, a protective device.

J. Sandler: You referred to the mechanisms as ready-made tools which have been developed for the protection of the ego, used specifically for that purpose, in normality or in pathology. Defensive measures might be any form of activity, which might well be normal ways of expressing a whole variety of things, which can also be used for purposes of defense. Would that then be your point?

Anna Freud: Yes.

The Mechanisms of Defense

Anna Freud points out in Chapter 4 that Freud had originally used the term "defense" for the ego's struggle against unpleasant ideas or affects. Later the term "repression" was used instead, but in 1926 Freud returned to the use of "defense" as the general term, while "repression" was used to designate the specific measure which had been originally called "defense."

She then suggests that we enquire into other specific modes of defense, and refers again to Freud's suggestion that there may be a special connection between forms of defense and particular illnesses, commenting that Freud has shown us that regression as well as reaction formation, isolation, and undoing occur in obsessional neurosis.

Anna Freud then refers to Freud's description of introjection (or identification) and projection as defensive mechanisms at work in neurosis. She reminds us that Freud described the processes of turning against the self and reversal, and sees these "vicissitudes of instinct" as also reflecting mechanisms of defense. She points out that "every vicissitude to which the instincts are liable has its origin in some ego activity" (p. 44).

Nine methods of defense had been described previously (regression, repression, reaction formation, isolation, undoing, projection, introjection, turning against the self, and reversal). To these must be added a tenth, i.e., sublimation (displacement of instinctual aims). The ego "has these ten different methods at its disposal in its conflicts with instinctual representatives and affects. It is the task of the . . . analyst to discover how far these methods prove effective in the processes of ego resistance and symptom formation . . ." (p. 44).

Anna Freud points out that in practice repression is usually combined with other techniques of defense. She quotes the case of a patient with a repressed wish to bite off her father's penis, who replaced this idea by a disinclination to eat, which was accompanied by feelings of disgust. The part of the patient's instinctual life represented by the oral wish had been dealt with, but the wish to rob her father remained until it was later re-

pudiated by her superego. The urge to rob was changed into "a peculiar kind of contentedness and unassumingness" (p. 49). This resulted in a substratum of hysteria on which was imposed a specific ego modification.

Repression has a special place in relation to the other methods of defense in that it is effective in a way in which the others are not. It represents a "permanent institution demanding a constant expenditure of energy" (pp. 49-50), whereas the other mechanisms have to be employed again and again whenever the instinctual urge arises. Repression is also one of the most dangerous mechanisms of defense because whole areas of instinctual and affective life become dissociated, and the integrity of the personality may be destroyed. But the other defense mechanisms may also produce serious consequences, resulting in all sorts of transformations and distortions of the ego.

Anna Freud now refers to Freud's suggestion that there may be differences between defenses according to the age at which they first develop. Thus the child needs to have achieved a differentiation between ego and id in order to employ repression. In the same way, projection and introjection depend on a differentiation of self from the external world. Sublimation requires the existence of superego values, and it follows that repression and sublimation cannot be used until relatively late. Regression, reversal, or turning round upon the self seem to be independent of the stage of development. It may well be that they are the earliest defense mechanisms used by the ego.

Discussions

J. Sandler: Miss Freud, in Chapter 4 you refer to Freud's view that introjection (or identification) and projection are defenses which are important "neurotic mechanisms." We can add identification and sublimation to introjection and projection and comment that all such mechanisms also play a part in normal development. For example, introjection has been seen as the mental counterpart of oral "taking in," an essential element in building up the child's inner

world. It seems that we have a whole group of mechanisms which may at times be used for defensive purposes, but need not always function as defense mechanisms.

Anna Freud: Introjection and projection are nearer to the id than are other defense mechanisms. When they are close to the primary process they are not defensive. But such mechanisms may make another appearance when used by the ego for defensive purposes.

J. Sandler: When you speak of introjection and projection as being primary-process mechanisms, are you not really speaking of condensation and displacement?

Anna Freud: That's very near to it. But although we can give the processes other names, they are very much the same. So displacement on the primary-process level is projection on the ego level.

J. Sandler: Could you elaborate a little on the relation of the defense mechanisms to primary-process functioning?

Anna Freud: The person who first develops primary and then secondary process is still the same person, and the earliest defense mechanisms of the ego are based on primary processes. The experience gained by the individual from his primary processes is used by him in the elaboration of the defense mechanisms. Of course, later defenses are much more sophisticated, and much more under the influence of the ego. But if we look at the very early stages of development we can see how close the little child's projections are to primary-process functioning. We know how insecure the boundaries are in the small child, and it is much easier for him to say "I haven't done it, you have done it" than later on, when the boundaries are more efficient.

J. Sandler: It is often said that the earliest defense mechanisms are introjection and projection. But for these mech-

anisms to be effective as defenses, surely a very definite boundary has to exist between the self and not-self? Introjection is often described as a defense against loss of an object, and projection as a defense against feelings the child doesn't like and wants to remove from his own self-representation. Can we call such processes defenses before boundaries exist?

Anna Freud: If you project something and it is still felt to be yourself, it is an unnecessary exercise. You haven't gained anything.

J. Sandler: We hear a lot about primitive projection and introjection in the extremely young infant. Is not what is meant something other than what we understand by the defense mechanisms of projection and introjection?

Anna Freud: Yes, the primitive id processes get taken over only later by the developing ego as defense mechanisms.

J. Sandler: We come now to the question of whether the list you have given in this chapter should be regarded as a definitive one. I wondered why, for example, you had not included displacement as a defense. We know that displacement is part of primary process, but we also know that it has a defensive function when used by the ego. It can protect the person from, for example, a conflict of ambivalence. In fact you describe it in Chapter 4 in regard to the patient who "displaced outward one side of her ambivalent feeling" (p. 45). Did you have any special reason for not including displacement in the list of nine defense mechanisms (to which you added sublimation as a tenth)?

Anna Freud: I suppose it was partly because displacement is so clearly a primary-process mechanism. When you ask whether the list is a definitive one, I would say of course it is not. It seemed the best I could do at that time. I remember that I was very reluctant to say there were nine mechanisms, because I had the feeling that if I said there

were nine there might by then be ten. One should never count these things.

M. Berger: I should like to ask about introjection, because you have used it interchangeably with identification. Do you differentiate between the two?

Anna Freud: At the time there was a great deal of discussion about the difference between identification and introjection. Someone came up with the idea that introjection really meant the mental counterpart of physical "taking in." I hadn't at that time become accustomed to using the two terms for different processes.

J. Sandler: I think that the situation must have been complicated by the way the term "ego" was used. Of course we now see that it is necessary to differentiate the self-representation from the ego as a structure. In your book there are times when you use "ego" where I think that you quite clearly mean "self." This double meaning in psychoanalytic usage must have caused a lot of problems at the time. If we recall some of the discussions we have had about narcissism, we can see how so many complications arose in the past because the word "ego" was used for oneself as an object.

Anna Freud: And, of course, there is no word for the noun "self" in German.

J. Sandler: The French have tried to introduce *le soi*, but it doesn't seem to have worked very well. I think that in other languages the English word "self" tends to be used where there isn't an appropriate word.

S. Rosenfeld: At some point in the book there is a reference to introjection enriching the ego. I wonder whether we ought not to distinguish more precisely between the defensive aspects of introjection and the ego-building aspects.

J. Sandler: This problem is also connected with the need

to distinguish between the ego and the self. One can say that identifications can change the self-representation. But learning has a very strong component of identification in it, so one can say that identification enriches the ego as a structure, too. Whether introjection can be distinguished in this way, I don't know. Of course, it was also used in a different sense to refer to the internalization of the parents to form the superego. There is here a double meaning of the term introjection, because it refers on the one hand to very early "taking in," and on the other to superego formation when the child is about five. Students of psychoanalysis have pondered for years about the famous reference in Freud to the ego as the precipitate of abandoned object cathexes. What does this famous phrase mean?

Anna Freud: What is meant is very simply that every abandoned object relationship leaves its residue in the self, or the person, or the ego, and enriches it thereby.

M. Berger: I was rather surprised, Miss Freud, to find that identification with the aggressor as a defense was not included in your list of defense mechanisms. Did you think of it as being included in the concept of introjection?

Anna Freud: No. I didn't list it here because I thought only of the recognized defense mechanisms, and I felt modest about this new one. I didn't think it had a claim to be introduced yet.

T. Lopez: When we speak of abandoned object cathexes, this does not actually mean that the person goes away, does it? Is it not that certain ways of relating are abandoned?

Anna Freud: No, it doesn't mean that the person is really lost, but rather that the object cathexis is withdrawn and replaced by an identification. It is very important that the object libido can be changed back into narcissistic libido, that the libido can then take the self as an object.

J. Sandler: If we use the model of libido and its transfor-

mation and displacement, would we not then say that the building up of secondary narcissism is an essential part of development? It involves a withdrawal of investment from the object and an attachment of the affection felt for the object to the self-representation. Identification would then be the vehicle for secondary narcissism. If one copies an admired aspect of the object, then some of the admiration, affection, and esteem for the object can be transferred to the self, adding to secondary narcissism. It goes hand in hand with identification.

Anna Freud: Yes, that's right.

J. Sandler: Perhaps we can now return to some of the specific defense mechanisms. I wonder how you saw them at the time, Miss Freud. You mention regression as a defense, and again we have a mechanism which is at times a defense, and at times not. Presumably this double aspect can apply to all the mechanisms. You have often referred to children regressing toward the end of the school day, and I suppose we would not call this regression a defense. In fact, one could conjecture that we have to do a certain amount of work to prevent ourselves from regressing at any time, and when we get tired we can't do that work as well, so we give in to the pull toward childhood modes of behavior.

Anna Freud: We know how children regress to more and more infantile modes of behavior in the period just before they go to sleep.

A. Holder: I have always had problems with the concept of regression as a defense. It seems to me, Miss Freud, that you refer here to libidinal regression, rather than to regression as a defense on the side of the ego. I think that regression, as it is usually described, takes place outside the ego. What I mean is that after the ego defends against some unacceptable impulse, instinctual drive regression may follow and earlier drive contents be revived. The ego has then

to deal with a regressively revived derivative which tries to force its way through again. I have always thought that the ego does not *actively* institute the regression, as it does, for instance, in the case of repression or reaction formation. Rather, regression is something that happens as a *consequence* of the ego defending against an impulse. This makes me question whether it is a defense at all.

Anna Freud: I remember it being said that regression is the most efficient way for the whole personality to adapt to an intolerably difficult situation. I don't know whether it occurs outside the ego, so to speak, or whether the ego institutes it actively. But certainly the return to a lower form of functioning is a way of avoiding intolerable stress.

J. Sandler: Perhaps we can say that it is a way of *attempting* to avoid something intolerable, by reverting to a mode of functioning characteristic of an earlier time when such conflicts didn't exist. But this can get the individual into trouble because, as you have often pointed out, a new conflict may arise as a result of the regression, a conflict with a superego which hasn't regressed. I am reminded of a patient of mine who became increasingly angry with his mother-in-law after she came to stay, but was not aware of his anger. His repressed angry wishes revived childhood sadistic impulses which had been relatively dormant. The patient then had a greater conflict because of his revived or reinforced sadistic wishes. His anger with his mother-in-law had aroused, quite unconsciously, the wish to kill and to maim her. Regression had reinforced a neurotic conflict, but I don't think that the regression was a defense in this case.

Anna Freud: What you describe is more a revival than a regression. I wouldn't call it regression. I think that the new experience touches off the former one, revives it, brings the emotions of the past into the present.

J. Sandler: Would you not say that the child who is angry,

who then loses control and who resorts more and more to throwing things around and making a mess as he gets angrier and angrier, is showing a regression?

Anna Freud: I would call it an overwhelming of the ego's controls by the strength of the emotion.

J. Sandler: This raises the interesting point of whether the instinctual drives which may be seen as regressively revived are normally active but kept in control. Or are they dormant but reactivated? Or do both happen? It seems to me that we do need to distinguish between, on the one hand, something which is active but is being successfully defended against all the time, being held back under pressure or being diverted in some way, and on the other something which is there in a relatively latent form only, but which can become stronger when it is revived (in terms of the energy theory, I suppose one would say recathected).

Anna Freud: What about the crime of passion, when somebody kills someone else in a rage? How would you define it? The person does not need to be someone who is usually given to rages, or who knows about his murderous impulses. On the other hand, we know that these murderous impulses are there, are present in everybody, but are kept under repression and are controlled. But at some point passion may overwhelm the individual, and the ego's control is lost. I think that it is essentially a quantitative matter, and what we see is that for the moment the affect and the impulse are stronger than any of the restraints which usually keep them in check.

J. Sandler: I wonder if you could comment on the clinical significance of the difference between those children in whom there is a weakness of control on the part of the ego, so that infantile modes of expression are allowed through, and those cases in which there is a reinforcement due to regression or to a sudden stimulation of an infantile wish for some reason.

Anna Freud: We know both situations. The result is the same, because the balance is disturbed. The balance can be disturbed on the one side or on the other. It can be disturbed because the impulse becomes overwhelming for some reason, or because the ego becomes unduly weakened. The reasons are different, but the effect is the same.

J. Sandler: Could you say something, Miss Freud, about the question of superego regression? We usually say that the superego doesn't regress, yet we speak of more archaic forms of superego functioning returning; or we say that the superego has become more sadistic because of regression.

Anna Freud: One usually doesn't call this regression, but rather a dissolving of the superego—as in the saying that the superego is that part of the mental apparatus which dissolves in alcohol.

J. Sandler: I was thinking of the change in the superego which we see in melancholia, in the self-reproaching type of depression.

Anna Freud: It becomes more cruel.

J. Sandler: Wouldn't one call this a regression?

Anna Freud: I think you could very well call it a regression.

R. Evans: Could you say something about regression of the ego? It is said that it follows different laws, but I have never really got that straight in my mind.

Anna Freud: This is a subject which we have discussed a lot. The ego follows quite different laws as far as regression is concerned. Regression is really a different concept here, but we use the same name. The earlier idea was that in regression the libido returned to fixation points, to earlier stations where some libido had been left behind. This notion cannot, of course, be used for the ego. With the ego

what we see is a regression merely to earlier stages, but without the idea that it is the libido that pulls it backwards to specific fixation points.

J. Sandler: If one wanted to argue the point, one could say that there are certain modes of ego functioning which gave particular forms of satisfaction at particular points in development. We could then speak of a functional fixation of the ego, and say that in ego regression the person goes back to, for example, earlier defense mechanisms, or to earlier modes of thinking, which were satisfying or reassuring at the time. This would be different from the way in which you have described ego regression as following a progressive path backwards, something which I think is more characteristic of organic states.

Anna Freud: I still feel that there is a difference between a mode of functioning that gave pleasure or satisfaction or reassurance on the side of the ego, and the actual libidinal fixation to a libidinal phase. I think that there we have something more direct and basic, but I can quite see the other side.

J. Sandler: I have been thinking a lot lately about the way in which the urgent need to deal with anxiety, or with some threat, a need which can be as great as the urgency of an instinctual wish, may also contribute to regression. The push to function in a particular way characteristic of an earlier period of development, as well as the relief gained by functioning in that way, could be seen to be as great as that which we associate with the drives. But, of course, the pleasure gained may not be as great.

Anna Freud: The pleasure is not the same. What you get is the most effective way of escape from an intolerable situation of strain or anxiety.

I. Hellman: When we observed the babies in the Hampstead Nurseries during the war, we didn't think of ego regression

so much in terms of the pleasure gained, but rather of reducing the stress. This was very evident in those phases where the strain resulting from having to function at a higher level was too great and the baby returned to more infantile ways of speech, thought, and motor control. The step back seemed to me always to be the essential way in which the child could reduce the strain. Then the child could move forward again after a fairly short time.

M. Berger: There must be an interrelation between ego and libidinal regression. Can we have libidinal regression without ego regression or vice versa?

J. Sandler: If we differentiate ego and id for the purpose of conceptualizing aspects of behavior involving the total apparatus, when there is a conflict of interests between different aspects of the mind, then this must affect our thinking about regression. Miss Freud spoke earlier of the ego collaborating with the id, and I think that in this collaboration there might well be a tendency for the ego to regress when the id does. The derivative of the instinctual impulse would involve functions of the ego, and when a child regresses he may well turn to more primitive methods of doing this. But naturally children will vary a great deal in this regard. Some will have much conflict where there has been drive regression and others will have egos which regress alongside the drive regression, which accept the drive regression.

Anna Freud: I think Mrs. Berger meant something different. Could we imagine, let's say, an adult remaining on the genital level and still regressing heavily on the ego side?

M. Berger: I was thinking of children in very stressful situations where the child may give up speech for months on end, or gives up walking and reverts to crawling. Does the ego regression here carry with it a drive regression?

J. Sandler: In response to Miss Freud's question, it seems

likely that some people with organic disturbances may show a genital level of functioning but have an ego regression. But apart from that I am sure that many cases of ego regression allow pregenital impulses, which have been defended against, to come through. For example, the arteriosclerotic old man who exhibits himself in the park is letting something through which may have been very much alive before, but had been dealt with in some way.

Anna Freud: Yes, such impulses would be allowed through to the surface rather than having been brought up by regression.

J. Sandler: What seems to have been coming out in the discussion is a distinction between release and regression, which might be worth pursuing further.

Anna Freud: And that would give us the answer to the question of the crime of passion. It is a release, not a regression.

J. Sandler: May we move on now to the question of repression? One of the things we can ask is whether or not repression is an element in all the defenses, one of the basic building blocks in every defense described. In the first phase of psychoanalysis, when Freud placed so much emphasis on childhood traumas, the defense of repression was introduced in relation to the dissociation of affect and the memories connected with that affect. What would one say now about the question of the repression of feelings? You have spoken, Miss Freud, of reaction formation in relation to feelings. Would you say that repression, as we see it now, operates only against ideational content, so that as a consequence associated feelings are not aroused, or would you say that one can in fact have repressed feelings?

Anna Freud: You know, at the time I wrote this book, I was under the influence of the papers and ideas that existed then, and there was much confusion about the whole question of unconscious affect.

J. Sandler: The problem must have been made difficult because while we can obviously have preconscious feelings, or feelings in the unconscious part of the ego, as Freud showed in *Inhibitions, Symptoms and Anxiety* in 1926, this does not necessarily mean that we have feelings in the system Unconscious, in the dynamic Unconscious, or in the id.

Anna Freud: This is a difficulty I have always had with Kleinian theory, in that they speak of the deep anxiety in the unconscious, but we only get anxiety if the threatening material reaches the ego.

J. Sandler: I think that the Kleinians equate what is descriptively unconscious with what is dynamically unconscious. This leads to a lot of theoretical difficulty.

Anna Freud: Unconscious anxiety is not the same as anxiety in the Unconscious. We would have to say that it is only material which reaches the Preconscious or the unconscious ego which can be defended against, but this certainly includes feelings, because censorship does not stop at the border between the Unconscious and the Preconscious. The ego does the defending, including defending against feelings, and this work of defense is done in the unconscious part of the ego.

J. Sandler: I just want to say a brief word about reaction formation at this point. This mechanism has been discussed at length in the Hampstead Index, and we were particularly concerned about a possible difference between defensive attitudes based on reaction formations and those reaction formations in which feelings are changed into their opposite. In the first case, the sort of change we see is where an enjoyment of dirt gets turned into a highly critical attitude toward dirt and an overvaluation of cleanliness. In the second, there is much more feeling involved, as in the transformation of sadistic enjoyment into pity.

Clearly there is a great deal which needs to be clarified in regard to reaction formation.

Isolation has always caused some difficulty. Sometimes we refer simply to isolation, at other times to isolation of affect. When you spoke of isolation, Miss Freud, did you refer to something which is tolerated in consciousness only because the associated feelings have been removed, and which would otherwise be repressed?

Anna Freud: Yes, that was the meaning.

R. Evans: There is also a conceptualization of isolation as an artificial separation of two contents that belong together.

Anna Freud: I don't think that was the original meaning. The original meaning was the isolation of an affect from the idea that it was originally connected with.

J. Sandler: Perhaps what Dr. Evans has referred to is something which we put under the heading "splitting," but this is a term which has several meanings.

H. Kennedy: One of the problems with regard to splitting is the question of what happens to the affect. Is a repression of affect involved? Isolation is certainly one of those mechanisms that draw on other defenses.

Anna Freud: Yes, the affect is usually displaced, warded off, changed into the opposite, or denied. The important thing is that the result is that the affect isn't connected with the original source, with the original idea.

J. Sandler: We come now to the mechanism of undoing, which we often refer to as "doing and undoing." The question comes up of whether we should distinguish between simple undoing on the one hand, and doing and undoing as a specifically obsessional mechanism, on the other. We sometimes speak of "undoing" when people have to undo something they have done because they subsequently feel

guilty, which is certainly not an obsessional mechanism. We hear occasionally of the person who has a "ruined by success" or "negative therapeutic reaction" type of personality, who has to undo his success because he feels guilty. One wonders whether or not we should use the term "undoing" for this, or rather keep the term for the doing and undoing of the obsessional.

Anna Freud: Certainly the obsessional who puts a thing in a certain place and removes it again is doing and undoing, but there is something else which obsessionals do. An obsessional I treated was very afraid of any sort of aggression leaking out, and he would go over incidents innumerable times in his mind. This was a sort of undoing. He would go through an event up to the moment when the dangerous thing happened, and then he would mentally undo what happened afterwards. He would put something else in its place so that the danger was avoided. In this way he was undoing events which had happened.

J. Sandler: Does one have to be an obsessional to do that?

Anna Freud: Yes, I think so. Or at least to have an obsessional character.

J. Sandler: You mean because it is compulsive.

Anna Freud: Yes, he had to do it compulsively until the dangerous event was removed altogether, until it was really blotted out.

J. Sandler: That would be quite different from the sort of symbolic compromise shown in obsessional doing and undoing, where the wish is gratified by an action of some sort, the defense showing itself by the undoing.

Anna Freud: With my patient it was really a belief that an event could be undone psychically after the event.

J. Sandler: So you don't mean the obsessional doing and undoing.

Anna Freud: When I spoke of doing and undoing I really meant both.

J. Sandler: Would both of these mechanisms be mechanisms of defense?

Anna Freud: Yes, certainly. In some patients who are not obsessional we find symptoms like compulsive eating followed by vomiting. Is this not a way of undoing what has been taken in?

J. Sandler: You mean the psychic significance of the event is undone.

Anna Freud: Yes.

R.L. Tyson: Are there any precursors that we can see in those children who subsequently develop the defense of undoing?

J. Sandler: To my mind the anal child shows the normal activity of doing and undoing, which is very characteristic of his play. He will constantly put beads in a bottle and take them out and then put them back in again and take them out again. This is part, I think, of his developing a means of testing and controlling his environment. It is a very normal activity, and it seems to me that the defense grows out of this normal activity.

Anna Freud: Yes, he has learned that he can undo. It is very interesting to see the activity shared between two children. I once watched two little ones in the Nursery School, and one of the children was very intent on removing all the dishes from the dining room cupboard. The other child was equally intent on putting them all back. Neither interfered with the other, but the doing and undoing fitted together perfectly.

M. Berger: Are the symbolic acts of, say, an obsessional latency child, such as touching something three times in order to undo a thought, of the doing and undoing type?

Anna Freud: Yes. You know, children are taught in what is really a very funny way. Let us say that a little child of two or three years of age has hurt another child, then the nursery school teacher or the mother will say, now you must go and do this or that, and then it will be all right again. This is really very much like the obsessional symptom, isn't it? A child goes up the staircase and handles the banisters roughly. Then he is told he has to go back and stroke the banisters to take away the hurt he has caused it.

I. Hellman: The question remains of whether there is not a difference between undoing and what one calls reparation, making something "good" again. I think that the two are not quite the same. For instance, if a child strokes a child he has just hurt, there is a feeling of remorse attached to it. It is not the same as just putting the hair back in order to undo the act. There is a feeling that the hurt has to be compensated for in some way. He tries to make the other child feel better again, not just to put the hair back.

Anna Freud: For the child I believe it means to undo the whole event and to give the hair back again. For the adult it means to make good the hurt feeling. What is most interesting is when there is a transition from the physical action into the thought process, with attempts to undo thoughts, as in the obsessional.

One sees certain children who have as much pleasure in tumbling building blocks down as in building them up, and these are perhaps the children who will become obsessional later. It's very difficult to say whether one should call this a pre-stage rather than a precursor of obsessional activity, but certainly defense mechanisms have always to be built on abilities of some sort. Whether or not these are abilities of the ego or something which comes from the primary process is another question.

J. Sandler: I am convinced that the defense mechanisms

relate to what has been referred to as the perceptual and cognitive style of the individual. A person can have a style of thinking and perceiving which shows the modes of functioning of defenses in latent form. For example, we may see a style of thinking in which there is a great deal of categorizing, and while this is not really obsessional, it may show a predisposition to develop obsessional defenses. There are other people who, in their normal perception and cognition, show a great deal of what could grow into the mechanisms of denial and repression.

Anna Freud: Yes. You remember it was Hartmann who was the first to point out that what we call the obsessional mechanisms are there very early in order to create order in our thoughts.

J. Sandler: It might be useful to discuss projection now. At present we restrict the use of projection in the Index to the attribution of an unwanted impulse to another person, and the impulse is then felt as coming back against the person himself. So if someone is angry with another person and uses projection in the way we have defined it, he will feel that the other person is angry with him. We use the term "externalization" in the Index for anything else which does not have this "reflexive" quality. We have, in fact, a very narrow definition, and there would be a good case for arguing that it is far too narrow, for in the general psychoanalytic literature the concept of projection tends to be used to refer to all sorts of externalizations. For example, a person might project an aggressive wish onto a second person, then feeling that the second person has aggressive intentions toward a third person. This does not have the "reflexive" quality, and at present we tend not to call this projection. We would use the general term "externalization." I am not sure, Miss Freud, that this is the way you saw it when you wrote about projection.

Anna Freud: Historically, the return of the projected impulse back against the self was the first sort of projection

which was discussed, and the term externalization was not used. We tended to study only those situations in which the projected aggression or some other impulse was returned to the sender. The idea of externalization or other forms of projection came later.

J. Sandler: Historically, then, the concept would apply to paranoid people and to people with phobias, who felt that a situation was too dangerous because they had projected, for example, their own hostile wishes onto it. It would apply to Little Hans.

Anna Freud: Yes. At the time the concept was introduced and first used, it was the pathological and not the normal which was studied. What we now call externalization refers much more to what we discuss in relation to normal development.

J. Sandler: Of course, we also see it in the treatment situation, particularly where superego introjects are externalized onto the analyst. This tends to be differentiated from ordinary transference when we call it externalization. We can also see various forms of externalization as aspects of the self-representation being attributed to others, both in pathology and in normal life. A child may write a story and externalize a conflict, inside the session or outside it.

Anna Freud: What you described first as externalization onto the analyst would, I think, have at the time been called transference. It would not have been distinguished sufficiently from the object relationship which develops in the analysis and which we now call transference.

J. Sandler: In recent years you have emphasized this distinction, I know.

Anna Freud: But it was not commonly made at that time.

J. Sandler: What do you feel, Miss Freud, about whether we should restrict the definition of projection to the nar-

rower meaning in which there is a turning back of the wish or impulse against oneself?

Anna Freud: My feeling is that the division into projection and externalization really covers all the manifestations, so long as one distinguishes clearly between the two.

M. Berger: I should like to come back to the point about a clear differentiation between self and other being necessary for projection. I wonder if the child's generalizations, and such thoughts as "he wants to do the same to me as I want to do to him" do not in fact originate in the phase when there is still a sort of twilight of differentiation present, with boundaries not fully established.

Anna Freud: Yes, but to get rid of an unwanted wish by putting it into the other person only makes sense if the other person has been differentiated from you. If the impulse is still inside yourself you have accomplished nothing. The mechanism can only work as a defense so far as there is a distinction, because if there is no distinction there is no gain.

J. Sandler: I want to add the idea (about which I am quite convinced) that a form of very primitive and fleeting primary identification normally persists in adult life. I believe that when we perceive an object we are momentarily confused with it, although the ego then sets boundaries almost immediately. We could call this the boundary-setting function of the ego. We see such persisting primary identification in the way we move when we see people riding horses, skating, and so on. If we are not particularly on our guard we move in sympathy with the person we are perceiving. The primary confusion of very early childhood persists in some way. In certain psychotic states, or in toxic states, or when one is not fully awake, we do not set the boundaries so quickly, and can become consciously aware of the confusion.

Anna Freud: There is an interesting parallel to this because we know that with persecuted minorities, against whom atrocities are committed, the atrocities are preceded by a withdrawal of the feeling of sameness. We get the substitute feeling of "we are not the same, you and I." It is a sort of dehumanizing process applied to the victim. Without this preliminary withdrawal or boundary setting what happens afterwards could not happen, because of the feeling of sympathy and empathy, of sameness, which has to be done away with.

J. Sandler: I should like to clarify whether in projection it is always the same impulse that is felt to be directed back at one. In some cases it seems to be the same and in other cases it gets modified. Someone might say that the other person is angry with him, but what is being defended against is a death wish which has a different content.

Anna Freud: If you are angry enough it becomes a death wish. I wonder whether it is ever wholly changed. I wouldn't think so. We wouldn't call it projection if it were.

J. Sandler: I have never fully understood the projection that Freud spelled out in regard to homosexual wishes in paranoia. The process ends up with a person feeling a sort of penetrating attack. The change from "I love him" to "he loves me" and then to "he hates me" has often been referred to as projection, but it involves a transformation which we do not usually associate with projection. It seems to be more complicated than simple projection.

Anna Freud: Yes, because if it were simple projection the forbidden love for the other man would come back as a forbidden love from him for the original person. But what happens in between is as you described; the love is changed to hate.

J. Sandler: I've never really understood that bit as part of the projection.

Anna Freud: It's not part of the projection, but a reversal process which gets involved in the projection.

J. Sandler: One sees the simpler form of projection in those people who believe that others are out to seduce them.

Anna Freud: I think this is more of an externalization. We see it sometimes in prepsychotic states. Someone travels on the bus or on the subway, and believes that all the girls are making secret advances to him. These are only his own wished-for secret advances to the girls. We don't call this projection. It is really an externalization of the impulse. The girl does it instead of the man.

J. Sandler: In paranoid people there is an increase in the narcissistic supplies of the individual because he becomes the center of attention. So a person's idea that all the girls are making eyes at him refuels his narcissism, and perhaps temporarily does away with the feelings of inadequacy and helplessness which go along with the recognition of his own unfulfillable sexual wishes. I think that there is also a wish fulfillment through a sort of unconscious basic identification with the persecutor, even though the boundaries between self and other are well established.

Anna Freud: I remember a patient who actually noticed the sexual excitement in these other people, instead of noticing her own. This isn't quite the same as projection, but there seem to be so many marginal phenomena we want to label. I think that one of the problems of constructing a definition is that we feel the need to define the process so that it includes all impulses. Even though the use of the term "projection" in a wide sense is the common usage, perhaps we ought to stick to externalization for the general class of these processes, and reserve projection for the externalization of a disowned impulse in one's self onto another, an impulse which is felt to be coming back at oneself.

R. Edgcumbe: Freud gives the example in his paper on

"Jealousy, Paranoia and Homosexuality" of someone who has the temptation to be unfaithful and then believes his wife to be unfaithful. Freud calls this projection, but says that it is not simply putting one's own impulses onto the other person. Also, it involved a libidinal rather than an aggressive drive.

J. Sandler: If we follow what was said earlier, we would have to call it externalization, although the term "projection" was certainly used earlier on.

Anna Freud: There is an element of the impulse returning, because the end of the story is that the husband is not unfaithful to his wife, but rather that she betrays him.

J. Sandler: Yes, in that sense it would be projection in the strict sense of the definition. But if one were to say that the person is not having conscious thoughts about other women, but believes that the wife is having thoughts about other men, then it would be externalization.

Anna Freud: Yes.

J. Sandler: It is a completely arbitrary division, but I suppose that it is necessary.

I. Hellman: I see projection in agoraphobia quite regularly. I had an agoraphobic woman as a patient, and she told me that every man she passed in the street became sexually excited. What she experienced was her fear of being in the street. It was quite obvious that she projected her wishes and felt them to be coming back at her.

J. Sandler: Would we not say that there is always a projection or an externalization in the classic phobic situation? The impulse is located in the external world, and then it can be avoided and controlled, whereas if it were to be recognized as one's own, it would not be so readily controlled. But *what* is projected—is it the wish or is it the danger situation, the threat? And isn't it really an externalization rather than a projection?

Anna Freud: I remember a child with a school phobia where it was quite clear from the work in the analysis that the danger for the child was her death wish against her mother. She was unable to move from mother to father, because this meant killing the mother. But this first appeared as a school phobia, as a fear of a boy she felt to be aggressive in the playground. Of course, this means for us that she was an aggressive little girl, but in her fear she refused to go out and play in case he hurt her. We would say that she was afraid that she would meet her own aggression in him. She then had a fear of a girl at school who had actually told her some aggressive fairy stories, and from then on she refused to go to school. In both instances she feared to meet her own aggressive death wishes in the outside world, but externalized them onto other people so that she could avoid them.

J. Sandler: I think that people will have to have the license to use projection or externalization interchangeably.

Anna Freud: Until we know better.

J. Sandler: One often sees in paranoid people the exploitation of a piece of reality for purposes of projection. Of course there is projection, but often something real is grossly exaggerated. This can lead to difficulties if one has a paranoid patient, because he can always find the evidence that the persecution he is talking about is really there. We also see it in certain character cases, who are not anywhere near being psychotically paranoid, but who have a capacity for selecting particular aspects of what other people do, so that they always produce a bit of reality to justify their own attitudes. They use the reality selectively in order first to externalize, and then to rationalize. Some people do this so skillfully that one can be convinced for a while that what they say is correct. This isn't quite the same as projection, and I've always thought it really needs to be labelled as a mechanism in its own right—this sort of differential selection or hyper-investment.

Anna Freud: Aren't we really talking about a heightened empathy for what goes on in the other person, as something which is part of the necessary background for the mechanism of projection. The reality is detected and used for projection.

While the psychotic person may be very empathic and extremely sensitive about what goes on in other persons, he may equally often be completely out of touch with reality. On the other hand the neurotic picks out bits of reality which substantiate his fantasies, and this does not necessarily have anything to do with projection.

J. Sandler: I should like to begin with a discussion of introjection. You mentioned, Miss Freud, that introjection was seen as an instinctual activity at the time you wrote the book. At that time, too, the term was used relatively synonymously with identification. From what I understand, this did not give rise to great difficulty, because it was clear from the context when Freud was using introjection to refer to the setting up of the parents in the form of the superego at the time of the resolution of the Oedipus complex. This was clearly quite different from the use of the term for the infant's oral "taking in" of his surroundings. We have these two quite clearly different meanings of the term introjection, but things are made more complicated because there has been a tendency in recent years to distinguish between introjection on the one hand and identification on the other. We are somewhat clearer now about identification, because it can be linked with changes in the self-representation, one's own psychic representation of oneself, which is a basis both for perceiving oneself and for action. Things are not quite as clear in regard to introjection, because the double meaning of the term has persisted. In our Index work on the superego we limited the term introjection to the internalization of parental authority at the time of superego formation. However, you listed introjection as a defense mechanism, and my guess

is that you had in mind the way the person coped with the pain of detaching from the object, with maintaining the tie to the object by internalizing it through identification. Possibly you also thought of it as producing a sort of inner companion which would then form part of the superego. Would that be a correct understanding?

Anna Freud: Not quite. I know very well that at the time I certainly had not thought through the difference between the two terms, or the differences between the processes covered by them. According to my feeling then, the term introjection was rather forced on us, and I know that I didn't feel comfortable with its use, but when writing about identification I felt an obligation to add introjection, because people were using it more and more as a synonym for identification. So I would ask you not to take what I have written very seriously in this connection, because I wasn't very clear about it at the time. Certainly, as you know, the attitude to the term changed later with the introduction of the whole idea of introjects and internal objects, which seems to be a broader idea than identification.

J. Sandler: As identification is not mentioned in your list, I suppose we could proceed as if you had put identification there rather than introjection. Wasn't the idea of identification in its defensive sense in current use at that time?

Anna Freud: There is the enrichment of the ego by identification on the one hand, and the defensive use, as in identification with the aggressor, on the other.

J. Sandler: Would the ordinary defensive use of identification have been seen at the time as a way of dealing with object loss?

Anna Freud: No, that wasn't the idea at all. That belonged to the area of enrichment of the personality. One loses the object, but retains something inside, so one's own person changes and grows as a result of the object loss. The em-

phasis was rather on the enrichment through loss and not on the defense against the feelings of loss. There was very much the idea, as you know, that one couldn't get rid of objects except by retaining something of them.

J. Sandler: What would be the defensive aspect of identification?

Anna Freud: Identification with the aggressor.

J. Sandler: I would like to clarify what aspects you had in mind, Miss Freud, when you included introjection as a defense in your book.

Anna Freud: I suppose I meant a defense against feelings of helplessness, of smallness, of impotence in the child, who then appropriated qualities of the adult in order to bolster up the self. I went on to pinpoint this more in the idea of identification with the aggressor. I got the idea from Aichhorn, who was able to show how there could be an identification with a sort of ideal object, a positive object, a powerful object like a hero.

J. Sandler: We see identification very much as a defense in connection with the next item on your list, the turning against the self. I think we are all familiar with the way in which the child may resolve ambivalence by identifying with the ambivalently loved object, then turning the aggression directed toward the object onto himself. So there identification would be one aspect of turning against the self as a way of resolving a conflict.

Anna Freud: There was a little girl in the Hampstead Nurseries who said to her little brother who was afraid of dogs: "You be doggie and no dog will bite you." She invented the idea.

J. Sandler: A number of people have asked if we could take up a point which is often found difficult. That is the precise distinction between the internalization (or the introjection)

of the parents at the time of superego formation, and the internalization of conflict. You often speak of conflict with the external world being replaced by internalized conflict. Do you link this specifically with superego formation, or is there a separate process in regard to the internalization of conflict? We tend to speak of internalized conflict occurring after about five years of age, more or less at the same time as superego formation.

Anna Freud: I certainly meant that what has been in the outside world before has become internal, so the external part of the conflict, part of the outside world, has in the meantime become part of the internal world. Because of that the conflict with the external object is not an internal conflict with a part of the self.

J. Sandler: The idea has been put forward that one can have an internalized conflict before the formation of the superego proper.

Anna Freud: I am sure that this is so. There again it was Aichhorn who brought the idea up first. The internal authority works better in the presence of the external object who is the originator of the prohibition. On his own the child may come to terms quite easily with the conflicting wishes.

J. Sandler: This is the story of the child who wanted to steal the fruit—

Anna Freud: —then he thinks of his father, which means he strengthens his internal superego by the thought of the external figure from whom it's derived. He can have a representation of the conflict, or of the external figure involved, the one that prohibits, but this does not yet mean that we have an internalized conflict.

J. Sandler: Fenichel has pointed out that before the superego exists there is a sort of "watchman" set up to assess the

reaction of the external world. Of course the assessment is distorted by fantasy, by the talion principle, by projection, and so on, so that the child does not have a direct representation of the external world, but for the child the punishing agency is still located outside. This would be different from the externalization of an internal agency, when the child deals with an internal conflict by putting one of the agencies involved in the conflict outside, because it is easier to feel that one has an external conflict than an internal one. So, in a sense, because the child learns to anticipate the reactions of people in the external world (even though these anticipations may be grossly distorted) he has an internal representation, but the conflict is not an internal one.

M. Berger: There are pre-stages of internalizing conflict. I remember two little girls who were in the nursery when the teachers were out in the garden. One girl dipped her finger in a jug of fruit juice, and licked it. The other said: "I won't do it, my mummy won't like it." I think her conflict was still with the external world, but already there was an internal prohibition. I think she was on the verge of saying "I don't like doing it."

Anna Freud: I think there are three stages. In the first the prohibiting agent has to be actually present. In the next stage the prohibiting agent can be removed from the scene, but is thought of. In the third phase the prohibiting agent is inside.

J. Sandler: There is a link here with the idea of object constancy, and with the point you have made elsewhere, Miss Freud, about the critical time in development at which irreparable damage can be done by loss of the object. Before that the object can be replaced without necessarily causing harm.

Anna Freud: In one of Róheim's studies of primitive peoples

he talked of the *tondi*. The *tondi* is a sort of ghost that governs the actions of the person, but we would really say that it is a superego. I remember when Róheim spoke of this for the first time he referred to people being alone with their *tondis* to guide their actions.

I. Hellman: I was going to say something rather similar about the pre-stages. We have had ample opportunity to observe the development of superego internalization in the Nursery, and it seems clear that the awareness of the external prohibition comes much earlier than four or five. We have so many observations of eighteen-month-old children finding a way of telling us "the other child has done it" or "the horse has done it." This shows an awareness that something is prohibited.

Anna Freud: I would say "somebody doesn't like it."

I. Hellman: Yes, but it is there at that early age without the prohibiting person being present.

J. Sandler: Surely there comes a point where one cannot argue the child out of his guilt feelings any more? Then one would feel that a firm introjection has taken place. Before that one can usually reassure the child in some way. But I think that we are left with the problem of when the superego introjection does occur, because although we say that the superego gets formed at a particular point, we know that it gets formed over a period of time. In connection with what we were talking about I am reminded of the nightmares of the two-year-old in which there are certainly reflections of the internalization of a prohibition against aggression. The aggression is then externalized onto the attacking figure in the dream. For me this has always been one of the patterns for later superego functioning. It seems that even in the child's sleep the prohibitions are effective internally. It is worth exploring to what extent the child can be reassured or argued out of

an internal prohibition at, say, the age of two and a half. I think of the child who has always pushed down his aggression, with the constant encouragement of his parents. Perhaps one can explain what goes on in terms of identification (because we know that identification can take place very early) but somehow it does not seem to be enough to account for this early internalization.

I. Hellman: Lots of people can be argued out of their superego convictions via identifications, because of some form of attachment to an object.

J. Sandler: Isn't there a big distinction between the sort of change one can see in a very young child, where one reassures the child, and the sort of arguing out you refer to, in which you usually provide the person with a formula so that he can ignore his superego prohibitions or gain alternative sources of narcissistic supply?

I. Hellman: I thought of it as something similar. The child who enters a delinquent group will sometimes give up certain things one would have thought were very much part of his superego standards at that point.

J. Sandler: I think this is certainly so. We know that drugs do the same. Miss Freud has pointed out that alcohol does it, and narcissistic supplies from the group will certainly do it.

Anna Freud: Sometimes children do it on their own. I remember a little boy of five who had an enormous wish to have a motorcycle. I explained to him that he wouldn't get it as his mother wouldn't like it. He said, "All right, then I'll wish for it for my birthday." I said, "No, I don't think they'll give it to you." "All right, I'll wish for it for Christmas; then one gets everything." I said, "No, I don't think you'll get it, it's not something you'll get." He said, "All right, I'll give it to myself, because I allow myself." He allows himself, which means that suddenly he was at one

with his superego, and his superego said "that's quite all right for you to have."

J. Sandler: One has to distinguish between superego prohibitions and the ego's assessment of reality. It may not be in one's superego to observe the speed limit [when driving], but the reality may make one do so.

Anna Freud: It *should* be in one's superego. It is really a question of whether the person is law-abiding. With the law-abiding person, it is in the superego, with others not. . . . I suppose the law-abiding person is law-abiding because he has an obsessional character!

J. Sandler: Or he may have a superego which says, "Obey laws, whatever they are."

Anna Freud: Yes. Another question, one that refers specifically to adolescence, is whether the superego in the developing person really becomes wholly independent of the external object, even after the superego has been internalized and the authority of the parent added to it. We have examples from the treatment of children who have gone wrong in their development because, at the age of eight or nine, confidence in the parents has been shattered because they have broken up. This in turn acts on the internalized superego. We have the example in adolescence where, with the loosening of the tie to the parents, the superego gets very shaken. And does that really coincide with our expectations of full internalization? Or does it show us that a link with the original objects and the tie to them always remains?

J. Sandler: I think we ought to try to bring the discussion back a little to the question of the defensive aspects of introjection or identification. Certainly we have to take into account the difference between the flexibility of the superego as a structure on the one hand, and the relation of the ego to the superego on the other. These are very

different things. In certain group situations the superego may remain the same, but one could say that the person doesn't respond to his superego at that time because he has been carried away by identification with the group. Perhaps it is the more conscious aspects of the superego that are more liable to change. Perhaps, too, after a certain point, external influence doesn't affect the unconscious operation of a sense of guilt very much. And then we ought also to take into account the point Miss Freud made about the superego continuing its development, the internalization of aspects of teachers and educators and so on. While I don't think we should go into the specific problems of adolescence here, it is perhaps legitimate to ask whether introjection as a defense might not occur in someone who has a particularly powerful superego and strong internal conflicts, and who may then internalize an alternative introject in a superego fashion. This would give an auxiliary superego, a sort of secondary superego to which the person can relate, as well as being a defense against the painful internal conflict with the original superego. Perhaps in such a case we could consider later superego-type introjection as a defense.

I. Hellman: Do you mean identifications with a new object in adolescence? For example, identification with the leader of a group who is then preferred to the father, identification with the rejection of much or all the father stands for and the adoption of a totally new set of values. While this often happens, I see it largely as a passing phenomenon, with very few residues to become thoroughly introjected.

J. Sandler: I suggest that we move on to the next mechanism, which is "turning against the self." I presume, Miss Freud, you meant turning aggression against the self, because if it were libido you would have spoken of the turning of object libido into secondary narcissism. In the Index we

have discussed the concept of turning aggression against the self at some length, and we found that there were many different varieties. I wonder if you would tell us what you had in mind at the time.

Anna Freud: I really took it from the then current psychoanalytic theory. The impulse, especially, of course, the aggressive impulse, first directed against the outside world, can be deflected from the outside world toward the self.

J. Sandler: Do you mean like the child who wants to push the therapist down the stairs, but falls down the stairs himself. This would then be an aggressive impulse of the moment, turned away from the object back against the self.

Anna Freud: Yes. Some people who commit suicide do that to the highest degree. That's the way they try to become good. "I don't murder you; I commit suicide." That's the defense I wrote about.

J. Sandler: I assume that you are also using the term here in a relatively broad sense, to include superego aggression turned against the self. There the defense is against the pain which would result from attacking the object.

Anna Freud: Yes.

J. Sandler: Shall we go on to the mechanism of reversal? I am not sure what you meant by reversal here, because nowadays so many different sorts of reversal are described.

Anna Freud: I meant reversal of roles. We had a very good example of a child of a partially sighted mother who was used by the mother as her eyes to guide her. This, of course, upset the whole mother-child relationship because the child had to mother the mother in certain respects, and in this child it led to a general tendency to reverse roles. For example, in the diagnostic interview, she began to question the diagnostician, as she evidently expected to be questioned. She asked, "What's your name?" "Where

do you live?" There can be reversal of roles in other contexts, between victim and attacker or between lover and loved. One always has to imagine a couple in a certain relationship where the individual in question assumes the role of the other and assigns his own role to the partner. That's what I meant by reversal here.

J. Sandler: Does one not see it also in those nurses who have had deprived childhoods and deal with their wish to be nursed and mothered by becoming nurses, by becoming a good parent to the patient and caring for the patient?

Anna Freud: I think more of the adults who treat their children exactly as they have been treated, only now they are the parents and can take the parents' role toward the child.

J. Sandler: In the Index we try to distinguish between reversal of roles, identification with the aggressor, and passive into active.

M. Berger: I was taught the meaning of reversal of roles by my very first patient. He was a highly intelligent child with a learning problem, and was terrified of the school situation, as he was probably also afraid of the treatment situation. He defended against his fear by becoming the teacher or a quiz master, but it wasn't enough for him just to sit opposite me in the treatment room and teach or quiz me. On the table he had to put the pouffe, on the pouffe he put the little chair. He would then sit high up and say he was the teacher and I was the pupil.

Anna Freud: This illustrates something else besides. If the defense of reversal isn't sufficient, it has to be repeated, exaggerated, and overdone. This shows it up for the defense it is.

J. Sandler: What this child does is also to get a tremendous boost to his self-esteem, as well as doing away with his anxiety. I think a very fine distinction will have to be drawn

between this and identification with the aggressor which, although superficially similar, is in fact a different mechanism.

Anna Freud: A more circumscribed one.

I. Hellman: I think that the big difference is that when it is identification with the aggressor there is the fantasy of the attacker rather than a re-enacting of a real experience. The two are very different.

Anna Freud: There is usually more than one defense involved. Let us take the child who has been to the dentist and who comes to the analytic hour and now plays dentist. One can say that he identifies with the aggressor because he is now the dentist. But you can also say that it is a reversal of roles. It can also be a turning of passive into active.

Of course, in reversal of roles, you can also reverse from active to passive, as in the patients who become addicted to masochistic experiences, taking the role of the victim, as a way of dealing with their own aggression. For one reason or another the reversal of roles is for them the most important or the most convenient mechanism.

J. Sandler: We have not proceeded very far into Chapter 4, but we come now to sublimation. You say, Miss Freud, that we have to add a tenth mechanism of defense "which pertains rather to the study of the normal than to that of neurosis" (p. 44). I think that we will have many things to say about sublimation, but I would like to begin with the question of whether this was the first time sublimation was regarded as a mechanism of defense, because you say in the text that we now have to add it to the list. I think we must all be aware that this mechanism is rather like identification in that it is, on the one hand, an aspect of normal ego functioning and important for normal development, and can also be a defense. I suspect that there is still a lot of controversy over whether sublimation is a defense or

not. You speak of the displacement of instinctual aims, but there is also the question of the change of aims to a so-called "higher" level associated with sublimation. This has, of course, led to difficulty about defining what we mean by "higher." Do we see sublimation in terms of what society regards as "higher?" Is this the first time the mechanism was regarded as a defense? What is its position as a defense in relation to its being also a normal developmental mechanism? Finally, do we need to amplify the formulation you have given in relation to displacement of instinctual aims to bring in the notion of "higher" aims?

Anna Freud: Before responding to your questions I want to say one thing about our last discussion. Those present seemed to assume that the formulations about the mechanisms were original contributions made by me, whereas what I did in Chapter 4 was really to sum up the opinions current at the time. I simply took the position as it was then—I needed to prepare the reader for the later chapters—and I summarized the position at this point. I think that didn't quite come across.

Of course one would say today that it is not only sublimation which belongs to the sphere of the normal, rather than to the neurotic or abnormal. We know very well that regression is normal, that repression is an absolutely essential mechanism in normal development, that reaction formation is normal in character formation. Isolation, undoing, introjection, all also appear in normal development. It is very much a quantitative question whether the outcome is a normal one or leads to pathology. But perhaps sublimation has a separate and special position in that it is ordinarily always normal, or rather leads to what is normal. If it appears as something pathological, then it has a compulsive quality. If it is used to keep down anxiety, it tends to be overdone, and we would not call it ordinary sublimation. The reason we call it a defense mechanism at all is because if we look at it from the point of view of

the drive derivatives it is an interference with a direct gratification which would otherwise arouse anxiety. A sublimation is usually very pleasurable, but can the pleasure
derived from sublimation really compete with the pleasure
from direct instinctual gratification? I suppose not, and
for that reason we need to see it as a defense mechanism.

J. Sandler: If I understand you correctly, as a defense it
must have something to do with the resolution of conflict.

Anna Freud: Yes.

J. Sandler: And the displacement to so-called higher aims
would be a way of resolving the conflict. For example, if
someone is guilty about some crude and primitive sexual
wish, or an aggressive one, your point would be that in
resolving the conflict a certain amount of pleasurable gain
is lost. A price is paid for sublimation in terms of giving
up some of the direct pleasurable gratification of the instinctual wish. Some of us have a problem in regarding
sublimation as a defense because it is so difficult to distinguish the defensive aspects from normal ego development.
I imagine that at the time of your writing this chapter the
whole notion of adaptation was not in people's minds as
much as it has been in the period after the second world
war.

Anna Freud: No, it wasn't. But let us take a very simple
example, which was used a great deal at that time. Take
the child who smears his feces. If, instead of this, the child
plays with sand and water, or with plasticine, and begins
to build things, then you can compare the pleasures the
little child gets from the two activities. What is lost in sublimation is surely some of the direct sensual pleasure in
the primitive activity, the wish to enjoy the dirty object, the
feeling on the skin, on the hands, the smell of the feces.
On the other hand, the child then has to cope with the
disapproval, the external disapproval followed by internal
disapproval. So he does a deal. He gives up some of the

pleasure, thereby avoiding some of the disapproval. He has a lesser pleasure, but what he does is much more approved of, and in the end he is better off. But the drive is not better off. The drive has been cheated of some of its gratification. I think it depends very much from what side you look at it.

J. Sandler: Would you say that the instinctual wish gets a symbolic gratification?

Anna Freud: A displaced gratification, yes.

J. Sandler: There would also be some sensual gratification if we think of the child modeling clay instead of playing with feces. That would be nearer to the original activity. But if one thinks of the example, say, of stamp collecting, which has been regarded as a sublimation of anal retentiveness or of hoarding, this is rather more removed from physical pleasures. Of course, not every stamp collector displays an anal sublimation.

We can approach sublimation in terms of a transformation of the instinctual energy and a desexualization. But we can also suggest that behind every sublimation there is, at some level, an unconscious fantasy gratification of the instinctual wish. This aspect has not been brought into most writings on the subject, certainly not in the writings of the ego psychologists, where sublimation is linked so much with the neutralization of instinctual energy. I would guess that the unconscious fantasy which might be unconsciously gratified would be much closer to the original activity than the overt sublimation appears to be.

Anna Freud: You are quite right, because Hartmann was very intent on pursuing his idea of secondary autonomy. He believed that the sublimated activity, once removed from the drive, becomes the property of (and part of) the ego, that it gets its new roots there and gradually gives up its original roots in the id.

J. Sandler: We have to dissect out several things here. We have learned from Hartmann that an ego activity which may not be derived from a particular set of instinctual impulses may be sexualized or aggressivized so that it has a completely new meaning and function. This then poses the problem of distinguishing between such a reinstinctualization on the one hand, and on the other the breakdown of a sublimation so that its original instinctual roots and sources show themselves again. In the first instance we have a change of function, and in the second a regressive breaking down.

Anna Freud: We also have to distinguish here between the breakdown of reaction formations and the breakdown of sublimations. The two are very easily confused.

There is still the question about the displacement of the aim in the activity of sublimation. You will remember the story my father liked so much of the little girl in a village, who walks along followed by a flock of geese. A benevolent traveler comes along and begins to talk to the little girl, and finds out what an intelligent child she is. He feels that it is a terrible pity that her life is wasted in such simple activities, so he pays for her education so that she becomes a teacher. This story was told in a cartoon strip in a newspaper, and the last picture showed the girl, now grown up, walking in exactly the same way as she did when she was a child, followed by a long line of children as she had been followed by the geese. That is sublimation.

J. Sandler: By your definition she would be getting less pleasure from the children than from the geese!

Anna Freud: It's harder work, you know.

J. Sandler: Can we touch on the question of what we mean by "higher" aims in sublimation?

Anna Freud: Well, that is very easily answered. One can answer it in two ways. The aims would be more approved

of by the superego, or more approved of by the outside world. This is what we mean by "higher."

J. Sandler: Would you say more removed from direct instinctual gratification?

Anna Freud: But the closeness to the direct instinctual aims would be the reason for the disapproval.

J. Sandler: Freud took the term sublimation from chemistry, so we should regard it as meaning a purifying and refining of something cruder. The baser elements, namely the sexual and aggressive elements are excluded.

Anna Freud: Or are refined.

When Aichhorn dealt with delinquent boys, he maintained that it was extremely important to find a sublimated activity in which to train them that was not too far removed from their instinctual aims. They should not have to take a big step in refining the instinctual aims, but rather a small one which was perhaps possible for them to take. For instance, a very violent boy would be placed in a butcher's shop; a boy who was near the homosexual level might be an excellent tailor. Aichhorn was very successful with this policy. In this we can really see the displacement.

J. Sandler: I have always held the view that for something to be regarded as sublimation it should be treated as an extension of the self or of the object. For something to be a sublimation people should care for the activity or its products, should be able to pursue and enjoy the activity even when the instinctual drives are not aroused. There is some degree of attachment, of affection and concern for the activity, something which parallels the relationship to an object. This seems to me to be a necessary factor added to the skills involved. From this point of view, certain activities which don't involve great skill might be classed as sublimation.

Anna Freud: What you have in mind is a kind of object

constancy towards the activity which then becomes independent of the immediate pleasure gained.

J. Sandler: Yes, exactly. In contrast, one could have a sort of need-satisfying relation to activities. Then the activity becomes something which is only undertaken from time to time, and the person doesn't treat it as if it is something important in his life. This is in contrast to the constant attitude to a sublimation which parallels object constancy as you have described it.

Anna Freud: This is very much along the lines of what Hartmann meant by secondary autonomy, although I was always unhappy when Hartmann took the stand that what we really had to deal with was a change in the energy, from sexual or aggressive energy to neutralized energy. My feeling is that thereby one loses the idea of the compromise character of the sublimation, and the whole question gets pulled over to problems of energy alone, to questions of the quality of the energy.

J. Sandler: I would agree very much that the concept of neutralization falls down because it is essentially a descriptive concept which has been given the status of being an explanation. This gives the illusion that it is useful. One starts with the description that there is no sexuality or aggression shown in the sublimated activity, and moves to the point that the process of change is one of desexualization and deaggressivization, in other words of neutralization. This is parallel to saying that someone is not working and therefore he is lazy, and going on to say that he does not work *because* he is lazy.

Anna Freud: In particular, the dynamic side gets lost because in reality a sublimation is a bargain. There is the wish to keep as much as possible of the original pleasure and to avoid as much as possible feelings of prohibition, disapproval, or guilt. The sublimation strikes a bargain,

but it is a very tricky business. Sometimes something emerges which is near to the original aim; sometimes it is much further removed.

J. Sandler: Miss Freud, some people have said that sublimations are essentially the same as reaction formations. Certainly we disagree with this, but there does seem to be an area of overlap. I remember a man who used to advertise in a weekly newspaper that if you wrote to him he would send details of a hundred ways to kill rabbits painlessly. This advertisement appeared week after week. Now I don't think we need to look very far to see the underlying wish and preoccupation of the advertiser. What we see is a reaction formation, and I am sure that this man felt very strongly that rabbits have to be protected from pain. Can we call his activities and his interest in the painless killing of rabbits a sublimation? He was doing something which is socially on a "higher" level, doing "good" one might say, and obviously his work was very highly invested and gratifying to him. Where do we draw the line between the reaction formation and the sublimation?

Anna Freud: Sublimation is much more an activity, and a reaction formation is part of the character and personality.

J. Sandler: Why is it that we often see excellent sublimations in people who have a full sexual life (normal or perverse)? There doesn't seem to be an economic balance between the amount of sexual gratification and the amount of sublimation.

Anna Freud: The answer once given to this point was that we have to distinguish between pregenital and genital activities, and to restrict the idea of sublimation and reaction formation to the pregenital drive derivatives.

J. Sandler: But this is why I mentioned perversions, because they have the pregenital component, and yet at the same time one sees sublimations. One has only to think of highly successful people in the theatre and in the arts generally.

Anna Freud: We probably see two quite different efforts to deal with the same drive material.

J. Sandler: We talk about sublimation within a framework which derives from a period when the consideration of the regulation of narcissism and self-esteem was not so intensely studied. So many activities, including artistic activities, have as much to do with self-esteem and narcissistic regulation as they have to do with the drives, although developmentally one might be able to argue that they are drive derivatives. In the "here-and-now" they may not have all that much to do with the drives. We make a mistake if we think that there has to be a quantitative relation between the amount of sublimation and the amount of sexuality. We should remember that the idea of sublimation was put forward, as were so many other concepts, in the attempt to understand relatively gross phenomena, such as the case of someone who is unable to gratify himself or herself sexually, or feels guilty or inhibited about the gratification and finds an alternative form of expression, which is more "refined" from a social point of view. When we begin to look microscopically at the concept, then, as with many other concepts, our theory may break down.

Anna Freud: That applies to all the defense mechanisms. If you look at them microscopically, they all merge into each other. You will find repression anywhere you look. You will find bits of reaction formation or identification. You will find five or six defenses compressed into one attitude. The point is that one should not look at them microscopically, but macroscopically, as big and separate mechanisms, structures, events, whatever you want to call them. Then they will stand out from each other, and the problems of separating them theoretically become negligible. You have to take off your glasses to look at them, not put them on.

J. Sandler: Ideally one should have bifocals! Then one could switch from one to the other.

Anna Freud: Yes.

H. Kennedy: I think it ought to be said that we should be very careful about judging what the processes are behind any one activity, because the activity can have different meanings. Certainly it is impossible to say from the activity itself whether it is sublimation or a reaction formation.

J. Sandler: It might be worth going back to Miss Freud's point that in speaking of a sublimation we refer to the activity, and when we speak of a reaction formation we refer to an attitude of mind. The two may, it follows, go together, as in someone very involved with the Royal Society for the Prevention of Cruelty to Animals, or who campaigns against cruel ways of killing rabbits. The sadism of the people who rage against fox hunting comes through, of course, in their physical attacks on the fox hunters, which are sometimes extremely vicious. If we consider nursing, we can think of reversal of roles, but at the same time the activity might be a sublimation.

Anna Freud: Yes. I think of a patient who is a vegetarian because she cannot stand the idea of killing or eating animals, of being cruel to animals in any way. At one time she even contemplated not eating vegetables because she felt so sorry for the plants. Now that goes, of course, rather far as a reaction formation or an inhibition—let us call it a reaction formation—against cruelty. On the other hand, she is fascinated by the reports of concentration camps and prisons. She has asked herself whether that is a morbid interest, which means to her that she asks whether the cruelty she pushes down in one part of her life shows itself in another part. But then, when she thinks further, she feels so identified with the victims that she is sure it could not be her own cruelty. When she read the stories about the concentration camps she compared herself constantly with the victims and felt a certain relief at the thought that they were worse off than she is. The whole thing is quite

complicated, and it only seems simple if we look at one side of it at a time.

I. Elkan: I should like to ask whether we still accept that sublimation is concerned with pregenital impulses only?

J. Sandler: I am sure that Miss Freud has been involved in many arguments about this, because it is a topic which has come up over and over again, and which has not really been settled. Do you want to comment, Miss Freud?

Anna Freud: I would rather let you answer the question!

J. Sandler: But I don't know the answer either. I do believe that phallic impulses can be sublimated, and that much confusion has arisen because phallic and genital are often confused. By definition something cannot be genital unless it expresses itself in a mature sexual relationship, which involves not only direct instinctual wishes but important object relations aspects as well.

Anna Freud: There is another point, an open question. We can ask how early in life sublimations are formed, and whether it is possible to develop sublimations in adult life when genital sexuality exists. Is it at all possible then to make new sublimations? Or do all sublimations date back to a much earlier time in childhood, to pregenital times?

J. Sandler: We have to distinguish here very strongly between a skill and a sublimation. Skills can start very early, but it must be relatively late—four, five, or six years of age, I would say—before the child can use the skill for purposes of sublimation. Even then perhaps one has to ask whether or not the gratification is a narcissistic one rather than a more direct instinctual one. You have linked sublimations, Miss Freud, with latency, which is the time that many skills develop. But the prelatency boy of four or five who plays the piano to admiring relatives and friends may be enjoying enormous pleasure in mastery, in control, in exhibitionism, and so on.

Anna Freud: We used to say to child analysts that they should be careful not to disturb budding sublimations in the child, because if you begin to interpret them, to show up their sexual or aggressive sources, you may nip the whole thing in the bud.

J. Sandler: I think some people do not agree with the attitude of leaving sublimations alone in child analysis.

Anna Freud: We used to think that, in the therapeutic process, elements the child could not deal with otherwise should be given a push toward sublimation. We felt that we had to be careful of these elements, that something might be going on which does not belong to what one has to analyze. But after a while we saw something else during child analysis, that there are many beginnings of sublimation which come to nothing, or which are transitory. Now we would say that it is far too optimistic to think that a child of, say, five years or so, who develops a special attachment to an activity, will keep that attachment in his later life. On the other hand, I remember analyzing a little boy about forty years ago, who was then six years old. He was a clever little boy, with divorced parents, and at times his mother would come to visit him. Whenever she left him again he fell into a sort of depression, and in that state he produced poetry. Well, he dictated the poetry in his analytic sessions. It was very nice poetry, and this boy, after a very stormy career, became a professor of literature. I heard from him recently that he was very interested in seeing his early poems, and as I had treasured them, I had them copied and sent to him. They are quite impressive, and there is no doubt that his present profession and his poetic ability as a child have a very definite link. But at the time we analyzed his poetic tendency, partly in relation to his mother and his feelings of extreme longing and sadness, and partly in relation to his very intense fear of being hurt which caused him to turn all his attention away from bodily accomplishments to intellectual ones.

J. Sandler: This seems to be a very nice example of change of function. The skill develops and is then used for purposes of sublimation, although it was not necessarily a sublimation at the time it started.

Anna Freud: If he had been a less clever little boy, or less gifted, I suppose he would just have been a little coward because of his fear of physical hurt, and not a poet.

J. Sandler: From a developmental point of view, practically everything can be reduced to instinctual impulses, and we could certainly say a person's superego is sadistic. However, what entered its formation *then* need not be operative now. It would not be correct, I believe, to say that every time the superego acted strictly, it was expressing, in indirect form, an instinctual sadistic impulse. We have to draw a sharp distinction between what is genetically true, developmentally true, on the one hand, and what is functionally true in the present, on the other.

Anna Freud: Reaction formations get mixed up with what you have described. If we look too closely we may find that several defense mechanisms are contributing to the effect. The source of the behavior might be an underlying sadism, but it also represents other things.

J. Sandler: There are many activities, such as teaching and nursing, where one speaks readily of sublimation, but if we look at the activity itself, we may find that it is not, in the strict sense of the definition, a sublimation.

Anna Freud: With some of these activities, you will find that they don't qualify as sublimations if you take them as a whole, and that only certain aspects can be called sublimation. I was thinking of a remark made to me by a little boy patient, six or seven years old. He was very clever, and in his analytic hour discussed his nursery school teacher. We talked about various methods of nursery school teaching. When we spoke of the Montessori method, in which

the children are given a great deal of freedom, he told me that his woman teacher really enjoys commanding the children. He had picked up that what was sublimated in her teaching was the wish to dominate.

H. Kennedy: Perhaps he did that because it was not so well sublimated.

Anna Freud: Perhaps, but I think he had a good eye for it. On the other hand, there are many things the teacher has to do which have nothing to do with controlling or domineering. One could say the same about nursing, of course.

J. Sandler: It is worth discussing the idea that the so-called aim-inhibited drives are more constant in their pressure than the original instinctual drives. Presumably aim inhibition (in the sense in which Freud used the term) is an integral part of sublimation. We can well ask why we can have a more constant pleasure in a sublimation than the sort of pleasure we associate with the id.

Anna Freud: Yes. We used to discuss this point a lot. It also arose in regard to masturbation fantasies in which direct sexual discharge was experienced, as compared with derivative fantasies in which the sexual discharge did not end the fantasy; they were much more drawn out and were a more or less constant feature of the person's life, due to the aim inhibition which existed in the fantasy derivatives.

J. Sandler: Surely the striving for certain forms of gratification may get an impetus, a motivation, which does not entirely come from the drives, but might be motivated as well by the ego's need, for example, to deal with anxiety by chasing after pleasure. And can we not say that certain activities which yield pleasure, initially by virtue of their relation to the id, to acquire a more constant pleasure-giving quality, so that they become enjoyable in themselves? I am thinking of hobbies, activities and other pleasurable interests which people maintain, in which it is

almost as if the activity acquires something of the stimulus properties of the drive itself.

Anna Freud: The activity is taken over by the ego. It gets a secondary function, a secondary autonomy. It would be good here to go back to the basic question of what happens if a drive is denied its aim, is denied discharge. Two things can then happen, which are quite opposite to each other. One is what we discuss now as sublimation, namely that the ego gets hold of the drive, modifies it, moderates it, makes it different and acceptable, reduces some of the pressure, and finally offers the impulse a moderate, displaced and reduced satisfaction. That's what we call sublimation. Then it becomes incorporated into the ego, becomes ego-syntonic and part of the personality. But an opposite thing can happen, which has always impressed me very much. An aggressive or sadomasochistic, sexualized aggressive fantasy—a masturbation fantasy in childhood—may be denied its outlet in bodily activity, and then exactly the opposite of a sublimation can happen. The fantasy can stay as it is, can swamp the personality, creating a sort of psychopathic personality.

J. Sandler: Is that the so-called impulse-ridden character that Fenichel spoke of?

Anna Freud: Impulse-ridden, but ridden by one impulse only. An impulse-ridden character is a person who cannot control any of his impulses, whereas these people usually repeat only one and the same impulse and fantasy endlessly. This is, for me, the formula for the psychopath. But I know it is not a generally accepted idea.

J. Sandler: Of course there are problems because of the different uses of the term "psychopathic." I am sure that we would agree that not all impulsive behavior, nor all antisocial behavior, can be regarded as a breakthrough of a drive. Such activity might, for example, represent a need

for punishment or a way of dealing with anxiety. We seem to be speaking here only of those people (rather like the cases of traumatic neurosis) who appear helpless in the face of the need to repeat, over and over, a pattern which was drive-gratifying in childhood. Could that be the point, Miss Freud?

Anna Freud: Yes, it's that. But my feeling is that if one looked very closely at any individual psychopath, one would find a pattern of this kind.

J. Sandler: We can have people who are labeled aggressive psychopaths for many other reasons.

Anna Freud: For different reasons, yes. But what strikes me so strongly about cases of this kind is the monotony of the repetition, which is the same monotony we find in masturbation fantasies, which are always the same for any one individual.

J. Sandler: Of course we see the same sort of monotonous repetition in other forms of activity. I am thinking of a patient who is a scientist and who is always late in producing his work. It has become clear in his analysis that he needs to enact the fantasy of his mother screaming at him to get his work done in time, to get in this way a gratification of a sadomasochistic fantasy of being assaulted by her. He repeated this in the transference, and does it in many other situations, with monotonous regularity.

Anna Freud: What is interesting here is to see that the same situation, involving the aim inhibition of a sadomasochistic fantasy, can create two quite opposite results.

J. Sandler: Perhaps we could add, in the light of our discussion, that the inhibiting of an instinctual wish or fantasy is an active process on the part of the ego. Sometimes the ego may falter in its process of inhibiting or displacing, and the original impulse, or a derivative close to the orig-

inal impulse, may break through. Alternatively, the impulse may come through in another derivative, in a joke, for example, or in a dream.

W.E. Freud: I have always found the concept of "sublimation potential," as we use it at the Clinic, very useful. If we can get an idea of a person's sublimation potential, I think this tells us something about the whole defensive organization.

Anna Freud: Yes, the idea was used in the Diagnostic Profile. It was Kurt Eissler who first suggested that we shouldn't only speak about the child's sublimations, but also of his capacity, his *potential,* for sublimation. This can be picked up rather early, as we have seen from looking at babies, by assessing the willingness of the individual to accept substitutes. A young patient of mine said the other day that she had rather high demands, and if she couldn't have the food she wanted, she would much rather starve herself. If she couldn't have the boyfriend she wanted, she'd rather have no boyfriend at all. This isn't quite true, of course, but she described something important, namely an unwillingness to accept substitutes. If this happens very early in life, it is an ominous sign in regard to the development of later sublimations. It is interesting to see how some children can gain satisfaction from a substitute offered to them, and others can't. They go on screaming until they have their original wish fulfilled. What I think of as sublimation potential is something built up very gradually. It is certainly influenced a great deal by the environment, but I think that there is something basic and fundamental in it as well. Of course, if a baby is too content with the substitute or with the person who acts as a replacement, this is also an ominous sign.

J. Sandler: In Chapter 4 you describe, Miss Freud, the case of a woman who split her ambivalence, so that her mother was kept as a good object and someone else became the

object of the child's hate or anger (p. 45). I wonder whether you meant to include the splitting of ambivalence among the defense mechanisms proper, since you refer to it as a "method of defense" (p. 46). Nowadays, of course, we distinguish between defense mechanisms on the one hand, and other defensive methods, measures, or maneuvers on the other. I wonder whether this distinction was beginning to crystallize in your mind at that time, because although you call the splitting of ambivalence a method of defense, you don't actually call it a mechanism of defense. I don't know if you were conscious of making any such distinction at the time of writing.

Anna Freud: I also don't know what the translator did and what I did. I certainly didn't make such a distinction myself.

J. Sandler: In the original German you spoke of the *Abwehrtechnik* in this context, so "technique of defense" might be a better translation.

Anna Freud: I didn't count it as a mechanism.

J. Sandler: We have been speaking about the drives and the aim of the drives in regard to sublimation. We know that the object of the drives must come into it, and the relation to the object is very closely connected with the aim of the drive, yet we speak of sublimation in terms of the vicissitudes of the drive and of the drive aim, but we do not verbalize the fact that there is also a displacement of object and a disguising of the relation to the object in the formation of a sublimation.

Anna Freud: The whole idea of defense is that it is an intrapsychic process, not one connected with the object world. So to the extent that we pursue how the ego defends itself against id derivatives, the object doesn't come into it, except as an instigator—or one of the instigators—of the ego's criticisms of the id.

J. Sandler: But what about the intrapsychic object representations?

Anna Freud: They are in the superego, of course.

J. Sandler: Or in the ego.

Anna Freud: Or in the ego, obviously.

J. Sandler: In fantasy.

Anna Freud: Only at that point they are not within the scope of the discussion. I do not feel that we have ever neglected object relations.

J. Sandler: I don't think we have, but we neglect talking about them sufficiently. I remember your reminding me once that when one talks about the ego one should always say something about the id, and not assume that the reader is going to take the id for granted. Perhaps the same applies to object relations.

S. Rosenfeld: I recall that Ernst Kris, in his paper on sublimation, traced the defenses used by two little girls to their relation to the object. He did this in a very detailed and meaningful way, and I wanted to draw attention to it because of your comment, Miss Freud, that the defenses are not immediately connected with the object.

Anna Freud: Well, they are not immediately tied up with the object, but they are indirectly connected with the object, insofar as we cannot think of the ego and superego development without object relations.

J. Sandler: I suppose that one should differentiate here between the motives for defense and the mechanisms of defense as such. When we think of the motives for defense, and the change of aims involved, this must very often involve the object, but the mechanism, the sort of mental machinery involved, might be regarded as independent of

the particular object concerned. But, of course, the symbolic aspect of sublimatory activities is very often intimately tied to the person's unconscious fantasies in relation to his objects. This has come out in our discussions about sado-masochistic tendencies.

At this point I would like to ask you to clarify, Miss Freud, what you understand by successful defense.

Anna Freud: Others have raised it [the question] with the idea that I meant "successful" in terms of the external world. Of course, I meant nothing of the kind. When I speak of successful defense I look at it from the point of view of the ego. If the ego defends itself successfully, it means that it achieves the aim of not allowing the forbidden impulse to enter into consciousness and that it does away with the anxiety connected with it and escapes unpleasure of any kind. That is a successful defense, although it may also have disastrous consequences for health and for later development. But from the point of view of defending oneself it is successful. You know, if somebody attacks you and you kill that person, the defense has been immensely successful, but it may not be approved of and have very disagreeable consequences. It all depends on your viewpoint. That is what I had in mind.

J. Sandler: Perhaps one could add that a successful defense need not have disastrous consequences. Repression can be successful, provided the impulse defended against is not too strong.

Anna Freud: I would call repression successful if every conscious knowledge of the item concerned has really gone. If the impulse returns from repression, then the defense has not been successful.

J. Sandler: But the subsequent defense, which might be projection, for example, might then be successful.

Anna Freud: It might be very successful, although it might also turn the person into a paranoiac.

M. Sprince: Don't we really need some way of differentiating between a defense which doesn't in fact result in pathology, which in a sense would be a successful defense, and a defense which would lead to pathology?

Anna Freud: A wholly successful defense is always something dangerous. Either it restricts the area of consciousness or the competence of the ego too much, or it falsifies reality—we see this best in projection. The defensive mechanisms and measures really undo the excellence of the ego's functions. And I don't think we should introduce values of health or pathology here, but should rather look at the battle between intact ego functions, at the unpleasure or anxiety they generate, and at the defenses used against the anxiety. And then we would see who wins, and the consequences for health or illness.

J. Sandler: It seems that there is a close parallel here with physiological defense mechanisms. On the physical level people can deal with stress successfully by physiological adaptations. They can deal with excess heat, for example, in various ways, but at some point the defense mechanism may break down, and the person may faint from sunstroke. Other adaptations to stress may not produce symptoms, but the so-called successful defense may lead eventually to pathology which starts because the defense, although successful, leads to an imbalance without the person being aware of it. This brings us to the double meaning of adaptation. From the ego's point of view we can have successful adaptation, which can be very unsuccessful from the point of view of the external world.

Anna Freud: I can give you an example. Nothing is more dangerous to the later health of the individual than the situation, for example, that we used to meet very often in former times, in which the child defends completely against masturbation in latency, so that it disappears from the scene. This individual may become highly neurotic or

even, as I suggested before, psychopathic. We might also get frigidity or impotence, and all sorts of other pathological results. But the breakdown of the defenses every so often during latency, with the breakthrough of normal masturbation, may be a saving feature for mental health.

J. Sandler: Is it not almost universal nowadays in latency children?

Anna Freud: It should be universal, but it isn't.

J. Sandler: There is the implication in what you have been saying, Miss Freud, that when we come to treat a patient we should bear in mind that his defensive adaptation, from the point of view of his ego, is really a "here-and-now" adaptation, which is as successful as he can get it to be at the time even though it may result in later pathology. If one approaches the patient with this point of view in one's analytic work, it means that one has to bear in mind that one is intervening as the analyst in a system which represents the best adaptation the person can make at the time, given the resources at his disposal.

Anna Freud: That is why patients resent analysis and the interference of the analyst so much, because the analyst is interfering with the patient's best defenses. Only, as far as health is concerned, these defenses have been inadequate attempts and have had disastrous results.

J. Sandler: All of this has implications for the way in which we phrase our interpretations.

Anna Freud: Yes.

J. Sandler: Miss Freud, in this chapter you use the phrase "love fixation" (p. 45), and I should like to raise the question of the current status of the word fixation in regard to an object. We know that Freud spoke of a fixation to an object, as when he referred to a father fixation, in addition to speaking of libidinal fixation during the course

of psychosexual development. Of course, when you use the phrase "love fixation" in regard to the child, it is very clear what you mean.

Anna Freud: Yes, it is also clear what the translator meant, but never mind.[1]

J. Sandler: I wonder whether you could say something, Miss Freud, about the use of the word "fixation" with regard to father fixation, mother fixation, and the like. We still use the term a great deal, meaning, I think, that there is a very strong instinctual or emotional investment in the person concerned.

Anna Freud: You know, the term means more, since the word is used in contrast to the free movement of the libido. Fixation always means that one is tied to a point in time, or to an object, when by rights one should have moved further away. So we wouldn't call a relationship a father or mother fixation if we are referring to the time when we expect the child to be attached to these objects. We call it a fixation when the child should have moved on. It always means that an undue amount of libido has been left behind.

J. Sandler: The meaning now seems very clear. I've always been struck by the fact that we tend to use the term only when the phenomenon to which it applies is overt. We speak of the grown-up man who still lives with his mother and doesn't want to leave her to marry as being mother-fixated. But the man who does leave, and who has defenses against his equally strong attachment to his mother, and who carries this unconscious attachment into his later life and into neurotic conflicts, is not usually referred to as having a mother fixation. We would have to speak of an

---

[1] Love fixation is a translation from Anna Freud's German phrase, *Liebesbindung an die Mutter* (literally, "bond of love with the mother"). In writing elsewhere in the book of pregenital fixations (p. 148) Anna Freud used the German phrase *prägenitale Fixierungen.*

unconscious fixation on the mother, but for some reason we don't often use the term in that sense.

Anna Freud: I think it is equally applicable to both situations. It always means the libido is tied to the object, whether consciously or unconsciously.

J. Sandler: In describing the case of the young woman early in Chapter 4 (p. 45) you write "In order to solve the problem of ambivalence she displaced outward one side of her ambivalent feeling." Would it be correct to assume that the word "outward" means "away from the mother," as opposed to the sort of displacement outward we see in projection?

Anna Freud: Yes. If I were to write this today I would say "She displaced elsewhere," not "outward." What I describe is really the splitting of the ambivalence.

J. Sandler: You use the term ambivalence in a very precise way, referring to two opposite instinctual attitudes toward an object existing at the same time, and to the conflict over these two separate attitudes.

Anna Freud: I think it always means two opposite feelings existing on the same level, whatever the level may be.

J. Sandler: Like love and hate, these being derivatives of sexuality and aggression?

Anna Freud: Yes, but not all ambivalence gives rise to conflict, and certainly not all conflict is over ambivalence.

J. Sandler: You speak of the little girl's ego resorting to a further mechanism. You say (pp. 45-46), "It turned inward the hatred, which hitherto had related exclusively to other people. The child tortured herself with self-accusations and feelings of inferiority and, throughout childhood and adolescence . . . did everything she could to put herself at a disadvantage and injure her interests, always surrendering her own wishes to the demands made on her by others."

To all outward appearance she had become masochistic since adopting this method of defense." We have recently been discussing the concept of aggression turned against the self, and it would be very useful if you could help us to consider some aspects of the topic. You speak here of the hatred of the child, which represents an object-related feeling, as opposed to the aggressive drive itself. I wonder whether you were taking it for granted that the derivative of an aggressive wish toward someone might be a feeling of anger or hatred, and that when you speak of the turning against the self of the hatred, you are in fact speaking of the content of the aggressive wish, including all the feelings and attitudes associated with that wish. Did you mean to make a distinction here?

Anna Freud: I suppose I used the word hatred instead of aggression because she felt so guilty for her feeling, even if it was not accompanied by any action. It was this feeling which she turned against her self. Recently we had a similar case of a child being unloved and unhappy, evidently re-acting to the situation with anger, hatred, aggression, and death wishes. But what we saw in that child was a very strong reaction against the death wishes, shown by great anxiety when the parents went out. She worried about what would happen to them, and couldn't go to sleep. She had a younger sister, and when she had to cross the street with that sister, she was afraid. She didn't want to cross the street because the sister might be run over. She didn't want to be left alone at home with the little sister, apparently afraid of what she would do to her. So she had reaction formations against her death wishes and her hatred. When provoked by other children at school, she would have sud-den uncontrollable outbreaks of aggression, when she would hit, pinch, bite and really hurt the other children. She couldn't control herself. She was afraid of these out-bursts, and felt very guilty afterwards. But simultaneously this nine-year-old girl would turn the whole feeling against

herself and would break into tears, saying, "I'm a total failure, I'm no good, no-one loves me, I'm bad." Then she became her own victim, the victim of her own aggression. We felt, although we could not confirm it, that some masochism might have become mixed up with this whole sequence so that she was forced to repeat it over and over. Whenever somebody approached her lovingly she would bring things to the point where that person would then dislike her. Descriptively, we would say this *is* masochistic, but we do not know whether it is really masochistic.

J. Sandler: You would restrict the term "masochistic" to situations in which there is a libidinal component in the suffering?

Anna Freud: Yes, so that the suffering becomes an aim in itself.

J. Sandler: It is important to clarify this, Miss Freud, because many people use the term masochism for all forms of aggression turned against the self, and if I understand you correctly, the term should really only be used where in some way the suffering has been erotized. People who habitually damage, hurt, or punish themselves may not be masochistic in the strict sense of the term.

Anna Freud: Quite right, because they may just look for relief from guilt, which of course they can get when they turn aggression against the self. That would not yet be masochistic, because they would have to have the secret enjoyment of being the victim. Only then should we call their turning against the self masochistic. Then it is especially difficult to treat, because one has to interfere not only with the painful situation, but with the pleasure.

J. Sandler: Some years ago I suggested that the outlook was less hopeful when there was a masochistic sexualization, but you felt then that although the patient might be more difficult to treat, the outlook was more hopeful than in

cases of turning aggression against the self purely because of guilt. You felt this was because the superego is so difficult to change, and if there is a sexual reinforcement, one can get on to that in the analysis.

Anna Freud: Yes, especially because one can interfere with the pleasure by making the whole process conscious. Of course the patient doesn't like to be interfered with because of the pleasure he gains, and he can turn the situation into one in which he becomes the victim and the analyst becomes the attacker. But if one succeeds in unraveling it, one has a chance.

J. Sandler: I have always felt that some of our more active analysts, who interpret a great deal in a very active way, so that they have a sort of to-and-fro conversation with the patient, foster a sadomasochistic relationship, and this may be one of the reasons that their patients stay in analysis for so long.

Anna Freud: I think that is true.

J. Sandler: There is another point. The problem we have had about feelings and drives is perhaps not such a big one if we remember that the drives are hypothetical constructs, and that what you refer to in your book essentially is the *wish*. With wishes go all sorts of feelings, as well as representations of the objects or the self toward whom the feelings are directed or with whom they are connected. When you speak of the vicissitudes of the drive, it seems clear that you speak of the vicissitudes of the wish, and if you then postulate that the drive takes a certain path, you simultaneously mean that the wish is modified. So turning aggression against the self automatically involves the displacement of an aggressive wish from an object to self. There is an advantage for us to talk of the wish rather than the drive, for then the feeling aspect can be taken as part of the wish. So when you speak of the vicissitudes of the drive, we could take it that you are speaking at the

same time of the vicissitudes of the wish, together with all the feelings involved. Would you go along with that?

Anna Freud: Yes.

J. Sandler: I think it may be useful to make some distinctions in regard to the clinical material we have been discussing. In the first place we have the child who specifically does to himself what he wishes to do to the object. So if the child wants to push the object down the stairs, he, in turning the wish against himself, falls down the stairs. The content of what he does to himself gives us the clue to what he unconsciously wants to do to the object. On the other hand, there are the children who punish themselves because they feel guilty, and what they feel guilty about need have no relation to the punishment they inflict upon themselves. They may feel as guilty about a sexual wish as they do about an aggressive wish, and punish themselves aggressively for that sexual wish. Here the content of the self-punishment gives us no clue to the unconscious wish which aroused the feelings of guilt and caused the child to punish himself. There are also the children who denigrate themselves, who suffer from intense feelings of inferiority or inadequacy. We cannot be sure that this is the result of aggression turned against the self, except perhaps in a descriptive sense, for the child may be identified with a denigrated object, may have problems in regard to the regulation of his self-esteem, to the provision of narcissistic supplies. I don't think that we should call this last group aggression turned against the self, because of the big narcissistic component. We may be misled about the pathology.

Anna Freud: I am reminded of a case we had recently of a child who tortured herself, was full of self-reproaches, and who left all the people who interviewed her with a feeling of unease. They felt accused by her in some subtle way, and I am sure that the parents of this child feel ac-

cused by the depressive self-torture of the child. So the wish to torture or to punish the object returns in a roundabout way. This is a good diagnostic sign of self-reproaches being deflected from the object. In that child too there was a low self-esteem because the child is unloved, because she is a devalued object in the eyes of the parents. The mother wanted a boy and she is a girl, and so on. Against this background of feeling devalued and having a low self-esteem, which comes from the past, there is then added the aggression which by rights should go outward to the people who denigrate her, who frustrate her and don't love her enough. It is very difficult to say, when we have the result, which part of it comes from the feeling of denigration from her identification with the parents' image of her, and which is added afterward by aggression turned inward. When you look at the individual case it is always more complicated than whatever it is we try to extract from it. The position is made even more complicated because the child's attempts to deal with her aggression are so inadequate. In reality she cannot get rid of it, she cannot cope with her aggression, or hate, or whatever you want to call it, against the parents, especially the mother. She tries to repress, she tries reaction formations, and both work to some extent. But then there are breakthroughs and breakdowns; so she becomes desperate. Then she tries to turn the aggression against herself, but it is still turned outward to some extent.

J. Sandler: Then you would not see the aggressive aspect of the child's self-reproaches as a secondary gain, as something discovered to be of use by the child.

Anna Freud: No, the aggression that remains toward the parents is part of the whole process.

H. Kennedy: I think of the child who talks of killing himself or committing suicide following a wish to attack the parent, and who uses the threat of killing himself as a provocation, or as a way of making the parents anxious or guilty.

Anna Freud: Yes, both. The little boy you have in treatment thinks that it is very bad to kill somebody else, and if one is good one kills oneself. But if one kills oneself, the parents are really guilty. So the suicidal thought is an attack, a punishment for the parents.

J. Sandler: Perhaps this is important in regard to suicides in children, which seem to be so very different because they often involve the fantasy of punishing the parents.

Anna Freud: Yes, they think how guilty and sorry the parents will be afterwards, and how nice it would be to watch that.

R. Tyson: I was thinking of the forms of self-torture due to the erotisation of anxiety which we see in adults.

Anna Freud: You see this sort of thing in children when it has very much the quality of a flirtation with anxiety. I once described a little boy patient of mine who had terrible anxiety attacks when he was in bed at night because he was sure that a robber was hidden behind the curtains. He was sure that as soon as he moved at all in his bed or, worse still, as soon as he got out of bed to fetch something or to reach for a glass of water, the robber would pounce on him and destroy him. One felt quite sorry for the child. I asked him once, "What do you do if the robber doesn't come out?" And he said: "Then I say: robber, come." Obviously the fantasy was a sexualized one, and playing with the anxiety was a sexual activity.

J. Sandler: I remember a patient who had eczema as a child, and his mother would come and put a soothing lotion on him at night. His later life consisted in large part of having little irritations and to scratch away. He couldn't bear the thought of not having something in his life go wrong. I think that the pain from the eczema was erotized very early on in his life, and this must be true for many children with skin complaints, where there has been painful scratching, or something similar.

Anna Freud: Of course, the pain may be erotized, but also the ministrations to the pain. In the Hampstead Nurseries, we saw that many young children stopped reacting to pain the moment the pain stopped, but in others the reaction dragged on long after the pain had stopped, as if the child could not disengage himself from the pain. I think this is a step along the path toward erotization of the painful situation.

J. Sandler: I should like to note the role of the maintenance of feelings of safety in people repeating what looks like purely masochistic behavior. The behavior may create an unconscious feeling of the presence of the love object, even though in order to do this the person has to do something unpleasant to himself. Somehow what is conjured up in fantasy is the feeling of the existence of the object close by, and this can produce a feeling of safety, in addition o other gratifications.

In describing the patient who turned her hatred inward (p. 45), you speak of the girl's ego finding relief from the sense of guilt by using a defensive mechanism. To what extent should we think of defense mechanisms in connection with doing away with guilt feelings? Do we oppose the defensive measures or defensive maneuvers used when guilt is involved to other defense mechanisms? You speak of projection giving the child relief from the sense of guilt, and yet I have a feeling that sometimes we hesitate to speak of defense mechanisms when guilt is being dealt with.

Anna Freud: It depends on how you look at it. Let us say the child has a sexual or aggressive impulse, and that this is followed by guilt. Now the child would like to remove the guilt, but I think the best way to remove the guilt is for the child to institute a defense against the impulse. So if we start at the end of the impulse, we can speak of a defense proper. The impulse may be defended against by projection, and the child who feels guilty for a certain

impulse then has no need to feel guilty about it if someone else has it. It would be incorrect here to say that the defense is against the guilt. The defense is against the drive derivative.

J. Sandler: I suppose I really want to get you to extend the formulation in Freud's *Inhibitions, Symptoms and Anxiety* about the anxiety signal initiating defense to any painful signal as the instigator of defense. This would include guilt, fear of the outside world, and so on.

Anna Freud: I think I say that in another chapter.

J. Sandler: So that a stab of guilt could equally bring into play defense mechanisms against the impulse which gives rise to it?

Anna Freud: Yes. People can do different things in relation to guilt. Some people cannot turn against the impulse that makes them feel guilty, but indulge in the guilty action and then deny or repress the guilt. What they really ought to do is attack the reason for the guilt feeling, and not deal with the outcome, the conflict.

J. Sandler: I am rather puzzled when you speak of what people should *really* do.

Anna Freud: When I say things like "what they should really do" I always speak from the point of view, not of the outside observer, but of the internal conflict. What certainly works best is to remove the reason for the guilt. But to remove the reason for the guilt means a great loss of pleasure, satisfaction, or relief of tension. So some people are quite reluctant to do that, and want to have their pleasure, but their pleasure makes them feel guilty. Sometimes patients come for analysis, and say—especially homosexual patients—"all I want to do is to continue with the things that give me pleasure and not to feel guilty about them." They have tried using measures that didn't work. And

what did they do? They went on with the activities that make them feel guilty, and then denied the guilt, or used a rationalization—only these methods didn't work.

J. Sandler: Are there cases in which they can work?

Anna Freud: I think rationalizations work very well. But there are other methods too. For instance, such people may provoke their environment to actions which then justify them in reacting with the impulse they would otherwise feel guilty about. I suppose there are thousands of ways of defending like this, and, I suppose, the individual tries them out until he finds one that suits him. It doesn't really suit him, of course, because he wouldn't want to be in analysis if it worked.

J. Sandler: Yes, I suppose that is the point. There are many people who do in fact manage, by some trick or defensive method, to deal with their guilt feelings, and don't end up in analysis, don't develop symptoms, and feel they are coping quite well. Also, if the guilt arises from some wish which is not necessarily put into action, and the person then deals with the guilt in one of the ways we have been discussing, the way of dealing with the guilt might be called a successful defensive activity and be regarded as quite normal. For example, the guilt might be dealt with by the use of projection within the person's fantasy life. If this works, then the person is in luck, and we don't see him in our consulting room.

Anna Freud: One could add that the patients who come for help, but who try to keep their pleasure and have the guilt removed, usually get greatly disappointed in analysis at the start, because the more one analyzes them, the more guilty they feel. They lose the methods they have used so far against the guilt, and feel the full weight of the guilt. So in the end it all comes back to dealing with the impulse, and to seeing whether it is appropriate to the present situation.

J. Sandler: If we take into account the distinction between what is descriptively unonscious and what is dynamically unconscious, we can speak of feelings which are descriptively unconscious. So anxiety or guilt can be kept away from consciousness, and people with unconscious guilt may go through life either punishing themselves or dealing with the guilt feeling in some other way. They are not aware of feeling the guilt, but it is in fact there. Such people may appear on the surface to be anxiety-free or guilt-free characters, and analysis may transform them into people who experience guilt and anxiety acutely. Would you say that if they have these feelings after analysis, this is better for them although somewhat less comfortable?

Anna Freud: Yes.

J. Sandler: You say (p. 47), "The aggressive impulses associated with hatred and the sexual impulses associated with penis envy may be transformed into bodily symptoms, if the patient possesses the capacity for conversion and somatic conditions are favorable." Presumably the defense involved is repression. But what about the so-called phobic defenses? We know that many defenses enter into phobias, yet we seem to treat "phobic defense" as if it were a unit in itself, worth giving a title to, even though a number of defense mechanisms may be involved.

Anna Freud: We could also call it an avoidance. It is an avoidance of the situation in which the conflict or feeling arises, and the consequences of that avoidance, or the way in which it is carried out, we call the phobic mechanism. It involves a withdrawal from the situation.

J. Sandler: So one should speak of phobic avoidance.

Anna Freud: One should speak of phobic avoidance, yes.

M. Berger: Does this not give us a bit of a problem because such avoidance has the features of a symptom?

Anna Freud: It has and it hasn't. If you look at it from the normal side, we don't know how many of our moves in life are really avoidance of situations we dread. If we look at this closely we would have to call it phobic avoidance, only the required intensity for it to be a symptom isn't quite reached.

M. Berger: What does such avoidance defend against?

Anna Freud: In my book I give an example of a little boy patient who developed much castration anxiety on the football field, and in every sport. He was so afraid of bodily hurt, especially hurt to his penis, that he became quite unable to do any sport. But this never became a phobia in the usual sense, because he simply avoided the area of sport altogether and developed great intellectual and poetic abilities instead. So he wouldn't have noticed that he was phobic. I knew in his analysis that if he weren't so afraid of the situation of being hurt, he would probably be less of a poet and a better sportsman.

J. Sandler: When does a food fad, for example, become a symptom? Wasn't it Wilhelm Reich who said that behind every character trait lies a phobia? I think he took the view that one could trace every character trait and character attitude to a childhood phobic anxiety.

Anna Freud: There is an avoidance of something, so you develop something else instead. It is a very interesting line to follow.

J. Sandler: Especially in regard to the question of what is normal and what is pathological. Here we have a mechanism which is in a sense quite irrational, but is so frequent that it can be normal. It certainly has a function for the ego.

Anna Freud: What people call, rather optimistically, all-round development, really means that no aspect of development is interfered with by such little phobias. But who

can achieve that? If one looks at people, there are always things they avoid and things they favor.

J. Sandler: This is where your concept of phase dominance is so useful, because it points to the most crucial thing being whether the child has moved into the next developmental phase. All these little symptoms or near-symptoms are not as important as making the transition to the next phase.

Anna Freud: What we are talking about also lies at the basis of what I have called ego restriction. As the ego develops it tries to avoid the worst and to go into the most comfortable areas. This is very interesting for normal psychology.

H. Kennedy: Is it not a question of how widespread such restrictions are within the individual? I think, for instance, of such things as a failure in sports getting involved in conflict. If the child particularly wants to be a good footballer, then he may have real difficulties.

Anna Freud: He doesn't entirely want to be a good footballer, because at the same time he restricts the wish. But let us look at it in another way. If, for instance, what he is afraid of in sport is the competition with others, because to lose means to him a complete destruction of his whole personality, he might then withdraw from the sports field and turn to the intellectual field. But then there is every chance that the fear of competition will follow him there, not any more in the physical sense, but in the mental sense, and he will feel just as destroyed if someone writes a better essay or a better poem. So he has to leave this particular area, and again look for another one, and in the end he will not find safety from competition anywhere. There are all shades of normality and pathology in these things.

J. Sandler: Freud distinguished between an inhibition and a neurotic symptom, but it is often difficut to make the

distinction. It is clear that a central aspect of the inhibition is stopping the activity which represents the gratification of an instinctual wish. By not entering into a particular area, the conflict is not aroused, and I understand how this is opposed to the idea of the symptom as a compromise formation. But so often what is, descriptively speaking, an inhibition, as we see it in our clinical work, has the qualities of a symptom in the sense of being a compromise formation. We speak loosely of all these things as symptoms. But it gets very difficult, for example, when we see a withdrawal from a situation because of a phobic anxiety. From one point of view we see an inhibition, but from another viewpoint the phobia is a symptom.

Anna Freud: I think an inhibition is really meant to be an unfinished symptom, because there is the move forward of the wish, and then there is the counterforce against it. That is the inhibition. The characteristic of the inhibition is that the wish is kept alive, and very often remains conscious. People are very unhappy about their inhibitions because they want to perform well. With the phobic withdrawal, the person is not unhappy any more. He has given up the wish, at least in consciousness. The symptom is only formed if a compromise is found between the wish and the guilt, so it is a step further removed. For instance, the boy who is so afraid of the football field might become an umpire. He can stand in a safe position and judge what the others do, he can send them off the field, and so on. Or he may become one of those boys who are crazy about watching football on television, and be quite safe in that. He fulfills some of his interests and at the same time guards against injury. That's a compromise. I suppose one might even call it a sublimation.

J. Sandler: It might be a sublimation if he is an umpire. If he throws bottles at the players at football matches, we wouldn't call it sublimation. But if, for example, a man is

impotent, we say he has a sexual inhibition, but we know it isn't always an inhibition. The person who can't approach girls, who is afraid, may turn out in analysis to be phobic, with the women representing a vagina dentata, or a castrating mother. He has put an enormous amount of unconscious fantasy distortion into the situation of being with the girl. What we really see is a phobia which shows itself like an inhibition. I have the feeling that when we get down to analyzing patients with inhibitions, it very often turns out that they have phobic avoidances.

Anna Freud: With the young man you describe, we would choose a term for his disturbance according to how near he can get to the girl. If he can never go anywhere where girls are, we would call this a phobia, a phobic retreat. If he goes much further and can even dance with them, only can't have intercourse, or if he is ready for intercourse but can't have an erection, we would probably call it an inhibition. The terminology is quite elastic.

J. Sandler: Anxieties which are essentially phobic can be of defensive or adaptive value. I think of someone with a street phobia in which he is repeatedly exposed to the phobic situation, but always retreats from it. We can see the way in which he has to deal over and over with the conflict aroused by the impulse represented by being in the street. But if, in contrast, we think of someone who has a fear of heights, which we also call a phobia, the fear may not be experienced at all unless the person goes to the top of a tall building. He might do this once a year or once in five years. There seem to be some anxieties which look phobic in structure, but don't appear to have an ongoing function in dealing with some persistent or frequently recurring unconscious wish. This seems different from the person who always thinks about his need to go out into the street and then always feels frightened and doesn't go out, so he constantly avoids the activity which represents something forbidden.

Anna Freud: I would put the question the other way round. Why are these people able to choose situations they meet so seldom? Why is such a person afraid of an insect which does not exist in Europe at all, and not of the common fly or a bee or a wasp which he might meet all the time? I have the feeling that the centering of the fear on something that is easily avoided is really a clever move of the ego. Think of the fear of heights as an example. We find it very often in our patients. Perhaps if the man wouldn't have the fear of heights, he'd be a mountain-climber! I have a feeling that if he chooses the height to be afraid of, then it is something which he does not actually have to experience. It is far away and can easily be avoided. It therefore lends itself to symbolization. I remember one highly obsessional patient who had obsessive avoidance symptoms which were very cleverly placed. They never interfered too much with his life. He would say to himself, for example, if it involved my books, then how could I study? So he chose something that lay a little outside an important area—a chair, for example, because he could then sit on another chair. He was highly plagued by his symptoms all his life, but his professional and daily life were not really actively interfered with, because he placed his symptoms that way.

J. Sandler: But he would have to be in contact with these situations regularly. I wonder whether an approach to such things as fear of heights might be to say that finding oneself on top of a tall building might concretize something which was previously contained in fantasy. Then one finds oneself suddenly in a situation in which the threat is much greater and cannot be contained by the fantasy, so there is an anxiety attack. Then it might not really be a phobia.

Anna Freud: I remember my obsessional patient saying (he had fears of pollution by different objects), "Of course my key doesn't bother me. If it did I wouldn't be able to get

into my apartment." So the key was free from pollution, and something a little less necessary to his life was polluted instead. But one could say that he was a highly developed obsessional who knew how to manage his obsessions in his life! What he did with his obsessions some people do with their phobias.

J. Sandler: Could you elaborate, Miss Freud, on the question of concern about the other person's safety as a reaction formation (pp. 47-48)?

Anna Freud: Worrying about safety is a form of concern for the object, and the most frequent examples are to be found in those children who can't go to sleep whenever the parents are out in the evening. They worry that something might happen to the parents. If they are in the theatre, a fire might break out. If they are in a car, they might have an accident. If the parents are on a trip and flying somewhere, the plane might drop out of the sky. This means the child is afraid of its own death wishes coming true and so develops an overconcern for the safety of the object. On the other hand, we know that those mothers who are overly concerned for the child's safety also have a reaction formation against their hostile wishes.

J. Sandler: Would you not say that one should only use the term reaction formation as long as it refers to an aspect of character?

Anna Freud: The fears of the child become ego-syntonic. What the child feels is, "I love my mother or my parents so much that I couldn't stand it if anything happened to them. I have to be continually concerned for their safety." This is completely ego-syntonic, and it is on the border between a character trait and a symptom.

Now we make more subtle definitions and would have to say that something is a reaction formation when it extends from the original objects for whose sake it was

erected to a general attitude to other people. Then it becomes part of the person's character or personality, so that the person is tender toward everybody, overconcerned for everyone's safety.

J. Sandler: The link between reaction formation and character is clearly important. It brings us to a technical point we have discussed often, that such character traits or attitudes might come into the analysis very early, even in the very first session, and we are faced with the question of how to deal with them. They don't represent transference proper, even though they may involve attitudes to the analyst, because they are general features of character. It seems to be important to distinguish between these and that concentration of object love or hate or ambivalence on the specific person of the therapist which characterizes transference proper.

Anna Freud: Yes, it's an important feature of the reaction formation that its aim is to keep an opposite part unconscious or repressed, and of course overconcern does exactly that. Instead of having the bad wishes toward the object in consciousness, the child has good wishes in their place, and in that sense it is a reaction. It acts as a counterforce against the repressed.

J. Sandler: Just as with aggression turned against the self, reaction formations, particularly against aggressive wishes, can nevertheless result in the child or the adult being aggressive in the end, although they have the reaction formation as well. I remember a lady who was very obsessional, who had had many abortions but never had any children. She hated children and babies as she had hated her younger siblings, but was passionately devoted to her dog. When she was in her menopause she decided that the dog—a bitch—was sexually frustrated and had to be mated. The dog gave birth to puppies, and she was very concerned that these puppies should survive. In order to

ensure this she regularly cleaned the nipples of the mother with a strong disinfectant to make sure that they were free of germs, and all the puppies died as a consequence of being poisoned. It seems that even though there was a strong reaction formation against cruelty, the unconscious wishes broke through.

Anna Freud: Yes, one often sees that.

J. Sandler: I should very much like to hear your comments, Miss Freud, on the relation of reaction formation to superego formation. You speak in your book of the moral code of exaggerated strictness as being a reaction formation. Presumably this is because of the exaggeration, but I think that we all feel that there is a strong link between superego functioning and ordinary reaction formations. When we speak of superego development, we refer so often to cleanliness and bowel training. We know that reaction formations begin in the anal phase, before the formation of the superego proper, but it is not yet clear to me what the continuity is between the reaction formation which a child establishes relatively early in development and the later superego. It seems to me that there is a whole area here which is worth going into, because so many of our ideals and our moral prohibitions are in the nature of reaction formations. We feel the injunction to be kind, to be concerned. I think we would have to call these things reaction formations, even if they are not excessive. Would you comment on the connection between reaction formation as a defense mechanism and an aspect of normal character development, and superego formation?

Anna Freud: It was Ferenczi, I think, who talked about sphincter morality, which we would call the child's response to a pre-superego demand, to a command which has been taken over from the parents, especially the command to be clean. The predecessor of the superego is there to be seen. But the mechanism by which the demand is

fulfilled is the reaction formation. The demand alone wouldn't bring the cleanliness about.

J. Sandler: I've always understood something different by sphincter morality, Miss Freud, but I might be quite wrong about this. I have always assumed that the child on the pot, experiencing what has been called the "battle of the bowel," will obey during the anal phase on a purely pragmatic basis. In other words, I see it not as a real belief of the child that he does this or that because he knows it to be right, but he does it because he knows he will get disapproval if he doesn't do what the parents think is right, and it is entirely tied to that approval or disapproval coming from the real parents. In more than one sense it is morality on a business basis.

Anna Freud: Sphincter morality is, so to say, a lower form of morality.

J. Sandler: It seems to be almost an "as-if" morality. That is the way I understand it to be in the period before the child becomes fully identified with the parents' morality.

Anna Freud: It isn't meant that way. As far as I remember, it meant that the earliest form of morality is to be clean, to control the bladder and the bowels. And what is built up at that time is repeated on a higher level in regard to functions which are no longer bodily functions. Also, in regression, the higher commands are thrown off first, and in psychosis even the sphincter morality is lost.

J. Sandler: So the reinforcement of a repression by its opposite, as in a reaction formation, would in your view be seen as beginning with regard to the control of messing in the anal phase, with the same mechanisms being later applied to other impulses. And then the aspect of the superego which relates to the ego's own attitudes to the self and to the child's own impulses, attitudes based on reaction formations, would be something which has grown out of this. Would that be a correct statement?

Anna Freud: Yes. Ferenczi added something very interesting which always impressed me. He said that all morality begins as hypocrisy, which is certainly true. He illustrated it in the anal sphere with the child's first liking the smell of its own excrement, and being quite uninterested in the smell of a flower. But then the child learns to imitate and later to identify with the adults who show him a rose and say "how nice," and who say that the smell of excrement is "nasty." And the child imitates hypocritically, but gradually acquires that attitude.

The inhibition of the biting impulse of the child goes very differently. The child likes to bite, and the child bites the mother. There are some simple and primitive mothers, even in our society, who have the idea that the child will never stop biting unless the mother bites it back. In the Nurseries during the war we had to dissuade many mothers from using that method, which was based on the idea that the child would be taught that biting hurts. Well, without necessarily doing that, mothers do give signs of displeasure when they are bitten by the child, and the child will then respond to the displeasure of the mother. "I mustn't do it or mother will get angry." But I think that's all that happens there. The child will then, in spite of that inhibition, use biting as a weapon with other children until, I suppose, the second or third year of life. We get worried if this behavior lasts longer, but the biting impulse as such is not disapproved of by the child after its first experience with the mother. We would never speak of a reaction formation to the biting impulse when it is only inhibited in certain situations.

J. Sandler: It's hard to imagine a reaction formation to biting. What could it be?

Anna Freud: Certain eating disturbances, where the child won't chew, I suppose. But that is more of an inhibition than a reaction formation.

J. Sandler: I think that what complicates things is that struggles over feeding are at their height in the anal phase. You have pointed out very often, Miss Freud, that the battle over food is very much an anal struggle, although in analytic reconstruction some analysts see these conflicts as much earlier. So perhaps reaction formations might be set up during the anal phase against all forms of aggressive behavior, including biting. I suppose one might get a reaction formation against hostility which is so widespread that the child becomes a passive child who appears to have given up his aggressiveness altogether. What I find particularly interesting is the idea that one could get reaction formations against derivatives of early oral impulses. For instance, a later derivative of biting might be sarcasm, and I could imagine a reaction formation then developing in which there is excessive concern about the effect of one's words on other people, as a defense against the aggressive wish, which is in turn a derivative of the original biologically based wish to bite. And again, there is the danger of the genetic trap in reconstruction. Something may start off being oral, but become very much anal or phallic while still retaining the oral mode. As you have put it, Miss Freud, there is a change of tool involved. And, conversely, the same tool can be used for different purposes.

Anna Freud: I once tried to show how wrong it was to look at both anal training and the handling of feeding difficulties in the same way, because the wish for food is something that always remains, whereas pleasure in anal matters has to be removed altogether in the course of development. There is an enormous difference between the two. By the way, should we call the symptom of hysterical vomiting, which is, after all, the opposite of taking in, a reaction formation? I don't suppose it is.

J. Sandler: We could say that it is a symptom because it is ego-dystonic, representing an unconscious expression of the wish to get rid of a baby, in a pregnant woman, for

example, or a fantasied baby, or whatever else might have been felt to have been taken in which was unwanted.

Our use of the term "ego-dystonic" is not always consistent. Perhaps we should speak of "consciousness-dystonic," because the term usually refers more to consciousness than to the ego as a whole. Freud used the term "ego-dystonic" long before he put forward the structural theory. If we look at it from the side of the gratification, we might find that there is an unconscious gratification in an impulse, but it is at the same time ego-dystonic, in the sense that the person does not want to accept the impulse consciously as part of himself. From this point of view the ego may play a very big part in the development of a symptom, which may finally represent a solution which is quite acceptable to the unconscious part of the ego, but because it is not in accordance with the person's conscious standards and ideals, it is felt to be alien, ego-dystonic.

We see symptoms as reflecting an activity of the unconscious ego. Could we not say that the unconscious ego, which creates the compromise formation, takes an active role in constructing the symptoms and in permitting the "breakthrough"? Not all neurotic symptoms have to be seen as compromise formations, and certainly certain psychosomatic symptoms, the symptoms of affective states such as depression, need not be concealed forms of an instinctual wish finding gratification in the shape of a compromise with the defense or with the punishment. You make the point, Miss Freud, that the formation of symptoms relieves the ego of the task of mastering its conflict because it has found a solution. Do you not mean the "conscious ego" is relieved?

Anna Freud: The ongoing battle really ends with the formation of the symptom, because then the symptom exists, if it is permanent, as a solution offered once and for all. Nothing further needs to be done about it, except that the person now suffers from the symptom, and has further

reactions, which depend on the particular symptom. But the conflict is solved. It is a bad solution, but it's a solution. In analyzing children, we very often get them at the stage before a solution—the formation of a symptom—has been found. We get them while the battle is still raging, and that is so very different from adult neurotics. It is perhaps a difference that we don't discuss sufficiently. We often see in our diagnostic evaluations of children that the child hasn't found the solution yet. The ego doesn't yet know what it will make of the conflict, which might still end up either in an obsessional neurosis, or in delinquent acts, or in a depression or a suicidal attempt. We don't know because the process hasn't yet been brought to a solution.

R. Tyson: I've often wondered about the developmental position of repression in regard to the other defenses. Is it early, or does it appear relatively late in development?

Anna Freud: That is a question that's been asked very often, and is very difficult to answer. We know it's not terribly early. It seems likely that all the major repressions in a particular individual are probably set up within a certain period—perhaps the oedipal period. Because later on you can't repress, except in highly abnormal states.

J. Sandler: I should have thought that a certain amount of repression was normal in ordinary functioning throughout life.

Anna Freud: It goes on from the past, but repressions are not newly established. You can re-repress what returns from the repressed, and in treatment, when people suddenly forget what has happened in the treatment hour, what has occurred is that you have opened up something with a patient, but some patients have the ability to close it off again immediately. This is certainly a repetition of repression, and not a new thing.

J. Sandler: I think there may be a confusion about the way

the term is used. The question would be, it seems to me, whether the defense mechanism of repression can be employed later on in life, and I think the answer must surely be "yes." If we speak of the content of what is repressed, which might otherwise be preconscious, one could say that it gets attached to the impulse which is in itself the subject of repression, or has just been released from repression, and so the defense mechanism of repression is brought into play, and represses as well the newer content which has become connected with what had previously been repressed. Surely we need to be constantly repressing derivatives of the past which threaten us?

Anna Freud: The question is whether we make new repressions of areas which have not been repressed before, or of instinctual matter that has not been repressed before. But what I had in mind is that the big repressions come early.

J. Sandler: We have often asked ourselves whether the essential conflicts in later life are revivals of earlier conflicts over oedipal and preoedipal wishes which have returned from repression. Is what comes later simply a derivative of what occurred earlier? It has been said that in adolescence fresh wishes which may be conflictual may emerge. It has been questioned whether all adult conflicts are simply childhood conflicts being reenacted on a different stage, so to speak. I personally think it is a caricature of psychoanalysis to say that we see everything the patient brings in the present as being a replication of something from his early childhood.

Anna Freud: There is a mistake in the book in this connection where I call repression the less normal or the more pathogenic of the defense mechanisms (p. 50). I shouldn't have said that, because all normality is based on the availability of repression at early ages. It can then easily lead to neurotic conflicts, but I agree that what is so abnormal

in the borderline children is that they do not have repression at their disposal in the usual way. I will give you another example which can be judged from that point of view. We know what happens to infantile death wishes against the love object, especially the parents: such wishes can be repressed, reaction formations can be built up, they can be displaced, they can be turned against the self, they can be answered phobically, or all sorts of other things can happen. But one of the things that can occur is that they are merely repressed, so that the individual knows nothing about these wishes. Now take a man of, let us say, thirty or forty, a fairly peaceful man all his life, who has good reason for developing hate and death wishes toward a rival, perhaps someone who has a superior position to him. He battles with that death wish because he does not want to become a murderer. But can he repress it? I think he can only repress it if that wish or impulse emerges with the old death wishes against the parents, and then he can treat those in the same way. If it is only a new impulse, and it might easily be a new impulse, I don't think he can repress that any more.

J. Sandler: What happens if he doesn't want to be a murderer in regard to the new impulse?

Anna Freud: He has many ways to deal with it at his disposal. He can avoid his enemy, he can leave the country, he can try never to see him again, he can hide his hostility, he can become superficially friendly, he can avail himself of the other defense mechanisms at his disposal. But I don't think he can repress the impulse.

J. Sandler: If such a wish arises toward a competitor, it will appear to be very much more dangerous if childhood death wishes are revived. In that case the person has to deal with a much more intense wish, one which has a much more primitive form for him. He has then the very urgent task of defending against the wish, and his first attempt

may be to throw both the new and revived wishes out, to keep them under, to put them under lock and key, just like the old ones. So he uses repression, but if that is unsuccessful, he may resort to other mechanisms. He may become persecuted, for example. A lot must have to do with the intensity of the impulse he faces because of infantile wishes having been revived and added to the new death wish. But this is not quite the same as saying that all adult impulses are new editions of the old ones. We are talking about the old wishes becoming mixed in with the new ones, which is something quite different.

Perhaps we should not link together inextricably the use of repression and the formation of the superego, because one could imagine a child in whom repression doesn't work well, but who has a very critical superego. Superego formation will occur in most children in one way or another by about the age of five or six, whether or not the Oedipus complex has been resolved, whether or not they have experienced the normal massive repression at about the age of five. Somehow the superego seems to some extent to have a life of its own. Possibly this was because it was originally observed as occurring at the same time as the massive childhood repression and superego formation, together with the so-called resolution of the Oedipus complex, and consequently it seemed that these were all parts of the same process, with no part occurring on its own. Perhaps nowadays we would say that they are separate processes which are very much interconnected, and which normally occur at the same time.

Anna Freud: And we have to think of the different borders between the psychic structures, because what is out of order in these children is not the border between ego and superego, but the border between id and ego. The repression—or rather the censor, if we can still call it that—lives on that border.

J. Sandler: And there are also children who have very

strong guilt feelings, but have to react massively in what looks like an impulse-ridden way in order to deal with their guilt feelings, because they can't deal with their guilt in any other way.

You once told us, Miss Freud, of the experiences you have had with the children of analysts. You said that at one time it seemed to analysts that it was the best thing for the child to let him do everything he wanted in order not to encourage any inhibitions.

Anna Freud: Yes, that was bad, because the child's ego then was afraid of being destroyed by the id impulses. This is different from the fear of the ego that has not obeyed the commands of its superego.

J. Sandler: Miss Freud, you say (pp. 49-50) that repression should be placed side by side with the other specific methods of defense, but it nevertheless occupies a unique position. You point out how strong a defense it is, that "it is capable of mastering powerful instinctual impulses, in face of which the other defensive measures are quite ineffective." You then describe how repression acts through the application of an anticathexis, and represents "a permanent institution demanding a constant expenditure of energy." The other defense mechanisms, unlike repression, are brought into operation "whenever there is an accession of instinctual energy." There's a problem, isn't there, about the nature of the permanent barrier, the permanent anticathexis, because in the energic theory, if it is permanent it would have to be considered to be "bound" cathexis, but this contradicts the idea that the instinctual impulses behind the repression barrier are free-floating, subject to primary process, and pushing forward for discharge. Would we not have to say that repression represents a barrier which can, at any time, be applied and reapplied? But then one has to wonder how this differs from the other mechanisms which can be applied and reapplied. Should

one conceive of repression as a sort of heightened stimulus barrier? A further question arises in regard to the possibility that certain mechanisms have to be used when repression fails. How does one reconcile this idea with the notion of repression being the most powerful form of defense? Do you think of "powerful" in the sense of the strength of the energies involved, or in the sense of effectiveness? Projection can be seen to be more effective in certain circumstances than repression, and certainly it involves less of an expenditure of energy. It is true that it involves more violence to reality, because one distorts the external world so much, and it might be more effective then, although in a sense less powerful. Something has to be clarified here.

Anna Freud: I think the meaning is pretty clear. Repression is a one-time happening. It isn't done whenever the instinctual demand comes up. On the other hand, what secures the repression demands a constant expenditure of energy. I think I can't say it in different words than those I used in the book, but there is to my mind quite a difference between the process of repression, which happens once, with a constant countercathexis, which is an ongoing process or an ongoing structure, and the other methods of defense. If we are dealing with a reaction formation, it is certainly a structure which has to be maintained, but it doesn't work in the same way as repression has to work constantly to keep the instincts down. As regards the question of effectiveness, my idea was that repression can deal with more powerful quantities. But, of course, even a powerful process doesn't always work, and every so often the machinery is defective, and we know then that we get a return of the repressed. It may reach consciousness, but invite re-repression, as it does very frequently in analysis, or it may call for the action of some other defense mechanism. We find an initial attempt at repression at the basis of most other defense mechanisms.

J. Sandler: Is it that repression, after a certain level of

development has been reached, is the first mechanism which is tried, perhaps with the exception of denial, which is after all a simple withdrawal of attention.

Anna Freud: Of course, developmentally repression is not the first. Other mechanisms like projection are used long before repression.

J. Sandler: Presumably because repression needs a considerable amount of strength on the part of the ego in order to work.

Anna Freud: Well, it needs structuralization of the personality, which isn't there in the beginning. If you haven't yet built the house, you can't throw somebody out of it.

J. Sandler: We know that, as the topographical model developed, Freud found it necessary to postulate a censorship between the system Unconscious and the Preconscious, and a second censorship between the Preconscious and the Conscious systems. So a wish which found its way past the first censorship was still liable to modification in the Preconscious before it reached the second censorship, at which point the final decision would be made about whether it should be admitted into consciousness or not. Now, if we transfer this to the structural theory, which is your essential frame of reference in the book, we would have to say that there is a repression barrier on the periphery of the ego, on the border with the id, which is the reservoir of instinctual wishes. The properties of secondary-process thinking and other means of transformation to form derivatives which were previously ascribed to the Preconscious would now be allocated to the unconscious ego. The ego would be aware that a wish or its derivative might constitute a threat to consciousness, because of the arousal of the anxiety signal. Then further defenses, including repression, might be instituted. This then provides a possibility for the repressed being constantly added to by derivatives which have been formed in the unconscious

ego but which have not been allowed to reach consciousness or motility. They may have had quite an elaborate development before being re-repressed and added to the original infantile wishes which had earlier succumbed to the major repression we associate with the resolution of the Oedipus complex and superego formation. The question which then comes to mind is how the ego knows what to repress. Does it not first sample the instinctual wish by allowing it some entry, and then because of the anxiety signal say "no"? Doesn't this process have to occur over and over, because the repressed wish has to be recognized in order to be defended against? Not all instinctual wishes are repressed, so some sort of selection must occur. I think we have to ascribe such a process of recognition and selection to the ego.

Anna Freud: I don't see any difficulty here, although evidently you do. But I'd like to correct one thing. You say I use the structural model in my book. But I never know whether I use the structural or topographical theory because I take from each what is useful. Does the conflict look so different when you look at it from the point of view of the two theories? Whatever way we use the theory, it has always contained the idea that there is constant movement in two directions in us. There is an upward movement toward consciousness, which implies the striving for satisfaction, whether it is in the id or in the Unconscious—it does not matter which way you want to put it. On the other hand, there is a reaction from the unconscious ego to push down impulses or memories, or whatever, which are trying to rise up. We have to take both movements into account, and certainly my idea would be that there is a great sensitivity at the border. We don't take it for granted within the analytic process that the patient becomes anxious before material that we are trying to make conscious has really risen into consciousness. He feels it coming; the resistance against it arises with it; and we take this as a sign

that something is going to happen of which he is afraid. Of course, the anxiety really begins before full consciousness is reached, and this is, I think, what you have in mind.

J. Sandler: I suppose my thoughts about this are affected by an increasing realization of how important the Preconscious system or the unconscious ego (of the structural model) is in mental functioning. The more we know about how the mind works, the more we see the extent to which there is unconscious functioning which involves secondary process. This unconscious activity is involved in the formation of derivatives of infantile wishes of all sorts; it forms and elaborates highly organized fantasies. We are much more aware nowadays of the role of the Preconscious or of the unconscious ego, both from a theoretical and a technical point of view. Earlier on, because the term "ego" referred so much to consciousness, or to the conscious self, the ego tended to be confused with consciousness. One even sees it in something you have said, namely, "Repression consists in the withholding or expulsion of an idea or affect from the conscious ego. It is meaningless to speak of repression where the ego is still merged with the id" (p. 51). Isn't there a contradiction here, if you maintain that repression must occur ultimately at the border between ego and id? Or would you agree that repression can also represent a holding back of a threatening impulse or wish at any point in its path through the ego or through the Preconscious system, a holding back directed against the wish or whatever is associated with it reaching consciousness?

Anna Freud: Yes. You introduce here the question of quantity. Something may come toward the border of consciousness, but because it is of low instinctual quantity it is not considered to be a danger until it is near consciousness. Whereas if it is highly cathected at that time, then it is a great danger, and is reacted to more quickly. We cannot

think of these movements without taking into account the quantities involved.

J. Sandler: Is it not more than a quantitative question? Isn't it as if the ego might say, "I will tolerate this as a preconscious thought, but I will not allow it into consciousness"? What I have in mind are such thoughts as those which patients have between sessions, thoughts which are repressed, presumably in the same way that infantile material is.

Anna Freud: Children say it quite openly. They don't mind some things as long as they are not put into words, which really means put in secondary-process terms. And they warn you, or they get furious, if you put it into words for them in the session. They get furious because the words arouse anxiety. But if the anxiety is only there on a vague level, they can tolerate it.

J. Sandler: What about repression in the forgetting of a name, for instance. Is it the same mechanism?

Anna Freud: It is a loss from consciousness, but into the Preconscious.

J. Sandler: Therefore in the structural model into the unconscious ego.

Anna Freud: Yes.

J. Sandler: I think that we should consider repression a defense mechanism the ego uses outside consciousness like all the defense mechanisms, one which is applied in proportion to the threat the wish represents. If the threat is recognized very early on, as a dangerous oedipal wish, for example, then it might be repressed more or less as soon as it is recognized. Or it might be tolerated as part of unconscious thinking, or of unconscious fantasy life in the ego, but if it comes too near to consciousness, a pushing back occurs. The content may reemerge, and then there

might be a re-repression, and this could happen over and over again.

Anna Freud: There are some patients who are threatened all the time by a low but worrying amount of anxiety. I think they feel threatened because what should be quietly in the id, in the unconscious system, rises all the time to be very near to consciousness. It isn't quite there, and we don't know why they feel so threatened. Of course, they are quite right to feel that at any moment something may break through. It is already at the door, and I suppose you would say it has become preconscious and near enough to consciousness to arouse anxiety but not near enough to be perceived.

J. Sandler: This would be an active holding back, but fairly late in the passage of the wish through the unconscious ego.

Anna Freud: Yes, but if in the person we are talking about there is a reaction formation, as in the obsessional, what he would do, quite instinctively and automatically, is to reinforce the reaction formation. He'd become more orderly or more clean or more slowed up, because he feels that the dam isn't quite strong enough. He says, "I must add another stone to it; perhaps it will then keep the flood back." Now this is certainly at a fairly high level of mental activity. We lose too much if we leave out the topographical view altogether.

J. Sandler: It seems that a great deal was gained with the structural theory, but the dynamic of the back-and-forth movement in the system Preconscious seemed somehow to be lost with the introduction of the concept of the ego as a structure.

Anna Freud: But it is lost only for the people who confine themselves to the structural theory.

J. Sandler: There is the story of the poor Jew who wanted

to get into the synagogue at the high festivals, but had no ticket. There was an imposing commissionaire standing outside to see that nobody without a ticket would get in. The poor man pleaded he had an important message for someone who was inside. The commissionaire wouldn't let him in, but the man finally said, "Let me in for just a minute. I'll give the message, and come right out again." The commissionaire said, "All right, go in and give the message, but if I catch you praying, God help you." I have a feeling that a struggle rather like this goes on in the preconscious. The threatening impulse is recognized, various forms of it are tested out, there is a back-and-forth struggle, and the form of the impulse changes into a derivative of some sort which is then allowed through.

Anna Freud: What the impulse that comes up really wants is satisfaction. Which means it wants to go over into motility, to reach a satisfying aim, and as long as there is no chance of that, if the motility is excluded, as in the dream or in the analytic hour, the danger isn't so great. But if the road is clear, the danger is very great.

M. Berger: I come back again to the point about repression acting once only. Did you mean that it acts at a point when a forbidden impulse wants to find expression, or did you mean by "once only" a particular stage of development?

Anna Freud: The latter.

J. Sandler: I think you must have in mind, Miss Freud, the massive repression which occurs before latency, and which leads to the infantile amnesia. At the same time, it seems clear that repression can be used again as a separate defense mechanism. Perhaps later it doesn't have the same force as it did early on, except possibly in regard to traumatic experiences. One gets the same sort of massive repression if a trauma has occurred, the defense being against the revival of the traumatic experience. Perhaps

the same massive repression leads to hysterical fugue states or to other things which are equally gross.

Anna Freud: What you mention in regard to traumas or fugue states is really the operation of something different from repression. It is a failure of the ego to perceive, which is not quite the same as withdrawing attention from something.

I once described a case I analyzed many years ago where a whole year between the ages of about seven and eight was absolutely blotted out from the memory of the patient, who otherwise had the normal childhood memories. What came out in her analysis was that she had lost her father very early, and had built up a theory of her mother being forever faithful to the father. During [that] year the mother had a relationship with a man who lived with the family, and was a very good father to my patient. But this man represented someone who could destroy the idea of the mother's faithfulness to the father in her memory. In order to keep an ideal she had built up, she had to remove a whole section of her life, all the evidence, positive and negative. I suppose that if something like this happened later in life, it would be similar to a fugue state, wouldn't it? There would be the removal of conscious awareness of a whole part of one's life for a certain period.

J. Sandler: When we consider the mechanism of repression and also its relation to denial we run into a number of problems. Classically we regard the mechanism of denial as being simply the withdrawal of attention from something significant which is unwelcome for one reason or another. But from a clinical point of view we have to consider a whole range of "denials" in which the withdrawal of attention is reinforced by a counterforce, by a counter-cathexis, if you will. If denial were simply the withdrawal of attention, then it would be relatively easy to point out to the person concerned what he is denying and to get him

to see it. But we know there are people who strenuously avoid looking at something painful or threatening, and even though it may be pointed out, maintain the denial. This is usually in regard to something in the external world, and seems parallel to the process of repression we normally conceptualize as involving both the withdrawal of attention and the application of a counterforce. But we don't usually speak of repression in regard to the perception of something in the external world. We also have the so-called scotomization, in which something which would normally be seen is blotted out. The person looks, but he does not see. This is somewhat different in quality from other forms of denial. And then there is repression proper, which is usually conceived of as a sort of "horizontal" repression, in the sense that attention is withdrawn from some mental content, a counterforce applied, and the offending content is then kept down. But there is also what we might call a sort of "vertical" repression—some people would call it a split—in which one part of the person's life is kept completely separated from another. I do not think this is at all uncommon. I remember a patient who kept out of her analysis a full-fledged obsessional neurosis which was restricted to the bedroom. When I finally quite accidentally got a hint of this, and managed to pull it into the analysis against severe resistance, she reacted with rage, maintaining that this part of her life did not really belong to the analytic work. Her defense had the force of a repression, except that she was conscious of the warded-off part. In a sense she had separated her consciousness, her life, into two areas. In energic terms, we could say that there seem to be a number of ways in which countercathexis is applied, repression being the most important of these.

Anna Freud: I remember a very lively discussion many many years ago when the term "scotomization" was first introduced, because scotomization meant not seeing something that was there. If it was not seen, it did not have to

be repressed. Current theory was that certain things were repressed because they had been perceived. It is a way of keeping things out of consciousness, but in order to keep something out it has to be there first. If it isn't there at all, then we don't need to repress it! We'd call it denial now, I think.

J. Sandler: Perhaps the problem has become more complicated nowadays because of the emphasis, in recent years, on unconscious awareness. This has perhaps been influenced by all the work on subliminal perception, and the knowledge that perceptual input is examined first in some unconscious way before being structured into a conscious percept. We would now tend to say that both scotomization and other forms of denial involve a recognition, but it is an unconscious recognition. With denial, we have the problem of whether we should regard it simply as a process whereby the unconscious ego pretends to consciousness that something isn't there, or is it a much more active rejection of the perception?

Anna Freud: Because the original German term *Verleugnung* really means disavowal, it implies that you've seen it and then you say you haven't. You say it isn't there when you first had the impression it *is* there. Disavowal is a much better term than denial.

J. Sandler: A word about the chronology of defenses. It is clear that no-one feels completely satisfied with the state of our knowledge about this. We could ask whether we should apply the notion of lines of development to defenses, rather than maintain a view of them as separate units which come into being at particular times. I don't know why we have such difficulty with chronology. Is it that the little child cannot speak?

Anna Freud: We know a little more about it now than we knew at the time of the book. I remember I warned myself

not to say more about it than I knew, which was very little. I suppose at that time it was not sufficiently brought into connection with structuralization. Nowadays we could probably say in much greater detail at what time every one of the defense mechanisms would have a chance to be used, because preparations for it have been made. You remember we said before that to speak of repression makes no sense before there is a division between conscious and unconscious ego, between ego and id, and so on. To speak of projection or externalization makes no sense before a differentiation between the inner and outer world has been established, because if there is no outer world for the child, you can't assign anything to it. On the other hand, the very fact that you can assign certain sensations or happenings to another place creates the distinction between inner and outer. We should ask what the preconditions are for the working of various mechanisms. Identification really makes no sense before the merging period is over, because then you and the object are one anyway, so why trouble to identify? You are already there!

J. Sandler: None of the mechanisms makes sense without the idea of displacement, which must be one of the very earliest mechanisms. For example, identification implies a displacement of a mental representation.

Anna Freud: Yes. I think that would be the way to go about it. But that is far further into the study of childhood reactions than we were then.

J. Sandler: One of the things we do need to straighten out is the whole concept of the "precursor," because it may be that we are using the wrong concept. Perhaps we ought to be looking for "necessary conditions," as opposed to precursors, because there is a tendency for the precursor of a defense mechanism to become equated with the mechanism itself. But there is a question I would like to ask in regard to the development of repression. How is it that

hysterical symptoms can occur in two-year-olds? I have seen a hysterical paralysis of the arm in a child of two based on an identification with the mother who had a sprained wrist and had her arm in a sling.

Anna Freud: There is no doubt that hysterical symptoms can occur in children of two, especially leg and arm symptoms. But I think that what the symptoms make use of very much is the easy interchange between mind and body in the first year of life, in the psychosomatic world of early childhood. This serves as the earliest basis for hysterical symptoms where the symptom has meaning. But we have never collected knowledge in regard to this in any systematic way.

J. Sandler: Perhaps because we tend not to get such young children in the Clinic.

I should like to ask about the link so often made in the literature between the defense mechanisms and the vicissitudes of the drives. Parallels are drawn between the expulsive and retentive aspects of the anal drives, and between defense mechanisms which show some of these qualities. As a result developmental links have been postulated between drive vicissitudes and defense mechanisms —projection linked with expulsion, and so on.

Anna Freud: There are some defense mechanisms which grow out of primary-process functioning. Displacement is a good example, and the turning of passive into active is another, where the opposites are really the same. There you can see the influence of the primary process. There are certain underlying models, shall we say, out of which the defense mechanisms can emerge. But I think that to equate projection with expulsion, as you describe, goes much too far. It destroys again the difference between id activity and ego activity, and by undoing the differences we don't get any further in clarification.

J. Sandler: If defense mechanisms can be taken over

through identification, then which mechanisms are more easily taken over? In a family of deniers, for instance, how much of the use of denial would be based on identification?

Anna Freud: We can ask the same question about a family of obsessionals. On the one hand there are underlying similarities of personality between parents and children, and on the other certain basic characteristics can be taken over by imitation and identification; out of that can grow similar defense mechanisms. But where defense mechanisms are really only taken over, first by imitation and then by identification, they are easily given up in analysis, because they are not the person's own.

J. Sandler: They must be very different qualitatively. But I suppose that there is a whole range of mechanisms which can be reinforced in a selective or differential way by other members of the family. These would then be mechanisms which actually belong in the first instance to the person concerned, but whose use would be greatly increased because of family support and reinforcement. This sort of differential reinforcement wouldn't be identification.

Anna Freud: No.

J. Sandler: Do you still hold the view that "repression is preeminently of value in combating sexual wishes, while other methods can more readily be employed against instinctual forces of a different kind, in particular, against aggressive impulses" (pp. 50-51)?

Anna Freud: It was a speculation, because I wasn't too sure then whether repression could equally be used against aggressive impulses. We knew so much less about the ego's dealing with aggression than with libido. Certainly repression can equally be used against aggression.

J. Sandler: The point you make is that possibly each defense mechanism is first evolved in order to master some specific instinctual urge. Do you think one could say that it is

evolved during a particular phase when a specific instinct dominates the picture? It might otherwise sound as if you postulate a special link between the mechanism and the partial instinctual drive, and I don't think you meant that. *Anna Freud:* I think I meant it as an open question. There are periods of life when particular instincts are dominant, and therefore also special dangers and special tasks of mastery for the ego. This certainly makes a link between the two.

Joseph Sandler

Sigmund Freud Center
Hebrew University
Mt. Scopus, 91905 Jerusalem
Israel

DEFENSE AND RESISTANCE IN PSYCHOANALYSIS AND LIFE

Leo Rangell, M.D.

RESISTANCE IS A DEFENSE AGAINST INSIGHT. This is not to be confused with obstacles to knowledge. Defenses are not inert barriers, but psychic configurations with dynamic force. Insight is not blocked, but actively opposed. And the knowledge that is kept from consciousness in the case of resistance is not out of reach because of its complexity, beyond man's cognitive ability to encompass or comprehend, but by virtue of its unacceptability to the ego.

The facts in repression are typically extraordinarily simple, such elemental concepts as "I love her" or "I hate him" or "I want what you have." It is not their cognitive complexity, but the affective accompaniments of such primitive constructs, with their anticipated retaliatory punishments or other consequences, which constitute the building blocks of the psychic armor around the forbidden thoughts or feelings which need to be kept captive, out of sight or conscious awareness.

The knowledge defended against by resistance to insight comprises the psychic elements maintained in repression. These include the fact of repression as well as the contents repressed. That a defense is itself defended against is not new or uncommon, but ubiquitous and typical. There is a motive to keep all aspects of conflict unconscious. In addition to defenses against forbidden impulses, there are defenses against subsequent in-

147

stinctual derivatives. There are defenses against unacceptable affects, unpleasurable affects other than anxiety, and against a hierarchy of other motivational drives, in a constantly changing dynamic layering of interacting motivational drives and defenses (Rapaport, 1953). There are defenses against anxiety, which is the motive for defense, against the superego, often the instigator of defense, and intrasystemic defenses of one part of the ego against another.

Both arms of conflict can be kept unconscious, and there are defenses against the compromise formations which result from the conflicting forces as well (Fenichel, 1945). It is common clinical experience that the undoing of repression can be followed by the emergence of hitherto repressed symptoms. A patient can learn after beginning analysis that he is anxious or phobic or compulsive. Arlow (1969) has stressed the importance of unconscious fantasy, which is as much of a compromise formation as a dream or symptom. And whole symptom complexes can come to light during analysis, which have been repressed. It can be a sign of progress when pathological formations which have been retained as ego-syntonic are dissociated from the ego to which they now become alien and dystonic.

With regard to the relation between resistance and defense, it is not the simple and neat formula that defenses occur in life and resistances in analysis. Both are operative in analysis and in life. Defenses can be strengthened or arise *de novo* during the course of analysis, and resistances occur in life situations as well as in analysis. These can occur whenever insight comes or threatens to come from any direction below the level of defense, from a teacher, an adversary, a chance encounter, or a friend. One patient, who prior to analysis had been through every kind of "wild therapy" extant in southern California, stated, "Every group is an encounter group. Everyone expresses judgments about everyone else." He was referring to a party he had just been at and what transpired when people were a little high. "This also refers to couples," he said.

But although resistance and defense are intrinsic to human

life, both occupy a special place within the psychoanalytic process. It was the advent of psychoanalysis, the first body of knowledge directed to the unconscious of man, which aroused resistance and defense in concentrated and pure form. And so it is with each psychoanalysis. Brenner (1982b), speaking of transference, which also occurs in life as it does in analysis, stated that the difference between transference in the two situations is that it is analyzed in analysis. The same can be said to be true of defense. There is, however, another crucial difference between the two situations, which is in fact what makes analysis possible. There is a difference in the phenomenology of transference that results from the analytic stance of the analyst, which differs from any other relationship in life. Transference, defense, and also resistances to each, as well as resistances to other elements of the unconscious, are brought to the fore in sharpened focus and in a specific and pathognomonic way by the analytic process. While both transference and defense occur in life, analysis isolates and highlights them in purer form, rendering them in a position to be observed and understood, and objectively and justifiably to be conveyed by the observer to the subject who demonstrates them.

The analyst oversees the patient in analysis and in his life. Unlike the analysis of transference only (Heimann, 1956), or the priority given currently to the here-and-now, as by Gill (1979), the analyst notes and brings into the analysis transferences, defenses, and resistances occurring in the extra-analytic life of the patient, current as well as past. The special task, however, is to subsume all of these within the psychoanalytic process and method. Behind the resistances and defenses, the contents being resisted are also pursued toward understanding throughout the patient's life, inside and outside the actual boundaries of the analysis. While analysis by definition centers on transference and resistance, these are to be utilized as means to the end, in the service of achieving the goal of analysis, to uncover the original conflicts which are the sources of them both. Toward this end the path is from the surface down; the analysis of resistances always come first.

From resistances to defenses to the contents repressed, there is a hierarchy of repressed elements, at the surface of which are the repressing forces themselves. The motive for maintaining the status quo, for supporting the equilibrium that the ego guards, is to keep anxiety in check unless and until the ego is equipped to substitute an improved solution. The removal of a defense below the resistance, either inappropriately in life or by a premature interpretation in analysis, results in the emergence of anxiety. A new cognitive-affective balance must then be achieved by the ego, with an altered combination of contents that are conscious and those that need to be repressed. Resistance is thus a defense against the undoing of a defense necessary to maintain an intrapsychic balance, to prevent a domino effect which would lead to anxiety and the need for a shift in relations between impulse and defense.

Freud's first insights as he approached the human mind as the subject of study was to dissect the whole into component parts. There was immediately conflict between opposing forces. I will pass over lightly how the course progressed with evolving theory to increasingly coherent explanatory formulations. From conflicts at first between the loculated affects associated with traumatic events and the moral prohibitions of society (Breuer and Freud, 1893-1895), conflicts were soon internalized, with instincts coming to replace affects and prohibiting forces also seen as existing within (Freud, 1900, 1905). Internal conflicts at the beginning were between sexual and ego self-preservative instincts (Freud, 1910, 1911a, 1914). When aggressive drives were added to the sexual (Freud, 1920), the nature of conflicts also changed, becoming instinctual drives versus defensive forces of varying types at different stages of theory formation.

Defenses were always less sharply defined by Freud than instincts, were mostly subsumed under the generic concept of repression, and went through a number of stages of conceptual definition of the motives and means of the repressing forces. These were far from clear in the early stages, during which psychic outcomes were divided into actual neuroses or anxiety

neuroses (Freud, 1895) and the neuropsychoses of defense (Freud, 1894, 1896). The concept of repression and its relation to defense was integrated at every stage with the prevailing theory of neurosogenesis, instinct theory, and the explanatory theory of anxiety at that particular phase of theory formation. Anxiety during this phase resulted from repression, without it being clear how or from where the repression came about.

Further clarification came with the introduction of the structural view (Freud, 1923) and Freud's (1926) definitive signal theory of anxiety. With these, defenses were clearly relegated to the ego and sharply defined in locus, motive and method, and in their function to keep forbidden instinctual impulses unconscious. The neuroses themselves resulting from these changing combinations of theoretical elements progressed from actual neuroses, through neuropsychoses of defense, to the current concept of psychoneuroses, with symptoms as compromise formations between instincts and defense. Anxiety in this phase, in an enduring formulation never since retracted or improved, was now the motive for defense, not its result.

In addition to repression as a general concept of defense, Freud had recognized and made explicit other defensive activities and measures which he had introduced from time to time into the theoretical armamentarium in connection with specific discussions of clinical syndromes. Thus Freud, along with Abraham (1921), Jones (1918), Ferenczi (1914), and other pioneers, connected reaction formation clinically to obsessive-compulsive and anal states (Freud, 1908, 1909b). Introjection, incorporation, and identification were described in oral syndromes (Freud, 1905), projection in paranoia (Freud, 1911b, 1922), displacement in phobias (Freud, 1909a), turning against the self in sadomasochism or scoptophilia-exhibitionism (Freud, 1915). Other mechanisms were exchanged with and borrowed from the dream work (Freud, 1900)—displacement, condensation, reversal into the opposite, the change from passive to active. In his reformulation of the theory of anxiety, Freud (1926), reduced repression to "a special method of defense."

Regression, isolation, and undoing were also made familiar intellectual terrain in psychoanalytic theory and understanding.

Although Freud had thus introduced many of the specific defenses, it remained for Anna Freud (1936) to do with defenses what her father had done with instincts, further subdividing the larger concept and organizing the results into an ordered range of specific instances and examples. She pursued the analysis of defenses with the same vigor, clarity, objectivity, and scientific purpose as her father did not only for instincts, but for the totality of mental functioning. What Freud had referred to at various times as defensive measures or methods, forms or modes of defense, or defensive techniques employed by the ego, Anna Freud designated as "the mechanisms of defense." Adding and elaborating upon sublimation and denial, and describing identification with the aggressor and a form of "altruistic surrender," she went on to systematize and classify the accumulated inventory of defenses into a series of defense mechanisms according to the sources of anxiety and danger, from the superego, the external world, or the dread of the strength of the instincts.

Completing the cycle of the interaction of impulse and defense, Anna Freud (1936) performed with repression what Freud had done with the repressed. Turning the higher power of observation and theoretical dissection onto the nature of the processes of defense, she proceeded to round out not only the theoretical body, but its implications for technique, to be able to analyze conflict from both sides, not one alone. By no means was this an academic exercise of intellectual conceptualization without practical goals. While from the theoretical side defenses were lifted to an equal role with instinctual drives, along with other forces from the superego and external world, to encompass the totality of human behavior, with the satisfaction of theory and understanding the most pragmatic motives guided and characterized this work. By defining further the tools of the analyst, the efficacy of analysis as a technical instrument was refined and its reach extended. Theoretical knowledge was

always in the service of increasing the mastery of treatment and technique.

It is frequently said and automatically felt that Anna Freud's classic monograph of 1936 initiated the period of ego psychology which followed Freud's emphasis before that time on the role of the id. It would be more accurate in my opinion to say that while Anna Freud elevated the position of the defenses to a coequal role in the genesis of conflict, it was only the defensive function of the ego that was confirmed and emphasized in her contributions. It remained for others to elaborate the wider functions of the ego, which led to what became commonly known as "ego psychology." This reached its full dimension in the works of Hartmann, especially with his (1939) monograph on the adaptive functions of the ego, which shortly followed Anna Freud's *The Ego and the Mechanisms of Defense.* With Hartmann's introduction of ego autonomy and the conflict-free aspects of ego functioning, and the important elaborations of these segments of human life by Kris (1955), Rapaport (1951, 1958), and Erikson (1950, 1956), it was not only the role of defense that was added to round out the pressures of instinctual drives, but the full-bodied role of the ego toward the id, superego, and external world.

To many the "ego psychology" that followed came to connote a role of the ego independent of the other psychic agencies, with the ego in control almost as it was in preanalytic days, before an ego had as yet been named. The concept connoted by ego autonomy fell on prepared and receptive ears. The fact was that Anna Freud, in giving due place to the role of defenses, did so only in relation to all other surrounding dynamic forces. Besides stressing this in her theoretical descriptions, she also pointed out that technically the analyst's stance, via an alliance with the patient's ego, was to be equidistant between all three psychic agencies and between these and the external world. The same was true for Hartmann, Kris, and Rapaport, all of whom, in their respective writings, sought and achieved a balance between all the forces emanating from and impinging upon the

human mind. It has typically been not the initiators of the above works but their followers who singled out the ego as though it stood alone, above the other psychic agencies and without their influence, as though man by virtue of his ego was free of forces not of his own making or control.

In each case—Freud, dividing instincts into specific subtypes, or dissecting symptoms into components of which they are the vectors, or Anna Freud, ordering defensive behavior into a spectrum of specific defense mechanisms—the principle followed was the same, the understanding of larger groups as composed of smaller ones. While the latter, upon deeper knowledge and more refined observations, could usually be seen to consist of another grouping of still smaller and more discrete elements, the goal was always toward the irreducible. Perhaps Freud (1920) felt he had come closest to this with his strongly cathected formulation of life and death instincts.

From the beginning and continuously into current history, along with the theoretical advance being achieved, there has been a simultaneous opposition and resistance to this procedure of differentiating part processes within the whole. Partly and originally this was due to the resistance of mankind, shared by many of the early deviationist analysts, to assigning a role in human behavior to mental functioning outside of conscious control. For the same reasons that the general population, including the scientific community, opposed the concept of the unconscious, some of the early analytic pioneers, such as Adler and in some respects Jung, objected specifically to libido theory, Adler preferring the ego—at least his early concept of ego, which was not what it is today—and Jung more cosmic forces over sexual impulses emanating from within. In more recent times a counterpart of this resistance could be seen in the similar objections of Alexander et al. (1946) and other modern theorists to libido theory.

Paradoxically, after the unconscious became common intellectual property, resistance to exposing it was also due to an opposite mechanism (Rangell, 1982). Besides the resistance

stemming from a threat to his control, man, some analysts included, resisted the increased responsibility that would come from making the unconscious conscious. With the advent and understanding of unconscious decision making (Rangell, 1969b, 1971), man was responsible for more, not less, than he knows or thinks. While resenting a lack of mastery, man at the same time fears an increase in responsibility. The discovery and addition of ego autonomy to human dynamics was not without its complicating effects. These two mechanisms, facilitated by the mutual enhancement of individual defenses which comes with group cohesiveness and group psychology, constitute major group resistances and defense, resistance to insight and defense against the contents of the unconscious.

Periodically and repetitively the scientific method of dissecting behavior into component parts has been objected to in principle and counterposed with the necessity to view the human subject or in particular his mental endowment as an undifferentiated whole. Implicit, or at times made explicit, has been the feeling that the process of differentiation, even if only in scientific understanding, does violence to the subjective integrity of the individual. From the nonanalytic "person" in the system of Rogers (1942), to Horney's (1937) environmental and Sullivan's (1953) interpersonal theories of etiology, to Kohut's (1971, 1977) theory of the self, to the more sophisticated objections to structural division by Klein (1973) or Gedo (1979), a common motivation in the followers of these theories is the feeling that scientific decomposition of the mental apparatus is somehow accompanied by a psychological fragmentation of the person or personality or, in the latest theory, of the self. Empirically there is typically less objection to the concept of defense, which remains accepted in some of the alternative theories, than to the contents of the repressed. Perhaps mankind in general, chronically defending against unwelcome elements, "experiences" an awareness of the process of defense in a primitive psychosomatic structural sense, or of preconscious fantasies poised between conscious and unconscious, in such a

way as to mitigate against a too-strong conscious intellectual objection to the theoretical possibility of a defensive process at work.

Within the mainstream of psychoanalytic theoretical development, during the entire history of id psychology followed by ego psychology, the importance of integration as a parallel process and principle alongside the process of differentiation was not lost sight of, but received equal attention in understanding and assessing presenting phenomenology. On the other side of the coin of the differentiating functions of the ego were the synthetic function described by Nunberg (1931) and the organizing and integrating functions described by Hartmann (1950). The issue of wholeness is not unaccounted for in psychoanalytic metapsychologic theory. The self as well as the system ego is encompassed within the structural view.

I would like now to pursue the subject of resistances and defense from the points of view of integration and differentiation as these are reflected in the phenomenology seen in analysis and life. Resistance, a phenomenon discovered and receiving prominence with the advent of psychoanalysis, is a defense againt insight, which is reacted to as a threat as well as a hope. This ambivalence, which is built in to the analytic procedure, is also intrinsic to the myth that is the central paradigm of psychoanalytic theory. Blum (1979) points out "the quest for insight has always paralleled the 'bliss of ignorance.' The hero of the oedipal myth moves and wavers between insight and blindness. Oedipus seeks the truth while asserting innocence of his guilt and ignorance of his identity. Analogous to the analytic process, the oedipal myth depicts the struggle between insight and resistance to insight" (p. 41).

A patient enters analysis because of the hope that insight will lead to mastery over anxiety, resists it because of the unconscious knowledge that along the way there will be the traumatic state. Resistance in analysis is aroused and activated when the patient unconsciously senses, from the analyst or analytic situation or from an inner process of readiness and, therefore,

imminence of insight, that an element hitherto unconscious has become potentially available to be rendered conscious. Typically this involves the imminent removal of a defense and constitutes a heightened defense both against the threatened defense and the contents about to emerge from repression. Resistance is activated by the ego in the service of defense as a second layer of defense to bolster a weakening pre-existing one.

Phenomena are discovered in analysis which are then seen to exist in life. Just as transference, which was first appreciated and received the full impact of understanding in the psychoanalytic situation, was later recognized as a general phenomenon in life, so does resistance play a part in life situations that share, in common with analysis, the threat of insight. Such was the case with the first appearance of Freud's psychoanalytic discoveries. The shock experienced and the negative reaction that ensued from the scientific community as well as the general population constituted a mass resistance to a global interpretation, a first interpretation to mankind of the existence of an unconscious mental life, along with the first glimmerings of the repressed sexual content it contained. This was a negative transference to psychoanalytic theory which was not limited to an initial reaction, but has played an ongoing role in psychoanalytic history (Rangell, 1982). One person suggesting to another what he is doing or feeling and why, or that he is defending against some unwelcome impulse or wish, arouses not only a defense, but a resistance, ranging from passive to more active forms. And the possibility of its being true in one stimulates a resistance to it in all. Such a reaction was institutionalized and made public in the film, *Never on Sunday*, when a man in a bar told another he loved his mother. The violent response that ensued was such that the physical well-being of the interpreter was in dire danger. The entire audience understood.

Novels are most successful when they walk a thin line, imparting insight subtly without arousing resistance or defense. The more they can achieve both, the more compelling and in demand they become. Crossing the line in either direction, to-

ward not enough insight or too much resistance, defeats the effect. Confrontations between individuals about long pent-up and mutual grievances invariably consist of interpretations fired reciprocally from one to the other, usually simltaneously or in quick succession. Delivered with passion and subjectivity on each side, the effect is of course what would occur in an analytic session if the countertransference of the analyst were uncontrolled and at a maximum intensity caused him to lose all restraints. Resistance is thickened, defenses strengthened, not weakened, and aggression enlisted to further their hold. Such interpretations are more common in life, in milder form below the level of resistances, than in analysis, where the resistances are anticipated, understood, softened, and interpreted first.

The patient presents an aggregate syndrome. It is the function and method of psychoanalysis to isolate and identify the separate elements. Clinically the patient enters analysis with a fused state. Impulses adhere to defenses, compromise formations cover and contain both, symptoms and character traits are usually admixed. In the occasional case, more rare in today's clinical world than it was in Freud's time, but still not uncommonly present, an ego-dystonic experience protrudes as a symptom from the conglomerate mass of psychic elements, serving the analyst as an entering wedge.

The analyst destratifies the fused mass into its component parts, differentiating symptoms from character, the defense within the symptom, the impulse behind the defense, one developmental level from another, the drive derivatives expressed via the object, etc., offering the patient's observing, analytic ego the analyst's reconstructions and interpretations toward their common understanding. No element alone is the goal of analysis, only the reciprocity and interdependence of contiguous and interacting forces. Neither defense analysis alone nor instinct analysis alone are the goals of treatment, any more than the exposure and analysis of the transference neurosis alone is the ultimate goal of the therapeutic procedure. All are means, paths, and way-stations to the end, the understanding of the

origins and genesis of the pathological aspects of the patient's presenting aggregate mental state.

Differentiation, besides being a factor in mental life, is central to the means of the analytic procedure. It can be normal or pathological, and be used for either purpose in analysis or in life. Just as normal differentiation can become pathological splitting in life, so during the treatment process can differentiation be used either in the service of analysis or be carried to a degree which can thwart its purpose, with undue separation of elements and inadequate cohesion and integration. While Hartmann (1950) has included the differentiating function in the inventory of ego functions, Needles (1978) has traced the vicissitudes of this function from normal to abnormal functioning in life and in the analytic process. The aim of analysis toward ego functions is to produce an optimum balance and capacity for both differentiation and integration. For an integrated self, one needs a functioning ego. The interest to maintain wholeness of the organism does not preclude separateness and harmony between internal parts.

Although integration and differentiation are intrinsic to growth and development, continuity and fusion, not discrete mechanisms or states, are the rule in life, biologically and psychologically. Mental products *in vivo* do not remain solitary and isolated, but adhere to contiguous and related states and conditions. This is true clinically and in theoretical concepts. A patient comes to analysis with a general overall complaint that she feels "weird." This major presenting symptom façade turns out, upon the microscopic process that is analysis, to be an aggregate affective-cognitive state, consisting of an undifferentiated experience of unpleasurable affects, depression, guilt, shame and anxiety, appropriate and neurotic, low self-esteem, self-punitive fears, fantasies with their accompanying affects, a diffuse inhibition of action, and symptoms which are global and diffuse and can only be described inadequately in verbal terms. Coursing behind them all is an anxiety of almost panphobic proportions, extending widely into the external and so-

cial world, with anxiety over uncontrolled aggression from within and the fear of retaliation as a consequence from without. In addition to numerous derivatives and accompaniments of anxiety, almost as a surplus, is a vague free-floating anxiety unattached to objects or situations. The total effect is a global agglutinated cognitive-affective experience of ego-dystonic unpleasure as the presenting symptom. I will not go further here into the findings of analysis, which not unexpectedly converge into common oedipal and preoedipal etiologic determinants.

I recently had an interesting related clinical experience in reverse. As a parallel syndrome in another patient was gradually being resolved during analysis, the patient reported feeling "numb," peculiar, in a suspended state, as anxieties were dissolving in significant increments. As overpowering insights into the origins of his symptoms fell into place, coming neither dramatically nor all at once, but in a series of cumulative uncoverings and intricate connections between his symptoms, memories, and dreams from past and current life, it was as if a load were lifting rather than, as in the previous case, pressing with full weight on the patient's ego and its functions. Subjectively, the first patient experienced an impairment of her will or ability to choose, while the patient who improved, as differentiation was being effected with increasing understanding, felt the change subjectively as the ability to make choices rather than to be swept along by automatic actions.

The same process of cohesion and integration is true theoretically as subjectively, in development as in clinical phenomenology. The ego and the id which come to be separable and separated are originally part of an ego-id matrix (Hartmann, 1950). The superego borrows strength, energy, and characteristics from the id, both libidinal and aggressive components, to become either loving or harsh or a combination of both. The ego ideal is a bridge that links the ego with the superego. Drives can be used for purposes of defense, and defenses can be instinctualized and convey characteristics of drives. Yet although the psychic agencies overlap, they are also separate, in life and

in the analytic process devoted to understanding them. Mental elements merge and yet remain apart.

The same phenomena take place horizontally in a moment of current time, as vertically and longitudinally in historical time and space. Perceptions newly coming into the ego are instantaneously linked with related memories, activate old fantasies or elicit new ones, associated by motives of drive or defense. As dreams are conceived and constructed at night, latent as well as overt daydreams play themselves out continuously or successively upon the mental surface during the day. Representing the same fused final psychic products as dreams of the night, they are similarly composed of disparate streams of thought and affect, synthesized before they can claim consciousness by the same secondary revision as dreams. Lewin's (1946) "dream screen" is available throughout the diurnal cycle, not only to serve as a backdrop at night, but during the day as well. This includes especially the transitional periods of falling asleep, waking up, dozing off, states of fatigue, boredom, musing, or drifting. And when daydreams fail and anxiety threatens, a "daymare" can come to the same abrupt end as a nightmare.

Both ego functions, of differentiation and integration, are goals of mental health, in appropriate qualitative and quantitative relational forms. And integration and differentiation can each be normal or pathological, in states of equilibrium or in progression or regression. Regression can cause either pathological defusion or dedifferentiation, in the opposite direction of what has been achieved adaptively during the course of progressive development. Integration as an aim and principle of mental functioning does not exclude differentiating activity; each can regress and be enlisted in the service of psychopathology.

The road to healthy integration in analysis is differentiation and reintegration, by destratification of clinical aggregates and their resynthesis into more stable and adaptive wholes. Only through the separation of elements into their discrete internal

components can the patient's ego more adequately identify and master the pathological ingredients. The woman patient reported above, within her diffuse unpleasure is afraid to be angry, guilty to be afraid, ashamed of being afraid, guilty and angry. The analyst destratifies the layers of repressed affect, each time by removing the defense against the particular affect, and always by first removing the resistance against insight into the defense. Not only the abnormal affects, but their interrelationships are exposed and rendered subject to reevaluation and change.

The same considerations about the whole and its parts obtain for the central subject matter of this paper, defenses and resistance. Defensive activities are still seen and treated clinically in their more diffuse aspects as in the general form first recognized by Freud. Just as Stone (1973) pointed out that resistances can vary from large complex actions to the most circumscribed forms, "from falling asleep to brilliant argument" (p. 42), the same holds for defenses, which also traverse a range in practice from diffuse behavior to limited thoughts or acts. Although the presenting pictures clinically are the results of fusion, and integration is part of the aim of mental health, the task in analysis is from the whole to its parts, from symptoms to their components, from conflicts to the forces of which they are composed. Toward this end the analysis of resistances and defense is similarly from the global or diffuse to the specific and circumscribed.

In connection with this theme of proceeding from higher to lower systems of organization, Brenner (1981), in a radical revision of psychoanalytic theory, has recently taken the position, differing from the classic contribution of Anna Freud (1936), that there are no special defense mechanisms, that the term "is incorrect and misleading" (p. 568). Opposing what he himself describes as one of the "most widely accepted parts of the psychoanalytic theory of conflict" (p. 558), Brenner argues that since all ego functions can serve the purpose of defense and there are no special ego functions used for defense alone,

"to discuss defense in terms of defense mechanisms, as Freud and every analyst since has done, myself included, is wrong" (p. 561). The observations that serve as the data for Brenner's present conclusions are the same as those I have pointed out, mainly the fusion and interchangeability of psychic elements. These are also intrinsic to the principles of multiple function (Waelder, 1930) and overdetermination, which have long been parts of accepted psychoanalytic theory. I, however, come to different conclusions than Brenner from the same phenomena, that is, while such multiple usages, overlap of functions, and diffusion of borders exist, they do not preclude the simultaneous presence of separate and separable functions, processes, structures, and mechanisms.

I agree with Brenner that any ego function can be used for defense, and go further that an even more elaborate organization such as a symptom can be similarly used. While Brenner disagrees with Schafer (1968) that defense is a compromise formation, I would say that it is not so by definition but that it can be. That a symptom can be used for defense, which Brenner states about an ego function which can also have other uses, indicates that in certain instances a defense can itself be a compromise formation. This would be similar in principle to Brenner's (1982a) conception, with which I agree, that the superego is a compromise formation born of conflict which can then function as a major component of subsequent conflicts.

Such a sequence is consonant with the concept of hierarchy I have described and applies at all levels of structures and functions. Defenses are imbued with characteristics of the drives they defend against and are in turn repressed or otherwise defended as derivative drives. This is what Rapaport (1953) meant by a hierarchy of motivational drives and defense, what Fenichel (1941a) described in the process of "taming of affects," and what Jacobson (1953) pointed to in the development of subtle and modulated affects and moods. Organs exist although they interact and combine into larger systems or functions. The ego is composed of substructures and internal functions and

yet can be usefully considered a separate agency distinguishable from other psychic structures.

Advanced systems do not preclude the more simple, but consist of them. And at all levels, in pursuit of psychological functions, processes and the interactions of psychic structures, the path of analysis is from the diffuse toward the elemental. Dreams and symptoms, to be analyzed, are separated into their components. Psychic structures overlap, interact, and combine, but are separated analytically. The metapsychological points of view integrate and enhance each other reciprocally and as explanations, and converge on the phenomena being explored; yet they too are logically and usefully separate.

The same is true of defenses. Defenses are not seen in the pure state, in life or clinic, any more than are instincts, which Freud (1915) pointed out are seen only in their derivatives. While from this view one can never be sure of arriving at original formative elements, the goal is toward as close to the irreducible as one can get. Perhaps it is similar to Winnicott's "good-enough mothering"; a pragmatic approximation to the ideal goal will do. Defenses, to be sure, can be global and generalized and can even merge with what they defend against, but analysis into primary components as much as one can, here as elsewhere, is in the service not only of clarity but mastery.

There are defense mechanisms even though there is defensive activity. Freud's original defensive measures, methods, modes, and techniques can be reduced, with more precise understanding, to specific defense mechanisms, which Freud himself began to use, and which Anna Freud carried to further completeness. The path of analysis from the diffuse to the specific proceeds from defensive behavior to the defense mechanisms underlying it. Anna Freud's own demonstrative clinical examples were of larger defenses, which she analyzed to their more basic discrete elements, the mechanisms of defense which were the center of her (1936) book. The issue is not rendered any clearer, in my opinion, by the suggestion of Wallerstein (1976) who distinguishes between "defense mechanisms as a

construct and defenses as actual phenomena" (p. 220). The defensive aspect cannot be observed any more directly in diffuse behavior than in a discrete and circumscribed mechanism. Both depend equally on theoretical inference. Mechanisms do not mean mechanical—another concern of some analysts who object to metapsychology on similar grounds (Klein, 1973). Mental mechanisms, as psychic structures, are psychological, not somatic. Although they may present a theoretical face toward the natural sciences, they are not of natural science, nor do I see how this could be a valid objection if they were.

The analyst, to analyze, teases apart the mass, destratifies the presenting behavioral picture into its component parts. As the symptom or dream is broken down into its individual streams, perceptions are separated from memories, fantasies from reality, aspects of the self from images of others. In the field of affects, unpleasure is also divided into specific affective experiences, affects are separated from each other, anxiety from depression, shame, guilt, or other affects. A model for such separation of affects was recently provided by Wurmser (1981) for the ubiquitous and etiologically important affect of shame. While describing the relation of shame to anxiety and other affects, Wurmser does not fail to separate it metapsychologically and clinically from all other affective states of unpleasure.

The same is true especially of anxiety. While Brenner (1979) places depressive affect on a par with anxiety, and feels that defense is instituted to avoid unpleasure (1981), I would not minimize the special role of anxiety even in connection with other affects of unpleasure. Anticipation of the future and the expectation of danger bring with them automatically the affect of anxiety. Just as the definitive and microscopic analysis of the defense mechanisms of the ego by Anna Freud still holds and illuminates more diffuse clinical states, the same is true of Freud's (1926) final parsimonious theory of anxiety. I have pointed out (Rangell, 1978) that anxiety continues as a motive for defense behind all other states of unpleasure, and is still,

as Freud stated, "the fundamental phenomenon and problem of neurosis."

The unpleasure defended against and the resistance to approaching it need to include, in the dynamic series of which it is a part, the anxiety it engenders and what this represents. The unconscious anxiety behind increasing unpleasure is of psychic tension mounting and getting out of control. A patient defends against guilt or depression because of the anxiety of its progressing beyond the ability of the ego to master or contain it. The danger of the spiraling unpleasure is that it will get worse or never stop (Rangell, 1955, 1968). The ultimate fear, similar phenomenologically to Freud's original description of the state of unconscious tension, is the traumatic state of psychic helplessness in which the ego will be completely overrun.

Psychoanalysis effects the localization as well as differentiation of affects. A patient did not know whether the affects she was experiencing belonged to her or the person she was speaking to. The same blurring and ambiguity took place in the transference. The concentration of repressed unconscious elements in the transference is a means by which localization and destratification can take place. The analysis of transference, however, is the means to the end, not the end in itself, the road to the infantile neurosis via the intermediate plateaus en route to this goal. On this path defense analysis points the direction and precedes the analysis of the repressed contents being defended. Defense before content, as stated by Freud, Anna Freud (1936) and Fenichel (1941b), still obtains. I do not agree with Gill's (1978, unpublished)[1] suggested change from Fenichel's "defenses first" to "transference first." The transference is a means for the identification of displaced conflict. If defense outside of the transference stands in its way, it comes first. Defense can of course also be related to the transference, in which case this defense, either a defense against the transfer-

[1]"The Transference in Fenichel's *Problems of Psychoanalytic Technique*." Panel on "Psychoanalytic Classics Revisited." American Psychoanalytic Association.

ence or within it against other elements, is the first way-station to be met.

A person's behavior deals with object relations, not only in the psychology which takes that name as its center, but in general psychoanalytic metapsychologic theory. The merging into final psychic products is not only of internal psychic elements, but of images crossing the internal-external border from and to the external world. Psychic elements are expressed, acted as well as acted out, into the "average expectable environment" (Hartmann, 1939). In the center of this expectable environment is the human object. Psychological object relations, however, are not limited to the external world, the visible arena of human action. A person carries his objects with him in the object representations within the ego. And a patient brings his objects, as he does his self, into the analytic situation in the form of his self- and object representations. A patient's objects people his free associations, and constitute a large part of the field upon which internal psychic forces are played out.

Defenses operative toward objects and brought into the treatment for analysis similarly exhibit fusion rather than separation. I have studied these ubiquitous interactional and interpersonal defenses both as they occur in group relations, up to mass behavior, and as they are operative and demonstrable in individual intrapsychic life, where the ego interacts with its object representations (Rangell, 1976, 1980). A typical defensive reaction, which was seen both in the mass and in individuals of whom it was composed, to unacceptable behavior of their elected representatives during the unprecedented crisis of the Nixon administration, was the commonly heard reaction, "Everybody does it," which incidentally did not preclude in the same individuals and mass a simultaneous claim that nobody did anything. The total condensed defensive reaction, in this living group situation, could be seen to consist not of one discrete defensive mechanism, but a fused combination of repression, denial, rationalization, defense by generalization, and other mechanisms which played a part and could be identified

separately. Loeb (1982) has described generalization as a defense from the clinical direction.

The superego, projected from individuals to their leader, or in a more diffuse way to the aggregate of one's peers, can be suspended between the participants in such groups, with an ambiguity as to whom it belongs, and with no one needing to claim it as his own. The task during the opportunity of an individual psychoanalysis, within the group situation that comprises any patient's object relations, is precisely to effect a differentiation of one defense mechanism from another, with the superego, if it has been projected into the social group, having to be drawn back and retained to bring it under the potential mastery of the ego.

The same mechanisms apply to small as to large group processes, to actions of individuals in committees, within scientific societies, including psychoanalytic, in small groups, triadic down to dyadic behavior. Ordinary conversations or actions or other social exchanges can be seen on analysis, where there is such an opportunity, to consist of automatic distortions which are fusions of discrete defense mechanisms instantaneously applied and combined together. Slips of the tongue and "the psychopathology of everyday life" (Freud, 1901), can be due as much to superego lapses or temporary faults in ego judgments as to instinctual breakthroughs, to defenses against the superego as regularly as toward the id. Such slips and errors are almost routinely in the direction of elevation of the "self" and derogation of "the other." Errors in check-writing most often benefit the writer of the check, not the recipient.

Defenses can maintain as unconscious an entire formed psychic product, rather than being limited to the instinctual wish that started the intrapsychic sequence on its way. Such a product, for example, is the unconscious fantasy, comprised of instinctual impulses, superego prohibitions, the feared reactions incorporated from the external world, the array of defenses selected to keep in check the forbidden drives, the dangers fantasied as coming from inside or out, from superego

or reality. A symptom with its similar underlying internal composition is another final product that can be kept entirely unconscious. This can then include not only the original symptom, but its subsequent secondary and "tertiary" (Rangell, 1954, unpublished)[2] gains—the latter resulting from a fusion of the symptom with the self-image or self-representation. All of these come to be protected together by the defensive and now self-preservative interests of the ego.

The mental presentation retained in repression can be a self-representation consisting itself of compromise formations. Grossman (1982) has referred to the self as fantasy. This would be more accurately stated as the self-representation; and the same could be said of the object representation. This points to the distortions of which these can be composed, brought about by defenses against instinctual wishes that bend perceptions of reality, inner and outer, to create images of the self or object composed of the same ingredients as symptoms are made of, except in this case maintained as ego-syntonic and constituting part of the character and its images. Always the memories and images that become the self-representation concern concepts and fantasies of interaction with objects, upon whom libidinal and aggressive drives and ego and superego components are played out.

Defenses *in vivo,* by the time they reach clinical view, exist against the total repressed product, which can be a complex psychic formation even in the unconscious state. Secondary revision, the same organizing process that gives a dream its final look, operates in synthesizing and shaping any other repressed mental presentation, fantasy, symptom, self- or object representation. And the last layer of defense of a sequential series keeps the whole together, whether as a stable or unstable unit. Freud (1937), in describing interminable analysis, notes the same layering of defenses as "resistances against the uncovering of resistances." Within the individual psychic formations there

<hr/>

[2]"Tertiary Gain of Symptoms." Presented to American Psychoanalytic Association.

are hierarchic defenses against all the ingredients of which they are composed, instinctual impulses, derivative affects, the anxiety that presages danger, the dangers foretold by the signal anxiety, the intrapsychic trial experiences of such dangers from the superego or external world, the psychic trauma envisioned if instinctual discharges were to be permitted, and defenses against intermediate levels of symptom formation before a final symptom or resolution or other solution comes about. The chronic frustration and limitations intrinsic to such states are also repressed. Frequently they are substituted by an opposite, even cheerful self-image, although usually at the expense of a dampened and restricted affective register. This is in the same direction as may occur with other distortions of the self-representation. Such chronic, often successful, defensive distortions may or may not be uncovered by analysis.

Psychic traumata, chronic and cumulative as well as acute, fantasied and anticipated as well as actual, and layered defenses which keep them neutralized and repressed, are built into ongoing mental life. In addition to repetition compulsion, there is a strong repression compulsion, which to my mind has not been described or sufficiently emphasized. A person frequently represses and keeps at bay, without being psychotic, a piece of reality and its intrapsychic consequences which play a large part in shaping a character or a life—the existence, for example, sometimes nearby, of an illegitimate child, or an act or decision that had permanent unwelcome and unabsorbable effects. The potentiality of exposure or disruption of such defenses, where the balance is precarious, may be part of a latent paranoia. This may either threaten chronically to emerge or be overt from time to time in small doses. The entire construct is repressed, its origins and its outcome retained in the unconscious as a latent symptom, in the same dynamic state as an unconscious fantasy, or unconscious aggression, or unconscious anxiety before any content is superimposed.

More commonly such a layered defense overlays a phobic structure, with displacement to a phobic object or objects from

the original sources of anxiety. A grown woman whose father had abandoned her in childhood, and who always feared that her mother, although excessively devoted, would similarly abandon her, lives with a barely repressed anxiety of potential trauma against which a significant amount of defensive energy needs to be permanently deployed.

The psychoanalytic process narrows down to the analysis of the intrapsychic process (Rangell, 1969a), the unconscious cognitive-affective sequence from impulse to anxiety to defense to psychic outcome. Two of the key segments in understanding this model intrapsychic sequence come from Freud's (1926) signal theory of anxiety and Anna Freud's (1936) definitive contribution of the role of defense. Resistance and defense comprise one half of the two arms of intrapsychic conflict. The half that remains consists of the contents defended against.

REFERENCES

ABRAHAM, K. (1921). Contributions to the theory of the anal character. In *Selected Papers on Psycho-Analysis*. New York: Basic Books, 1953, pp. 370-392.

ALEXANDER, F., FRENCH, T. M. et al. (1946). *Psychoanalytic Therapy: Principles and Application*. New York: Ronald Press.

ARLOW, J. A. (1969). Unconscious fantasy and disturbances of conscious experience. *Psychoanal. Q.*, 38:1-27.

BLUM, H. P. (1979). The curative and creative aspects of insight. *J. Amer. Psychoanal. Assn.*, 27 (Suppl.): 41-69.

BRENNER, C. (1979). Depressive affect, anxiety, and psychic conflict in the phallic-oedipal phase. *Psychoanal. Q.*, 48:177-197.

——— (1981). Defense and defense mechanisms. *Psychoanal. Q.*, 50:557-569.

——— (1982a). The concept of the superego: a reformulation. *Psychoanal. Q.*, 51:501-525.

——— (1982b). Transference and countertransference. In *The Mind in Conflict*. New York: Int. Univ. Press, pp. 194-212.

BREUER, J. & FREUD, S. (1893-1895). Studies on hysteria. *S. E.*, 2.

ERIKSON, E. H. (1950). *Childhood and Society*. New York: Norton.

——— (1956). The problem of ego identity. *J. Amer. Psychoanal. Assn.*, 4:56-121.

FENICHEL, O. (1941a). The ego and the affects. In *The Collected Papers of Otto Fenichel*, ed. H. Fenichel & D. Rapaport. New York: Norton, 1954, pp. 215-227.

——— (1941b). *Problems of Psychoanalytic Technique*. New York: Psychoanalytic Quarterly.

——— (1945). *The Psychoanalytic Theory of Neurosis.* New York: Norton.

FERENCZI, S. (1914). The ontogenesis of the interest in money. In *Sex in Psychoanalysis.* New York: Brunner, 1950, pp. 319-331.

FREUD, A. (1936). *The Ego and the Mechanisms of Defense. Writings,* 2. New York: Int. Univ. Press, 1966.

FREUD, S. (1894). The neuro-psychoses of defence. *S. E.,* 3.

——— (1895). On the grounds for detaching a particular syndrome from neurasthenia under the description "anxiety neurosis." *S. E.,* 3.

——— (1896). Further remarks on the neuro-psychoses of defence. *S. E.,* 3.

——— (1900). The interpretation of dreams. *S. E.,* 4 & 5.

——— (1901). The psychopathology of everyday life. *S. E.,* 6.

——— (1905). Three essays on the theory of sexuality. *S. E.,* 7.

——— (1908). Character and anal erotism. *S. E.,* 9.

——— (1909a). Analysis of a phobia in a five-year-old boy. *S. E.,* 10.

——— (1909b). Notes upon a case of obsessional neurosis. *S. E.,* 10.

——— (1910). The psychoanalytic view of a psychogenic disturbance of vision. *S. E.,* 11.

——— (1911a). Formulations on the two principles of mental functioning. *S. E.,* 12.

——— (1911b). Psychoanalytic notes on an autobiographical account of a case of paranoia (dementia paranoides). *S. E.,* 12.

——— (1914). On narcissism: an introduction. *S. E.,* 14.

——— (1915). Instincts and their vicissitudes. *S. E.,* 14.

——— (1920). Beyond the pleasure principle. *S. E.,* 18.

——— (1922). Some neurotic mechanisms in jealousy, paranoia and homosexuality. *S. E.,* 18.

——— (1923). The ego and the id. *S. E.,* 19.

——— (1926). Inhibitions, symptoms and anxiety. *S. E.,* 20.

——— (1937). Analysis terminable and interminable. *S. E.,* 23.

GILL, M. M. (1979). The analysis of the transference. *J. Amer. Psychoanal. Assn.,* 27:263-288.

GEDO, J. E. (1979). *Beyond Interpretation: Toward a Revised Theory for Psychoanalysis.* New York: Int. Univ. Press.

GROSSMAN, W. I. (1982). The self as fantasy: fantasy as theory. *J. Amer. Psychoanal. Assn.,* 30:919-937.

HARTMANN, H. (1939). *Ego Psychology and the Problem of Adaptation.* New York: Int. Univ. Press, 1958.

——— (1950). Comments on the psychoanalytic theory of the ego. In *Essays on Ego Psychology: Selected Problems in Psychoanalytic Theory.* New York: Int. Univ. Press, 1964, pp. 113-141.

HEIMANN, P. (1956). Dynamics of transferences. *Int. J. Psychoanal.,* 37:303-310.

HORNEY, K. (1937). *The Neurotic Personality of Our Time.* New York: Norton.

JACOBSON, E. (1953). The affects and their pleasure-unpleasure qualities, in relation to the psychic discharge processes. In *Drives, Affects, Behavior,* ed. R. M. Loewenstein. New York: Int. Univ. Press, pp. 39-66.

JONES, E. (1918). Anal-erotic character traits. In *Papers on Psychoanalysis.* Baltimore: Williams & Wilkins, 1948, pp. 413-437.

KLEIN, G. S. (1973). Two theories or one? *Bull. Menninger Clin.,* 37:102-132.

KOHUT, H. (1971). *The Analysis of the Self.* New York: Int. Univ. Press.
—— (1977). *The Restoration of the Self.* New York: Int. Univ. Press.
KRIS, E. (1955). Neutralization and sublimation: Observations on young children. *Psychoanal. Study Child,* 10:30-46.
LEWIN, B. D. (1946). Sleep, the mouth, and the dream screen. *Psychoanal. Q.,* 15:419-434.
LOEB, F. F. (1982). Generalization as a defense. *Psychoanal. Study Child,* 37:405-419.
NEEDLES, W. (1978). Notes on the differentiating function of the ego. *J. Amer. Psychoanal. Assn.,* 26:49-68.
NUNBERG, H. (1931). The synthetic function of the ego. In *Practice and Theory of Psychoanalysis.* New York: Int. Univ. Press, 1948, pp. 120-136.
RANGELL, L. (1955). On the psychoanalytic theory of anxiety: a statement of unitary theory. *J. Amer. Psychoanal. Assn.,* 3:389-414.
—— (1968). A further attempt to resolve the "problem of anxiety." *J. Amer. Psychoanal. Assn.,* 16:371-404.
—— (1969a). The intrapsychic process and its analysis: a recent line of thought and its current implications. *Int. J. Psychoanal.,* 50:65-77.
—— (1969b). Choice-conflict and the decision-making function of the ego. A psychoanalytic contribution to decision theory. *Int. J. Psychoanal.,* 50:599-602.
—— (1971). The decision-making process. A contribution from psychoanalysis. *Psychoanal. Study Child,* 26:425-452.
—— (1976). Lessons from Watergate: a derivative for psychoanalysis. *Psychoanal. Q.,* 45:37-61.
—— (1978). On understanding and treating anxiety and its derivatives. *Int. J. Psychoanal.,* 59:229-236.
—— (1980). *The Mind of Watergate.* New York: Norton.
—— (1982). Transference to theory: the relationship of psychoanalytic education to the analyst's relationship to psychoanalysis. *Ann. Psychoanal.,* 10:29-56.
RAPAPORT, D. (1951). The autonomy of the ego. *Bull. Menninger Clin.,* 15:113-123.
—— (1953). On the psychoanalytic theory of affects. *Int. J. Psychoanal.,* 34:177-198.
—— (1958). The theory of ego autonomy: a generalization. *Bull. Menninger Clin.,* 22:13-35.
ROGERS, C. R. (1942). *Counseling and Psychotherapy.* Boston: Houghton Mifflin.
SCHAFER, R. (1968). The mechanisms of defence. *Int. J. Psychoanal.,* 49:49-62.
STONE, L. (1973). On resistance to the psychoanalytic process: some thoughts on its nature and motivations. *Psychoanal. Contemp. Sci.,* 2:42-73.
SULLIVAN, H. S. (1953). *The Interpersonal Theory of Psychiatry.* New York: Norton.
WAELDER, R. (1930). The principle of multiple function. In *Psychoanalysis: Observation, Theory, Application,* ed. S. A. Guttman. New York: Int. Univ. Press, 1976, pp. 68-83.
WALLERSTEIN, R. S. (1976). Psychoanalysis as a science: its present status and its future tasks. In *Psychology versus Metapsychology,* ed. M. M. Gill & P. S. Holzman. *Psychol. Issues,* Monogr. 36. New York: Int. Univ. Press, pp. 198-228.

WURMSER, L. (1981). *The Mask of Shame.* Baltimore: Johns Hopkins Univ. Press.

456 North Carmelina Avenue
Los Angeles, California 90049

ON THE CONCEPT
OF PRIMITIVE   Martin S. Willick, m.d.
DEFENSES

IN CURRENT PSYCHOANALYTIC THEORY AND PRACTICE there
seems to be a general acceptance of the idea that there are
certain defense mechanisms employed by the ego very early in
life, and others that do not come into use until later, when a
greater degree of ego organization is present. The former are
frequently referred to as "primitive" defenses and are believed
to operate primarily before the age of two or three. The latter,
often referred to as "higher-level" or "more mature" defenses,
are associated with a later stage of development, after object
constancy has been achieved and the child has reached the
phallic-oedipal phase. This idea is designated as the chronology
of defense mechanisms or the developmental hierarchy of defenses.

The term "primitive" defenses is *also* used to characterize
the defenses used by patients who are considered to be psychotic
or borderline, or patients who are experiencing severe regressive states during the course of treatment. As a corollary to this
view, the terms "higher-level" or "more mature" are used to
describe the defenses used by normal individuals or patients
with neurotic conflicts who are generally considered to be functioning with a greater degree of ego integration and organization.

There is, in addition, a formulation about the development
of psychopathology which links together the two uses of these
terms. This formulation proposes that sicker patients continue

to use the primitive defenses of very early childhood and that the presence of such defenses in an adult is indicative of early pathology and trauma.

I shall examine the concept of primitive defenses, especially as it is currently used in clinical psychoanalytic work. The aims of this paper are: (1) to trace the history of the idea of a developmental hierarchy of defense mechanisms and of the concept of primitive defenses; (2) to clarify the use of the term primitive defenses and to point to some mistaken assumptions when the term is applied to clinical phenomena and theoretical formulations; (3) to utilize clinical examples of projection and denial to illustrate some deficiencies in the concept of primitive defenses; (4) to offer an alternative way of conceptualizing the nature of defensive processes which does not depend on classifying them as more primitive or more mature.

My thesis is that the terms primitive and mature have a place in psychoanalytic theory and observation, providing the assumptions and criteria about their use are sound and are in accord with clinical experience. We speak of primary process to designate an earlier form of thinking and of secondary process to denote a more mature form. We utilize the terms primitive and mature to describe the organization of the ego, the nature of the object relations, and the integrity of ego and superego functioning. However, when applied to defensive processes, the term primitive currently carries with it assumptions that may interfere with our clinical work and theoretical understanding. One assumption is that a so-called primitive defense used by adults is the same as a defense used by a young child. Another is that the use of such primitive defenses means that the patient's pathology can be traced back to an early period of childhood when that defensive operation is presumed to be predominant. A third is that the presence of such a defense is indicative of serious psychopathology.

The alternative view expressed in this paper is that defenses should not be designated as primitive or mature without an evaluation of the total ego organization. What appears to be the

operation of a primitive defense in an adult depends not merely on the type of defense employed, but on the nature of the ego involved. The sicker a patient is, the more we see poor ego integration, poor ego organization, and breakdown of ego functions. The defensive processes called into service in such patients appear primitive primarily because of the low level of ego functioning.

This conceptualization is related to the view suggested by Brenner (1982) who emphasizes that there are no special ego functions used for defense and defense alone. He concludes that the notion of specific "defense mechanisms" is incorrect, despite the fact that it has been generally accepted for many years. He states, "Whatever ensues in mental life which results in a diminution of anxiety or depressive affect—ideally in their disappearance—belongs under the heading of defense. Defenses are not special mechanisms of the ego, as they are customarily considered to be" (p. 1). Brenner is not advocating the view that there are no defensive processes or defensive operations, but that these same processes may also serve to promote the gratification of unconscious wishes.

The point of view expressed in this paper is that defenses are aspects of ego functioning and cannot be described as primitive or mature in and of themselves. It is the integrity of ego functioning that will determine, among other things, the operation of the defensive activities.

Concept of a Hierarchy of Defense Mechanisms: Historical Review

Freud's first comment about the chronological classification of defenses appears in *Instincts and Their Vicissitudes* (1915a). He refers to certain vicissitudes of the instincts, such as turning around against the self and reversal into its opposite, as early modes of defense against the instincts themselves. A few years later, in the Addenda to *Inhibitions, Symptoms and Anxiety* he states, "It may well be that before its sharp cleavage into an ego

and an id, and before the formation of a super-ego, the mental apparatus makes use of different methods of defence from those which it employs after it has reached these stages of organization" (1926, p. 164).

In her classic monograph, *The Ego and the Mechanisms of Defense,* Anna Freud (1936), describes the specific defense mechanisms learned by every student of psychoanalysis. She elaborates upon Freud's idea, and, following a suggestion made by Helene Deutsch, proposes that it might be possible to develop a chronological classification of defense mechanisms. She states, ". . . possibly each defense mechanism is first evolved in order to master some specific instinctual urge and so is associated with a particular phase of infantile development" (p. 51). She goes on to say that repression and sublimation cannot be employed until relatively late in development, while such processes as regression, reversal, or turning around against the self are probably among the earliest defense mechanisms used by the ego. She comments that projection and introjection are, like repression, methods that depend on the differentiation of the ego from the outside world, thus placing these two defenses later in the developmental hierarchy. She also notes that the English school of analysis believes that projection and introjection "are the very processes by which the structure of the ego is developed and but for which differentiation would never have taken place" (pp. 52-53).

Later in her monograph she turns her attention to the defense of warding off of affects. She writes, "This simple defense against primarily painful affects corresponds to the defense against the primarily painful stimuli which impinge upon the ego from the outside world. We shall see later that the methods employed by children in these primitive forms of defense, which are governed simply by the pleasure principle, are themselves more primitive in character" (p. 62). Although she refers to the mechanism of denial as a "primitive" one, the case illustrations appear to be taken from neurotic children using denial during their latency years. Anna Freud did not attribute

this defense to the period of infancy, but she did note: "This mechanism belongs to a normal phase in the development of the infantile ego, but, if it recurs in later life, it indicates an advanced stage of mental disease" (p. 80). She goes on to say that excessive use of such a mechanism is inconsistent with another function of the ego which gradually develops during childhood—namely, reality testing. One can infer that she is pointing to the necessity of evaluating defensive function along with other functions of the ego in order to determine the strength of the total ego organization.

Fenichel, in his encyclopedic text (1945), describes defense mechanisms as successful or unsuccessful, depending on whether they bring about a cessation of that which was warded off. He also classifies them according to whether they are defenses against instincts or against affects. He indicates that denial, projection, and introjection are more primitive defenses, and especially considers projection to be archaic or at least modeled on "that early stage of development of the ego which Freud has called the purified pleasure ego in which everything pleasurable is experienced as belonging to the ego while everything painful is experienced as being non-ego" (p. 146). He also notes that "this primitive mechanism of defense can be used extensively only if the ego's function of reality testing is severely damaged by a narcissistic regression, thus blurring the boundaries between ego and non-ego once more" (p. 147).

In his *Elementary Textbook of Psychoanalysis*, first published in 1955, Brenner describes the mechanisms of defense, but even at that early date emphasizes that the ego "can and does use all of the processes of normal ego formation and ego function for defensive purposes at one time or another" (p. 88). He does, however, say that projection normally plays its greatest role early in life and, like Anna Freud and Fenichel, points to the impairment in reality testing if projection is used to a very great extent in adult life.

The work of Fairbairn (1954) and Klein (1946) brought a new and important emphasis to the concept of primitive de-

fenses. These analysts noted defensive operations in adults from which they reconstructed the presence of early modes of defensive organization in the infant. Klein's analytic work with children and adults led her to describe the defenses of splitting of the object and the impulses, splitting of the ego, idealization, denial of inner and outer reality, stifling of emotions, projection, introjection, omnipotence and projective identification. She believed that these defenses came into operation at the age of three months during the paranoid-schizoid position and specifically stated that failure to overcome their use would not only interfere with the child's reaching the depressive position at six months, but would result in these same defenses being used throughout life.

Many other authors have written in this area. Bak (1954, 1971) considered regression to primary narcissism or dedifferentiation of the ego to be among the most important defenses. This regression would lead to the loss of differentiation between the self- and object representations—a return to the undifferentiated phase of id-ego development. He also mentioned the archaic mechanisms of an introjective-projective nature. He, too, was careful to point out that it was not possible to discuss the defenses used by schizophrenics or patients with perversions without simultaneously discussing the nature of the object relations and the integrity of various ego functions.

Hartmann (1953), when he specifically referred to primitive defenses in schizophrenics, seemed to follow Freud's early ideas. He listed turning against one's person, reversal into the opposite, and projection. He also mentioned detachment of libido, which Freud had described in the Schreber case as the crucial factor in psychosis.

Mahler and her co-workers (1968) are among those analysts who, using direct child observation, have described defenses employed by very young children. They cite denial, splitting, deanimation, and autistic withdrawal. Very early defensive maneuvers are considered to be coping or maintenance mechanisms. Warding off is described as a defense against symbiotic engulfment (1968).

Frosch (1970) differentiates primitive and mature defenses on the basis of the type of danger that calls them into operation. He states that repression, displacement, reaction formation, and conversion are called into operation against the anxieties of separation, castration, and superego punishment. In order to ward off anxieties over what Frosch considers the more profound dangers of preservation and survival of self and object and loss of identity, sicker patients resort to regressive dedifferentiation, introjective-projective techniques, projective identification, fragmentation, splitting, massive denial, and somatization. Thus he puts forward the view that more disturbed patients use more primitive defenses because they are dealing with more primitive dangers—dangers that appear earlier in childhood.

Kernberg (1975, 1976), in his comprehensive account of the symptomatology, ego structure, object-relations, and genetic-dynamic factors in borderline patients, asserts that these patients use specific primitive defenses which distinguish them from neurotic patients who primarily use higher-level defenses. These primitive defenses are splitting, projective identification, primitive idealization, denial, and omnipotence and devaluation.

According to Kernberg, these defenses, when found in adult patients, along with a characteristic type of internalized object relation which follows from their use, are, in fact, pathognomonic for what he identifies as the borderline personality organization. He derives his formulations from observations gathered during the treatment of borderline patients and hypothesized the presence of these defenses early in life. The main process is splitting, which keeps apart the mental representations of the good and bad self and object. Kernberg feels that during the first year of life splitting is due to the incapacity of the child's mind to bring these two images together. During the latter part of the first year and into the second year, splitting functions as a defense to ward off hostility toward the object and to protect the positive introjections and identifications.

Kernberg suggests that in borderline patients these primitive defenses persist because of ego weakness and in turn contribute to further ego weakness. In healthier children, primitive defenses are no longer used; the child instead begins to utilize the higher-level defenses of repression, reaction formation, displacement, and isolation.

It might be useful at this point to summarize the conclusions we can draw from this brief selective review of the history of the concept of primitive defenses. Which defenses are generally considered to be primitive and which are considered to be more mature? Although Hartmann mentions turning around against the self and reversal into its opposite, these defenses mentioned by Freud are not frequently cited today. Turning around against the self is used more often to describe the role of the superego in conflict, while the idea of reversal into its opposite was Freud's attempt to deal with the problem of sadism and masochism before he formulated the dual instinct theory. Occasionally turning around against the self is used to describe the clinical phenomena of self-destructive acts such as self-mutilation, wrist- and arm-cutting, and head-banging. These actions, often seen in very sick patients, are viewed as primitive defenses against aggression directed outward.

In general, the most frequently mentioned primitive defenses are denial and projection. More recently, splitting and projective identification, along with projective introjective techniques, are often included under this heading. Dedifferentiation or fragmentation, which seem to be aspects of ego regression, are also sometimes included. In contrast, repression, displacement, reaction formation, isolation, conversion, and sublimation are thought of as defenses used by neurotic patients, which come into use later in a child's development.

Use of the Term Primitive Defenses

Problem of Reconstruction

I have already mentioned that the term primitive defenses is used to designate both those defensive operations employed by

the child very early in life and those used by psychotic and borderline patients. The reason that it is used in both instances is that regression indicates a return to earlier modes of functioning. Therefore, in general our assumption is that the sicker a patient is, the more likely we are to see regression in ego functioning as well as the eruption of more primitive drive derivatives and a tendency to resort to defenses which were utilized very early in development.

A similar view is that primitive defenses are an integral part of normal early development but are gradually supplanted by more mature defenses. In severely disturbed children, however, these early defenses are retained as a permanent part of the ego's defensive equipment, thereby predisposing them to further difficulties. These defenses have the quality of fixations and continue to operate into adult life, where they are associated with severe ego disturbances.

Defenses such as denial, projection, and splitting were first described by analysts treating severely disturbed adult patients, and were assumed to be the same as or similar to those defenses utilized by the small child. This type of reconstruction, based as it is upon observation of older patients, has been an essential part of the psychoanalytic understanding of psychic development. Freud derived his theories about infantile psychosexual phases from the study of the dreams, fantasies, and symptoms of his adult patients (1905). Later, he used the same approach to hypothesize such early states as autoerotism and narcissism from the clinical manifestations of psychotic patients (1911).

In addition to the use of reconstruction from adult patients, the understanding of the development of defenses in childhood has been derived from child analysis and child observation. Since Anna Freud's pioneering work on defenses, child analysts have continued to describe and assess defenses used in childhood and have attempted to trace their development from childhood into adult life.

In all likelihood, however, defenses used by adult patients, even in a state of severe regression, are not the same as the

ones used by a very young child. Bak (1954) addressed himself
to this problem when he stated: "The methodological pitfalls
of reconstructing biological phases of maturation through ex-
trapolation from adult phenomena into a genetic frame are
well known. It is our basic approach that in pathology we deal
with regressive phenomena, but we should certainly keep in
mind that owing to the complexity of the disease process which
affects the ego and its functions to a varying degree and only
in parts, the genetic aspect can only be observed together with
the alterations of the above-mentioned functions" (p. 129). He
went on to say that the picture seen in an adult undergoing
regression is entirely different from the one we hypothesize in
early infancy.

Because of the maturation and development of the ego
and of psychic structures, the defenses we see in adults are
much more complex and varied than those of the young child.
Defensive processes themselves partake in the general growth
and development of the ego. They do not remain the same;
their form and use most likely change as maturation and development take place. This point is emphasized by Lichtenberg
and Slap (1972) who state, "Our view is that defense mechanisms, like other processes of the cognitive apparatus, are sus-
ceptible to development and refinement" (p. 788).

It is obvious that a one-and-a-half-year-old toddler cannot
have the same defensive capacities available to him as does an
adult. Rationalization and intellectualization, to take some obvious examples, cannot be used very early in life. The child may
use turning away or withdrawal as early defenses, but an adult
who uses such mechanisms is most likely not behaving in the
same way as he did as a small child. The manifestations of such
turning away and withdrawal in an adult will be much more
complicated and include elements of aggressive drive gratification and self-punitive trends.

I am not proposing that we do away with the concept of
a developmental hierarchy of defenses or defense organization
in childhood. A genetic frame of reference must be applied to

defenses as well as psychosexual phases, object relations, and ego maturation. I am, however, warning of the "genetic fallacy" in psychoanalytic theory whereby it is believed that we can easily use reconstructions to derive a correct chronological development of defenses in children. More important, I am arguing against the view that the presence of a particular defense such as projection or denial should lead to the conclusion that the use of these defenses is derived from severe early psychopathology.

The Theory of Countercathexis

Another aspect of the attempted differentiation of primitive and mature defenses is derived from the theory of countercathectic energy. It seems to be generally accepted that repression requires a good deal of countercathexis. Therefore it is assumed that it does not operate successfully until neutralized energy is available to the ego at the time of the resolution of the Oedipus complex, when important identifications take place and the superego is formed. It is argued, in contrast, that the infant or toddler, not having this countercathectic energy at its disposal, cannot use repression and must resort to other defenses—operations such as splitting and early forms of denial and projection.

Along with this assumption about the developmental sequence of the operation of defenses which, like repression, require the ego's countercathectic energy, is the observation that borderline and schizophrenic patients frequently show a breakdown in the capacity to repress. While this is certainly true in acute psychotic states, my own observations based on working over a long period of time with such patients is that, in fact, a great deal of repression *does* occur. Sometimes one sees massive childhood amnesias in very sick patients. One borderline patient had a total amnesia for the ages of nine to eleven, which encompassed her mother's pregnancy and the birth of her sister. The Kris Study Group on Borderline States (Abend et al., in

press) confirmed the observation that repression was indeed an important defensive operation along with many others. In addition, when one sees repeated projection and denial in such patients, one can only be impressed with the fact that the ego is defending itself in a profound way against anxiety and depressive affect. One must assume that these defenses, too, require a great expenditure of the energy of the ego. It seems that the idea that we can differentiate primitive and mature defenses on the basis of the degree of countercathectic energy available is not in accord with clinical experience.

Relation of Primitive and Mature Defenses to Diagnostic Categories

The idea that more mature defenses are not used by psychotic and borderline patients is clearly not correct. Repression, reaction formation, isolation of affect, and displacement are commonly seen in very sick patients. At the same time, denial and projection are used by neurotic patients as well as psychotic ones. What should impress us is not the particular type of defense used, but the maturity of the total ego organization.

This is not to say that there are no distinctions to be made between the defensive operations of psychotic and neurotic patients, but I believe we can achieve greater clarity if we rest these distinctions upon the maturity of the ego organization rather than on specific defense mechanisms. For example, it seems to me that schizophrenic patients use defenses that may accurately be described as reaction formations. We may see the sudden development of asceticism or the gradual appearance of excessive preoccupation with neatness. Often, in an acute state these defenses break down and we see the eruption of the impulses which have been defended against. Although we do not see the same breakdown in a stable obsessional neurotic, it seems that reaction formation is an acceptable term to describe defenses used by both types of patients. What is different is the breakdown of the defense which occurs along with the acute

regression in the sicker patient. With this understanding we can proceed to a detailed examination of the ego functions in both instances rather than qualifying the *type* of reaction formation that is present.

Use of this approach also enables us to avoid such designations as psychotic denial and neurotic denial, which are really attempts to describe the interrelation between the defensive process and the integrity of other ego functions such as reality testing. I am aware that shifting the emphasis from the defense process itself to the nature of the ego organization does not do away with the problems and complexities involved in the assessment of defensive functioning. For one thing, one could ask whether the term primitive can be applied to the nature of the ego organization in a more useful way than when it is applied to defenses themselves. In addition, the same problem involved in reconstructing early defensive operations from adult pathology is present if one tries to understand early ego organization or early object relations on the basis of the regressive phenomena observed in adults. Nevertheless, by eliminating the terms primitive and mature as a designation of defenses, we can focus our attention on a careful assessment of all the ego functions involved in the use of various kinds of defenses as well as on the influence of specific conflicts on the integrity of the ego functions themselves.

The issue of defense and diagnostic categories is taken up by Lichtenberg and Slap (1973) when they discuss splitting of representations which they acknowledge as an early defense. They state, "Conflicts marked by intense ambivalence as well as by the use of splitting as a defense are not, however, confined to any specific diagnostic category or development stage. Splitting of representations, like other defenses of the infantile period, such as introjection, projection and denial, occurs in normal and neurotic persons, as well as in psychotic patients. The specificity of any given diagnostic category depends on the nature and quality of object relationships and of the whole defensive organization, rather than on any specific defense

mechanism" (pp. 781-782). It should be noted, however, that in their writings about defense organizations, these authors adhere to the view that some primitive defense mechanisms retain a primitive form because they are not integrated into the continuous process of cognitive maturation and development.

Clinical Examples of Projection and Denial

Projection

It is not unusual for analysts to think that patients who use projection are more disturbed and to feel that this defense is one of the more primitive ones, although any experienced analyst would acknowledge that projection is a ubiquitous defense, used by normal people, neurotics, and psychotics alike. One need not rely only on Freud's (1922) description of its use, since this observation can be confirmed by any analyst. There is, therefore, some question about asserting that projection is not to be classified with the other higher-level defenses used by neurotics.

There is no adequate way to separate one ego function from another. When we focus our attention on defensive processes, we are looking only at one of the many aspects of ego functioning involved in the person's adaptation to the world. If it appears that projection predominates in sicker patients, we can attribute this to the nature of the ego organization of the person utilizing the defensive process. If there is severe regression in ego functioning or profound disturbance in object relations, projection will appear to be more "primitive" than the same defensive mode used by a healhtier ego.

This view is in contrast with the opinion of those who consider projection to be a more primitive operation mainly because they believe that it is derived from a time of life when there is poor self-object differentiation. If we were to adopt that view—namely, that every projection involves poor self-object differentiation, since a part of the self is attributed to another person or an inanimate object—we would have to

acknowledge that everybody functions this way to a certain extent, and we would surely be diluting the clinical significance of the concept of poor self-object differentiation. There are clearly distinctions to be made between the psychotic patient who believes that people around him are full of hatred and murderous intent and are putting evil thoughts in his mind, and the neurotic patient who feels that a friend's affectionate arm around his shoulder indicates homosexual tendencies. We see all kinds of gradations of projection and its use in all levels of ego functioning. It is therefore not so much the presence or absence of projection, but the degree of ego integrity of those who resort to projection as a defense.

Projection is frequently cited as one of the most common defenses in psychotic states because of its close association with impairments in reality testing. However, we should not make the error of asuming that it is the operation of a "primitive" defense such as projection which *leads* to faulty reality testing. The defense used is only *one* aspect of what is a complicated interaction of drive, defense, ego, and superego functioning and the quality of object relations.

There are other problems involved in such considerations about defenses. For purposes of discussion, we are accustomed to talking about "defense mechanisms," and we attempt to describe them. Actually, when one is listening to clinical data, such as detailed descriptions of analytic sessions, it often is very difficult to say precisely which defense is operating at any given time. In addition, some defensive operations seem simple, or easily described, while others appear to be complex interactions of various defensive processes, ego and superego functions, as well as expressions of id gratifications.

During the discussions of the Kris Study Group on Borderline States (Abend et al., in press) it became clear that we were evaluating much more than the particular defense used by a given patient. We were taking into consideration the pervasiveness of its use, its inflexibility or modifiability, and the degree to which it promoted the ego's capacity both to deal with

anxiety and adapt to the outside world. In evaluating our borderline patients, we noted that some defenses, such as projection, were persistent and resistant to change despite considerable
analytic work. Our examination of the defensive processes necessitated an overall view of the patient's ego organization.

When Anna Freud (1965) once again took up the issue of
the status of the defensive organization, she asked us to consider
whether defense is employed specifically against individual
drives or, more generally, against drive activity and instinctual
pleasure as such; whether defense is balanced, i.e., whether the
ego has at its disposal the use of many of the important mechanisms or is restricted to the excessive use of single ones;
whether defenses are ego-adequate, too primitive, or too precocious; whether defense is effective, especially in its dealing
with anxiety; whether it results in equilibrium or disequilibrium,
lability, mobility, or deadlock within the structure; whether and
to what extent the child's defense against the drive is dependent
on the object world.

A closer examination of projection indicates that what may
also be of great importance is the exact nature of what is projected. We know that many different unconscious thoughts and
feelings can be attributed to others. Aggression, hatred, and
sadistic fantasies seem to be most commonly cited in descriptions of severely disturbed patients. However, we know from
our clinical work that envy, greed, and sexual wishes, as well
as superego attitudes, can be and are often projected. Is it
possible that projection takes on a more pathological form when
it has been used early in childhood to ward off aggression
against the earliest caretaker? It was Melanie Klein's view that
projection was necessary for the infant to protect himself from
the death instinct. Kernberg emphasizes its use in dealing with
aggression which is either constitutionally excessive or an outcome of faulty early mothering. Projection used to ward off
sexual wishes or superego condemnation might appear, then,
to be less pathological. At present, we cannot be certain of such
a distinction. In states of severe regression, projection of su

perego attitudes is quite common, often playing an important role in the content of auditory hallucinations. The idea that certain drive derivatives are coupled early in development with specific defense mechanisms leading to specific drive-defense organizations has been emphasized by Pine (1970) and Lichtenberg and Slap (1970, 1972).

A brief clinical vignette might prove useful to illustrate some of the ideas presented about projection. A young man, considered to be a borderline patient, was in analysis for ten years and achieved a moderately good resolution of his severe characterological problems. Of all the defenses at his disposal, projection was the most prominent. He felt older men would be too competitive with him and that they wanted to humiliate him, but he was completely unaware of his wishes to do the same to them. He was suspicious of his male friends' affectionate embraces and thought that his friends had latent homosexual tendencies, while his own considerable homosexual longings were unacknowledged. His primary fear, however, was that women wished to ensnare or entrap him and restrict his freedom.

He had an obligatory masturbation fantasy wherein he lay passively while a woman played with his genitals and excited him. However, she would not let him have an orgasm unless he turned into a little girl. It was important in the fantasy that this was the woman's wish and not his. He was not aware that he would have female genitals, only that he would be a little girl in a dress. The woman was always an older one.

Analysis revealed that his fantasy, much like the manifest content of a dream, had many latent thoughts and served many purposes. If he were a girl he would not have to fear his father's wrath and be castrated. If he were a girl he could not harm his mother with his phallic weapon, which contained his considerable aggression toward her for preferring his older brother and for disappointing his oedipal and dependency wishes.

But the patient had another compelling reason for projecting onto his mother the wish that he turn into a girl. When

he was four years old, his mother gave birth to a sister who died a few hours after childbirth. A reconstruction was made during analysis that she suffered a significant depression after the loss and had difficulty caring for her son for about six months. This reconstruction was subsequently confirmed by his mother. Thus the patient desperately wanted to be the little girl his mother had lost in order to restore her to him as a nurturing, dependable caretaker.

The patient also had the idea, although it was not a fixed delusion, that his mother actually might want to do something sexual with him. His illness broke out when his parents separated and he was left in his home alone with his mother at age twenty-three. The patient occasionally expressed the fear that if he got too close to a woman, she might suck him up into her as though she were a vacuum cleaner. In addition to expressing his fear of being devoured and his sense of dirtiness, this fear concealed his wish to be inside the mother's body so as never to be separated from her.

When this material was presented to the Kris Study Group on Borderline States (Abend et al., 1983), a number of people pointed to the pervasiveness of the projection and its paranoid quality, forming the conclusion that there was significant impairment in his development and his object relations in the first two years of life. The fact that his father was away in the war for his first three years reinforced their view because they believed that the mother must have been disturbed at that time.

My own feeling was that there was insufficient information to lead to such a conclusion and that it was derived from the idea that if there is a great deal of projection, there must have been early failures in mothering. That is to say, the presence of a "primitive defense" led to the belief that early difficulties in self-object differentiation must have been prominent.

Despite his strong projective defense, the patient maintained, by-and-large, good self-object differentiation in the face of all the distortions caused by his conflicts. During the course of his analysis, significant progress was made. He married, be-

came professionally successful, and with a growing awareness of his wishes and fears there was a considerable diminution in his use of projection. I must acknowledge, however, that I cannot supply an answer to the very important question of why projection was so prominent in this patient. We are faced once again with the usual questions about choice of neurosis, and we remain unable to supply adequate answers. The question is clearly an important one, but I am suggesting a greater degree of caution in reconstructing the presence of severe early difficulties in order to account for the presence of a particular defensive process. It is less helpful to label projection as primitive than to define in detail the operation of all the ego functions, the nature of the object relations, the developmental vicissitudes of the drives in relation to the objects, and the quantitative factors involved in intrapsychic conflict.

Denial

Let us now turn to a closer examination of the use of the term denial. In clinical discussions it comes up most often as an indication of serious pathology and is frequently designated as a "primitive defense." I believe that denial is currently used in so many different ways as to render it almost meaningless in clinical and theoretical discussions. The term is used to refer to a denial of external perception and reality, or to a denial of inner emotions, and to designate any and every attitude or verbal expression of a patient when he says "no" to an analytic interpretation. It also is being used to describe various attempts to ward off painful affects.

Freud's (1894) example of a woman who believed the man who rejected her was there to see her, and his description of a mother carrying a piece of wood in her arms after she lost her child are obvious examples of denial of external reality. Brenner (1982) believes that the greatest clarity is achieved if we use the term in this way. So used, it leads some analysts to assume that it must be associated with a major disruption in

reality testing and therefore can be designated as psychotic. Nevertheless, there are degrees of faulty reality testing, and we must acknowledge gradations or degrees even of denial of external reality.

This leads us to yet another way of thinking about the classification of defenses. Would it be useful to assume gradations of primitivity within each defense mechanism? That is to say, would it be useful to say that some forms of each defense are more mature ones while other forms of the same defense are more primitive? We would then be describing earlier and later forms of projection, denial, and reaction formation, for example. As I have mentioned, Kernberg makes this distinction in calling projective identification an earlier form of projection. He does the same with denial. According to him, the primitive form of denial is "exemplified by 'mutual denial' of two emotionally independent areas of consciousness" (Kernberg, 1975, p. 31). He considers it to be intimately associated with splitting. He states, "Denial, then, is a broad group of defensive operations, and probably related at its higher level to the mechanisms of isolation and other higher level defenses against affects (detachments, denial in fantasy, denial in 'word and act') and at its lower level to splitting" (pp. 32-33). He also includes negation as a higher level of denial.

One can readily see that it is difficult to label different forms of the same defenses as more primitive or more mature without bringing into consideration a number of other aspects of ego functioning. This same issue was taken up by Lichtenberg and Slap (1972) when they asserted the mechanism of denial changes with development. They state: "As each develops, the cognitive structures and the defense mechanisms are integrated into the functioning of the defensive organization. Each defense mechanism undergoes further refinements with further psychic development. In infancy, gross denial of distressing perceptual stimuli is the rule. With development, this becomes progressively refined to more subtle disavowals of the drive derivatives and of the memory links associated with the percept" (p. 785).

Denial presents us with some further difficulties as well. It is commonly used to describe the defense used by people who have real physical illnesses. It ranges from mild forms to gross distortions of reality. I am reminded of a story a colleague told me about visiting his friend, a physician, who was dying of cancer in a hospital. My friend found him sitting in a wheelchair. When asked how he was feeling, he pointed to his swollen edematous legs and said, "I'm getting better—look at my legs. I've begun to put on weight!" We can certainly agree that the defense is denial and that faulty reality testing has occurred. But the patient was not psychotic; furthermore, the denial here served an adaptive function. Is it a primitive defense in the sense that it corresponds to a hypothesis about the purified pleasure ego? Is it really less healthy or more pathological? As a matter of fact, there are some indications that patients with some degree of denial of physical illness do better than those who experience significant depression or anxiety. Should we call this "denial used in the service of the ego"? Clearly, labeling the defensive process without placing its use in a proper perspective is not very useful.

A very intensive, thoughtful, and stimulating discussion of the mechanisms of denial is presented in the Kris Study Group Series (Fine et al., 1969). A brief review is provided of the important contributions of Lewin (1950), and Jacobson (1957). The members of the group believed that denial is one of the more primitive defenses. Lewin felt it operated mainly to ward off painful affects, and traced its origin to the phenomena of sleep and hallucinatory wish fulfillment. Jacobson, acknowledging that denial refers to the turning away from external reality, felt that denial of inner reality could occur if the ego had regressed partially to a "concretistic infantile stage" in which external and internal (self and object) were treated in the same manner. That is to say, because of the regression, introjective and projective mechanisms account for the treatment of unacceptable inner reality as though it were external. Other members of the Kris Study Group on Denial noted its relation

to closing of the eyes in infancy and spitting out bad feelings, such as postulated by Freud in the concept of the purified pleasure ego.

In that discussion, Loewenstein commented that there are normal analogues to every defense mechanism, and Brenner stressed the importance of keeping separate the normal precursors, prototypes, and analogues from the defense mechanisms proper. These points are relevant here because all too often the appearance of the defense of denial in an adult patient is assumed to be derived from very early life experiences. I have seen cases where denial was used extensively, although not in a way to disrupt reality testing severely, by patients who had prolonged life-threatening hospitalizations during latency.

For example, a man came to analysis becase, among other things, he felt as though he were living in a dream. He had been hospitalized for polio for about one year at the age of seven and had a residual, very obvious deformity of one leg. This defect was frequently denied.

During the course of analysis, the patient recovered the memory that throughout his hospitalization he believed the whole experience was "only a dream" and that he would wake up and have no defect whatsoever. This belief was transferred to the analysis, which he believed would cure him. We have no adequate reason to search for the origin of this man's extensive use of denial in some early predisposing trauma. Everything I could learn about him in the course of the analysis led to the conclusion that the crucial determinant in his use of denial was the year-long illness and hospitalization and the physical deformity which remained.

It could be argued that in order for this particular defense to be chosen by this patient he would have had to be predisposed to its use by earlier traumata. Certainly people with similar experiences do not necessarily use denial as a way of warding off painful affects. It is likely that the defense of denial is at everyone's disposal and that certain life-threatening experiences can bring it into use. It also may be said that even this

patient did not use denial in every aspect of his functioning, but only in those areas that touched on his illness and its sequelae. Nevertheless, it is just such considerations as these that warn us to look at the complexities involved rather than labeling a defense primitive and drawing oversimplified conclusions from its use.

Two other brief vignettes might prove useful in this discussion of denial. A forty-nine-year-old woman was hospitalized in a psychotic state two days after her husband died suddenly of a coronary at their twenty-fifth wedding anniversary party. She was extremely agitated, claimed her husband was alive and that we were keeping her from seeing him. She recovered within two weeks and began a more usual mourning process. As far as we could determine, she had been a warm, loving, fairly healthy woman (although she was not studied in enough detail to understand her prepsychotic personality). The psychosis was marked by the prominence of the defense of denial as it applies to the denial of external reality.

Another woman, thirty-five years of age, was hospitalized two days after her three-year-old daughter suddenly died in an accident. This woman had developed a complete retrograde amnesia which lasted for five days, until her family located her. As with the other patient, there was no history of severe mental disturbance. This illness, labeled dissociative reaction, is not considered to be psychotic. It is characterized by massive repression which caused her to lose her awareness of her own identity. We might consider the first patient sicker because of the psychotic state, but I do not believe it is helpful to consider that one patient used the more primitive defense of denial as contrasted with the defense of massive repression. Furthermore, are we prepared to say that the defense of denial used by the woman who lost her husband is derived from an early period of life when the infant turns away from painful external stimuli? All too often this is, in part, what we are implying when we call a defense primitive.

It may very well be that the psychotic patient used milder

forms of denial throughout her life, while the other developed predominantly repressive mechanisms. Although we must try to understand why one defense was used in preference to another, and we must be interested in learning more about the development of defensive processes, we should be cautious about reconstructing their origins. In addition, we might have to distinguish between the transient use of a defense, such as in these examples of denial and repression, and a chronic characterological use of a given defense or set of defenses. It also should be noted that although we use the term denial to describe the defense used by the patient with polio as well as the patient who became psychotic when she lost her husband, we are really describing two different kinds of pathology. Once again, we must be impressed with the fact that only a full consideration of the functioning of the ego will enable us to adequately assess a patient's defensive operations.

Summary

There are difficulties in devising a chronological classification of defenses in the sense of being able, through reconstruction, to determine which defenses are used primarily by the infant and toddler and which are used by the older child. We must be cautious when we claim that these same early, so-called "primitive" defenses are used by psychotics and people with borderline disorders, while the more mature defenses are used by neurotics and normal people. It seems more accurate to acknowledge that all kinds of defensive operations may be used by all kinds of individuals. The idea that there are specific primitive defense mechanisms and specific higher-level defense mechanisms does not seem to be in accord with clinical phenomena. These phenomena are better understood by examining the degree of ego regression, the intactness of ego functions, the quality of object relations, and quantitative factors involved in intrapsychic conflict.

When we examine a patient's defenses we must take into

account whether they are adaptive, or lead to further impairment; whether they are rigid and not modifiable, or flexible and changeable; whether they are pervasive, or can operate in discrete ways; whether they are associated with faulty reality testing and are unstable, or whether they are stable and promote further ego integration. Such examination properly shifts the emphasis from whether a particular defense is primitive or mature to a broader conceptualization about the nature of the patient's ego organization and the intactness of the ego functions.

REFERENCES

ABEND, S. M., PORDER, M. S. & WILLICK, M. S. (1983). *Borderline patients: Psychoanalytic Perspectives.* Kris Study Group, New York Psychoanal. Institute, Monogr. 7. New York: Int. Univ. Press.

BAK, R. (1954). The schizophrenic defense against aggression. *Int. J. Psychoanal.,* 35:129-134.

———— (1971). Object relationships in schizophrenia and perversion. *Int. J. Psychoanal.,* 52:235-242.

BRENNER, C. (1955). *An Elementary Textbook of Psychoanalysis.* New York: Int. Univ. Press.

———— (1982). *The Mind in Conflict.* New York: Int. Univ. Press.

FAIRBAIRN, W. R. D. (1954). *An Object Relations Theory of the Personality.* New York: Basic Books.

FENICHEL, O. (1945). *The Psychoanalytic Theory of Neurosis.* New York: Norton.

FINE, B., JOSEPH, E. & WALDHORN, H., Eds. (1969). *The Mechanism of Denial.* Kris Study Group, New York Psychoanal. Institute, Monogr. 3. New York: Int. Univ. Press.

FREUD, A. (1936). The ego and the mechanisms of defense. *Writings,* 2. New York: Int. Univ. Press, 1966.

———— (1965). Normality and pathology in childhood. *Writings,* 6. New York: Int. Univ. Press.

FREUD, S. (1894). The neuro-psychoses of defense. *S. E.,* 3.

———— (1905). Three essays on the theory of sexuality. *S. E.,* 7.

———— (1911). Psychoanalytic notes upon an autobiographical account of a case of paranoia (Dementia Paranoides). *S. E.,* 12.

———— (1915a). Instincts and their vicissitudes. *S. E.,* 14.

———— (1922). Some neurotic mechanisms in jealousy, paranoia and homosexuality. *S. E.,* 18.

———— (1926). Inhibitions, symptoms and anxiety. *S. E.,* 20.

FROSCH, J. (1970). The psychotic character. *J. Amer. Psychoanal. Assn.,* 18:24-50.

HARTMANN, H. (1953). Contribution to the metapsychology of schizophrenia. *Psychoanal. Study Child,* 8:177-198.

JACOBSON, E. (1957). Denial and repression. *J. Amer. Psychoanal. Assn.*, 5:61-92.

KERNBERG, O. (1975). *Borderline Conditions and Pathological Narcissism.* New York: Aronson.

—— (1976). *Object Relations Theory and Clinical Psychoanalysis.* New York: Aronson.

KLEIN, M. (1946). Some notes on schizoid mechanisms. *Int. J. Psychoanal.*, 27:99-110.

LEWIN, B. D. (1950). *The Psychoanalysis of Elation.* New York: Norton.

LICHTENBERG, J. D. & SLAP, J. W. (1970). On the defensive organization. *Int. J. Psychoanal.*, 52:451-457.

—— —— (1972). On the defense mechanism: a survey and synthesis. *J. Amer. Psychoanal. Assn.*, 20:776–792.

—— —— (1973). Notes on the concept of splitting and the defense mechanism of the splitting of representation. *J. Amer. Psychoanal. Assn.*, 21:772-787.

MAHLER, M. (1968). *On Human Symbiosis and the Vicissitudes of Individuation.* New York: Int. Univ. Press.

—— & MCDEVITT, J. (1968). Adaptation and defense in statu nascendi. *Psychoanal. Q.*, 37:1-21.

PINE, F. (1970). On the structuralization of drive-defense relationships. *Psychoanal. Q.*, 39:17-37.

970 Lincoln Place
Teaneck, New Jersey 07666

DEFENSES, DEFENSE MECHANISMS, AND THE STRUCTURE OF THE MIND

ROBERT S. WALLERSTEIN, M.D.

T HE WORD "DEFENSE" WAS FIRST USED BY FREUD in his (1894) paper, "The Neuro-Psychoses of Defence." There he said, "For reasons which will soon be evident, I shall call this form *defence* hysteria', using the name to distinguish it from *hypnoid* hysteria and *retention* hysteria" (p. 47). The reason for this usage—"soon to be evident"—is elaborated as the designation of the ego's response to "incompatible ideas"; "the patients can recollect as precisely as could be desired their efforts at defence, their intention of 'pushing the thing away', of not thinking of it, of suppressing it" (p. 47). The linked concept "repression" had been introduced a year earlier in the "Preliminary Communication" (Breuer and Freud, 1893), where in talking of the memories of psychic traumata that had not been sufficiently abreacted, among the reasons given is that "it was a question of things which the patient wished to forget, and therefore intentionally repressed from his conscious thought and inhibited and suppressed" (p. 10).

As many authors have pointed out, including Anna Freud (1936), Freud then used "defense" and "repression" interchangeably, and at times, confusingly, until he undertook, in *Inhibitions, Symptoms and Anxiety*, to clearly differentiate them and to establish what has been since then, the accepted usage. Freud (1926) said:

201

In the course of discussing the problem of anxiety I have revived a concept or, to put it more modestly, a term, of which I made exclusive use thirty years ago when I first began to study the subject but which I later abandoned. I refer to the term 'defensive process'. I afterwards replaced it by the word 'repression', but the relation between the two remained uncertain. It will be an undoubted advantage, I think, to revert to the old concept of 'defence', provided we employ it explicitly as a general designation for all the techniques which the ego makes use of in conflicts which may lead to a neurosis, while we retain the word 'repression' for the special method of defence which the line of approach taken by our investigations made us better acquainted with in the first instance.

Even a purely terminological innovation ought to justify its adoption; it ought to reflect some new point of view or some extension of knowledge. The revival of the concept of defence and the restriction of that of repression takes into account a fact which has long since been known but which has received added importance owing to some new discoveries [p. 163].

He went on to describe several other defense mechanisms —isolation, regression, reaction formation, undoing—and then summarized, "These observations provide good enough grounds for re-introducing the old concept of *defence,* which can cover all these processes that have the same purpose—namely, the protection of the ego against instinctual demands—and for subsuming repression under it as a special case" (p. 164). With this statement, Freud definitionally established repression as but one among many mechanisms of defense, but since it is characteristically operative alongside (almost) every other defense mechanism it has also always been considered *primus inter pares*; indeed one can postulate that other defense mechanisms only come into play when repression alone does not suffice. Gill (1963) put this same thought as follows: "Substitute formation can be distinguished from repression only in the instance of

completely successful repression—using the term in its limited present-day connotation of the defense of keeping something out of awareness. All the other defenses show some degree of return of the repressed, and indeed this is the basis of the formulation that the other defenses come into operation only after repression has failed" (p. 103).

It was within this framework that Anna Freud constructed her own landmark contribution in this area, *The Ego and the Mechanisms of Defense* (1936). In her book she reviewed this prior history, citing the 1894 and 1926 contributions of Freud, and then listed the various defense mechanisms previously described in Freud's work, mentioning *Inhibitions, Symptoms and Anxiety* (1926) where Freud described repression (in relation to hysteria), isolation, regression, reactive alteration of the ego (reaction formation) and undoing (all in relation to obsessional neurosis); "Certain Neurotic Mechanisms in Jealousy, Paranoia and Homosexuality" (1922), where he described introjection (or identification) and projection; and finally "Instincts and Their Vicissitudes" (1915), where he described turning against the self and reversal. Anna Freud then stated:

> To these nine methods of defense, which are very familiar in the practice and have been exhaustively described in the theoretical writings of psychoanalysis [the list is then recapitulated], we must add a tenth, which pertains rather to the study of the normal than to that of neurosis: sublimation, or displacement of instinctual aims.
>
> So far as we know at present, the ego has these ten different methods at its disposal in its conflicts with instinctual representatives and affects [p. 44].

She also offered tentative "Suggestions for a Chronological Classification" (p. 50) of defense mechanisms, trying to link their origin and evolution to the successive developmental phases, but after reviewing the various controversies around such efforts came to the pessimistic conclusion that "These differences of opinion [with the Kleinian views on projection and

introjection particularly] bring home to us the fact that the chronology of psychic processes is still one of the most obscure fields of analytical theory. . . . It will probably be best to abandon the attempt so to classify them and, instead, to study in detail the situations which call for the defensive reactions" (p. 53).

It was Valenstein and his co-workers (Bibring et al., 1961) who first sought systematically to expand beyond the ten basic mental mechanisms which according to Anna Freud ("So far as we know at present. . . .") were all that the ego had at its disposal in its conflicts with impulse and affect. In their Glossary of Defenses (pp. 62-71), these authors listed 24 basic or "first-order" *mechanisms,* such as Anna Freud's already familiar repression, projection, etc., as well as additions such as acting out, avoidance, denial, etc.; and 15 more complex or "second-order" *complex behavior patterns,* such as aestheticism, altruistic surrender, clowning, compliance, counterphobia, whistling in the dark, etc. The distinction between these two groups (basic and complex) was stated as follows:

> Defensive activities of the ego include not only specifically describable unconscious mechanisms but also complex unconscious functional responses which are more or less specific and recurrent and yet of a defensive nature. It appears that there is a *continuum* of defensive measures making up the defensive organization of the ego. The extremes can be readily distinguished from each other, but there is an indeterminate middle range which defies exact specification regarding those defensive functions which justify explicit specification as *defense mechanisms,* and those *more complex measures* made up of various combinations and sequence of defense mechanisms and admixtures of other ego functions. However, they are so closely related to those relatively irreducible defense mechanisms as to justify inclusion in a tabulation of defenses [p. 62; italics added].

In making this distinction between basic (first-order) mech-

anisms and complex (second-order) measures Valenstein et al. acknowledged that "a variety of classificatory problems emerged: for example, between basic and complex, pure and composite, including the greater or lesser admixture of instinctual elements, ubiquitous and specifically determined, archaic and mature" (p. 62). But they said of their "tentative" arrangement that it was "not meant to suggest mutual exclusiveness, but only the more or less quality of basic irreducibility, and complex synthesis of various ego-defensive functions" (p. 62). It was this same overall statement and same justifying rationale that Valenstein in effect reiterated in a later contribution (Panel, 1967).

It was at this point that I felt a serious confounding to have arisen between defense *mechanisms* as constructs or conceptual abstractions and defensive *behaviors* as observable phenomena, empirically demonstrable—a conceptual issue I discussed in response:

Wallerstein . . . drew a distinction between *defense mechanisms,* as constructs that denote a way of functioning of the mind, invoked to explain how behaviors, affects, and ideas serve to avert or modulate unwanted impulse discharge, and *defenses* as the actual behaviors, affects, and ideas which serve defensive purposes. For example, an exaggerated sympathy can be a *defense* against an impulse to cruelty. The postulated operative mental *mechanism* by which this is explained is called reaction formation. Defenses can range from discrete attributes or aspects explicable by reference to the simple operation of a single defense mechanism (as in the example just cited) to complex behavioral and characterological constellations that are likewise specific, recurrent, and serve defensive purposes, like clowning, whistling in the dark, sour-grapes attitudes, etc. These more complex configurations are variously called defensive operations, patterns, maneuvers, etc. They are made up of various combinations and sequences of behaviors, affects, and ideas, the operations of which are explicable by reference to a variety of the classically described defense

mechanisms, admixed with other ego activities. The Glossary of Defenses published by Grete Bibring, Valenstein, and their collaborators, from their investigation of the psychological processes in pregnancy, is the most comprehensive classification yet attempted. It encompasses both the most discrete defenses explicable by reference to a single defense mechanism and the more regularly recurring of the more complex defensive patterns; but it does not maintain the sharp conceptual distinction here advanced between defense mechanisms as a construct and defenses as actual phenomena [Panel, 1967, p. 135].

This sharp distinction delineated by me in effect broke up the classificatory continuum of hierarchical complexity posited by Valenstein and his co-workers between first-order, "basic" mechanisms and second-order, "complex" behavior patterns in favor of a separate hierarchic organization of increasing complexity in both realms, the conceptual, and the empirical.

. . . defense *mechanisms* can be of different degrees of hierarchic complexity; and so can defenses as *behaviors*. Repression is conceptually among the simplest of defense mechanisms; the linked behavior is a negative behavior, an absence of something expected. Reaction formation is a more complex defense mechanism; an exaggerated sympathy (as a cover against the underlying impulse to cruelty) would be the defining behavior. Altruistic surrender is a defense mechanism of the highest degree of complexity; the whole character and behavior style of a Cyrano de Bergerac advancing the love claims of his friend Christian comprise the relevant behaviors explained by recourse to this construct. In these senses . . . "whistling in the dark" [is] a complex of defensive behaviors and *not* a mechanism; the main defense mechanism by which this complex could be explained is that of denial . . . it is confusing to combine *both* defense mechanisms (constructs) and defenses (behaviors) in the *same* hierarchy from simple to complex.

Each has its own hierarchy [Wallerstein in Panel, 1967, p. 138].

What follows from this conceptualization is the differing relation to the possibility of *consciousness* or conscious awareness derived from our understanding of the structure of the mind:

> Since defense mechanisms are theoretical abstractions describing a way of working of the mind, they cannot of course be conscious. Freud [1900] made this same point in *The Interpretation of Dreams*, stating that the psychical systems are only assumptions in accord with which the phenomena of the dream may be more meaningfully ordered and understood, "the systems, which are not in any way psychical entities themselves and can never be accessible to our psychical perception" [p. 611]. On the other hand, the contents of the defenses, the simple or complex behaviors, affects, and ideas that serve defensive purposes (explained in terms of the operation of the postulated defense mechanisms) can be either unconscious or conscious . . . in all their combinations, it is these behaviors, affects, and ideas that serve defensive purposes that can be and usually are unconscious in their defensive working and can be rendered conscious by psychoanalytic work [Wallerstein in Panel, 1967, p. 136].

It is just this differing relation to the possibilities of (phenomenal) consciousness that was so fundamental in Gill's formulations. In the introduction to his (1963) monograph, he made this same crucial point:

> It is not easy to define a mental "process"; nor is it entirely justifiable to use it interchangeably with mental "content" in discussions of access to consciousness, since, logically speaking, one can become conscious only of a content which is the *outcome* of the working of the mind, not of the working itself. Although Freud often discusses *mental processes* reaching or not reaching consciousness, I have at-

tempted to describe only mental contents as doing so [p. 2].

Gill also made this point specifically in regard to defense *mechanisms*: "To say that the defense itself is unconscious cannot mean that the defense *mechanism* is unconscious, since a defense mechanism is a theoretical abstraction of a way of working of the mind, which of course cannot become conscious" (p. 96). He returned to this point again, stating: "Both mental mechanisms and structures must, of course, always function with specific content. What comes to consciousness are not mechanisms and structures as such but contents the discharge of whose cathexes is regulated by such mechanisms and structures. A content may or may not have undergone some alteration, depending on whether the mechanism or structure is one which distorts the original content" (pp. 114-15).

This distinction between what Gill calls mental process and content, or between what I call construct and phenomenon, was more elaborately developed in terms of its fuller implications for a model of the mind by Sandler and Joffe (1969), who delineated it as the distinction between the "experiential" and the "non-experiential" realms of the mind:

A great deal of confusion has arisen in psychoanalytic theory because of a failure to take into account a fundamental distinction between two very different areas, and we would propose that a sharp distinction be made between what we would like to call (for want of better terms) the experiential and the non-experiential realms. . . . The realm of subjective experience . . . refers to the experience of the phenomenal content of wishes, impulses, memories, fantasies, sensations, percepts, feelings and the like . . . experiential content of any sort, including feelings, *can be either conscious or unconscious.* . . . In sharp contrast is the *non-experiential realm.* This is the realm of forces and energies, of mechanisms and apparatuses, of organized structures, both biological and psychological, of sense organs and means of

discharge. The non-experiential realm is intrinsically un-knowable, except insofar as it can become known through the creation or occurrence of a phenomenal event in the realm of subjective experience. From this point of view *the whole of the mental apparatus* is in the non-experiential realm, capable of becoming known to us (only to a limited extent) via subjective experiences of one sort or another. . . . The more stable components of the non-experiential realm can be considered to be *structures* . . . organizations which are permanent or have a relatively slow rate of change. . . . There is an intimate relationship between the experiential and the non-experiential realms. . . . Apart from the ma-turational influences, the mental apparatus develops only through conscious or unconscious awareness of changes in experiential content and related attempts to control that content. Thus the elements in the non-experiential realm are employed, mobilized and changed—all outside the realm of experience—although changes in the non-expe-riential realm are mediated by experience and their mod-ification provides, in turn, new experiential data [pp. 81-82].

Here then is a model of the mind which distinguishes (properly) between a realm of both conscious and unconscious experiences, a realm, that is, of subjective or mental *phenomena,* and a realm of explanatory *constructions* that order and establish sequences of regularity and interdependency among those kinds of phenomena. It is such constructions that of course represent the efforts of Freud and the ego psychologists who came after him to develop a comprehensive scientific theory of the mind or, as it is usually called, a structure of the mind, or of the psychic apparatus. As an example of this distinction, and at the same time relatedness between the two realms, Sandler and Joffe considered *fantasying* as an organized way of mental functioning "which falls wholly within the non-experiential realm" (p. 83), and contrasted this with *fantasies,* "The image and feelings which are the products of fantasying [which] fall

within the realm of experience (conscious or unconscious)" (p. 83). And they underscored the conceptual and heuristic confusion that can arise when this distinction is not firmly adhered to, "a study of the concept of fantasy . . . showed that an enormous amount of confusion existed in relation to the use of the term 'unconscious fantasy'. It was necessary to distinguish between the process of *fantasying* and the products of this process. These included conscious fantasies (daydreams), preconscious (but descriptively unconscious) fantasies, and fantasies which had once been wish-fulfillments but which were now repressed or otherwise defended against" (p. 80). This distinction (and relation) between fantasying (in the non-experiential realm) and a fantasy (in the experiential) is incidentally very akin to that made in a very different context by Seymour Kety, the noted biochemical researcher in psychiatry, in his oft-quoted statement that "there can someday be a biochemistry of memory but never of memories."

Clearly, this elaboration of their model of the mind by Sandler and Joffe extends and deepens the conceptual basis for the distinction they make between the *process* of fantasying and fantasies as the *outcome* of that process, between what I have called defense mechanisms as *constructs* and defenses or defensive behaviors as observable and demonstrable phenomenal events, and between what Gill called mental *processes* and mental *contents* as the outcomes of the processes, the workings of the mind. Unfortunately, despite their elaboration and clarification and their valiant effort to counter the conceptual confusions that result from confounding of the experiential and nonexperiential, Sandler and Joffe have inadvertently introduced an arena of potential severe confusions by calling both of them realms, as if they were to be considered fully conceptually coordinate. My own preference, and this was also Gill's, is to maintain a semantically noncoordinate nomenclature, the distinction between a construct (Gill's process) that describes a *way of working* of the mind, which is logically inferred from a (sequence of) behaviors or events, and the behaviors or events

(Gill's contents) themselves. Since the constructs are not entities, they do not constitute a coordinate realm and they have no status as existing consciously or unconsciously; that question is simply irrelevant. On the other hand, the realm of experiences (including, of course, behaviors, affects, ideas, etc.) can be either conscious or unconscious; and it is the established work of psychoanalysis as therapy to bring more fully into the ken of the individual whatever experiences have been, for whatever defensive or adaptive reasons, disavowed.

Both this distinction and the conceptual and definitional confusions around it have both a prior and a subsequent history. Gill in fact drew attention to an earlier statement by S. Sperling (1958): "When affects, percepts, memories, attitudes, or behaviour patterns are designated as *defences,* one may be perplexed as to whether these *phenomena* are considered the *defensive process itself* or an abbreviated symbolic nomenclature for the attendant defence. For instance, abnormal cleanliness, as so frequently designated, is certainly not the *defence mechanism* against impulses towards dirtiness, but the *resultant manifestation* of the operative defence mechanism—reaction formation" (p. 35, italics added). At the same time and despite this distinct conceptual clarity we find the following in the same article and on the very next page:

> The term (A) *defence mechanism* should be limited to those elementary, pathological, counter-cathectic psychodynamisms by which the unconscious ego, in trying to subserve the ego's synthetic function, primarily prevents the direct cathectic psychic representation of instinctual strivings or superego demands from gaining access to consciousness and discharge. The term (B) *defence* should be confined to not too complex, pathological, counter-cathectic dynamisms previously utilized by the unconscious ego to inhibit perceptual stimuli, instinctual impulses, or superego demands from gaining direct access to consciousness and discharge, in which the defensive expression *per se* simultaneously affords some, but not very much, direct cathectic outlet [p. 36].

This second statement is very akin to Valenstein and his co-workers (Bibring et al., 1961) making one continuum of hierarchically increasing complexity out of basic (first-order) defense mechanisms and complex (second-order) defensive behavior patterns.

And looking forward to the very contemporary literature, Brenner (1981), in a current effort at expansion (or conceptual alteration) of the term defense mechanism, nonetheless repeated this same conceptual confounding between construct and phenomenon (e.g., p. 565). But before turning to Brenner's contribution, I want to describe two prior efforts, those of Gill (1963) and of Schafer (1968), at the significant broadening of, and the adding of multidimensional complexity to, the concept of defense mechanisms and their central role in the array of explanatory constructs describing mental processes, and thereby configuring what we call the structure of the mind or of the psychic apparatus. Both Gill and Schafer spoke to the same two issues, defenses and defense mechanisms as layerings and also as compromise formations, though with significantly different thrusts. Gill's main emphasis was on the "hierarchical *layering*" of the defensive apparatus as part of his overall perspective on the organization of the total psychic apparatus. In short:

> Any behavior simultaneously has impulse and defense aspects. . . . It is well understood that defensive behavior will provide some discharge of what is being defended against: the sadism of reaction formation against sadism is a classic example [pp. 120-121]. . . . What is defense in one layer is impulse in relation to another layer. . . . In general, a behavior is a defense in relation to a drive more primitive than itself, and a drive in relation to a defense more advanced than itself. . . . It becomes clear that there is a hierarchical layering of both impulse and defense. . . . If the defenses exist in a hierarchy, the lower levels must be unconscious and automatic, and may be pathogenic. The defenses high in the hierarchy must be conscious and voluntary and may be adaptive (p. 123).

In all of this Gill was clearly talking of the hierarchical layering of *defenses* as behaviors, affects, and ideas that can be either conscious or unconscious, that can serve defensively against "impulses" or "drives" which are merely (in that context) more "primitive" behaviors, affects, and ideas, and can *at the same time* serve as "impulses" or "drives" in relation to a more ego- or socially syntonic (Gill says "advanced") behavior, affect, or idea which serves defensively against *it*. It is not the defense mechanism that is here considered to be constructed hierarchically. By contrast, Gill's other, less emphasized formulation is that of defense and defense mechanism considered as a compromise formation:

> What in fact does it mean, to say that substitute formation is at the same time an anticathexis? That the return of the repressed in distorted form prevents any more direct expression of the repressed, which after all amounts to saying that a compromise is both a partial victory and a partial defeat. We may safely conclude, then, that, except in the instance of completely successful repression, anticathexis and substitute formation in the "Papers on Metapsychology" are compromise formations and therefore equivalent to what we described as dream work, censorship, and distortion in our discussion of dreams, even though at first consideration anticathexis seems to refer to the second party to the conflict alone [p. 104].

Here, in contrast with the discussion on hierarchical layering, it is not the defensive behaviors but the defense mechanisms that are the subject of discussion as compromises or compromise formations. What links the two perspectives, that of hierarchical layering (of defensive behaviors), and of compromise formations (defense mechanisms), is that both encompass (though differently) the conjunction of defense and impulse. The concept of hierarchical layering permits us to view the same *behavior* as both defensive and impulsive simultaneously, defensive in relation to a "lower," and impulsive in re-

lation to a "higher," stratum. The concept of compromise formation permits us to view the same *mechanism* as serving both defensive and impulsive purposes, again simultaneously, and in compromise of varyingly counterposed inner urges.

Schafer (1968) also dealt with these same issues of layering and compromise, but with a sharply reversed emphasis. Schafer focused on the elaboration of defense mechanisms as constructs that embody concepts not just of defense, but also of dynamic instinctual urge and drive, and as therefore in their very nature, *compromise formations.* He made but one specific reference to the idea of the hierarchical *layering* of defenses:

> to be aware—in the psychoanalytic sense of to have insight—of a mechanism of defense is to be aware of certain threatening tendencies, assertions, and gratifications that have been set in opposition to other, even more threatening tendencies, assertions, and gratifications. The hierarchic concept of defences as being layered, of a series of defences from the most archaic ones to the easily accessible preconscious ones, refers to *a continuum of conflicted positions.* . . . As Rapaport (1951) and Gill (1963) have already proposed, Freud's formulation implies a series of hierarchically ordered id-ego positions, each of which acts as a defence against the position below it in the hierarchy, in which view the line between id and ego becomes a fluid and relative matter . . . [p. 60].

Mostly Schafer dealt with the spelling out of the conception of the defense mechanisms as inherently the compromise resultant of dynamically conflicting forces, as "double agents" (p. 55) so to speak, rather than as just static barriers against unwanted and warded-off drive discharge. He set his thesis as "a special instance of a general problem in psychoanalytic ego psychology. Briefly, this general problem has to do with a lag in the explicit and systematic development of *dynamic* propositions concerning the ego system" (p. 49, italics added). Schafer talked here, within the context of the prevailing ego psychology

and Hartmann's centrally biological-adaptive theorizing, of the concomitant "*relative* neglect of dynamic propositions concerning the ego" (p. 50). He emphasized the word relative in view of the place, within the overall edifice of ego psychology, of ego motives, interests, values, ideals, and moral codes—of an ego that sets aims and goals.

Nonetheless, Schafer did aver that ordinarily we do speak of id wishes and ego *defensive functions*. "Briefly, it is the wish pitted against the function" (p. 50), and "What we miss is an internally consistent dynamic formulation. This formulation would speak in terms of ego wishes pitted against id wishes" (p. 51). From this it follows that, "this entire development left Freud with an unsolved theoretical problem, namely, how to account for the dynamically unconscious status of defences themselves" (p. 51). What Schafer then developed *is* a *dynamic* conceptualization of the functional defense mechanisms, the reading of motives or wishes into the very operation of the specific form of defensive activity, as it were. He initiated it thus:

This introductory survey has been meant to set the scene for conceptualizing the mechanisms of defence as motives or wishes, that is, as dynamic tendencies having mental content. The gap in theory I referred to in my opening statements is the absence of a dynamic view of the defence mechanisms themselves. To fill this gap it is necessary to rediscover the dynamic, meaningful content that is the referent of the abstraction *mechanism*. This content includes wishes, fantasies, alterations of representations and shifts of emphasis. One might call my objective a dynamic microanalysis of defence mechanisms [p. 51].

From this point Schafer essayed this "microanalysis" in some detail, in a point-by-point elaboration of the specific kind of dynamic intent that can be read into the operation or the invocation of each of the classical defense mechanisms in turn. For example, regarding isolation, after quoting Freud's (1926)

definition, Schafer stated, "what, on a taxonomic level, we call obsessional isolation is, in dynamic terms, an intrapsychic enactment of not touching, hence not engaging in the anal-sadistic acts of masturbating, soiling, killing, playing, observing the primal scene, making babies, and so forth. This enactment is disguised. . . . Touching and not touching, or engaging and not engaging in certain activities: this way of putting it implies that the 'mechanism' is simultaneously the instinctual act and the defence against it. The implication is intentional" (p. 54). Similarly, he described undoing in relation to fantasies about "blowing away" (p. 54); defensive altruism with its "reliefs of tension that come pretty close in certain respects to direct instinctual expression" (p. 54); projection with its "wishful disguised fantasy of being penetrated homosexually" (p. 55); and an array of others (introjection, reaction formation, regression, and displacement) ending with repression and the statement that "as Freud noted more than once, to repress the name or memory of a person may express the wish that the person die or the wishful fantasy that he has died" (p. 58). Schafer said in summary of all this: "I submit that the study of defence mechanisms will remain incomplete so long as they are regarded chiefly as wardings off, renunciations and negative assertions; their study will have to be rounded out with an account of defences as implementations, gratifications, and positive assertions. In other words, they must be viewed as expressing the unity of the ego and id and not just the division and enmity of the two" (p. 58).

Schafer has by this point persuasively made out his case. Just as Gill has emphasized the concept of the hierarchical layering of behaviors (including affects, ideas, etc.) that can (should) be viewed as defensive and impulsive simultaneously (in relation to "lower" and more archaic versus "higher" and more syntonic, respectively), so Schafer has emphasized the concept of dynamic compromise, of the same *mechanism* serving defensive and impulsive purposes simultaneously. In both instances there has been an appropriate (in the sense of theoret-

ically and clinically useful) broadening of the conceptions of both defensive behaviors and defense mechanisms, each in their dynamic two-sidedness, a conceptual breaking out finally from the originally simpler and more static mold in which they had been cast. None of this implies any alteration in the distinction I have tried to draw so sharply between defensive behaviors as observable phenomenal events that can be conscious or unconscious, and defense mechanisms as theoretical constructs that denote a way of functioning of the mind invoked to explain *how* those defensive behaviors serve to fulfill their defensive purpose—and which, being abstractions and not entities, do not "exist" either consciously or unconsciously.

This overall theoretical thrust in the direction of conceptual broadening, all of it very much in the spirit of Waelder's (1930) quintessentially psychoanalytic conceptions of multiple function and overdetermination, has been further extended in a current very substantial and, from the definitional standpoint, quite radical, reconceptualization of the nature of defense and defense mechanisms by Brenner (1981). Before developing Brenner's further enlarged perspective, I want to turn to Sandler's (1974) comparable endeavors in reconceptualization in the related area of psychological conflict. Like defense, the concept of conflict is one that has been central to theory and technique from the beginning of psychoanalysis; indeed the two concepts are indissolubly interlinked. An essential element in the concept of intrapsychic conflict has been what Sandler called "the *unconscious peremptory urge*" (p. 53), usually associated with instinctual wishes or their direct derivatives.

Sandler's own (broadening) point in this connection was that "this so-called peremptory tendency is not confined to the id, but may be regarded as a function of various aspects of the apparatus. The concept embraces derivatives of instinctual impulses, but includes as well compelling urges of a different, noninstinctual character, as for example the automatic and impelling unconscious tendency for an adult to use a childhood defensive manoeuvre in particular circumstances, or the au-

tomatic and imperative ego response of anger and rage in circumstances of externally aroused frustration" (p. 53). That is,
there is "a whole *class* of peremptory urges *where we may have
previously considered unconscious instinctual impulses alone*" (p. 53)
and it follows that conflict can therefore arise "between different functioning aspects of the total mental apparatus. The unconscious peremptory urge can involve any aspect of this
apparatus" (p. 58). From this, "it is evident that a large number
of 'peremptory', 'automatic', 'urgent', and 'compelling' tendencies arise within the apparatus *which are not drive-motivated
at the time*" (p. 58). It is in this context that we speak so familiarly
of "interpretation of 'defences against defences' " (p. 60) and
"conflict over the previous solutions to conflict" (p. 57). In summary, "any unconscious impulse ('unconscious' is used here in
a purely descriptive sense) occurring within the apparatus,
whether it be instinctual or non-instinctual in its immediate
origin (for example, the automatic use of a particular defence
mechanism or adaptive manoeuvre) may arouse conflict" (p.
59). This was capped much more tersely in a subsequent paper
where Sandler (1976) made the generalization that "we can in
a sense regard all conflict as being a conflict of wishes of one
sort or another" (p. 61)—a seeming far cry from the tight specificity of the original concept of intrapsychic conflict being (just)
between id impulse and ego defense. This is all in full keeping
with the developmental perspective on the human life span and
its progressive unfolding. "The development of new adaptive
structured solutions during the course of development implies
the continual creation of new wishes for which new solutions
are found" (Sandler, 1976, p. 61)—"new solutions" that are new
compromises of inevitably conflicting tendencies.

It is in this same broadened sense of *conflict* being between
"wishes of one sort or another" that Brenner's current effort
at revision and expansion beyond the narrower traditional conceptualization of *defense* mechanisms should be placed. It is not
that this is entirely new with Brenner. Two decades earlier
Valenstein, in the textual elaboration of his Glossary of Defenses

(Bibring et al., 1961) stated what was already an established truism, the "considerations concerning the *dual* aspect of defenses, namely, the warding off of anxieties in relation to unconscious conflict; and second, the actively autonomous, adaptive function in the service of constructive, maturational, progressive growth and mastery of the drives" (p. 63, italics added). It is this conception of the same mechanisms serving both defensive and adaptive purposes, either singly or together, sequentially or simultaneously, that has long found its way into the entire so-called "coping" literature in both psychoanalytic and nonpsychoanalytic contexts. A well-known psychoanalytically based example is Vaillant's (1977) book *Adaptation to Life,* in which he discusses, "what is the difference between pathological defense mechanisms and adaptive coping mechanisms?" (p. 76) or, "When is a given adaptive mechanism coping and when is it pathological?" (p. 85). And Vaillant has a whole chapter entitled, "*Adaptive* Ego Mechanisms—a Hierarchy" (italics added).

It is within this already established and overall familiar context that Brenner placed his self-styled "radical revision." He proposed his thesis thus:

> Despite their familiarity and wide acceptance, the time has come for a major, even a radical revision of this part of conflict theory [having to do with the customary psychoanalytic formulation of the relations between intrapsychic conflict, unpleasurable affect, and the "classical" defense mechanisms], an alteration which is based on a reappraisal of the psychoanalytic data having to do with psychic conflict. As I shall show, those data substantiate the conclusion that there are no special mechanisms of defense. Whatever ensues in mental life that results in a diminution of unpleasurable affects—ideally in their disappearance—belongs under the heading of defense. . . . Defenses are not special mechanisms of the ego, as they are customarily considered to be [p. 558].

What then are defenses? Brenner's answer was that "De-

fense[1] is an aspect of mental functioning that is definable only in terms of its consequence: the reduction of unpleasure associated with a drive derivative, i.e., with an instinctual wish, or with superego functioning" (p. 559). Brenner expanded this central point as follows:

> The ego does not develop in isolation from the drives or in opposition to them. . . . It develops as part of the means of drive satisfaction. The same aspects of mental functioning which we observe clinically in the psychoanalytic situation as defenses against drive derivatives are those which further the gratification of other derivatives at other times. There are no special ego functions used for defense and for defense alone. Thus to discuss defense in terms of defense *mechanisms,* as Freud and every analyst since has done, myself included, is wrong. To do so implies that there are special ego mechanisms of defense, used for defense and nothing else. This is not the case. To do so also implies that only some ego functions—the defense mechanisms—are used for defense, while the rest of the range of ego functioning is not. This is also incorrect . . . the ego can use defensively whatever lies at hand that is useful for the purpose. It can use any ego attitude, any perception, or any alteration of attention or awareness . . . the ego can use for defense anything that comes under the heading of normal ego functioning or development. Modes of defense are as diverse as psychic life itself. [For example:] It can use the promotion of another drive derivative which arouses less unpleasure than the derivative to be defended against, in which case the one drive derivative masks and supplants the other [p. 561].[2] To repeat . . . no aspect of ego functioning—no ego function—is "a defense mecha-

---

[1] For the most part, where Brenner used the word "defense," I would use "defense mechanism," in the interest of conceptual clarity.

[2] Here of course it will be clear that, in terms of my preferred lexicon, Brenner is talking of (defensive) behaviors, one behavior (or affect or idea) masking another, rather than defense mechanisms so doing.

nism." All aspects of ego functioning are all-purpose. They can as well be used to further the gratification of a drive derivative or to enforce an aspect of superego functioning as to prevent or minimize the unpleasure associated with either. Anything that comes under the heading of ego functions can be used either way [pp. 566-567].

Brought to this point, Brenner has indeed provided a significant broadening of our customary conception of defense mechanisms as specially segregated mechanisms of the mind, specifically and almost exclusively (aside from their uses in the service of adaptation of which we have been aware) devoted to purposes of defense. He states this in an unnecessarily provocative language that can inadvertently imply that the *conception of the defensive activity* itself is being undermined, and even that Anna Freud's fundamental contribution to this area is being called into question. My own reading of its intent and value however is in just the same developmental broadening and conceptual breaking out of a simpler and more static frame that I have already marked in Gill (the same *behaviors* as both defensive and impulsive simultaneously, defensive in relation to "lower" mental strata, impulsive in relation to "higher"), in Schafer (the same "mechanisms" as reflecting compromises of defensive wishes or needs and impulsive wishes or needs), and Sandler (the clash of "peremptory urges" from whatever psychic sources delineating conflict, and the assignation then of the terms impulse and defense to the arms of that conflict). In this same contextual frame, Brenner advocates viewing any mental function or capacity (mechanism) as potentially in the service of defense as well as other ego needs. When defensive uses and needs are being scrutinized, the selfsame defensive mechanisms can be invoked for heuristic and explanatory purposes as when they were originally described by Anna Freud. In this sense I feel the historical developmental line to be straightforward but also incremental.

Where then does all this bring us in this review of the current conceptual status of defenses and defense mechanisms

in relation to our understanding of the structure of the mind now, nearly a half-century after the publication of Anna Freud's (1936) seminal book? At the time, that book was widely acclaimed as the definitive, almost last, word on the nature (or structure) of defense mechanisms. Today we see it as but the influential inauguration of this major chapter in our (meta)psychology. I shall recapitulate the major steps of development in our theoretical understanding of the concepts of defense and defense mechanisms in a series of statements that will successively amplify and at the same time modify the prior statements.

1. Defense mechanisms are constructs that denote a way of functioning of the mind. They are invoked to explain how behaviors, affects, or ideas ward off or otherwise modulate unwanted (impulse) discharge. Since they are theoretical abstractions, not entities, they are neither conscious nor unconscious; the question is not relevent.

2. Defenses (or defensive behaviors, patterns, constellations, etc.) are the specific behaviors, affects, or ideas, that serve defensive purposes; their defensive functioning is explained by recourse to the array of mental *mechanisms* designated defense mechanisms. Since defenses or defensive behaviors are *behaviors* (within a broad psychoanalytic mentalistic definition of behaviors) they are observable or inferable phenomenal experiences that can be conscious or unconscious. In theory they can all be brought into consciousness, and it is a large part of the work of psychoanalytic therapy to do this.

3. Both defense mechanisms and defenses (or defensive configurations) can be conceived within hierarchic organizations of increasing complexity (for defense mechanisms ranging from simple repression to such complicated structures as reaction formation, projection [see Waelder, 1951] and altruistic surrender; for defenses ranging from simple forgetting to such complex behavioral constructs as counterphobic behavior, clowning, whistling in the dark. The two hierarchies are separate but roughly parallel: e.g., a simpler defensive act, simple

forgetting, is matched by a simpler explanatory defense mechanism, repression. Implicit in all the above is the potential for inadvertent confounding between mental mechanisms (theoretical constructs) and behavioral events (observable phenomena).

4. Defenses or defensive behaviors can be viewed as complexly *layered* and, depending on whether the perspective is "upward" toward the more syntonic and conscious or "downward" toward the more archaic (infantile) and unconscious, can be seen to serve impulsive discharge pressures in relation to the higher psychic layerings or defensive avoidant needs in relation to the lower psychic layerings. Defenses are therefore not simply defenses, but depending on one's view, are both defensive and impulsive (behaviors), simultaneously and/or sequentially.

5. The counterpart defense mechanisms can be comparably viewed as complex *compromise formations* embodying both a way of defending against unwanted impulse discharge while at the same time offering a disguised pathway for expressing that very same unwanted impulse pressure. Defense mechanisms are therefore both defensive and impulsive, simultaneously and/or sequentially, depending on how one view them.

6. Just as the concept of psychic conflict can be usefully broadened (in terms of both theoretical and clinical considerations) from the narrowest construction of simply ego versus id to the far more encompassing, between wishes ("unconscious peremptory urges") of "one sort or another," and just as the concept of defensive functioning has through usage already come to encompass the adaptive capacity as well, depending on whether one is looking "inward" or "outward," so the concept of defense mechanism or defensive purpose can be usefully broadened from the narrowest construct of simple ego defense against id impulse to the broadest conceptualization of "ego mechanisms" available simultaneously and/or sequentially for whatever organismic need or pressure—defensive, adaptive, impulsive, etc.—is perceived (at some level) as most salient at any given moment and in whatever complexly configured

expression. In this sense, it is true that there are no special defense mechanisms, just ego mechanisms, or better, ways of functioning of the mind designed to give the most effective compromise expression to the varying external and internal, past and present, needs and pressures being experienced by the individual at each successive moment in time. Similarly, there would be no special defenses or defensive behaviors, since any behavioral expression (conscious and observable or unconscious and inferable) can in exact counterpart serve defensive, adaptive, impulsive, or whatever other purposes, again simultaneously and/or sequentially. This brings us then to a model of the mind today considerably less "specific," hence far less prone to reification, than that given expression in Anna Freud's (1936) milestone contribution, yet traceable in a reasonably direct developmental line to her work upon which each subsequent step has been successively built.

REFERENCES

BIBRING, G. L., DWYER, T. F., HUNTINGTON, D. S. & VALENSTEIN, A. F. (1961). A study of the psychological processes in pregnancy and of the earliest mother-child relationship. *Psychoanal. Study Child*, 16:9-72.

BRENNER, C. (1981). Defense and defense mechanisms. *Psychoanal. Q.*, 50:557-569.

BREUER, J. & FREUD, S. (1893). On the psychical mechanism of hysterical phenomena: preliminary communication. *S. E.*, 2.

FREUD, A. (1936). The ego and the mechanisms of defense. *Writings*, 2. New York: Int. Univ. Press, 1966.

FREUD, S. (1894). The neuro-psychoses of defence. *S. E.*, 3.

———— (1900). The interpretation of dreams. *S. E.*, 4 & 5.

———— (1915). Instincts and their vicissitudes. *S. E.*, 14.

———— (1922). Certain neurotic mechanisms in jealousy, paranoia, and homosexuality. *S. E.*, 18.

———— (1926). Inhibitions, symptoms and anxiety. *S. E.*, 20.

GILL, M. M. (1963). *Topography and Systems in Psychoanalytic Theory. Psychol. Issues*, Monogr. 10. New York: Int. Univ. Press.

PANEL (1967). Development and metapsychology of the defense organization of the ego. R. S. Wallerstein, reporter. *J. Amer. Psychoanal. Assn.*, 15:130-149.

RAPAPORT, D. (1951). *Organization and Pathology of Thought: Selected Sources*. New York: Columbia Univ. Press.

SANDLER, J. (1974). Psychological conflict and the structural model: some clinical and theoretical implications. *Int. J. Psychoanal.*, 55:53-62.

——— (1976). Actualization and object relationships. *J. Phila. Assn. Psychoanal.*, 3:59-70.

——— & JOFFE, W. G. (1969). Towards a basic psychoanalytic model. *Int. J. Psychoanal.*, 50:79-90.

SCHAFER, R. (1968). The mechanisms of defense. *Int. J. Psychoanal.*, 49:49-62.

SPERLING, S. J. (1958). On denial and the essential nature of defence. *Int. J. Psychoanal.*, 39:25-38.

VAILLANT, G. E. (1977). *Adaptation to Life.* Boston: Little, Brown.

WAELDER, R. (1930). The principle of multiple function: observations on overdetermination. In *Psychoanalysis: Observation, Theory, Application,* ed. S. A. Guttman. New York: Int. Univ. Press, 1976, pp. 68-83.

——— (1951). The structure of paranoid ideas: critical survey of various theories. In *Psychoanalysis: Observation, Theory, Application,* ed. S. A. Guttman. New York: Int. Univ. Press, 1976, pp. 207-228.

Langley Porter Psychiatric Institute
401 Parnassus Avenue
San Francisco, California 94143

RESISTANCE AND CHARACTER THEORY: A RECONSIDERATION OF THE CONCEPT OF CHARACTER RESISTANCE

DALE BOESKY, M.D.

THE CONCEPT OF CHARACTER RESISTANCE suffers from ambiguities in character theory. I shall argue that the term "character resistance" is a theoretical anachronism reflecting the fact that the concept of character as prevalently applied in psychoanalytic theory is nonphenomenal in connotation. I shall illustrate that the clinical phenomena designated by this term are better understood by utilizing the concepts of multiple function and compromise formation in the context of the tripartite structural model to identify and detail phenomena better categorized as character *traits*. I shall argue for the advantage of preserving the concept of discrete, descriptively concrete character traits. Failure to recognize the conceptual incompatibility of character as a supraordinate concept of the mind with modern structural concepts has important consequences for psychoanalytic technique and for our understanding of resistance. Such failure leads to incorrect descriptions of how the modern psychoanalyst usually deals with resistance, and it has important implications for psychoanalytic nosology.

Psychoanalytic theories about character have played a de-

cisive, evolving role in the history of our science. Freud's (1908) revolutionary paper, "Character and Anal Erotism," had a bombshell impact on nonpsychoanalytic theories of personality development. Almost from the beginning, the developmental point of view informed the psychoanalytic theory of character and quickly became imbricated in various nosologic typologies, originally oriented to infantile drives. As psychoanalytic theory continued to evolve, most authors gradually designated character as the seat of ego-syntonic resistance (Lazar, in Panel, 1980); character structure became the crucial area for technical interventions with patients.

It was, of course, Wilhelm Reich (1933) who epitomized this view which survives to the present day. When I speak of character as *structure,* I am referring to *conceptual explanations* of the continuity, stability, and predictability of "characteristic" behavior patterns. Throughout this paper, I shall distinguish between character as a disguised and unarticulated model of the mind, i.e., character as a supraordinate, nonphenomenal, global concept, and character *traits.* Except where individual character traits are specifically designated, I shall be referring to character in the supraordinate sense.

I shall deal only with the narrow aspect of character resistance and shall give no consideration to the vast literature devoted to resistance, and only very selective attention to the literature on character. In order to develop my assertions about the theory of character resistance as a compromise formation, I shall first have to discuss issues that relate to the evolution of character concepts in psychoanalytic theory.

Character as a term is in one respect exactly opposite to transference in its position between psychoanalytic theory and all other descriptions of human behavior. Whereas transference was a term that originated in psychoanalysis and was discovered to have profound relevance for all mankind outside of analysis, character was a term borrowed from the nonscientific sphere and applied as an improvised conceptual tool within psycho-analysis as a then-necessary conceptual plank in Freud's theo-

retical scaffolding. It is also useful to recognize that, in addition to some two dozen dictionary definitions for character as a noun, there is an uncommon usage of character as a transitive verb in the sense of engraving something in order to distinguish it, or to imprint something distinctive.[1]

Whenever we describe a character trait, we are arresting and arbitrarily isolating one part of an enormously complex behavioral ensemble. We are reifying a process. Freud was obviously thoroughly aware of this, but when he introduced (1908) his revolutionary triad of anal character traits, he needed a conveniently ambiguous protostructural concept to describe the stable linkage between certain infantile sexual drives and later observable adult behavior which could be predicted. Science is, of course, the "pursuit of predictability," and the notion of character was readily at hand. Character could be formed by the transformation of libido. Permanent character traits were either unchanged prolongations of the infantile drives, sublimations of them, or reaction formations against them (Freud, 1908). It is the dual function of models of the mind to account for stability (structure) and to describe change (dynamics) (Compton, 1981). To these ends character served Freud during the era of his topographic hypothesis as a protostructural model of the mind. The supraordinate concept of character is actually, therefore, an inchoate model of the mind which has never been explicitly so designated and which remains as a shadowy, unofficial, approximate alternative to aspects of the ego. Character structure has become a vague synonym for psychic structure. Both terms refer to stability, continuity, predictability, and integration of complex behavior.

This unobtrusive and infrequently discussed introduction of character as a model of the mind during the era of Freud's topographic hypothesis has left us with some confusion in theory, technique, and nosology up to the present day.

The major conceptual problem is the tendency to equate character with the ego of post-1923 structural theory, or to fail

---

[1] Sterba (1951) also discussed this archaic meaning of "character."

to recognize that character concepts in the global-supraordinate or structural sense are on a different level of abstraction, and that character as a supraordinate, nonphenomenal structure is not easily integrated with the tripartite supraordinate structural model of the mind. Character as a supraordinate structure means that there is a nonphenomenal organization integrating human behavior, mediating between drive and considerations of reality, between drive and superego, simultaneously including drives and superego *yet propelled by drives and superego*. In short, character then must be nothing other than the psychic apparatus as a totality. Character as supraordinate structure is a crude model of the mind, a map of the entire psychic apparatus without coordinates; yet character is not the total person. There may be those who prefer such a model as a supraordinate hypothesis equivalent in scope, but separate from the structural tripartite model. The problem would then be to demonstrate the clinical advantage of one model over the other. Serious difficulties arise when we do not *recognize* that there are *two* models and that these are conceptually separate frames of reference (Boesky, in Panel, 1983).

Freud's Evolving Views of Character

Freud's views of character changed. It is insufficiently appreciated that he never attempted a definition of character. It was only eight years after his announcement of the classic triad of anal character traits, which he originally proclaimed to exemplify drive transformation exclusively, that he stated matters more cautiously (1917, pp. 126-133) and said that the traits of avarice, pedantry, and obstinacy only drew powerful contributions from anal erotism. It is widely known that an important component of Freud's genius was his preference for supple ambiguity in describing matters provisionally that were, for the time being, beyond conceptual clarity or terminologic precision. His allusion to character in one crucial passage of "The Ego and the Id" (1923, pp. 29-30) is, in my opinion, such an ex-

ample. Freud said "the *character of the ego* is a precipitate of abandoned object-cathexes and . . . it contains the history of those object-choices" (p. 29; italics added). Was the "character" of the ego to be construed as the distinctive characteristic feature of the ego *vis-à-vis* identifications, or did Freud mean to imply that a person's character should be viewed as a component or substructure of the ego?

Freud certainly did not mean the latter. He took the trouble nine years later, in his *New Introductory Lectures,* to explicitly correct such a simplistic view. He said: "You yourselves have no doubt assumed that what is known as 'character', *a thing so hard to define,* is to be ascribed entirely to the ego. We have already made out a little of what it is that creates character. First and foremost there is the incorporation of the former parental agency as a super-ego, which is no doubt its most important and decisive portion, and, further, identifications with the two parents of the later period and with other influential figures. . . . And we may now add as contributions to the construction of character which are never absent the reaction-formations which the ego acquires . . . when it rejects un-wished-for instinctual impulses" (Freud, 1933, p. 91; italics added).

Freud clearly warned that one cannot equate character with any one of the three major components of the psychic apparatus. In fact, in his view, character was "located" in all three systems of the psychic apparatus. We also know that throughout Freud's writings he viewed constitutional endowment as an essential aspect of human character. We cannot accurately describe Freud's views even by saying that in his estimation character was the whole psychic apparatus; we see that he was dealing with character in very different ways at different times. Character as a conceptual frame of reference remains a confusing concept. Very few analysts have dealt with this as a theoretical problem (Stein, 1969; Baudry, in Panel, 1983). Many of our leading theoreticians have preferred, for whatever reason, to ignore Freud's caveat that character cannot be reduced

to, included in, or equated with the ego. Waelder (1930) recognized this and gave a definition of character that stressed the role of compromise formation. He said: "Character is largely determined by the specific methods of solving problems, and these methods are peculiar to each individual. . . ." (p. 75).

Character Resistance and Technique

Wilhelm Reich's (1933) views advocating a technical assault against character resistances have been extensively criticized (A. Freud, 1936; Sterba, 1951, 1953). Still, some modern analysts consider Reich's ideas valuable because he called attention to the importance of character as a resistance. There is reason to believe that Reich's views about character resistances survive in the clinical and theoretical writings of Fenichel (1945, 1953) and Kernberg (1980a, 1980b).

For Reich, the task of the analyst was to confront the patient with his pathological character resistances and to insist on the "unfreezing" of these traits as an essential precursor to further analytic work. Reich viewed this as a task for the early phase of the analysis so as to enable conversion of character resistances into derivatives which would then be therapeutically accessible in the transference neurosis.

Anna Freud's (1936) classic book, *The Ego and the Mechanisms of Defense*, was, in one respect, a reply to Reich's excesses. She cogently warned against one-sidedness in psychoanalytic technique and advocated the now generally accepted "equidistant posture." The controversy between Reich and Anna Freud was well summarized by R. Sterba (1951, 1953). Sterba also argued (1953) that the concept of character resistance was confusing and technically misleading, and that it should be abandoned. Yet Reich's ideas die hard. Fenichel's work is an example of Reich's influence.

Fenichel's (1953) definition of character is still widely accepted: "Character, as the habitual mode of bringing into harmony the tasks presented by internal demands and by the

external world, is necessarily a function of the constant, organized, and integrating part of the personality which is the ego . . . the ego's habitual modes of adjustment to the external world, the id, and the superego, and the characteristic types of combining these modes with one another constitute character" (p. 467). Fenichel himself said his definition of character was nearly identical with his own definition of ego. This poses a useful question. Fenichel was undoubtedly aware of these issues. Why did he find it necessary to propose a global character roughly congruent with and identical to the ego? I think it can be argued that he was led to this in part by his effort to account for character resistances, which he chose to view in terms very similar to those of Reich (1933).

These notions of character expressed by Fenichel are the theoretical core of his technical interventions with character resistances. Fenichel (1945) said: "An acute resistance, one that is directed against the discussion of some particular topic, is far easier to handle than 'character resistances.' These are attitudes which the patient had previously developed in order to maintain his repressions, and which he now exhibits toward the analyst. These attitudes must first be *broken down* before the repressions can be resolved" (p. 29; italics added).

Fenichel's technical strategies were more subtle than Reich's *Blitzkrieg* technique against the character armor (Fenichel, 1953, 1954). But no matter what disclaimers Fenichel uttered, he believed that the sanctuary of resistances could be located in the character of the patient. Rangell (1965) has also commented on the influence of Reich on Fenichel's ideas.

I shall give one further example of Fenichel's apodictic, simplified, and linear description of technique with character resistance:

> If the mobilization of the old conflict succeeds, [the patient] will experience anxiety and subsequently the instinctual impulses in question, instead of his rigid and frozen attitude. Thus the character neurosis will be *changed* into a symptom neurosis, and character resistances into vivid

transference resistances; *afterward* they will be treated the way symptomatic neuroses and transference resistances usually are handled [Fenichel, 1945, p. 538; italics added].[2]

This is no longer an accepted description of optimal psychoanalytic technique. Most modern psychoanalysts would prefer to say that we help the patient to work through certain aspects of such transference resistances involving some of his character traits and that when this is successful, we observe a shift in compromise formation and the emergence of other transference resistances. Transference resistances are compromise formations (Brenner, 1981) and some transference resistances represent typical behavioral ensembles "characteristic" for that patient. Obviously, not all character traits will be imbricated with transference.

Kernberg's View of Character

Kernberg has contributed important observations on the interrelationships of object relations theory and the tripartite structural hypothesis in a series of closely reasoned, scholarly, clinically astute publications, most notably in his book, *Object Relations Theory and Clinical Psychoanalysis* (1976). He has also attempted the parallel reconciliation of character theory and the structural hypothesis in his introduction of a nosologic framework organized on levels of character functioning. I believe there are problems with some of his views of character theory.

   Kernberg (1980a, 1980b) discussed character resistance from the angle of his proposed (1976) nosologic classification based on three levels of character pathology. His classification attempts to establish criteria for diagnosis among three "levels" of organization of character pathology which he designated as higher, intermediate, and lower levels. Kernberg proposed this classification in part "to clarify the relationship between a de-

[2] See also Fenichel (1954), p. 210.

scriptive characterological diagnosis and a metapsychological, especially structural, analysis. . . ." (p. 139).

But the "descriptive characterologic diagnosis" and the "metapsychological . . . structural analysis" represent two very different conceptual frames of reference and cannot be reconciled as simply as Kernberg proposed. His three "levels" of character pathology conflate descriptive aspects of character-as-behavior with the supraordinate, nonphenomenal, theoretically postulated character-as-psychic structure. Then, in turn, this hierarchy of character pathology is viewed as on the same conceptual level as id, ego, and superego. Kernberg does not refer here to the more successful classification which Anna Freud achieved in her Diagnostic Profile (A. Freud, 1962; A. Freud et al., 1965). Kernberg is one of the minority of modern analysts to advocate the value of isolating from the total fabric of psychoanalytic technique the Reichian term character analysis (V. Calef, personal communication). Kernberg (1980a) prefers to retain the term character resistance and advises that optimum technique with character resistances requires careful evaluation of character pathology in the initial diagnostic study. Various authors have noted that it is not possible to easily reconcile the tripartite structural hypothesis with object relations theory (Calef and Weinshel, 1979; Klein and Tribich, 1981);[3] I believe that it is equally difficult to reconcile character as a supraordinate concept with the tripartite structural hypothesis.

Clinical Illustration

Obviously, character traits are of great significance in the analysis of almost every patient. The issue I shall consider next is how we currently understand character manifestations in our daily work and how we usually deal with character issues technically. The following vignette is offered to illustrate that it is useful to view an important character trait in relation to com-

---

[3] For other comments on Kernberg's work, see Heiman (1966) and N. Segel (1981). The issues considered go far beyond the scope of this paper.

promise formation and as the manifestation of an unconscious fantasy (Arlow, 1971, 1974). I will show that there was no need to view the character trait as separate in any way from the theoretical and technical considerations required by the usual concepts related to compromise formation, multiple function, and the tripartite structural hypothesis.

The patient began gradually, in the course of his analysis, to express himself in a facetious manner. Sometimes this took the form of a tongue-in-cheek tone; other times he was baiting and disparaging. He might report a dream and then offer associations with comments such as, "Well, here's a thought about the dream," as though he were doing a problem for a teacher who has given him a rather silly assignment. He was often supercilious and skeptical about the dubious scientific value of psychoanalysis. If a friend offered him a cigar, he felt that I would assume it was a phallic symbol.

On one occasion he began a session with a story of his frustration about the delivery of a gift he had ordered for his wife. It came from a distant city, and it was the wrong color. The item he ordered was expensive and fragile. He telephoned the store and got nowhere. The saleslady insisted this was what he ordered. It could not be returned; the owner was out of the country. He was furious and called his best friend who was an attorney. His friend told him it would do him little good to pursue the matter.

He next recalled an incident in the Army. He was in charge of a school facility and had a terrible fight with an unreasonable sadistic woman who had, in her job, duties that overrode his own. She refused to provide certain basic comforts for the youngest group of children. He insisted that the children were being neglected. He felt that the commanding officer of his own unit was an inept fool, so without consulting him, he went over his head to the commanding officer of the entire military base. Predictably, he was reprimanded but also relieved of this particular duty, so he simultaneously escaped this woman who frightened him, embarrassed his immediate superior officer, and was himself punished.

Next, he thought about an incident just before the hour, which had alarmed him. The safety device on the elevator door must have been broken. The patient was on the way up to my office in this elevator when a man on a lower floor put his hand between the closing doors as he rushed to catch the elevator. The safety opening device failed, and the man only managed at the last second to avoid mangling his hand. After a brief silence, the patient said facetiously that I certainly ought to notify the building management, and if I did not, I would be negligent. On the other hand, it seemed pointless to tell me. I would view anything he said as mere grist for the mill. Besides, he knew the owner of my office building, whose office was on the top floor. He would tell him directly.

Because I thought his facetious attitude represented an important transference resistance, I intervened first by drawing his attention to his viewing me as no more helpful than his father in his dangerous fantasy struggle with women. I was then able to show him that he had a defensive wish to prove the futility of appealing to men in authority for rescue from these castrating women. In this way he could relieve his fear by reversing passive into active. He could thus identify with the phallic, castrating mother. Just as he went over the head of his superior officer in the Army, he would now in fantasy literally go over my head to the owner on the top floor. At the same time his facetious tone represented a denial of his fear of castration by the dangerous, attacking mother in his fantasy. Since my highly valued analysis was only a game, he belittled and castrated me instead of suffering this calamity himself. Moreover, castration was denied by his facetious tone. Nothing need be taken seriously. The entire session was a mere game, a mock exercise.

Later in the analysis it was possible to interpret other aspects of this transference resistance. His facetiousness, for example, represented a fantasy of revenge against his father who was so often actually indifferent to the patient. His facetiousness at still other times represented a baiting, provocative wish to be

beaten for masochistic, sexual gratification as well as for punishment.

It was clinically useful to view the patient's facetiousness as a transference resistance and as a compromise formation. Thus he could be helped once again to see the link between his character trait, his childhood conflicts about his unreliable father who never came to his aid in his painful battles with his mother, and his previous need to identify with her in his attitudes toward me. His character trait of facetiousness was usefully interpreted as a communicative attempt to gratify but also to defend against unconscious transference fantasies. At no time did I find it necessary to *convert* his facetious attitude into a transference resistance or to rely on the idea of his character trait as a component of his "character structure" in the sense of character as an organization separate from the compromise formations integrated by the id, ego, and superego. I here suggest that this is generally the case.

Thus the trait of facetiousness represented the excrescence of a group of complicated wishes and unconscious fantasies, each of which was itself a compromise formation. The character trait was in many respects like symptomatic behavior, as is true of many "characterologic" manifestations. This is widely known, and it is also well known that the development of symptoms in childhood is inevitably associated with related character formations. Here we again see the congruence of the problem of character formation and the entire developmental issue of the formation of psychic structure. At bottom these are the same phenomena.

Character and Action

Character traits always imply action. Any attitude is a dispositional tendency. Viewed from the angle of action, the behavior of the patient in this vignette, when he teased me about ignoring a real danger, was an acting out in the sense of his effort to engage me in the actualization of his unconscious fantasy (Boesky, 1982).

We cannot achieve a systematic theory of character traits until psychoanalytic theory evolves a comprehensive theory of action. Much of the early writing on character utilized the topographic model of action described in Chapter 7 of Freud's (1900) *Interpretation of Dreams*. This was a very simplified view of action and behavior as the motor discharge of psychic energy. Irrational behavior was then seen as a manifestation of shifts in psychic energy distribution between the systems *Ucs.*, *Pcs.*, and *Pcpt.-Cs.* If there was a damming up of libido due to repression, certain thoughts came under the sway of the primary process because their *Pcs.* cathexis had been abandoned and their one aim was motor discharge (Freud, 1900, p. 605). Glover (1925) and others pointed out that the collateral discharge channel into character formation was analogous to perversion, in that both perversion and character formation spared repression. We have advanced since then in our understanding of action. Nevertheless, Hartmann (1947) observed that to this day we have no systematic theory of action and that such a theory of action, based on the knowledge of structural aspects of the personality and its motivations, is the most important contribution psychoanalysis will one day be able to make in this field.

The gaps in our understanding of character as disposition to action can be illustrated by a comparison. Just as we cannot predict the choice of neurosis from prior knowledge of developmental interference, so we cannot predict action from prior knowledge of thoughts. We use character traits clinically to represent our attempted predictions and our estimates of probabilities. Such clinical use of character traits serves us very well at present.

Supraordinate Concepts

Character and self are terms designating supraordinate concepts. The ambiguous theoretical relation between character and ego concepts resembles the confusion between the terms ego and self. Hartmann (1950, p. 127) distinguished Freud's

use of *das Ich* as ego from *das Ich* as self.[4] In this now historic distinction, Hartmann also pointed out that narcissism is "located" in all three systems. There is a good parallel between character and self, then, in respect to the fact that neither can be located only in the ego.[5] There are further similarities between character and self. Each may be viewed as an epiphenomenal resultant of the interplay of the structural systems. Part of the appeal of character and self-concepts has been their beguiling near-to-experience resonance—the quality of being at the heart of what we sense to be central to our intuitive experiencing of ourselves (J. McLaughlin, personal communication).

The conceptual and epistemological questions related to a coherent integration of partial and global mental concepts have been unresolved for millennia. It is no surprise, therefore, that they have been the basis for controversy since the beginning of psychoanalysis. It does seem rather surprising, however, that the parallel incongruence between ego falsely equated with self and ego falsely equated with character has received so little attention. It is clear that neither character, self, identity, personality, total person, or any other available term can be easily reconciled with the tripartite structural hypothesis. One can no more "locate" character "in the ego" than one could locate the soul in the ego. Character in the supraordinate sense was defined by Baudry (Panel, 1983) as: ". . . a nonphenomenological inner organization corresponding to the outer façade which we can identify as a structure on a *somewhat different plane* from that of the ego, id, and superego" (p. 213; italics added).

Character Traits

Individual character traits have their own ambiguities. First, the criteria for phenomenal definition of each character trait are

---

[4] Hartmann's distinction has been questioned by Spruiell (1981). It is not generally recognized that Loewenstein (1940) was the first to discuss this issue.

[5] Schafer (1979) discussed the conceptual confusion in prevalent definitions of character as an example of a category mistake in which an abstract term and its referents are confused.

highly arbitrary. Note the difference of connotation in Freud's original 1908 use of the word "parsimony" in his definition of the famous anal triad and his later use of the word "avarice." Second, as Baudry (Panel, 1983) pointed out, there are no restrictions on uniformity of levels of clinical generalization. Some authors describe observable behavior and others describe inferred defensive patterns. To further confuse matters, most character typologies, including Fenichel's sublimative-reactive as well as Freud's (1931) libidinal types, conflate adult character traits with complex developmental issues. This is only one reason why no psychoanalytic character typology has proven conceptually useful.

The further the character trait we wish to study is from the nodal structural conflicts, the less we can know about the trait from a psychoanalytic viewpoint. Without simplifying the relation of rational and irrational behavior, one can say that psychoanalysis has less to say about stable configurations of human behavior outside the sphere of conflict. Thus we may conclude a successful analysis without knowing much about certain successful character traits and modes of highly adaptive functioning in the external life of the patient (Stein, 1969).

Conventional definitions of character usually include reference to the ego-syntonic aspect of the character trait in contrast to the ego-alien quality of the neurotic symptom. This is clinically and theoretically incorrect. David Beres (1965, unpublished) observed that the term ego-syntonic dates to the days when analysts used the word ego as a synonym for self. Since the ego is a *group* of functions, character traits which were formed originally as compromise formations can only be syntonic with certain functions of the ego as opposed to others.[6] Clinical observation often provides evidence of a fluctuation of attitudes by patients toward their character traits and symptoms. For example, when my patient was facetious, he might have been amused, oblivious, or penitent. Although the tradi-

---

[6] See also Schafer's (1979, 1982) observations on ego syntonicity and character.

tional distinction holds at the extremes, careful attention to this question will also demonstrate important fluctuations and even reversals in so-called syntonicity or acceptance of symptoms as well as character traits. In a like vein the traditional distinction between autoplastic and alloplastic alterations to contrast symptoms and character neurosis simplifies the complex, oscillating, and reciprocal adaptive modifications the ego imposes on certain of its own functions versus efforts to impose certain roles on actual persons in the environment.

There is still another way in which our views of character have changed as a result of the refinement of observation and theory afforded by the structural hypothesis. It is true that there is something quite distinctive about a person's character as perceived by others. This distinctiveness is included in a closely related idea which also seems erroneous. I refer to the time-honored view of "a characteristic repertory of defenses." Brenner (1981, p. 568) has observed that "if one includes in one's assessment of each patient's defenses not just those which are part of his major symptomatology, but those which are involved in his dreams, his fantasies, his ambitions, his plans—in a word, in the entire gamut of his mental life, normal as well as pathological—one sees immediately how inapplicable is the concept of a limited repertory of defenses." In other words, character traits usually emerge with greatest visibility as we approach pathological intrapsychic conflicts. Any ego function may appear in any character trait, and the range of each person's character is as broad as his range of ego functions. It is only when we focus attention on particularly prominent symptomatic behavior and ignore the rest of the patient's mental functioning that we can argue for the few identifying features of some traits as representative of the total person.

Symptom and Character

The poor fit between Freud's evolving notions of the ego and the descriptive, nonsystematic views of character is the soil in

which misunderstandings also have arisen about the relation between character traits and symptoms. In a highly simplified and perhaps even schematically exaggerated way, this argument might be stated thus: character traits are developmentally, clinically, and theoretically discontinuous from symptoms, in that symptoms are always formed by the return of the repressed and character traits are not (Calef, 1981, personal communication). Nunberg (1956), Lustman (1962), Stone (in Panel, 1980), and Arlow (1964, 1966) have discussed various aspects of the interrelation between symptoms and character traits. The issues transcend the scope of this paper, but it has been widely recognized that both symptoms and character traits can be viewed as compromise formations. This was illustrated in my own clinical example cited above. It was clear that there was no advantage gained by making a distinction as to whether the patient's facetiousness represented a neurotic character trait or a neurotic symptom. Brenner (1983) has asserted that the distinction between neurotic character traits and neurotic symptoms is of little value. When a drive is used as a defense, what usually results is a perversion or a character trait (Brenner, 1957). Arlow (1971) illustrated the value of the notion of character perversions and extended Freud's idea that it is possible for symptom, character trait, and perversion to coexist in the same person. Here we can also observe the importance of related unconscious fantasies represented in different modes. Instead of the direct impingement of id upon ego, which would erroneously imply an isolated quantum of drive energy gaining access to motor innervations, we now speak of the multiple integrations of unconscious fantasies which are themselves highly complex compromise formations deriving from all levels of psychosexual as well as ego development, superego formation, and structural differentiation.

Summary

The time has come to re-examine what we mean by character structure, to determine to what extent we can reconcile our

views of character with the structural hypothesis, and to abandon the concept of character resistance. The clinical utility of
character traits as a concept is obvious, but the clear distinction
between character traits versus character as a global concept of
the mind is overdue. Character resistance as a concept is a
theoretical and technical anachronism. The value of character
trait formation viewed as a developmental concept resides in
the convenience of linking our ideas about the formation of
psychic structure to abiding behavioral and attitudinal configurations in adult mental functioning. It is misleading to suggest
that so-called character resistances should be dealt with differently than any other resistance.

REFERENCES

ARLOW, J. A. (1964). Symptom formation and character formation: summary
and discussion. *Int. J. Psychoanal.*, 45:167-176.
——— (1966). Character and conflict. *J. Hillside Hosp.*, 15:139-151.
——— (1971). Character perversion. In *Currents in Psychoanalysis*, ed. I. Mar-
cus. New York: Int. Univ. Press, pp. 317-336.
——— (1974). Some character problems in psychotherapy. E. Slakter, reporter. *J. Phila. Assn. Psychoanal.*, 1:158-161.
BOESKY, D. (1982). Acting out: a reconsideration of the concept. *Int. J. Psychoanal.*, 63:39-56.
BRENNER, C. (1957). The nature and development of the concept of repression in Freud's writings. *Psychoanal. Study Child*, 12:19-46.
——— (1981). Defense and defense mechanisms. *Psychoanal. Q.*, 50:557-569.
——— (1983). *The Mind in Conflict.* New York: Int. Univ. Press.
CALEF, V. & WEINSHEL, E. (1979). The new psychoanalysis and psychoanalytic
revisionism. Book review essay on *Borderline conditions and pathological
narcissism. Psychoanal. Q.*, 48:470-491.
COMPTON, A. (1981). On the psychoanalytic theory of instinctual drives. III.
The complications of libido and narcissism. *Psychoanal. Q.*, 50:345-362.
FENICHEL, O. (1945). *The Psychoanalytic Theory of Neurosis.* New York: Norton.
——— (1953). Concerning the theory of psychoanalytic technique. *Collected
Papers*, 1. New York: Norton, pp. 332-348.
——— (1954). Psychoanalysis of character. *Collected Papers*, 2. New York:
Norton, pp. 198-214.
FREUD, A. (1936). *The Ego and the Mechanisms of Defense. Writings*, 2. New York:
Int. Univ. Press, 1966.
——— (1962). Assessment of childhood disturbances. *Psychoanal. Study Child*,
17:149-158.

—— NAGERA, H. & FREUD, W. E. (1965). Metapsychological assessment of the adult personality: the adult profile. *Psychoanal. Study Child*, 20:9-41.

FREUD, S. (1900). The interpretation of dreams. *S. E.*, 4 & 5.

—— (1908). Character and anal erotism. *S. E.*, 9.

—— (1917). On transformations of instinct as exemplified in anal erotism. *S. E.*, 17.

—— (1923). The ego and the id. *S. E.*, 19.

—— (1931). Libidinal types. *S. E.*, 21.

—— (1933). New introductory lectures on psycho-analysis. *S. E.*, 22.

GLOVER, E. (1925). The neurotic character. In *On the Early Development of Mind*. New York: Int. Univ. Press, 1956, pp. 47-66.

HARTMANN, H. (1947). On rational and irrational action. In *Essays on Ego Psychology*. New York: Int. Univ. Press, 1964, pp. 37-68.

—— (1950). Comments on the psychoanalytic theory of the ego. In *Essays on Ego Psychology*. New York: Int. Univ. Press, 1964, pp. 113-141.

HEIMAN, P. (1966). Comment on Dr. Kernberg's paper. *Int. J. Psychoanal.*, 47:254-260.

KERNBERG, O. (1976). *Object Relations Theory and Clinical Psychoanalysis*. New York: Aronson.

—— (1980a). Character structure and analyzability. *Bull. Assn. Psychoanal. Med.*, 19:87-96.

—— (1980b). *Internal World and External Reality*. New York: Aronson.

KLEIN, M. & TRIBICH, D. (1981). Kernberg's object relations theory: a critical re-evaluation. *Int. J. Psychoanal.*, 62:27-44.

LOEWENSTEIN, R. M. (1940). The vital or somatic instincts. *Int. J. Psychoanal.*, 21:377-400.

LUSTMAN, S. (1962). Defense, symptom and character. *Psychoanal. Study Child*, 17:216-244.

NUNBERG, H. (1956). Character and neurosis. *Int. J. Psychoanal.*, 37:36-45.

PANEL (1980). Character structure and analyzability. *Bull. Assn. Psychoanal. Med.*, 19:73-119.

—— (1983). Theory of character. S. Abend, reporter. *J. Amer. Psychoanal. Assn.*, 31:211-224.

RANGELL, L. (1965). Some comments on psychoanalytic nosology: with recommendations for improvement. In *Drives, Affects and Behavior*, 2, ed. M. Schur. New York: Int. Univ. Press, pp. 128-160.

REICH, W. (1933). *Character Analysis*. New York: Noonday Press, 1949.

SCHAFER, R. (1979). Character, ego syntonicity, and character change. *J. Amer. Psychoanal. Assn.*, 27:867-892.

—— (1982). Problems of technique in character analysis. *Bull. Assn. Psychoanal. Med.*, 21:91-99.

SEGEL, N. (1981). Otto Kernberg's books. *J. Amer. Psychoanal. Assn.*, 29:221-236.

SPRUIELL, V. (1981). The self and the ego. *Psychoanal. Q.*, 50:319-344.

STEIN, M. (1969). The problem of character theory. *J. Amer. Psychoanal. Assn.*, 17:675-701.

STERBA, R. (1951). Character and resistance. *Psychoanal. Q.*, 20:72-76.

—— (1953). Clinical and therapeutic aspects of character resistance. *Psychoanal. Q.*, 22:1-20.

WAELDER, R. (1930). The principle of multiple function: observations on overdetermination. In *Psychoanalysis: Observation, Theory, Application*, ed. S. A. Guttman. New York: Int. Univ. Press, 1976.

755 West Big Beaver Road (Suite 510)
Troy, Michigan 48084

OBJECT RELATIONS THEORY AND CHARACTER ANALYSIS

OTTO F. KERNBERG, M.D.

T HE PRINCIPAL AIM OF THIS PAPER is to integrate new knowledge regarding the structural characteristics of and the
psychoanalytic approach to severe character pathologies with
Fenichel's (1941) theory of psychoanalytic technique. Within
his proposals of metapsychological criteria for interpretation,
Fenichel both incorporated and critically revised Reich's (1936)
technical approach to character resistances. My expansion of
Fenichel's theory of psychoanalytic technique as it applies to
character analysis is in line with my earlier efforts to enrich an
ego-psychological approach to technique with object relations
theory (see Kernberg, 1980, Chapt. 9).

According to object relations theory, unconscious intrapsychic conflicts are not simply conflicts between impulse and
defense. These conflicts are between two opposing units or sets
of internalized object relations. Each of these units consists of
a self- and an object representation under the impact of a drive
derivative (clinically, an affect disposition). Both impulse and

---

Medical Director, The New York Hospital-Cornell Medical Center, West-
chester Division; Professor of Psychiatry, Cornell University Medical College;
Training and Supervising Analyst, Columbia University Center for Psychoanalytic Training and Research.

Presented at the panel on "The Relationship Between Psychoanalytic
Theory and Technique" at the Annual Meeting of the American Psychoanalytic Association, Boston, May, 1982.

247

defense find expression through an affectively imbued internalized object relation.

Pathological character traits carry out dominant, chronic defensive functions in the psychic equilibrium of patients with severe character pathology. All character defenses represent a defensive constellation of self- and object representations directed against an opposite and dreaded, repressed self- and object constellation. For example, a man who is excessively submissive may be operating under the influence of a unit consisting of a self-representation submitting happily to a powerful and protective parental (object) representation. But this set of representations is defending him against a repressed self-representation rebelling angrily against a sadistic and castrating parental representation. These conflicting internalized object relations may, under optimal circumstances, become reactivated in the transference, in which case character defenses become transference resistances. Formulating the interpretation of these transference resistances in terms of their hypothesized internalized object relations may facilitate the reactivation of these component self- and object representations in the transference, thus transforming the "hardened" character defense into an active intrapsychic and transferential conflict.

The more severe the character pathology, the more pathological character traits acquire specific transference functions and become both character resistances and specific transference resistances at the same time (Fenichel, 1945, pp. 29, 537). Simultaneously, the compromise formation between impulse and defense represented by these pathological character traits also leads to more or less disguised impulse gratification in the transference. The more severe the patient's character pathology, the more prematurely and consistently do pathological character traits intrude in the transference situation. Under these circumstances, the patient seems to enter prematurely a stage of severe distortion in his relation to the analyst that resembles the ordinary transference neurosis, but differs from it in that it simply seems to reflect the patient's playing out in analysis a

pattern that simultaneously persists in the rest of his life. The typical transference neurosis in less severe cases takes some time to develop and is usually accompanied by a diminishing of the patient's neurotic manifestations outside the analysis. Further, the more severe the character pathology, the more pathological character traits are importantly expressed in nonverbal behavioral communications in addition to character disturbance expressed directly in free association.

To complicate matters further, the more severe the character pathology, the more the patient's nonverbal behavior, examined over a period of many weeks or months, also shows a paradoxical development: there may be chaotic shifts, from moment to moment in each psychoanalytic session, making the selection of the predominant material for interpretation very difficult, and yet, simultaneously, over a period of months or even years, there is a strange stability in that apparent chaos. A stable and unconscious, highly specific set of distortions emerges in the patient's relation to the analyst that reflects defensively activated internalized object relations which need to be resolved as part of the analysis of the transference in order to obtain significant structural intrapsychic change. Frequently, two contradictory sets of primitive object relations are activated alternatively, functioning as defenses against each other; sometimes their mutual dissociation is the dominant resistance that needs to be worked through. Or else one specific primitive object relation acquires a long-term, subtle, but controlling influence over the patient's relationship with the analyst and expresses itself more in a distortion of the psychoanalytic setting over time than in concrete developments that fluctuate session by session.

Clinical Vignette

The patient, a professional in the field of social rehabilitation, was a single man in his middle thirties who consulted me because of severe difficulties in his relation with women, great

difficulties in his work with clients, severe limitations in his capacity for empathy, and a general sense of dissatisfaction expressed in experiences of boredom, irritability, and uncertainty over the meaning life held for him. He suffered from a narcissistic personality, without overt borderline or antisocial features.

His initial attitude toward entering psychoanalysis and the method of free association was marked by strong ambivalence. On the one hand, he considered me one of the more desirable analysts in the relatively small local professional community where I worked; on the other hand, he thought that psychoanalysis was a rather old-fashioned and *passé* technique, and he considered what he experienced as my rigid maintenance of a psychoanalytic stance pompous and pedestrian. His own theoretical approach and background were almost diametrically opposed to psychodynamic views. In the early stages of his psychoanalysis, he was also extremely concerned about my interest in what he was saying, suspected me of total indifference to him, and interpreted any movement of mine behind the couch as secret engagements on my part with endeavors having no relation with him (such as balancing my checkbook). He would become very angry when I failed to remember a name or a circumstance he had mentioned in an earlier session.

His free associations centered on his relation with his latest girl friend, whom he considered very attractive and desirable at first, but in whom he gradually discovered shortcomings that made him feel she was getting much more from him than he from her and made him wish to terminate it. In this context, his general suspiciousness of women, his fear of women exploiting him, emerged as a major theme. This could gradually be traced to the relation with his mother, a locally prominent socialite who dominated his father, and whom he had experienced as dominant, intrusive, dishonest, and manipulative. The patient described his father as a hard-working and effective businessman, withdrawn and chronically unavailable during the patient's childhood.

During the first two years of his psychoanalysis, the connection between his experience of his girl friend, his mother, and of me became more and more evident. I was hypocritically pretending that I was interested in him while in reality using him for my own financial interest, or pretending to listen to him when I was engaged with my own activities; similarly, his girl friend pretended to love him, but was only interested in exploiting him socially and financially. It gradually also became apparent that in his treatment of her he was himself quite dominant and exploitative, expecting her to guess his moods and respond to his needs without his paying attention to hers. Whenever I tactfully tried to make him aware of his own contribution to their difficulties, the patient angrily accused me of trying to make him feel guilty and of acting the way his mother did toward him. He saw me with the same sly, intrusive, and dominant, guilt-raising behavior that enraged him in his mother.

In the transference, my enactment of the replica of his mother now seemed complete: I was either silent, indifferent and only pretending to be interested in him, or I was actually interested in brainwashing him with my views by means of inducing guilt in him, and sadistically enjoying that control. Efforts to convey to him that he was attributing to me aspects of his own behavior toward women that he could not tolerate in himself all failed. The relationship with his girl friend broke up and, several months later, was replaced by a relationship with a new girl friend that soon became a facsimile of his interactions with the previous one.

Over the next year, the same issues seemed to repeat themselves endlessly in free association and in his relationship with me. I gradually reached the conclusion that the enactment of the relationship with his mother in the transference and with his girl friends served powerful defensive as well as instinctual purposes. It was as if he managed to obtain some secret (at least partial) satisfaction from his girl friends of his unacknowledged needs for sadistic control. The girl friend also served as a receptacle for massive projection onto them of his mother, thus providing rationalization for his attacks on them.

In the third year of his psychoanalysis, I gradually reached the conclusion that the patient's relation with me in the transference had basically not changed since the beginning of treatment. Nor had his discovery of childhood experiences in relation to his mother (which explained, apparently, his present relations to his girl friends and to me) resulted in any change of his previously held conscious convictions about his present or past. I also noticed in the patient's continuing suspicion and anger toward me an easy activation of fantasies of stopping the treatment. Although he never actually stopped, I did not have the feeling of certainty about his engagement in analysis that I had with other patients who, when acting out negative transference reactions, might temporarily miss sessions without shaking my conviction that they would return. With this patient, I sensed both a frailty in our relation and a definite lack of deepening in it.

I also observed, over a period of months, that the patient listened to my interpretations eagerly enough, but he then either agreed with them with the implication that he had earlier reached those very conclusions himself, or he disagreed with them immediately, or he attempted to argue with me about them. He simply dismissed those interpretations he did not accept immediately. At other times, he would appear very interested in an interpretation and, in fact, attempt to use it in his counseling of his own clients, but not give any evidence of making use of it for deepening his own understanding of himself in his hours with me. In short, his reactions to my interpretations reflected a chronic incapacity to really depend on me for further exploration of his intrapsychic development, and, in contrast, a tendency to extract them from me as valuable knowledge to be appropriated for his own use. Abraham's (1919), Rosenfeld's (1964), and my own (Kernberg, 1975) observations on narcissistic transference resistances clearly applied to this case.

When I attempted to interpret these dynamics to him and to explore the functions of his attitude, it emerged that the

patient was protecting himself against intense feelings of envy of me by utilizing for his own purposes whatever he saw as new and good coming from me, so that what he saw as feathers in my cap could become feathers in his. These envious feelings and the defenses against them reflected both preoedipal and oedipal conflicts. It gradually became evident to him that, while he could thus protect himself from envious feelings about me, he precluded his utilization of my comments for his own self-exploration. This led us back into his initial derogatory and critical attitude toward psychoanalysis in contrast to his affirmation of his own very different approach to clients.

Eventually the patient began to understand that he was torn between valuing me highly as somebody who might be instrumental in helping him overcome his difficulties with women, but by the same token, somebody whom he would therefore feel extremely envious of, which was intolerable, or, not having to feel envious of me at all, which would reconfirm that nothing was to be expected from psychoanalysis. This analysis of his attitude toward my interpretations and, by implication, of the sharply contradictory attitude toward me (a constant oscillation between envious idealization and unconscious devaluation) intensified his sense of restlessness and loneliness in the hours. The patient felt that even if what I was pointing out to him was accurate, my doing it implied a grandiose triumph over him and showing off on my part; as a result he felt powerless, lost, and rejected by me.

In this context, in the fourth year of his psychoanalysis, the following rather protracted episode took place. The patient became more and more alert to whatever he could experience as my shortcomings, both in and outside the hours. Unbeknownst to me, he gradually developed a network of information about me that extended through various related groups in the small town where we both lived and culminated with his establishing contact with a particular group of disaffected members of the local psychiatric community who were very resentful of the institution I was in and my role in it. My patient began

to extract from one person who felt particularly bitter about me information the patient considered damaging to me, while feeding that person information about my shortcomings as an analyst. When this information came back to my patient in an amplified fashion through a third person, he became alarmed, and "confessed" the whole process to me. That he had been withholding all these developments from me for weeks, by itself illustrates the frailty of the therapeutic relationship, the limitations in the patient's free associations, and the chronic distortion in the psychoanalytic setting.

My immediate emotional reaction to the patient's confession was intense. I felt hurt and angry—particularly controlled by the patient and helpless. It took me several hours before I realized that the patient's relation with his mother had now become activated with reversed roles, that he was now identifying himself with the aggressor (his mother) and that I, in the countertransference, was identifying with the patient as the victim of his mother's manipulations. I also became aware of the patient's intense fear that I might retaliate or abandon him. This fear was clearly mixed with guilt feelings. After exploring his fantasies about my retaliating and rejecting him—he spontaneously remarked that this is what he would feel like doing in similar circumstances—I said that his description of his own behavior resembled descriptions he had given of his mother's treatment of him, which he could now accept. I also told him that his awareness that his curiosity about me had aggressive implications made it less necessary for him to deny these feelings. The patient then said that he felt that in his behavior throughout that time there had been an exciting, daredevil attitude. He had felt all along that he was transgressing our essential understanding about open communication, risking, as he saw it, the continuation of his relation with me, but also feeling a sense of freedom and power which was exciting, even intoxicating. In fact, he added, now that he was no longer afraid that I would throw him out, he could see something good in the entire experience.

Further exploration of this feeling led to his awareness that his sense of satisfaction, power, and excitement came from his feeling that he could successfully control and manipulate me, that I was really quite limited by my analytic attitude. He had never seen our relationship in this context before. This, in turn, led to further exploration of his now activated relation with me in which he dared to identify with his mother, with a profound sense of power and satisfaction expressing aggression he had never dared accept in himself, while I appeared in the role of himself, powerlessly dominated by him as his own mother. This aggression included elements of orally determined envy and anal-sadistic impulses condensed with castrating impulses (which became dominant only at later stages of the analysis).

For the first time, the patient was able to experience an identification with the image he had projected of his mother throughout all these years. Concomitantly, he achieved contact with the aggressive, revengeful qualities of his envy toward me. Over the next few months, it became possible to point out to him how his image of himself as powerless, empty, defeated, and lonely *vis-à-vis* exploitative women was a defense against the opposite self-image wherein he identified with his powerful mother, sadistically enjoying herself in relating to women and myself as his (her) powerless slaves. The result was an integration of the previously dissociated and repressed sadistic self-representation identifying with his mother and the empty impotent self defensively set up against it. As a consequence, and in the context of the integration of these contradictory affects and self-representations, the patient became better able to explore his relationship with me in depth and to deepen his understanding of his relationship with women and with his mother as well. Beyond that, a new image of me began to emerge in the transference. I became a tolerant and warm father toward whom the patient experienced dependent and sexual longings, marking, for the first time, a shift in his unconscious relation to me, in the nature of the predominant transference paradigm, and in his experience of the past.

Discussion

Several technical aspects of this case may be highlighted. First, the early activation of transference resistances (the patient's angry and suspicious concerns over my lack of interest in him, his angry outbursts when sufficient attention was not paid to him) repeated in relation to me aspects of his relation with women, and required or permitted an immediate integration of the analysis of character resistances with the main themes emerging through free association (his relation to his girl friends). Next, the partial nature of his self-representation, the related lack of capacity for deepening his emotional relation to me as well as to his girl friends, and the corresponding rigidly maintained version of his past gradually emerged as a self-perpetuating global resistance to further advance in the treatment. Now my focus on the patient's attitude toward my interpretations and, by implication, his chronically maintained, subtle but stable relation to me and the analysis, permitted the interpretation of the most pervasive characterological aspect of his narcissistic personality structure, namely, the identification with a sadistic maternal representation as a core constituent of his pathological grandiose self. The working through of that feature in the transference was a precondition for any further move in the psychoanalytic process.

It needs to be stressed that the excited and sadistic behavior toward me, connected with a dissociated self-representation, was available as a conscious experience in his relation to various women, but only expressed in temper tantrums and protracted emotional storms that were "justified" by his massive projection of mother's image onto the girl friends, so that this particular self-representation was conscious yet dissociated from self-experiences in which the patient felt lonely and inferior, highly rationalized, and protected by primitive defensive operations, particularly projective identification. The expression of this grandiose and sadistic pattern in the transference, and its integration, by means of interpretation, with contradictory self-representations of the defeated, exploited child, marked the

successful completion of a systematic analysis of the corresponding character resistances that had first emerged in relation to my interpretations. In retrospect, the patient could understand that, in rejecting my interpretation as well as in co-opting them, he had subtly enacted his mother's role, and also that of himself as a frustrated child.

This development also permits an illustration of one interesting difference between the narcissistic grandiose self and the dissociated or repressed, normal self-representations against which the grandiose self is defending. This patient's dominant self-concept was that of himself as a mistreated child, entitled to compensation. This concept was hidden behind a self-righteous and well-rationalized exploitation of women and a derogatory dismissal of whatever might stir up envy in him. In contrast, the sadistic, rageful, yet excited aspect of the self that emerged in the transference was also part of the normal aggressively infiltrated self-representations, paradoxically closer to authenticity and depth in object relation than the defensive surface self-representation. At the deepest level, his conception of his sadistic mother included the projection onto her of his own rageful feelings from many sources.

From a still different viewpoint, the sense of stalemate I experienced throughout an important part of the third year of treatment could retrospectively be interpreted as the consequence of the mechanism of omnipotent control, by which the patient was successfully interfering with my interpretation of the dissociated aggressive aspects of his self, angrily accusing me of attempting to raise guilt feelings in him every time I attempted to interpret aggressive aspects of his behavior that he could not accept in himself. It was as if I had to function as a dominant mother or else remain impotently in the background. My hurt and angry reaction following his acting out of the negative transference aspects, signaled, in addition to my own countertransference potential, the activation within me of his image of himself as the powerless, attacked, and hurt innocent little boy faced with an overpowering mother. My emo-

tional reaction could thus help me to further analyze an aspect of his experience of himself in relating to his mother, while pointing to his enacting the role of his mother in relation to me. This formulation makes use of the concepts of concordant and complementary identification in the countertransference proposed by Racker (1957), which emphasized an object-relations perspective in the analysis of countertransference.

Strategies of Character Analysis

By itself, the severity of character pathology is not sufficient to indicate whether interpretation of character resistances should be given early or later. In this regard, Fenichel's (1941, p. 67) proposal to examine character defenses in accordance with what is in predominance at any point in the analytic situation is a reasonable approach to the practical issue of when to interpret character resistances. He suggests to first work with the patient's character defenses that are habitual and continuous in order to "release the personality from its rigidity," even when active impulse-defense configurations emerge elsewhere, and to work with other character resistances only when they have become transference resistances (p. 68). But one first has to know whether what one is confronting is character resistance, and if it is, whether it is economically predominant at the time.

Fenichel suggests working ". . . at the point of the *most important* current instinctual conflicts. It is the point of the most important conflicts *at the moment*" (1941, p. 47). In my view, the economic criterium for interpretation is reflected by the point of highest affect disposition in the material of the hour. Insofar as drives (whether functioning as part of the defensive or the impulsive side of the conflict) are manifest as affectively invested internalized object relations, the affectively predominant object relation in the analytic situation represents the economically dominant instinctual conflict as well. But affective dominance is not equivalent to consciousness or surface manifestations. As Fenichel himself put it: "For we must operate at that point

where the affect is actually situated at the moment; it must be added that the patient does not know this point and we must first *seek out* the places where the affect is situated" (1941, p. 45).

I propose that the combined evaluation of (1) the content of free associations, (2) the prevailing nature of the interactions in the patient-analyst relation—including the patient's nonverbal behavior during the sessions—and (3) the patient's overall relation to the psychoanalytic setting over a period of months or even years makes it possible to discern whether pathological character traits have invaded the transference, resulting in a condensation of transference and character resistances, and whether these character resistances have become affectively predominant, thus justifying the highest priority as the focus of psychoanalytic interpretations. The following conditions illustrate the applications of these criteria.

1. If free association is proceeding satisfactorily, and if the resistances emerging in the context of exploring any restrictions of free association can be interpreted—regardless of whether these are directly linked to the transference—and if the patient's awareness of his intrapsychic life as well as of the emotional relation to the analyst deepen over time, then the interpretation of nonverbal behavior in the hours can wait until it can be incorporated naturally into the themes of the free associations and the transference.

2. Specific clinical situations are encountered in which nonverbal behavior strongly emerges in the sessions, and in which the affect and object relation implied by the patient's nonverbal behavior and the affect and object-relations configuration implied in his verbal communications are congruent or consonant or complementary. When a consonance exists between the nonverbal material and the verbal, the understanding of the transferential implications of both usually permits a deeper understanding of both. In other words, if verbal and nonverbal material complement each other, and both jointly indicate the nature of the issues that predominate affectively in the content

of the hour, the economic principle of interpretation can be applied. Simultaneously, the material can usually also be understood in terms of the dynamic principle, that is, of a conflict between impulse and defense, and the decision made which aspect of the defensive side of the conflict should be explored before the impulse aspect. Congruence between behavior and content and affective dominance in the hour usually indicates, by the same token, that the object relations "unit" involved is dominant in the transference as well. Clarification of the dynamic ordering of impulse and defense usually also has topographical implications, permitting an interpretation from surface to depth, from consciousness to the unconscious. We usually find a consonance of verbal and nonverbal communications in patients with well-consolidated tripartite intrapsychic structure, whose conflicts also tend to be organized in intersystemic ways. It is therefore possible to clarify which system—ego, superego, or id—the predominant defensive organization corresponds to, and which other system the impulse is stemming from. Thus, the structural criteria of interpretation apply as well.

3. By contrast, in other clinical situations the conflicts reflected in the verbal content and the interactional material in the hour seem strongly dissonant or incongruent. Strong affects in the verbal content and the development of acute or chronic affective interactions reflecting the patient's "frozen" character traits seem strangely unrelated to each other, thus raising the question of what is the predominant material in the hour. Under the latter circumstances, I propose that applying the criteria that follow usually permits one to arrive at a decision regarding which material should be dealt with first and how to approach it.

It is helpful to consider first whether the patient's free association is proceeding satisfactorily or whether there is significant conscious suppression of material. Whatever interpretive approach is indicated to facilitate understanding the motives for conscious suppression and the related transference implications takes precedence here. The analysis of the trans-

ference implications of the motivation operating against full compliance with free association usually also provides an answer to what is affectively predominant in the hour, and whether it relates primarily to the verbal content or to aspects of the patient's (nonverbal) attitudes in the hours.

Now, if free association seems to proceed satisfactorily, the question of what is predominant in the transference can be examined more easily and helps to decide whether verbal or attitudinal material predominates. I am suggesting that, with two simultaneous parallel object relations "units" revealed in the psychoanalytic situation (one in the behavior, the other in the verbal content), the one with both transference dominance and affective dominance takes interpretive precedence. If, however, affective dominance and transference dominance diverge, I think affective dominance (the application of the economic principle) should have priority. It needs to be stressed that all defensive and impulsive, verbal and nonverbal, self- and object-related aspects of the material have affective implications, so that "affective dominance" does not mean searching for a unique affect or a consciously dominant one or one linked with defense or impulse only. It is the predominant affect in the total immediate situation that counts, not its access to consciousness. A hysterical temper tantrum, for example, may defend against another dominant affect in the immediate transference situation.

The approach I am suggesting is in contrast to Reich's (1936) insistence that characterologically anchored transference resistances always be interpreted first. It is also in contrast to Gill's (1980, 1982) insistence that transference always be given the highest priority for interpretation, for there are times when affective investment is highest in extratransference issues or in the patient's exploration of aspects of his past. The fact that all analytic material has transference implications does not mean an automatic predominance of transference material. Sometimes, however, a theme that has strongly predominated in the transference for many hours, for example, a patient's chronic

dissatisfaction about "not receiving anything from the analyst," may suddenly shift into a displacement of that complaint onto a third person. Here, affective dominance and transference are still consonant, although the transference is temporarily displaced (which may actually facilitate its interpretation).

In addition, at times of rapid shifts in the transference itself, which complicates detecting incongruity between verbal and nonverbal communication, the analyst's waiting for a crystallization around one of the various affectively important issues present should eventually permit him to decide what is affectively (and, therefore, economically) predominant. Here, a "wait-and-see" attitude is preferable, in my view, to the rather prevalent exclusively topographical viewpoint—that is, regarding what in the material is closer to consciousness. There is never just one "surface" to the material: there are many surface configurations, and at which point to penetrate from surface to depth (the topographic criterion) depends on what is actually dominant in the total situation. Obviously, when the patient can be helped to acquire awareness of simultaneous, strongly unrelated emotional dispositions in the analytic situation, the exploration of his associations to this observation in itself illuminates the issues involved.

During periods of heightened resistance, the most important material may be relatively distant from consciousness (particularly in personality structures with strong repressive mechanisms). While I agree that, once one has decided what material is most important, the material should be explored from its defensive side or aspects (which includes consideration of some conscious or preconscious configurations linked to it), the access to consciousness does not in itself indicate thematic predominance.

I am here questioning a general tendency for the analyst always to proceed from the surface down, from conscious to unconscious material, disregarding what is economically predominant. By the same token, however, I also question the opposite tendency to arrive at premature genetic interpreta-

tions of the unconscious fantasies reflected in characterologically expressed object relations in the transference. To stay close to the surface manifestations of resistances is as problematic as the search for the "deepest level" of a certain conflict, "deep" usually meaning genetically early. I think the analyst should interpret in depth in the sense of focusing on the unconscious conflicts that are predominant in any particular session, the unconscious aspects of the transference in the "here and now."

In cases where important discrepancies exist between the implications of verbal and nonverbal communication, where free association seems to be proceeding satisfactorily but without any real deepening of the material, and where, in addition, there are indications of a chronic stalemate in transference developments—or a loss of previously gained understanding of the present nature of the transference—I have found it helpful to give clear precedence to the analysis of the object-relations aspects of the patient's attitudes over those derived from his verbal communications. The same precedence applies to situations in which the patient is either repetitively acting out, or where strong potential for acting out seems to be developing. Giving precedence to nonverbal communication also applies to situations where general emotional dispersal, an exacerbation of splitting mechanisms, results in affective fragmentation and becomes a major transference resistance, which occurs particularly in personalities with strong schizoid features.

Other situations in which I would give preference to the interpretation of behavior over that of dissonant verbal communications include patients with "living-out" life styles, or whose free associations remain fixed at a surface level, or in the absence of a thoughtful, cooperative attitude on the patient's part. In all these cases Reich's recommendation to interpret attitudes before verbal content, and to consider this a special application of the principle of interpretation of "surface" before "depth," "defense before content," still seems valid. By the same token, cases with borderline character pathology where severe acting out colors the initial stage of the treatment also require

rapid interpretation of the transference implications of pathological character traits.

In other words, when free association "gets stuck" in the context of important activation of pathological behavior patterns in the analytic situation or in the patient's external life, analytic exploration of these behaviors and clarification of their relation to the transference are indicated. To put it still differently, from an economic viewpoint, discrepancies between verbal and nonverbal behavior require an interpretive approach to the total picture generated by this discrepancy. In practice, therefore, character resistances in the transference should be analyzed early on.

4. In still other cases, severe distortions in the relation to the psychoanalytic setting become apparent over time. In the vignette presented earlier, after a period of progress in the third year of the analysis, a therapeutic stalemate highlighted the pathology of the patient's relation to interpretations and to the analyst in general (the subtle compromise solutions between envious idealization and devaluation). In still other cases, quite similarly to those described by Reich, the patient's free associations apparently develop well, with abundant information about present and past, and flexible shifts from affects to intellectual thoughts, from fantasy to reality, from the transference to the patient's external life, etc. (thus imitating Ferenczi's [1919] and Glover's [1955] description of optimal free association), but without any real deepening in the transference relationship, or any manifestation of a particular nonverbal behavior in the sessions that would lend itself to exploring the transference.

In these latter cases, as I have implied before, it is the total relation to the analyst that is usually highly distorted, a distortion that must be diagnosed, particularly as it affects the patient's relation to the analyst's interpretations. Here the interpretation of pathological character traits coincides with the interpretation of the attitude toward the interpreting analyst, and under conditions of such chronic stalemates, this subject

matter has high priority. Otherwise, these become the typical cases of the patient acquiring a superficial "learning" of the psychoanalyst's theories as a way of defensively resisting full awareness of his unconscious intrapsychic conflicts, with consequent limited therapeutic results.

Under these circumstances, it is important to clarify the unconscious implications of the patient-analyst interaction in the "here and now" as a crucial step to fully understanding the object relation that is being played out, without attempting prematurely to achieve genetic reconstructions. "Here-and-now" interventions should not be conceptualized as artificially cut off, dissociated from their "there-and-then" aspects. The issue of their past implications should be kept in abeyance, however, until the unconscious aspects of the transference are fully explored. Often the patient finds it easier to accept a transference interpretation if a tentative reference to the childhood origin of a certain attitude to the analyst is made; hence, genetic reconstructions should not be reserved for the final stages of analysis. Here, however, I am stressing the need to clarify first the unknown in the present: a process erroneously bypassed in many patients with severe character pathology.

To spell out a patient's unconscious fantasy on the basis of a specific object relation enacted by the patient's chronic nonverbal behavior in the hours corresponds to a psychoanalytic construction. But it is necessary to follow this construction with a genetic reconstruction only after the patient's associations gradually transform this fantasy into an antecedent object relation, with the appearance of new information regarding his past and a natural reordering of the new and old information in this area. Establishing the actual genetic sequence of such recovered material requires that the analyst actively order and reorder these genetic units of the patient's unconscious conflicts (Blum, 1980).

The analyst's exploration of his own emotional reactions to the patient under conditions of chronic stalemate may be crucial to diagnosing both chronic countertransference distor-

tions (which are more pervasive though less obtrusive than acute countertransference developments) and subtle but powerful transference acting out that might otherwise not have been diagnosed. In this regard, the analysis of the analyst's total emotional reaction is a "second line" of approach when the first line of approach to direct transference exploration proves insufficient (Heimann, 1960; Kernberg, 1975).

The analysis of an implicit and, for the patient, often completely unconscious "interchange" of role relations with the analyst highlights the advantages of the study of the analyst's moment-to-moment affective responses to the patient, while also pointing to the differentiation of countertransference reactions in a strict sense (reflecting the analyst's unconscious conflicts activated in response to the patient's transference) from the analyst's global emotional response to the patient. Although these two aspects of the analyst's reactions—the restricted type of countertransference and the total emotional response—enter into complementary relations, for practical purposes this distinction facilitates the analyst's more open exploration of the moment-to-moment shift in his affective responses to and fantasies about the patient's immediate attitudes and chronic attitudinal dispositions, thereby enriching the analyst's understanding of the verbal content of the patient's communication. By the same token, the analyst's *utilization* of his own emotional reaction to the patient certainly does not mean *sharing* his emotional reaction with a patient.

Metapsychological Implications

I now return to considering the interpretation of character resistances in the light of Fenichel's economic, dynamic, and structural criteria for interpretation, combining these with the interpretation of internalized object relations represented in such character resistances. Regarding the *economic* criteria, I have stressed the need to interpret first the material that is affectively predominant, while simultaneously questioning

whether closeness to consciousness is an important criterion for deciding such predominance of affects. This view is implied in everything I have said regarding the difficulty in choosing economically predominant issues when information stemming from the patient's verbal and nonverbal communications is contradictory.

Regarding the *dynamic* criteria for interpretation, I reported earlier (Kernberg, 1980, Chapt. 10) that, at levels of severe regression in the transference or in cases of analyzable borderline personality organization, the predominance of splitting over repressive mechanisms permits the alternation, in consciousness, of the dynamically opposed components of intrapsychic conflict, so that the access to consciousness *per se* does not help to decide which is the defense and which is the impulse aspect of the conflict. Defense and impulse can rapidly be interchanged in the alternating reversals of activated object relations that are typical of part-object relations, and conflictual impulses are conscious and mutually dissociated or split off rather than unconscious—that is, repressed. Here, consciousness and unconsciousness no longer coincide with what is on the surface and what is deep, what is defense and what is content. But, while the topographic approach to interpretation (the ordering of the material from surface to depth) no longer holds for such borderline structures, the moment-to-moment decision of which is the defensively activated ego state directed against which other "impulsive" ego state is very important. Hence, both the economic and dynamic criteria of interpretation as spelled out by Fenichel are still fully relevant. This brings us to my next point, the structural aspects of interpretation of character resistances at various levels of severity of psychopathology.

The *structural* considerations regarding the interpretation of character resistances refer to the organization of the predominant internalized object relation activated in the transference in the context of a particular character trait or pattern. When we diagnose predominant "units" of internalized object

relations, we are diagnosing substructures of the tripartite structure. We are, in fact, applying a structural perspective where the overall tripartite structure may not yet (or may no longer) be operative. The patient's attitude, as mentioned before, reflects the enactment of a self-representation relating affectively to an object representation or the enactment of an object representation (with which the patient appears to be identified at that moment) relating affectively to a self-representation (now projected onto the analyst). One primary consideration here is the extent to which both self- and object representations are rooted in broader characteristics of the patient's ego or superego, reflecting broadly integrated conceptions, values, and emotional dispositions of ego and superego or, to the contrary, the extent to which they are dissociated or split off from other self- and object representations. The latter, part-object relations, are more disruptive, bizarre, fantastic than the total-object relations, which reflect more ordinary childhood experiences, and which, although repressed, became integrated with the child's ego and superego development.

In the context of these elaborations of the structural aspects of pathological character traits in the transference, one important question is, does the object relation activated reflect *inter*systemic or *intra*systemic conflicts? And in the case of intersystemic conflict, to which agency do the self-representations and object representations correspond? Or, which object relation corresponds to the defense and which to the impulse side of the conflict, and in which agency is each imbedded? In the case of intrasystemic conflicts, split-off internalized object relations may at first appear mutually delimited yet intrinsically undifferentiated, intense yet vague, and always highly fantastic and unrealistic. They need to be translated into an intelligible affective experience in the here and now, a fantasy enacted by them within which, in turn, the defensive and impulsive aspects have to be clarified in terms of which split-off object relation acquires a momentary defensive function against an opposing (impulsive) one. Attention to the interchange between patient

and analyst of self- and object representations—the alternation of complementary roles in the transference—needs to be integrated into the interpretation of these expressions of the conflict. That often requires relatively rapid, imaginative "tracking" of what appear to be chaotic interactions. The analyst's systematically pointing out to the patient how he feels under the impact of a self-representation and the respective object representation activated at different times may permit the analyzable patient with severe character pathology to achieve a degree of integration and empathy with himself and with his objects, which will contribute to transforming part-object into total-object relations. In the clinical vignette presented earlier, the patient's gradually growing awareness of his identification with his sadistic mother image as well as with his mistreated and frustrated self-image led to his awareness and eventual tolerance and integration of contradictory tendencies in himself, of love and hatred, and of his exploitative and devalued self-experiences previously projected onto his girl friends.

As regressive transferences emerge in the treatment, the patient's observing ego may be temporarily swept up by them. It is important that the analyst maintain a clear image of how a "normal" person would respond under the current circumstances to the analyst's interpretive comments. That theoretically "normal" person is usually represented by the collaborative work of the patient's observing ego with the analyst, but may be almost totally missing temporarily in all patients, and chronically in patients with severe character pathology. With the latter, therefore, the analyst's evocation of a "normal" counterpart to the patient's actual regressive behavior becomes crucial. This means that the analyst has to "split" himself into an "experiencing" part, which accompanies the patient into regression and transforms his behavior into the construction of an enacted unconscious fantasy, and a "distancing" part, which maintains objectivity precisely at times when objectivity is most challenged. The boundary function in the analyst's mind between fantasy and reality requires his tolerance of primitive fantasies and

emotions, of internal discrepancies between the understanding of what is going on and the level at which the patient can be approached, a capacity for firm convictions combined with attitudinal flexibility.

In the long run, when character analysis is systematically pursued, a paradoxical situation may emerge: some patients find it much easier to talk about their past than about the unconscious aspects of their current relation to the analyst. The analyst himself may begin to wonder whether he is neglecting the exploration of the past in his emphasis on the present. Other patients may "jump" over the real past and link the conscious present with the assumedly deepest levels of his past conflicts: the patient "easily" connects present conflicts with, for example, "castration anxiety," but no concrete and painful aspects of his childhood emerge.

Careful working through of character resistances, maintaining constant alertness to whether the patient is changing not only his current experience of the psychoanalytic situation—thus indicating authentic shifts in transference paradigms—but whether there is also a significant shift in how he experiences his past—thus expressing the working through of transference paradigms—may confirm the authenticity of psychoanalytic work, in contrast to a mechanistic translation of current difficulties into the patient's own rigidly maintained myths regarding his past.

Summary

The economic, dynamic, and structural criteria for interpretation proposed by Fenichel (1941) are updated, reformulated, and applied to the interpretation of character resistances in patients with severe character pathology, in the light of object relations theory.

The priority setting for interpretation of verbal and nonverbal material, of transference and affects, is explored and guidelines for interpretive priorities are suggested. A clinical

vignette illustrates the application of these considerations to the analysis of character resistances in the transference.

REFERENCES

ABRAHAM, K. (1919). A particular form of neurotic resistance against the psychoanalytic method. *Selected Papers on Psycho-Analysis.* New York: Basic Books, 1953, pp. 303-311.

BLUM, H. (1980). The value of reconstruction in adult psychoanalysis. *Int. J. Psychoanal.,* 61:39-54.

FENICHEL, O. (1941). *Problems of Psychoanalytic Technique.* New York: Psychoanalytic Quarterly.

——— (1945). *The Psychoanalytic Theory of Neurosis.* New York: Norton.

FERENCZI, S. (1919). On the technique of psycho-analysis. In *Further Contributions to the Theory and Technique of Psycho-Analysis.* New York: Basic Books, 1952, pp. 177-189.

GILL, M. (1980). The analysis of transference: a critique of Fenichel's "Problems of Psychoanalytic Technique." *Int. J. Psychoanal. Psychother.,* 8:45-55.

——— (1982). *Analysis of Transference,* Vol. 1. New York: Int. Univ. Press.

GLOVER, E. (1955). *The Technique of Psycho-Analysis.* New York: Int. Univ. Press.

HEIMANN, P. (1960). Countertransference. *Brit. J. Med. Psychol.,* 33:9-15.

KERNBERG, O. (1975). *Borderline Conditions and Pathological Narcissism.* New York: Aronson.

——— (1980). *Internal World and External Reality.* New York: Aronson.

RACKER, H. (1957). The meaning and uses of countertransference. *Psychoanal. Q.,* 26:303-357.

REICH, W. (1936). *Character Analysis.* New York: Farrar, Straus, & Giroux, 1972.

ROSENFELD, H. (1964). On the psychopathology of narcissism: a clinical approach. *Int. J. Psychoanal.,* 45:332-337.

21 Bloomingdale Road
White Plains, New York 10605

THE EMERGENCE OF HOSTILE AGGRESSION AND ITS DEFENSIVE AND ADAPTIVE MODIFICATIONS DURING THE SEPARATION-INDIVIDUATION PROCESS

JOHN B. MCDEVITT, M.D.

I N THIS PAPER, I SHALL EXAMINE the emergence of hostile aggression, its precursors, and its adaptive and defensive modifications during the course of the separation-individuation process from five to thirty-six months of age. I shall examine the subphase-specific developmental unfolding of the manifestations of aggression and their vicissitudes in infants and toddlers, show how hostile aggression contributes to the onset of intrapsychic conflict as well as to defense and compromise for-

Based in part on research supported by NIMH Grant MH-08238, USPHS, and FFRP Grant 069-458, Foundation Fund for Research in Psychiatry: Margaret S. Mahler, Principal Investigator, John B. McDevitt, Co-Principal Investigator. Follow-Up Study supported by The Masters Childrens Center and The Rock Foundation, New York City: Margaret S. Mahler, Consultant, John B. McDevitt, Principal Investigator, Anni Bergman, Co-Principal Investigator.

This paper is a modified version of the Brill Memorial Lecture presented to the New York Psychoanalytic Society, November 25, 1980.

273

mation in the second year of life, and describe briefly the outcome of these developments in three of the children evaluated
in a follow-up study when they were eight years old. I shall also
examine the role aggression plays in the emergence of the sense
of self. Further, I shall discuss a view of the nature of hostile
aggression suggested by this study.

My views are based on observations and inferences drawn
from the interactions of mothers and their children who participated in a naturalistic observational research study (Mahler
et al., 1975). The design of the study—a nurserylike setting in
which middle-class "average" mothers had charge of their "normal" children and in which the children were free to come and
go and to explore—was uniquely suited for the observation of
the spontaneous expression of aggressive attitudes and interactions of mothers and their infants and toddlers. Although the
total study population consisted of 38 children in 23 families,
this particular study is based on the detailed analysis of the data
on 9 children in 7 families.

I choose to define aggressive behavior as ". . . the forceful
prosecution of one's ends" (Webster, 1978). The object-related
aggressive behaviors observed ranged in forcefulness from the
removal, with or without anger, of obstacles that interfere with
the child's aims to behaviors having more elaborate motives and
that have hurtful or destructive results. I use the term aggressive
behavior to refer to the forceful prosecution of libidinal aims
and such ego interests as exploration, mastery, and coping.

The frustration of these aims leads to anger. This anger
most likely contributes to the impelling or driving quality of
hostile aggressive behavior. The forceful prosecution of one's
aims and interests now becomes in addition the hostile prosecution of these same ends, and ultimately hostile aggression
becomes an end in itself, as in revenge.

Although nonhostile aggression is a major determinant of
successful separation-individuation, most strikingly so in the
practicing subphase (Mahler, 1979, 1981; Mahler et al., 1975),
my focus here is on the emergence of hostile aggression.

The Differentiation and Practicing Subphases

Although distress from inner sources (e.g., hunger) had become less disturbing by six months, frustrating experiences that came from the outside produced even greater distress, including anger, than heretofore. During these subphases, object-directed aggressive actions without apparent anger were also seen (e.g., pulling mother's hair or biting her shoulder).

By seven to eight months, however, anger was clearly visible. At the same time that the infant was becoming more attached to his mother, he was beginning to detach, differentiate, and distance himself from her. As he did so, the mother found it increasingly necessary—in fact even obligatory—to restrain him because of his carefree, exuberant, often dangerous exploration of the "other-than-mother" world. Real anger toward the mother usually accompanied the infant's struggle to counteract, even to fight against, his mother's restraints, beginning as early as eight to nine months. By nine months most infants would on occasion hit, bite, throw, push, scratch, kick, angrily demand and snatch toys, especially the more actively endowed ones and those whose mothers were unnecessarily stimulating, frustrating, or punitive (see Spitz, 1953).

The practicing infant was more capable of directing anger specifically toward the mother and other children by the ninth month because he was more advanced in his motor, emotional, and cognitive development. But even more important, he had achieved sufficient self-object differentiation by then to be aware that it was his mother who restricted him and caused him unpleasure.

The infant's angry behaviors did not occur spontaneously (Parens, 1979). They appeared in connection with a variety of unpleasurable restrictions and frustrations of his activity, usually brought on by the mother. When the cause of unpleasure was removed, the anger subsided. Even though the infant's anger was stimulus-bound, short-lived, and limited to the specific situation that brought it on, a brief developmental crisis occurred between nine and ten months in many of the infants,

particularly the more precocious ones: they clung to their mothers as if they were fearful of losing them.

The "hatched" (Mahler, 1963) infant's more alert, outer-directed sensorium and newly found ability to actively distance himself from his mother made him more aware of his separateness and caused him to become perplexed and distressed on finding that his aims were often at cross-purposes to hers. Many of the children not only began to anxiously anticipate separation from mother on those occasions when she left the room for an interview (McDevitt, 1975), they also become sensitive to and began to anticipate mother's concern with behaviors she did not approve of, especially angry behaviors. It was her critical reaction and the fear of losing her that caused the infants to cling.

As a result of this crisis, infants began to modify their angry behaviors. These ego modifications were clearly discernible throughout the practicing subphase (from nine to fifteen months). They included: fusion with libido, displacement, restriction of aim, denial or avoidance, turning on the self or reversal, regression, clinging, falling asleep, ambitendency, as well as more adaptive efforts at delay, control, mastery as well as taming of, and coping with aggression. It was striking how early in life anger became mixed with affection as the infant teasingly and playfully pulled the mother's hair; and how early the infant displaced or deflected (Parens, 1979) anger toward the mother onto a doll or turned it against himself. Instead of attacking when angry, the infant often inhibited his action and withdrew. Anger was also expressed as negativism, provoking the mother. The pain experienced by seeing the mother leave the room for an interview was often handled by denial or avoidance, particularly if the mother used similar mechanisms. Not infrequently anger alternated in rapid succession with affection in the older infant, for example, hitting and hugging, biting and kissing, crying and smiling. In this phenomenon, which Mahler termed ambitendency (Mahler and McDevitt, 1968), the infant seeks the reassuring love of the same mother with whom he is angry.

The constructive use of forceful activity, often accompanied by anger, provided an essential impetus to the developmentally essential shift from passivity to activity. In doing so it promoted appropriate distancing from the mother and, as a consequence, self-object differentiation and individuation. By contrast, excessive anger—which was often mixed with anxiety and was brought on by overly controlling, overly intrusive, or overly anxious mothers—interfered with appropriate distancing and self-object differentiation. The infant would move away, stay away, avoid his mother; or, as a beginning reaction formation to his anger, he would cling to her. In addition, we saw the practicing infant not only avoid and ignore his mother under conditions of considerable maternal neglect, but also regress from practicing to autoerotic behaviors.

These modifications of forceful, often angry behavior represented the beginning of ego control and modulation of aggression under the aegis of the maternal auxiliary ego. Although they began as isolated instances, they slowly assumed patterns of behavior characteristic for each child and each mother-child pair.

In contrast to the situation that has been described when the mother was in the room with the infant, a different situation existed when the mother left the room for an interview. By six to eight months the infant began to show distress even though he was cared for by a familiar observer. His attachment to his mother had become exclusive. No one else would do. By eight to ten months his distress was more marked and contained an element of helpless rage. The infant had by now not only established a recognition memory of his mother but also a recall memory of her when he experienced a physiological or a psychological need for her (Fraiberg, 1969; McDevitt, 1975). As a result he now began to connect his distress with the absence of mother. Sometimes when she returned, he would reveal his anger by starting to go to her and then veering away or ignoring her altogether (see Ainsworth and Bell, 1970). During her absence, of course, it was impossible for him to express anger

toward her directly because she was not there. Instead, anger seemed to be experienced in a passive, inward-directed manner contributing to a regressive withdrawal from the environment which we have called "low-keyedness" (Mahler and McDevitt, 1968). Later in the practicing subphase, once the child could express his anger, e.g., by banging on the door, "low-keyedness" did not occur.

In contrast to the infant's distress when the mother was out of the room, the infant seemed to deny feelings of loss or anger brought on by each step in self-object differentiation during the practicing subphase. He seemed to maintain the "illusion" that he and his mother were still undifferentiated and often treated her as an extension of himself. This illusion was made possible by the mother's presence and availability as well as by becoming interested in his own body, in the world around him, and in transitional objects (Mahler et al., 1975; McDevitt, 1975; Roiphe, 1979; Winnicott, 1969).

By twelve months, modified angry behaviors were more frequent, more differentiated, more integrated, and were expressed by all infants. Object-directed angry behavior was usually mingled with playful or affectionate behavior or was used to avoid mother rather than to hit her. There were even instances of the inhibition of aggressive impulses without immediate external impetus such as mother's disapproval. It seemed that the children were channeling or controlling aggressive impulses into forms acceptable to the mother. Often the mother turned a hostile act on the part of the infant into a game, giving the infant an opportunity to test out feelings of aggression, separateness, and autonomy in a relatively safe setting, that is, in mother's lap or arms when mother was in a playful or affectionate mood.

Although by twelve months the infant began to defend himself against the attack of others, something he had not been able to do earlier, the practicing infant's angry behavior did not as yet show any deliberate intent to hurt. The practicing infant seemed oblivious to or even surprised by any hurt he happened

to inflict on the mother or another child (see A. Freud, 1972). This reaction seems to invalidate the assumption that to inflict hurt is the original aim of the aggressive act. On the contrary, the aggressive action—which has the intent of removing an obstacle or forcibly attaining one's ends—is primary; its result—the pain inflicted—is initially secondary.

During Donna's practicing subphase, Donna's mother initially gave the impression of being optimally available. Gradually, however, we began to realize that the mother's guilt over her own aggressive impulses was subtly hampering Donna's development. Donna became cautious and inhibited. It was much more important for her to know where her mother was and to keep in touch with her than it was for other infants. This hampered her distancing behaviors, her self-object differentiation, and, most importantly, her individuation (McDevitt, 1975, 1979).

Between nine and ten months a crisis developed in Donna's relationship with her mother. This followed a trip during which Donna's routine was disrupted, and she reacted with anger and distress to prohibitions enforced upon her. In the research setting she clung to her mother for several weeks, behaving as if she were afraid she would lose her mother completely. At the same time, she began to anticipate with excessive anxiousness the fact that her mother might leave the room, and she became fearful of her mother's disapproval of any angry behavior she might express toward her mother or other children.

A few examples will illustrate how Donna handled aggression. During her eighth month, Donna grabbed a toy from another child without hesitation. During her ninth month, the same month she began to anticipate her mother's leaving the room, however, Donna looked at her mother quickly and searchingly after grabbing a toy from Peter. Instead of enjoying playing with the toy, she seemed bewildered, not knowing what to do with it. In her thirteenth month, after hitting Susan on the head with a hammer without any intent to hurt, Donna seemed confused when Susan cried. She backed away and

mouthed her fingers. Soon after this, when Susan reached for Donna's toy, Donna screwed up her face, seemed compelled to hand over the toy, said, "Bye-bye," and walked away, seemingly relieved.

What we see in these examples is how Donna, as a result of the mother's prohibition of aggression and the gradual identification with this prohibition, is first unable to enjoy a toy she grabbed from another child, and finally is unable to hold on to her own toy and even seems relieved to give it up in order to avoid a struggle.

Mark's relationship with his mother had become full of inconsistencies and conflicts by six to eight months, primarily because of the mother's extreme ambivalence, which caused her to automatically misread his clues. Her unpredictability discouraged both autonomy and closeness. Although Mark wanted to get away from her in order to explore and practice, he felt a pull back to her, which caused him to be indecisive. In the crisis that occurred between nine and ten months, Mark became less alert, poorly focused, showed little interest in people or things, and clung constantly to his mother. Finally, later in the tenth month, in order to engage more fully in locomotor exploration, he avoided looking back at his mother, because whenever he did look back, the mother inadvertently signaled him to return to her. Mark's effort at avoidance was an instance of object-directed anger being used constructively in the service of self-object differentiation. It followed soon after Mark's first expression of object-directed angry behavior—biting his mother and hitting his sister. As a rule, however, instead of expressing anger directly when his mother interfered with his exploratory play, Mark whined and fussed unduly, clung to his mother, and had mild temper tantrums. Aggression was expressed passively, was turned inward, and soon began to play a role in exciting sadomasochistic play induced by the mother. She played a game of chasing Mark, pretending to bite off his finger, which he would laughingly withdraw.

Mark was not able to mobilize or to express outwardly and

constructively the amount of angry aggression toward the mother that is so necessary for the infant's push toward self-object differentiation and individuation. Only occasionally was he able to defiantly move away from his mother.

In contrast to Donna and Mark, Peter, a well-endowed, active, and alert infant, coped with a mother who was overstimulating, unpredictable, and sometimes sadistically hostile, by playing at increasing distances from her. Fortunately, she did not interfere with his angry avoidance of her nor did she interfere with his individuation.

When he was provoked, Peter had no hesitation about expressing anger vigorously toward either parent. During his eighth month, when his father's arm interfered with his water play, Peter tried to push it aside and then bit it. Later, when his mother said, "No," when he started to bite her, he bit himself instead.

Peter's nine-to-ten-month developmental crisis was brief: the result of a struggle over autonomy. Otherwise, the frustrations Peter experienced in his relationship with his mother throughout the practicing subphase did not seem to interfere, in fact, may even have encouraged his ability to achieve autonomy. This was accomplished in part through his excellent endowment and his close relationship with his father, who spent considerable time playing with him and teaching him, unlike Mark's father, who was relatively unavailable (Herzog, 1982). Although Peter's mother was hurt by his ability to find his greatest pleasure in his own functioning and in the world around him, she did not interfere. She even supported the use of his "other-than-mother" environment for growth and development. Peter was better able to control, modulate, and channel aggressive impulses in constructive directions than were Donna and Mark.

The Rapprochement Subphase

During rapprochement, cognitive and other advances cause the toddler to become acutely aware of his separateness. Although

he longs for autonomy, he also at times feels helpless and lonely and therefore longs for closeness or "oneness" with his mother. Instead of interference with his activities, the main source of his frustration and anger now becomes rivalry, jealousy, and possessiveness. He becomes jealous of the interest mother shows in anyone or anything other than himself. He feels hurt, betrayed, disappointed, and angry with his mother who can neither permit full autonomy nor restore his former sense of omnipotence. These conflicts create an intermittent angry state of mind characteristic of this subphase which may contribute to the toddler's basic depressive mood (Mahler, 1966). They also bring on a crisis in the relationship during which the toddler clings to his mother—the rapprochement crisis (Mahler, 1971, 1974).

There are now frequent, more focused, more intentional, and especially more lasting expressions of object-directed hostile aggression. Anger resulting from conflicts with the mother no longer simply flares up and disappears as it did in the practicing subphase; it continues beyond the situation in which it originated and persists in the child's mind for longer periods of time. It is now possible for feelings, thoughts, and fantasies about the mother, however primitive, to be brought to mind and remembered whether she is present or absent. This ability to hold angry feelings in the mind, along with the newly acquired ability to empathize with the feelings of others, cause the toddler to begin to direct his anger toward others with the clear intent to hurt. Although his attacks on other children sometimes appeared to be unprovoked, they seemed to be either displaced expressions of anger or delayed responses to previous frustrations. When Mark, aged fifteen months, resented the attention paid to Linda, aged eight months, he said, "Bang," and then pushed and hit her. His interest in watching her cry suggested that, by belatedly imitating his older sister who had hurt him, he was identifying with the aggressor (see Parens, 1979). Mahler (1965) has called these attacks "directed aggression."

The three danger situations—fear of loss of the object, loss of the object's love, and castration anxiety—come together during the rapprochement subphase. Although interpersonal conflict continues to exist, as a consequence of advances in ego development we see the gradual beginning of intrapsychic conflict (Mahler, 1975; McDevitt, 1971, 1975, 1979; Nagera, 1966; Settlage, 1971). On the one hand, the toddler's ego becomes intolerant of ambivalence; on the other hand, intrapsychic conflict now emerges between the toddler's aggressive impulses and the internalized prohibitions brought on by the fears characteristic of the danger situations. Aggressive impulses which have all along been disapproved of by the mother are now, as a result of identification, disapproved of by the ego and superego precursors. As a consequence, they persist in the unconscious in the form of thoughts, fantasies, and wishes.

At the same time that the toddler's expression of angry thoughts and feelings have become more complex and more persistent, so have the ego modifications of his aggression. These now become early forms of defense mechanisms resembling the defense mechanisms familiar to us in the older child.

By now the junior toddler has progressed considerably along the lines of self-object, conscious-unconscious, and ego-id differentiation. Although projective and introjective mechanisms are presumed to be early processes leading to these accomplishments, they are not easy to observe in the infant's behavior. These accomplishments do seem to be necessary, however, for the more complex defense mechanisms observed during the rapprochement subphase. These included: selective ego identifications with mother's prohibitions and regulations (different from the mirroring, introjection, and imitation seen earlier); more complex displacements and projections of aggression from the mother onto the animate and inanimate, "non-mother" world, e.g., in renewed stranger and separation anxiety, in a variety of fears, and in blaming one's own bad behavior on a sibling or pet; and splitting when the toddler directs his anger toward the "bad" caretaker and reserves his

love for the absent "good" object, the mother. Most important, they also included the beginning emergence of repression and reaction formation. These will be illustrated in Donna and Peter. Some children showed a marked inhibition against playing with water, paints, or play dough. This was their response to anal, urinary, and masturbatory conflicts. Denial continued to be used to avoid the pain and anger brought on by many situations—e.g., the awareness of the anatomical differences between the sexes (Roiphe and Galenson, 1981).

Some children directed aggression toward the self in more complex ways than the earlier sudden biting of the self, which probably resulted from insufficient self-object differentiation and the inability to anticipate pain. Hostile aggression now resulted in low moods, accident-proneness, and, at times, temper tantrums. Most children, however, showed a greater tendency to control and inhibit the expression of hostile aggression, to be more compliant, and to express aggression in a more mature manner, for example, verbally and in symbolic play. Hostile aggression was occasionally intermingled with libido, resulting in sadomasochistic behavior. This was true of Mark. It was universally dealt with by identification with the aggressor—the frustrating mother—as indicated by use of the word *no* (Spitz, 1957, 1965). When anger became too intense, for example, during the rapprochement crisis or at times of severe castration reactions, regression to more infantile behavior occurred.

The same capacity to empathize with another child or adult that led to the overt expression of hostile aggression proper, as illustrated when Mark hit Linda, was also essential for the beginning capacity to have concern, to care, to feel sorry for another person who is in distress. These expressions of sympathy are reaction formations (reparation, undoing) and are forerunners of the benign superego. Furer (1967) described eloquently how a toddler's ability to say, "I'm sorry," to the mother involved an obvious identification with her, not as the aggressor but as a consoler and comforter.

During the rapprochement subphase, Donna became in-

creasingly ambivalent toward her mother. This ambivalence reached a climax at nineteen months when Donna blamed a mild infection and an injection on her mother. Donna developed a severe rapprochement crisis which was made worse by the mother's intolerance of aggression. In order to protect the relationship with her mother, Donna projected and displaced her anger onto the outside "non-mother" world and at the same time regressed to an infantile clinging relationship with her mother. As a result, she became an extremely fearful, shy, quiet, overly cautious, inhibited little girl who was quite possessive of her mother and who suffered excessive separation anxiety. When particularly upset, she turned aggression upon herself, chewing and biting her fingers, leaving distinct teeth marks.

Although Donna began to recover in the beginning of her third year, a marked castration reaction precipitated by a urinary infection and a traumatic physical examination when she was twenty-nine months old reactivated her extreme ambivalence and once again brought on regressive behavior and symptom formation similar to that present during the rapprochement crisis. Toward the end of the third year Donna appeared more at ease and happier. A positive oedipal attachment to her father and an identification with the maternal aspects of her mother were seen in play sessions (McDevitt, 1979).

At the time of a follow-up study,[1] Donna, aged eight and a half, showed the same marked timidity and inability to assert herself. Psychological testing revealed a fear of retaliation if she did not conform. This fear was the result of her projection of hostility onto the mother. Donna felt that if she were more assertive she would lose her mother (the maternal introject). Because of these fears, passive-dependent trends took precedence over more advanced developmental tasks. Even the rivalry of the positive oedipal complex, which showed itself in a passive oral form, was experienced as too dangerous to the

[1] The follow-up study of seventeen children consisted of three interviews with the parents, three with the children, school visits and school reports, home visits, and psychological testing.

positive relationship with the mother. The use of projection and identification led to a personality organization suggestive of altruistic surrender (A. Freud, 1936).

The extremely ambivalent, sadomasochistic relationship between Mark and his mother—which had earlier interfered with practicing, self-object differentiation, and individuation —continued into the rapprochement subphase. A rapprochement crisis began during the seventeenth month when Mark became extremely demanding of his mother and sought her constant attention, often by seeking to play provocative games with her. For several months a pattern of rapid alternation could be observed between extreme clinging and excessive withdrawal from his mother. Mark would insist on being picked up and then angrily demand to be let down. Once down, he would cry as if his mother had abandoned him forever. He responded to inevitable frustrations either by having temper tantrums or by hitting his mother. He coerced her and clung to her as if she might leave or withdraw her love at any time because of his hostility.

Aggression continued to create significant problems for Mark at the time of the follow-up study when he was eight years old. He was an impish, teasing, provocative child. His sadomasochistic relationships had been internalized and were now apparent in his interviews. Fears, at night, of sharks who might bite were the consequence of a displacement of oral-aggressive impulses. He was unhappy at school, had few friends, felt stupid, and his pent-up aggression made him so restless and impatient that he thought he might explode. Poorly neutralized and controlled aggression contributed to impulsivity, intolerance of frustration, and distractability. These were observed clinically, and they were confirmed by psychological and educational testing.

Psychological testing also revealed that the overpowering internalized relationship with the mother, along with the frequent absences of the father because of an incapacitating illness, created a more lively negative oedipal complex than a positive

one. Mark demonstrated some psychosexual confusion despite the fact that his gender identity was masculine.

In contrast to Donna and Mark, who represented the middle range of pathology of the seventeen children evaluated in the follow-up study, Peter fared better during the rapprochement subphase and at the time of follow-up, as he had during the first two subphases.

Peter's rapprochement crisis was precipitated by the birth of a sister when he was sixteen months old. He was initially sad, withdrawn, and somewhat intolerant of his mother's brief absences from the room. Within two months, however, Peter had used his active resources, which included language, to overcome his "depression." He now found great pleasure in his relationship with other people and in play.

At first Peter had alternated between attempting to hit and bite or pet his sister (ambitendency). Slowly we saw a definite change in his behavior; by twenty months he only petted her. The mother's admonitions had become internalized in the form of precursors of repression and reaction formation (Bornstein, 1935; Mahler and McDevitt, 1968).

It was characteristic of Peter to use play constructively whenever he seemed anxious or disturbed. He found a way of coping with his mother's unpredictability in the more predictable environment of inanimate objects and play. At the same time, his active masculine play revealed a strong identification with his father.

At the time of follow-up, Peter at age eight and a half appeared self-assured and confident. He had excellent rapport with both adults and children. He could stand up for himself and assert himself forcibly when it was appropriate to do so. He also showed the typical ego interests and attitudes of a latency boy, was enthusiastic about school work, and performed at a high level both at school and on psychological tests. Mild neurotic symptoms did not interfere with these achievements. His personality was said to be organized on neurotic lines on psychological tests, which also revealed that positive oedipal

themes and conflicts were exceptionally lively and that one of Peter's three wishes was to have a wife and children. We were pleasantly surprised to find that Peter had a good relationship with his mother and that he was friendly with girls his own age. There was an age-adequate assumption of masculine gender identity and a growing capacity to derive satisfaction and to extract genuine admiration from his father through identification and real achievements.

Discussion

I shall limit my discussion to four aspects of aggression and its modifications that can be inferred from this study: the onset of object-directed aggression and its modifications; the role aggression plays in the differentiation process; the relation of aggressive behavior to the aggressive drive; and the continuity and persistence of modifications of object-related hostile aggression.

Onset of Object-directed Aggression and Its Modifications

As we have seen, at as early as nine months, the infant begins to recollect the pain brought on by his mother's absences from the room and to become fearful that she might leave again. In a similar manner he now begins to anticipate his mother's critical responses to certain behaviors used to attain his ends, especially those behaviors that are contrary, are accompanied by anger, and are persistent. For both of these reasons the infant may develop a crisis during which he clings to his mother from roughly nine to ten months, acting as if he were fearful of losing her. The fact that angry aggression is involved in this developmental crisis is partially confirmed by the infant's beginning modification of his angry behavior.

We might ask why the mother's critical, often angry, response to the infant's contrary and angry behavior causes him to modify this behavior. Presumably he modifies it for two in-

terdependent reasons. First, the infant experiences unpleasure as a result of his mother's angry, scolding criticism. By this age the mother's criticisms are more severe because of the more marked struggle between her and her infant. At that same time the infant is more sensitive to his mother's facial expressions and attitudes, and therefore to her criticism. Second, it would appear that her critical behavior also causes him to fear and to anticipate object loss. There are several ways in which the mother's scolding and the fear of object loss may be related. The infant's anger may remind him of the anger he experienced when his mother was out of the room. His mother's angry criticisms may have become connected in his mind with occasions when she actually left him. Finally, the feelings he experiences when his mother scolds him, e.g., confusion, puzzlement, etc., may be similar to feelings he experienced when she was out of the room. If so, these feelings would cause him to fear object loss. When Donna, aged nine months, took Paul's toy, she looked at her mother quickly and searchingly. She seemed bewildered, not knowing what to do with the toy. At the same age she clung to her mother, fearing she would leave the room.

Benjamin (1961), writing about the fear of object loss (infantile separation anxiety), stated: "What is new, as I see our data, is the more definitive organization of the libidinal investment of the mother; the further development of the earlier made distinction between mother and others . . . as well as the greatly increased capacity of the ego to anticipate and predict. To these must be added what is at least a highly *contributory*, and possibly a *necessary condition* for these particular anxiety manifestations: the maturational organization of aggression as such into *object-directed* hostility and anger, with the resultant marked increase in fear of object loss" (p. 662).

Tennes and Lampl (1966) systematically studied the same data by rating eight variables. They concluded: "The best predictors of the intensity of infantile separation anxiety were found to be the mother's inhibition of the child's aggression and the mother's hostility toward the child" (p. 436).

The nine-to-ten-month developmental crisis occurs many months after the onset of stranger reactions and several months after the onset of separation reactions. It does occur at the same time as the beginning anticipation of object loss. It is not related to loss of the object's love, which does not appear until the rapprochement subphase.

Because this "crisis" occurs at the end of the differentiation process and because it seems in part to reflect a relation between separation anxiety and aggression, it might be called a "differentiation crisis," foreshadowing on a sensorimotor level of cognitive and affective development the rapprochement crisis that occurs later on a symbolic level and similarly reflects in part the relation between the vicissitudes of separation and aggression.

Many significant changes that occur in the infant's maturation and development in the third quarter of the first year are necessary underpinnings of this "crisis." Between eight and twelve months the infant reaches Piaget's fourth stage in sensorimotor development (Piaget and Inhelder, 1969). He acquires a beginning object permanence, anticipation, intentionality, and means-ends relations. He has now acquired the capacity to experience the emotions of fear and anger in his interaction with others (Emde et al., 1976).

At this age the infant has an increasingly complex network of interrelated memory systems, for example, recognition memory, motor memory, affective memory, imaginal memory, and beginning recall memory, e.g., of the absent mother. These memories and their associations are necessary for the development of anticipation and for the more alert sensorium of the hatched child who is more outer-directed (Mahler, 1963). His movements are more active, both away from and toward his mother; and he is both aware of and recollects his mother's comings and goings, often becoming fearful when she is not immediately at hand.

As we have seen, infants can now react to persons not visually present, affectively respond to their loss and recovery, and experience their affective reactions as being directly related

to the specific event, e.g., the mother's absence (Sroufe, 1979). Anticipation extends beyond the motor to the affective and cognitive realms, for example, anticipating mother leaving the room, and acts as a motivating signal to the infant, for example, to try to prevent his mother from doing so (Emde et al., 1976). As a next step in development, behaviors which bring on the mother's criticism begin to be modified, for example, by inhibition, displacement, turning on the self, or reversal, by fusion with libido or by ambitendency. The organization of infant behavior and the sense of self is now meaningful and is influenced by past experiences and anticipated outcomes (Sroufe, 1979).

The early struggle and its modifications between infant and mother over autonomy and closeness during the differentiation and practicing subphase is probably the forerunner of later struggles and conflicts: for example, rapprochement, sibling, and oedipal conflicts. How it is resolved may effect the ability to resolve later conflicts.

Aggression, Differentiation, Adaptation, and Individuation

Aggression, with or without anger, enhances turning passive into active and promotes distancing and self-object differentiation, enabling the infant to experience himself as separate and distinct from his mother, as an autonomous and independent person. Early in life this essential adaptive shift from passive to active is enhanced by primitive motor and gestural imitations, later by selective ego identifications. Aggression also enables the infant to reach out to and hold on to the libidinal object (A. Freud, 1965) and to successfully engage in a variety of activities.

The extent to which the infant is able to successfully summon his mother, and later to successfully overcome obstacles himself, will cause him to feel competent and effective and will enhance his self-esteem in an adaptive manner. The opposite situation leads to destructive aggression and diminished self-

esteem. It is not only, however, the nature of the infant's and toddler's ongoing experiences that determine his self-esteem. Even more important, as illustrated in Donna's case, is the effect of intrapsychic conflict.

The infant's libidinal attachment to the mother is more specific, more exclusive, and more stable than are his angry reactions to her when she frustrates his activities and his ends. These reactions certainly do not represent a specific aggressive attachment to the mother. Up until fifteen months the infant's anger disappears as soon as unpleasure has ceased. As Anna Freud (1972) has pointed out, aggression along with its coordinated affects of anger, hate, and resentment, remains anaclitic longer than does libido, that is, it remains more clearly tied to pleasure-pain and satisfaction-frustration experiences in relation to the mother. Aggression does not become enduringly invested in the love object as early or even in the same way that libido does under favorable conditions for development.

The existence of a secure and firm affectionate tie to the mother is a necessary means of protecting the mother-infant relationship from the onslaught of the infant's hostile aggression in the rapprochement subphase. Unless this libidinal bond occurs early and outweighs hostile aggression, the toddler's personality is highly vulnerable to disruption by hostility, irrespective of the use of defense mechanisms (A. Freud, 1965).

During the rapprochement subphase the toddler's new-found mental capacity permits him to see the complex interrelationships between himself, his mother, and a rival. It also contributes to the awareness of his rivalry, jealousy, and possessiveness as new and more persistent sources of anger. As a result, both the motive for and the cognitive ability to have a wish to hurt now exist. These wishes become part of hostile fantasies which may lead to intrapsychic conflicts.

Aggressive Behavior and the Aggressive Drive

Parens (1979) provides a comprehensive review of the literature as well as a discussion of the relation between aggressive be-

havior in young children and drive theory, based on a research study of the development of aggression in infants and toddlers.[2] For a wider-ranging approach to the phenomenon and classification of aggression and its relation to the dual-instinct theory, see Arlow (1973), Brenner (1971, 1983), A. Freud (1972), Freud (1915, 1920), Greenacre (1960, 1971), Hartmann, Kris, and Loewenstein (1949), Marcovitz (1973), Rochlin (1973), Roiphe (1979), Spitz (1953), Stone (1971, 1979), Waelder (1960), Weil (1978), and Winnicott (1969).

For the purpose of this discussion I shall assume that aggressive behavior defined as ". . . the forceful prosecution of one's ends" (Webster, 1978) is the manifestation of an aggressive drive (see Greenacre, 1960; Mahler, 1974; Mahler et al., 1975; Parens, 1979; Spitz, 1953; Weil, 1978). This behavior refers to maturational processes, biological urges, and to the attainment of psychological wishes by forcibly overcoming resistances and obstacles.

Sufficient frustration of these wishes (or helplessness, trauma, pain, and narcissistic injury) brings on anger and eventually hostility (see Parens, 1979; Rochlin, 1973; Stone, 1971). This leads to the forceful prosecution of hostile ends, as in revenge, or to defense and compromise formation. By this time the toddler is capable of having fantasies with the primary aim of hurting the object (see Greenacre, 1960; Mahler, 1965; Parens, 1979; Weil, 1978).

Anger and, later on, hatred and hostility are not simply the outcome of experiences of unpleasure and frustration; they are also the result of a biological and psychological "potential" or "readiness" of the ego to react to unpleasure with anger (Panel, 1957). In this sense anger and, later, object-directed hostile aggression are based both on an innate neurophysiological genetic and maturational blueprint and on the expectable conflicts with the mother which begin to be internalized during the rapprochement subphase. This developmental sequence is seen in

[2] There are many similarities, as well as differences, in the findings of this study and the findings of Parens's study.

the younger infant's distress and rage, the older infant's anger, and in the toddler's hate and anal sadism.

These considerations lead me to speculate that hostile aggression resulting from the interaction of different levels of maturational readiness, psychological development, and the inevitable experiences of unpleasure occurring during the mother's caretaking is a further development or expression of the nature of the aggressive drive, or at least of its aim, particularly as the concept is used in clinical practice—a development shaped by the affect of anger and its subsequent more complex elaborations. This developmental process would be similar to the gradual arousal of the libidinal drive by the mother's stimulation of the erotogenic zones which regularly occurs during her caretaking as each zone matures (see Loewald, 1971).

Many affects, ideas, and fantasies other than hostile ones are also internalized and expressed symbolically, but hostile impulses, particularly once they are held in the mind in a sustained manner during the rapprochement subphase, bring the toddler into such dangerous conflict with the mother that they must be forced into the unconscious by repression and other defense mechanisms as a result of intense anxiety over the loss of the mother, of mothering, and of mother's love. Hostility now seems to be brought on not only by external stimuli and conscious fantasies, but also by unconscious imagery, fantasy, and thought (Holt, 1976; Noy, 1982; Parens, 1979, pp. 6 and 106n.; von Bertalanffy in Panel, 1957, 1965). The persistence of these images in the unconscious is one explanation for the persistence of object-directed hostile aggression as a powerful motivational force or drive.

Hate and hostility as a form of aggression and as an aspect of ambivalence do not seem present before the existence of distinct self- and object representations characteristic of the rapprochement and fourth subphases. Hate may be said to differ from anger in the same way that love is different from a need-satisfying libidinal relationship (J. Sandler in Panel, 1972). Hate is an attitude of the ego toward the object, not

simply the result of object-directed aggressive impulses (Freud, 1915).

Insofar as hate becomes persistent in the mind during rapprochement, as does love, hate may come to have a quality of constancy similar to, if not comparable with that present in "libidinal" object constancy (J. Sandler in Panel, 1972). The balance between the two is important. In the reasonably healthy adult, constancy of love will far outweigh that of hate. If the reverse is the case, we would expect to find severe pathology.

The Continuity of the Modifications of Hostile Aggression

During the practicing subphase the defensive behaviors observed in this study were short-lived and stimulus-bound. They were closer to primary-process functioning, and they existed only momentarily—until the current conflict with the mother was resolved. Each involved a temporary modification of aggression directed toward the object, for example, by inhibition or displacement or by the influence of libido. Even though these early defenses only later became relatively autonomous of the environment, they may have had some bearing on subsequent defense formation in the rapprochement subphase—probably by shaping action patterns and prerepresentational feeling states and images.

During the rapprochement subphase, not only is the toddler able to hold angry fantasies in his mind for increasingly longer periods of time, but more complex, more lasting, more structured, and more persistent defense mechanisms now come into being as a way of dealing with internal conflict. The fact that these defense mechanisms are persistent is another reason to view hostile aggression as a persistent force.

Although it could not have been predicted, particularly because of the vicissitudes of life and of intrapsychic conflict, one of the most striking findings of the study was the continuity and persistence of modifications of aggression from the second half of the first year to eight years of age in many of the chil-

dren. This has been illustrated in Donna and Mark where regressive forces outweighed progressive forces (A. Freud, 1965). By contrast Peter demonstrated that neutralization, modulation, and the constructive use of aggression contribute in the third year to progress in reality testing, language, secondary-process thought, and more advanced, adaptive defense mechanisms, in particular selective ego identification and repression which replace the mechanism of splitting. These changes in the ego, which persisted into the eighth year in Peter, enable the senior toddler to integrate "good" and "bad" aspects of objects into one unified representation. Libido outweighs aggression, and the toddler achieves some degree of object and self-constancy (Mahler et al., 1975; McDevitt, 1975, 1979; McDevitt and Mahler, 1980).[3]

Summary and Conclusion

I have examined the ontogeny of hostile-determined and defensively shaped behaviors or their precursors during the course of the separation-individuation process, with particular emphasis on their impact on objects, on the self, and on the formation of intrapsychic conflicts, defenses, symptoms, and compromise formations. The aggressive potential in each child as well as his ability to modulate aggression depend on the child's endowment and on his relationship with his parents. The manifestations of aggression, as well as the success or failure in coping with aggression, become evident as they influence and are influenced by the characteristics of each subphase of the separation-individuation process. The subphase-specific changes in the manifestations and modifications of aggression are in part determined by the evolving establishment of self-object differentiation and of distinct self- and object representations and, in particular, on the development and nature of

---

[3] For a detailed description of these constructive changes during the fourth subphase, see Mahler, 1965; Mahler and McDevitt, 1968; Mahler et al., 1975, especially pp. 76-120, 225-230.

intrapsychic conflict along with the ego's ability to master and cope with conflict.

Under unfavorable conditions, problems in the development of aggression during the differentiating and practicing subphases contribute to failures to resolve similar problems which exist on a symbolic, intrapsychic, and conflictual level during the rapprochement and fourth subphase. This failure, in turn, enhances the conflicts in the oedipal phase of development and makes their resolution more difficult.

Under favorable conditions the child's libidinal investment in the mother outweighs his aggressive cathexis of her in each subphase. Development and adaptation proceed, and the toddler eventually attains some degree of object and self-constancy in the third and fourth subphases. These developmental advances prepare him to successfully resolve current and future conflicts.

REFERENCES

AINSWORTH, M. D. S. & BELL, S. M. (1970). Attachment, exploration, and separation: Illustrated by the behavior of one-year-olds in a strange situation. *Child Devel.*, 41:49-67.
ARLOW, J. A. (1973). Perspectives on aggression in human adaptation. *Psychoanal. Q.*, 42:178-184.
BENJAMIN, J. D. (1961). Some developmental observations relating to the theory of anxiety. *J. Amer. Psychoanal. Assn.*, Vol. 9: 652-668.
BORNSTEIN, B. (1935). Phobia in a two-and-a-half-year-old child. *Psychoanal. Q.*, 4:93-119.
BRENNER, C. (1971). The psychoanalytic concept of aggression. *Int. J. Psychoanal.*, 52:179-184.
——— (1983). *The Mind in Conflict*. New York: Int. Univ. Press.
EMDE, R., GAENSBAUER, T. & HARMON, R. (1976). *Emotional Expression in Infancy: A Biobehavioral Study. Psychol. Issues*, Monogr. 37. New York: Int. Univ. Press.
FRAIBERG, S. (1969). Libidinal object constancy and mental representation. *Psychoanal. Study Child*, 24:9-47.
FREUD, A. (1936). *The Ego and the Mechanisms of Defense. Writings*, 2. New York: Int. Univ. Press, 1966.
——— (1965). *Normality and Pathology in Childhood: Assessments of Development. Writings*, 6. New York: Int. Univ. Press.
——— (1972). Comments on aggression. *Int. J. Psychoanal.*, 53:163-171.
FREUD, S. (1915). Instincts and their vicissitudes. *S. E.*, 14.

—— (1920). Beyond the pleasure principle. *S. E.*, 20.

FURER, M. (1967). Some developmental aspects of the superego. *Int. J. Psychoanal.*, 48:277-280.

GREENACRE, P. (1960). Considerations regarding the parent-infant relationship. *Int. J. Psychoanal.*, 41:571-584.

—— (1971). Notes on the influence and contributions of ego psychology to the practice of psychoanalysis. In *Separation-Individuation: Essays in Honor of Margaret S. Mahler*, ed. J. B. McDevitt & C. G. Settlage. New York: Int. Univ. Press.

HARTMANN, H., KRIS, E. & LOEWENSTEIN, R. M. (1949). Notes on the theory of aggression. *Psychoanal. Study Child*, 3/4:9-36.

HERZOG, J. M. (1982). On father hunger: the father's role in the modulation of aggressive drive and fantasy. In *Father and Child—Developmental and Clinical Perspectives*, ed. S. H. Cath, A. R. Gurwitt & J. M. Ross. Boston: Little, Brown.

HOLT, R. R. (1976). *Drive or Wish? A Reconsideration of the Psychoanalytic Theory of Motivation. Psychol. Issues*, Monogr. 36. New York: Int. Univ. Press.

LOEWALD, H. (1971). On motivation and instinct theory. *Psychoanal. Study Child*, 26:91-128.

MAHLER, M. S. (1963). Thoughts about development and individuation. *Psychoanal. Study Child*, 18:307-342. New York: Int. Univ. Press.

—— (1965). On the significance of the normal separation-individuation phase. In *Drives, Affects, Behavior*, 2, ed. M. Schur. New York: Int. Univ. Press, pp. 161-169.

—— (1966). Notes of the development of basic moods: the depressive. In *Psychoanalysis—A General Psychology: Essays in Honor of Heinz Hartmann*, ed. R. M. Loewenstein, L. M. Newman, M. Schur & A. J. Solnit. New York: Int. Univ. Press, pp. 152-168.

—— (1971). A study of the separation-individuation process and its possible application to borderline phenomena in the psychoanalytic situation. *Psychoanal. Study Child*, 26:403-424.

—— (1974). Symbiosis and individuation: the psychological birth of the human infant. In Mahler (1979), Vol. 2, pp. 149-165.

—— (1975). On the current status of the infantile neurosis. *J. Amer. Psychoanal. Assn.*, 23:327-333.

—— (1979). *Selected Papers*. New York: Aronson.

—— (1981). Aggression in the service of separation-individuation: case study of a mother-daughter relationship. *Psychoanal. Q.*, 50:625-638.

—— & McDEVITT, M. D. (1968). Observations on adaptation and defense *in statu nascendi:* developmental precursors in the first two years of life. *Psychoanal. Q.*, 37:1-26.

———— (1982). Thoughts on the emergence of the sense of self, with particular emphasis on the body self. *J. Amer. Psychoanal. Assn.*, 30:827-848.

—— PINE, F. & BERGMAN, A. (1975). *The Psychological Birth of the Human Infant*. New York: Basic Books.

MARCOVITZ, E. (1973). Aggression in human adaptation. *Psychoanal. Q.*, 42:226-233.

McDEVITT, J. B. (1971). Preoedipal determinants of an infantile neurosis. In *Separation-Individuation, Essays in Honor of Margaret S. Mahler*, ed. J. B. McDevitt & C. G. Settlage. New York: Int. Univ. Press, pp. 201-226.

——— (1975). Separation-individuation and object constancy. *J. Amer. Psychoanal. Assn.*, 23:713-742.

——— (1979). The role of internalization in the development of object relations during the separation-individuation phase. *J. Amer. Psychoanal. Assn.*, 27:327-343.

——— & MAHLER, M. S. (1980). Object constancy, individuality and internalization. In *The Course of Life*, Vol. 1, ed. S. I. Greenspan & G. H. Pollock. Bethesda, Md.: NIMH, p. 407.

NAGERA, H. (1966). Sleep and its disturbances approached developmentally. *Psychoanal. Study Child*, 21:393-447.

NOY, P. (1982). A revision of the psychoanalytic theory of affect. *Annual Psychoanal.*, 10:139-186.

PANEL (1957). The theory of aggression. M. Ostow, reporter. *J. Amer. Psychoanal. Assn.*, 5:556-563.

——— (1972). Aggression. A. Lussier, reporter. *Int. J. Psychoanal.*, 53:13-19.

PARENS, H. (1979). *The Development of Aggression in Early Childhood*. New York: Aronson.

PIAGET, J. & INHELDER, B. (1969). *The Psychology of the Child*. New York: Basic Books.

ROCHLIN, G. (1973). *Man's Aggression: Defense of the Self*. Boston: Gambit.

ROIPHE, H. (1979). A theoretical overview of preoedipal development during the first four years of life. In *The Basic Handbook of Child Psychiatry*, ed. J. D. Call, J. D. Noshpitz, R. C. Cohen & I. N. Berlin. New York: Basic Books, pp. 118-127.

——— & Galenson, E. (1981). *Infantile Origins of Sexual Identity*. New York: Int. Univ. Press.

SETTLAGE, C. F. (1971). On the libidinal aspect of early psychic development and the genesis of infantile neurosis. In *Separation-Individuation, Essays in Honor of Margaret S. Mahler*, ed. J. B. McDevitt & C. F. Settlage. New York: Int. Univ. Press, pp. 131-154.

SPITZ, R. A. (1953). Aggression: its role in the establishment of object relations. In *Drives, Affects, and Behavior*, Vol. 1, ed. R. M. Loewenstein. New York: Int. Univ. Press, pp. 126-138.

——— (1957). *No and Yes: On the Genesis of Human Communication*. New York: Int. Univ. Press.

——— (1965). *The First Year of Life*. New York: Int. Univ. Press.

SROUFE, A. L. (1979). Socioemotional development. In *Handbook of Infant Development*, ed. J. D. Osofsky. New York: Wiley, pp. 462-516.

STONE, L. (1971). Reflections on the psychoanalytic concept of aggression. *Psychoanal. Q.*, 40:195-244.

——— (1979). Remarks on certain unique conditions of human aggression. *J. Amer. Psychoanal. Assn.*, 27:27-65.

TENNES, K. H. & LAMPL, E. D. (1966). Some aspects of mother-child relationship pertaining to infantile separation anxiety. *J. Nerv. Ment. Dis.*, 143(5): 426-437.

VON BERTALANFFY, L. (1965). Comments on aggression. In *Psychoanalysis and the Study of Behavior*, ed. I. G. Sarason. Princeton: Van Nostrand.

WAELDER, R. (1960). *Basic Theory of Psychoanalysis*. New York: Int. Univ. Press.

Webster's New Dictionary of Synonyms (1978). Springfield, Mass.: Merrian Co.

WEIL, A. (1978). Maturational variations and genetic-dynamic issues. *J. Amer. Psychoanal. Assn.*, 26:461-491.

WINNICOTT, D. W. (1969). The use of an object. *Int. J. Psychoanal.*, 50:711-716.

55 East 87th Street
New York, New York 10128

SPLITTING OF THE EGO AND ITS RELATION TO PARENT LOSS

HAROLD P. BLUM, M.D.

CONTEMPORARY VIEWS OF DEFENSE HAVE TAKEN into account the developmental history and hierarchy of defenses; the role of defense in normal as well as pathological development; the influence of defense on other ego functions, and vice versa; change in the means and functions of defense; the relation of defensive style to character and identification; and the complexity of the defense organization in inhibition, gratification, adaptation, etc. Anna Freud (1936) gave us the most specific, elaborate studies of defense with implications for a broad range of considerations that transcended the role of defense in psychological disturbance. Defense was related not only to ego constriction but to ego development, to coordination with, and to adaptation to the social environment and the object world. There is always a price paid for socialization and acculturation in terms of restriction and inhibition, proclivity to neurosis and guilt. But defense also has an essential protective function related to adaptation and survival, stressed in the antecedent formulation of ego instincts. Defense has intrafamilial and social-cultural dimensions and implications, and Anna Freud (1965, p. 177) pointedly noted, "all defense mechanisms serve simultaneously internal drive restriction and external adaptation, which are merely two sides of the same picture."

This paper deals with "splitting of the ego in the process

301

of defense" and with Anna Freud's emphasis in considering
that form of splitting in relation to adaptation to the environment. The form of splitting described by Freud (1927, 1938,
1940), associated with denial and a consequence of defense, is
different from other forms of splitting described in the literature. Splitting has other significant meanings. The "splitting"
noted in those papers, although related, is not identical to the
splitting that Mahler (Mahler et al., 1975) has described and
illustrated developmentally in the process of separation-individuation. Hostile aggression is "split off" from the primary
object representations to preserve and protect the "good object"
representation. This is the type of splitting of representations
that Kernberg (1975) explicates as a defense or as a defensive
use of failure of integration of libidinal and aggressive representations. "Splitting" as a primitive defense, and not consequent to simultaneous denial and acceptance of reality, has been
described by Kernberg in the continued maintenance of infantile contradictory—all good and all bad—self- and object representations and contradictory ego and affect states commonly
found and given special meaning in borderline states. The polarized affects are subsumed within contradictory ego states
which are kept separate and which may be alternately activated.
In the splitting of representations between all good and all bad
(emphasized in earlier literature by Melanie Klein in a different
developmental framework), neither set of representations is
realistic, whereas in the splitting of the ego, in Freud's sense,
reality is also partially retained and there is a simultaneous
struggle to both preserve and alter reality. The preoedipal concepts of representational splitting were placed in developmental
sequence and context during separation-individuation (Mahler
et al, 1975), and address other developmental and clinical issues
than the "ego split" of denial and acknowledgement of reality.

This "splitting" may be preambivalent if it results from a
developmental deficit in synthesis or is associated with intense
ambivalence which is not tolerated and defensively avoided.
Splitting is a metaphor; it does not refer to fragmentation of
intrapsychic representations or "part objects" but to dissociation

of affectively opposite preconscious psychic experiences. With ego development, repression and displacement of self and object directed aggression contribute to "split" or segregated good and bad, idealized and denigrated self or object images. Various forms of splitting may interweave, and in the preoedipal period may contribute to a developmental failure or instability of self- and object constancy.

Splitting has also been noted in other than borderline and narcissistic disorders (Segel, 1981; Rangell, 1982). Splitting occurs in normal oedipal development and is seen in the different imagesof the father as comforting and castrating, protective and punitive; similarly, the mother as virgin and as prostitute is found in universal oedipal fantasy. The splitting of parental imagoes between idealized and devalued is also part of a universal oedipal fantasy system, namely, the family romance. This form of splitting is coordinated with the child's actual perceptions of parental limitations and feelings of narcissistic injury and oedipal disappointment. In addition, there are many other meanings of splitting (Lichtenberg & Slap, 1973; Pruyser, 1975; Ross & Dunn, 1980). The form of splitting that Freud associated with denial will be the specific subject of this paper, a form of splitting in which the ego at once remains realistic and denies, disavows, and inevitably distorts reality. While various forms of splitting mechanisms are described by Freud,[1] the form of splitting he described in "Splitting of the Ego in the Process of

---

[1] Freud (1938, p. 77) also noted ego splitting in relation to trauma. This would historically and conceptually trace the splitting after traumatic object loss to the effect of trauma and not only to denial. Two related formulations were introduced earlier. The splitting of representations was described first (Freud, 1923a). "It does not need much analytic perspicacity to guess that God and the Devil were originally identical—were a single figure which was later split into two figures with opposite attributes. In the earliest stages of religion God himself still possessed all the terrifying features which were afterward combined to form a counterpart of him.

"We have here an example of the process, with which we are familiar, by which an idea that has a contradictory—an ambivalent—content becomes divided into two sharply contrasted opposites" (p. 86). Considering conflicting ego identifications, Freud (1923b) observed, "If they obtain the upper hand and become too numerous, unduly powerful and incompatible with one an-

Defense" (1938), deals with the struggle between the acceptance of or turning away from a painful, anxiety-provoking reality.

I shall refer particularly to cases of parent loss in childhood and to the splitting of the ego in such situations. I cite cases of object loss, where object constancy and the oedipal phase have been attained, recognizing that the consequences of object loss are crucially related to ego development and object relations. I shall refer primarily to parent loss because of death. Although parental death is unique, similar reactions may ensue with loss due to divorce, desertion, disappearance, etc. I shall take as a point of departure Freud's discussion of splitting in relation to fetishism and to parent loss, to denial of loss of the penis and of loss of the object. Freud (1927) stated:

> In the analysis of two young men I learned that each—one when he was two years old and the other when he was ten—had failed to take cognizance of the death of his beloved father—had "scotomized" it—and yet neither of them had developed a psychosis. . . . It was only one current in their mental life that had not recognized their father's death; there was another current which took full account of that fact. The attitude which fitted in with the wish and the attitude which fitted in with reality existed side by side. In one of my two cases this split had formed

---

other, a pathological outcome will not be far off. It may come to a disruption of the ego in consequence of the different identifications becoming cut off from one another by resistances; perhaps the secret of the cases of what is described as 'multiple personality' is that the different identifications seize hold of consciousness in turn. Even when things do not go so far as this, there remains the question of conflicts between the various identifications into which the ego comes apart, conflicts which cannot after all be described as entirely pathological" (pp. 30-31). A more normal, transient, ego-controlled form of splitting (possibly related to the therapeutic "split," or dissociation between the observing and experiencing ego) was also recognized: "the ego . . . splits itself during a number of its functions—temporarily at least. Its parts can come together again afterwards. That is not exactly a novelty, though it may perhaps be putting an unusual emphasis on what is generally known. On the other hand, we are familiar with the notion that pathology, by making things larger and coarser, can draw our attention to normal conditions which would otherwise have escaped us" (Freud, 1933, p. 58).

the basis of a moderately severe obsessional neurosis [pp. 155-156].

In cases of childhood parent loss, the ego split is coordinate with a subjectively distorted and divided object world. In the neurotic "ego splitting," denial is circumscribed, and reality sense and testing are relatively preserved. While the loss is partially denied, present reality is actually radically transformed from the past. In addition to the object loss itself and separation of the living and dead, the child's life situation has been irrevocably altered. Familial structure and living conditions are different from those antecedent to the loss. The sense of group familial cohesion, the combined parental image of care and protection, the child's security system, personal and familial narcissism, are all seriously injured. Depending on the child's developmental level and ego resources, there will be variable coping with the trauma and developmental strain, relatively controlled regressive tendencies, and efforts at ego synthesis of inner and outer change.

The relationship with the surviving caretaker will undergo new stresses and transformations, contributing to the division of life before and after loss of the other parent. When "splitting of the ego" occurs, it tends to be anchored in and reinforced by a parallel division and alteration of the object world. This "split" in the child's reality and experiential continuity is not identical with the child's personal or familial myth about the cause and consequences of the loss. Other forms of splitting often occur as parallel processes to "splitting of the ego." For example, idealization of the lost parent may be found along with denial of the parent's loss.

"Splitting of the ego" and related forms of splitting are also pertinent to conditions other than object loss, such as the cause and consequence of traumatic experience, the role of shared fantasies in development, the parent as model and identification with the parent in choice of defense and in pathogenesis, the secondary gain of certain defensive maneuvers and of symptom formation in object relations and adaptation. The bereaved

child, for example, may seek the privilege of the exception, exploit the sympathy or overprotection of the caretaker, etc.

Consideration of defensive ego splitting and impaired synthesis extends my own work (Blum, 1977, 1980, 1983) on the reconstruction of the consequences of object loss in childhood and adult analysis. I shall be particularly concerned here with denial and the altered ego and realities rather than the consequence of loss in terms of castration, narcissistic injury, mourning and melancholia. Denial of parent loss is inevitable in children because of the child's proclivity to the use of denial under stress, probably universal in all children dealing with such an overwhelming real loss. The child is confronted with a culmination of shock and strain or more accurately with a traumatic situation surrounded by extraordinary developmental stress and strain. The problems are exponentially increased if both parents are lost. With truly traumatic situations, the ego is temporarily overwhelmed, thrust into a state of helplessness, disorganization, and regression. The multiple traumata and chronic developmental disturbance are more likely to leave the personality vulnerable to than immunized against further trauma (Furst, 1967), although the long-range consequences depend on many other influences and further development. Doubtful that subsequent repetitive attempts of mastery can successfully eliminate traumatic injury of the ego, Deutsch (1966), while emphasizing a residual pathogenic disposition, noted that subsequent personality consolidation might result in new traumatic events being mastered, with positive value for further development. Persons with exceptional ego endowment seem to meet and master traumatic loss with renewed strength and capacities for substitution and sublimation (Kanzer, 1953; Pollock, 1970).

A time factor is involved here for both the mastery of trauma and for the mourning process. A special vulnerability to developmental disturbance and, in adults, to psychological disorder persists in those with incomplete or pathological forms of mourning. Engel (1961) views grief as a psychopathological

state and notes that pathophysiological changes may ensue leading to somatic disorders which may ultimately be partially psychosomatic in origin.

Many authors have noted the importance and prevalence
of denial in cases of childhood parent loss (e.g., Mahler, 1961;
Wolfenstein, 1966; Pollock, 1970; Furman, 1974). The use of
denial is much more intense, broadly based, and syntonic with
the rest of the personality in childhood than it is in adulthood.
While the adult may temporarily deny with a refusal to "believe
his eyes or ears" upon learning of a major loss, this reaction is
usually short-lived. For the child with an immature ego, the
need for the parent is so great that denial and other defenses
are obligatory to deal with the danger and, at least potentially,
if not actually, traumatic situations. Other defenses operate in
concert, and there are usually also various forms of regression,
subsequent developmental interference, and a tendency toward
developmental retardation of certain ego functions, such as
object relations (Fleming and Altschul, 1963; Altschul, 1968).
Areas of regression or of arrested development tend to be selective rather than global, and developmental arrest or fixation
is likely to be at the pre-loss level. In addition to the injurious
effects of regression and other defenses, denial itself interferes
with the reality testing necessary for mourning. The child has
to be able to deal with the massive separation anxiety, with the
need to separate himself from the loved and needed object who
no longer exists in reality, and with the task of disinvesting the
object representations for purposes of new adaptation and relations to substitute and surrogate objects. Denial of loss or of
its irreversability may sustain hope, but at the price of developmental interference, fixation, and failure. While some degrees of mourning are possible in childhood, particularly
dependent on the child's pre-loss personality strengths, a child's
level of ego development, and the quality of care provided by
surviving love objects, it is doubtful that the work of mourning
can be accomplished in childhood. In fact, it seems doubtful
that mourning can be truly completed by most adults, and the

analytic process itself and various life situations may reactivate the mourning for the lost parent and childhood throughout life (Blum, 1983).

The persistence of denial leads to a splitting of the ego since a part of the ego will then remain divorced from reality, developmentally immature, isolated and segregated from the rest of the ego, but also influencing the rest of the personality through denial in fantasy, word, and deed. The far-reaching effects of this type of denial, ranging from developmental imbalance and dysharmony to developmental deviation or arrest, coexist with ego acceptance of the loss with more or less resigned tolerance of the paradoxical contradiction. Freud (1940) stated:

> Disavowals of this kind occur very often and not only with fetishists; and whenever we are in a position to study them they turn out to be half-measures, incomplete attempts at detachment from reality. The disavowal is always supplemented by an acknowledgement; two contrary and independent attitudes always arise and result in the situation of their being a splitting of the ego. . . . The facts of this splitting of the ego, which we have just described, are neither so new nor so strange as they may at first appear [p. 204].

Even if the fact of death is consciously accepted, it may be unconsciously denied; more important, the emotional significance and consequences of the loss may be denied. And there are universally persistent efforts by the child to consciously and unconsciously maintain the object relation in fantasy and to treat other objects as though they were the lost and found object rather than a different object. The work of mourning permits acceptance of substitution, replacement, and eventually a relation to an object with its own uniquely different attributes and qualities. There are, inevitably, fantasies of resurrection, rebirth, and reunion, and one is reminded of the two attitudes (reversible and irreversible loss) that Freud (1900, pp. 254-255n) described, "I know father's dead, but what I can't un-

derstand is why he doesn't come home to supper." After this remark of a ten-year-old-boy, Freud further noted a four-year-old girl's statement that if an unwanted maid simply went away rather than being dead, "then she would come back again." Such observations, combined with later developmental studies of children's conceptions of death, show that these varied concepts color adult attitudes toward death. Death is equated with sleep, separation, and symbiosis as well as with the major anxieties and gratifications at all developmental levels. Death tends inevitably to be seen as the fulfillment of a death wish with the danger of talionic retribution. However, each death is different, sudden or gradual, accidental or suicide, etc., with the realities having their own influence and fantasy elaboration.

Denial of the fact of death and of the affects and emotions associated with the loss may take many forms. The child may talk or write to the dead parent, and while at the grave, knowing of death, ponder the feeling or experience of the body and spirit of the deceased. The idealization of the dead parent is supported by the cultural attitude toward such idealization and the cultural prohibition toward saying anything ill of the dead. Idealization of the lost parent may be associated with self-denigration and loss of self-esteem and with denigration of the surviving parent or caretaker. Jacobson (1971) noted that the loss of a parent in early childhood is a severe narcissistic injury leaving the child feeling degraded. This is denied along with the feelings of castration, and the child often develops a fantasy of reunion with the glorified lost object, which is simultaneously an attempt to recover a precious part of the "lost" self. The child, and later the adult, may become permanently insecure and fearful of the loss—a perpetual loser—by simultaneously denying and even provoking loss in an effort at mastery which usually miscarries (A. Freud, 1967). In the long run, the problem can only be resolved internally through gradual decathexis of the representation of the lost object. This depends on ego development, the development of the capacity to mourn, and the resolution of denial and defenses which obstruct the mourn-

ing process. Mourning may be abbreviated or protracted, with some individuals evading mourning and yet perpetual mourners sharing the sorrows of other "losers." Once object constancy has been established, it is doubtful that the object representation is ever permanently destroyed. The lost object is retained through identification and becomes an object of memory, while the personality regains freedom to also identify with and relate to the surviving object and new objects.

What is emphasized and elaborated here is the way in which the splitting of the ego, most especially the vertical split associated with denial, but also the problems of idealization and devaluation, fixation, and regression, have been supported by and anchored in the child's reality situation. This reinforced split then becomes a simultaneous split of the ego and of the object world. There is a discordance between the reality antecedent to the loss and the different "external" reality subsequent to the loss. The internal splits and external changes may be superficially bridged and covered through immediate unconscious, illusory reinstatement of the lost object relation. This occurs in the therapeutic transference and in life, e.g., in the well-known projection of the lost parent onto social and religious institutions with a transference of feeling from the lost object to groups and institutions, e.g., hospitals, universities, fraternities, etc. New families are found which are really unconscious reconstitutions of the old family with the lost object unconsciously recovered. Parenthood itself and the formation of the family has as one of its motives the replacement of lost objects, and many religions and cultures will demand or defend against the wish for the reincarnation and recovery of the lost love object. Denial of the finality of death and wishful fantasies of an afterlife are fundamental features of most religions.

The adaptive social and cultural responses to object loss are perhaps as variable as the vicissitudes of human imagination. However, unless the denial and ego splitting can be resolved, the intrapsychic conflicts and disturbance are likely to become anchored in reality. The child's denial may be fostered

by familial denial and facilitated by familial reactions to the same object loss which really contribute to the confusion and splitting of the ego of the child. The influence of the caretaking environment encompasses the impact of the fantasies, attitudes, and behavior of the surviving familial objects on the child and the mutual influence of the bereaved child on his surviving objects.

The older emphasis in the literature on the identification with the lost object in the resolution of mourning did not give simultaneous and sufficient attention to the parallel identifications with the surviving objects. The child's further personality development is crucially dependent on the availability of the surviving parent; the continuity and consistency of care; the quality of empathy, sensitivity, and concern; and the parents' understanding and capacity to bear with the child, their own, and the child's anxiety, depression, and guilt concerning the loss. Early intervention may assist the bereaved through dealing with denial and regression, clarifying areas of confusion and concepts of death and promoting verbal expression of feelings and attitudes toward separation, clinging, etc.

Each new family unit may favor certain defenses and adaptations in the child. One child, whose mother died when he was seven, cognitively knew that she was dead and yet continued to fantasy that she remained in the background like a guardian angel and would some day return. Another child was allowed to go to the funeral, was taken to the cemetery to visit the grave, and participated in anniversary religious rituals. Despite being repeatedly informed and confronted with the fact of death, he had imaginary conversations with his deceased father in the cemetery and sometimes before falling asleep. He imagined that his father was only asleep. His mother's speaking frequently and insistently about the dead parent did not alter the need to cling to the lost parent in fantasy as well as in memory and to retain the fantasy of reunion in both life and in death with isolation and reversal of unbearable affects. He came to recognize the powerful current of clinging to the same lost loved one

in his surviving parent. There are often intense, persisting shared fantasies of recovery and reunion with the lost object, as well as aggressive fantasies of revenge against the lost object and against the surviving object who, along with the self, is held responsible for the loss. Shared denial in fantasy and in action becomes part of a shared reality of bereaved parent and child. Denial of the loss may coexist with attempts to undo, expiate, repair, and finally master the loss in symbolic and developmentally shifting repetitions.

All these vicissitudes of the child's reaction are, in part, linked to the intrafamilial reactions of the survivors. It will make a great difference whether the surviving parent is "tuned in" and emotionally available or remains grief-stricken, apathetic, or depressed. The child identifies not only with the denial and other defenses of the surviving parent, but also with that parent's ideation and affective reactions. In a case described previously (Blum, 1980), the child's depressive reactions were not recognized or acknowledged by her mother who was herself depressed. Both parents were, therefore, unavailable. There was little opportunity to express or to openly and verbally share grief and guilt, sadness and sorrow. Mourning was, in effect, opposed from the outside, and she soon learned not to ask questions concerning her deceased father. Little information was provided about his life or his death, and the consequences and changes in the familial living arrangements, location, and lifestyle that ensued after his death. Once her mother remarried, references to her father's earlier life and to the earlier state of the family were avoided. The familial secret became a conspiracy of silence with conscious parental cues to avoid the deadly topic and unconscious parental prohibition to remember and to reflect upon the past life. In a sense, her father had not only died, but it was as if he had never lived; denial of his very existence was partially supported by her mother. Familial history was rewritten, at first by making her father an "unperson," and later by changing the legend, both in terms of happier endings and extreme punishment and retribution. The splitting

of the ego and of past from present reality was externally reinforced by the surviving parent.

The historical events of parental illness and death or abandonment and then adoption by a step-parent are critical areas
of life experience which become nodal points in a whole constellation of intrapsychic reactions and experience. There are
important differences between death wishes and actual object
loss, between fantasies of abandonment and the actual experience of abandonment, between death and desertion through
divorce. Not only does the reality have an activating and vali-
dating effect on the fantasy of the child, sometimes with alteration of crucial ego functions such as reality testing, but the
reality itself is different, is often radically transformed, with
powerful effects on the child. If the surviving parent remains
depressed, become anorexic or obese, turns to drugs or prom-
iscuity, this will influence the child's further development, com-
pounding the problems engendered by the death or
disappearance of the other parent. The upheaval for the child
and for the surviving parent can be immediately discerned in
the reactions following bereavement, e.g., when little boys are
often taken into bed by their bereaved mothers, replacing their
fathers. They may be told now they are the man of the house
and the seemingly innocent denial of childhood may be growth-
promoting in certain respects while impeding the child's acknowledgement of his continued dependency and increasing
demands to be "grown-up" as well as his incestuous temptation
and castration anxiety. The mother may turn to her son as a
resurrected husband, not only seeing all sorts of resemblances
and telling the child how much he looks, acts, and talks like his
father, but also using the child in the service of her own denial
of loss and urgency of object replacement.

The anxieties of the bereaved child and of the bereaved
parent are complementary and circular. The child worries who
will take care of him and becomes much more fearful as well
as increasingly dependent on the surviving parent, so that ambivalence cannot be dealt with as it was formerly. Oedipal and

dependency conflicts are intensified (Neubauer, 1960), and separation from, anger toward, and control over the surviving
parent become critical issues. These feelings are similarly trans-
mitted by the parent, e.g., the surviving mother who worries
who will take care of her, who will provide for her, and who
communicates her own psychological, social, sexual, and economic anxieties to the child. As the child worries about who will
take care of him in his mother's absence, she worries who will
take care of her child in her absence. Should anything now
"happen" to her, her children will be orphans. Both parent and
child may fear each other's desertion or death and the recurr-
ence of traumatic loss. This disruption and reconstitution of
the family after death, divorce, etc., inevitably becomes a developmental stress with its own field of forces for the child.
Parent loss transforms the familial structure and relationship
so that there is a discontinuity as well as a continuity of the
surviving family. Relocation, changes of surrogate objects and
of home and school, and loss of familiar surroundings are ordinary sequellae of parent loss.

In terms of unconscious wishes, there is no sense of time,
of loss, or of contradiction, so that the object does not have to
be found or regained since it has not been lost. The denial of
reality serves wish fulfillment, protects the ego from enormous
distress and the most painful affects (anxiety, grief, guilt,
depression), and attempts to maintain the illusion of intact object relation in this and other possible worlds. The child's illusion about the deceased parent will be related to the child's
own fantasy life, but also to the surviving parent's communications concerning the missing parent. The surviving parents'
idealization or denigration of the deceased parent, their feelings
about the former spouse, and their feelings about life with and
without the spouse will influence the child's attitude toward the
lost parent. The child may identify with the remaining parent's
attitudes or develop a contradictory set of attitudes based on
feelings of loyalty and disloyalty toward the present and absent
parents. The child may identify with a depressed, surviving

parent's own self-reproach and join the surviving parent's idealization of the dead parent in a "splitting" of love and hate
toward the parents. Identification with the self-accusation or
the reproach of the surviving parent toward the child favors
the child's turning aggression on himself. The splitting tendencies will therefore be influenced by the surviving parent-
child relation as well as by the pre-loss personality and identifications with the lost object.

Jacobson's (1971) statement that the actual or supposed
desertion in fantasy had not been the fault of the lost parent
who is fantasied as a wonderful person, but had been caused
by the surviving child or parent's bad character or worthlessness
can be amended and amplified in several directions. Death is
not always followed by idealization of the lost or surviving objects.

The splitting of the representation and idealization of the
lost parent may be incomplete and unreliable. There may be
persistent fantasies of loving reunion and angry attack on the
"deserter." The child may project anger and blame from the
absent to the present parent, as so often occurs with foster
parents, but may also display hostility to the lost parent. Rage
at the parent for dying may be disguised in terms of the parent's
character or sibling preference.[2] The hostility connected with
fantasies of abandonment and murder may be inferred in the
linked representations of the denigrated object and despised
self. The child's self-blame and self-hatred may protect the relation with the surviving parent and the fantasy relation with
the lost parent. Sometimes the child's self-blame coincides with
the parent's mutual recrimination prior to death or desertion.
In the face of severe narcissistic injury, hatred, guilt, and self-
accusation, the defensive idealization of the lost parent and
clinging to the idealized fantasy parent may also be used to
bolster self-esteem at the expense of reality testing and new
object relations.

---

[2] Shakespeare, in *Julius Caesar*, provides an example of poetic splitting
with a manifest representation of denigration of the dead, "The evil that men
do lives after them, the good is oft interred with their bones."

The problems associated with the splitting of the ego include those of different realities or different dimensions of reality. The child's sense of reality, especially that of the younger child, is intimately tied to the sense of reality conveyed by the parent. Even after the superego has been formed, the child remains dependent on the auxiliary superego of the parent to lesser degrees throughout childhood. And superego sanctions codetermine what will be regarded as real, true, and worthwhile (Nunberg, 1932). After the child has lost contact with the parent, and the child's age and development at the time of loss will always be an important variable, the child's memories and fantasies of the lost parent will be colored by those of the surviving parent. In fact, many memories of the missing parent are mediated among the survivors, and the child preserves contact with the lost parent through the continuing contact and sharing of memories with the remaining parent. This helps preserve a sense of continuity, even in the face of death or disappearance. And the child who may in fantasy or reality actually resemble the lost parent, may have the same meaning for the surviving parent, so that both may feel that the lost parent lives on in his or her child. The feeling of contact and continuity with the lost parent depends on the capacity for shared identifications and expressions of affective memory which also may promote mourning and reciprocal adaptation to the new realities of life. The child will sense what the surviving parent feels, whether "Tis better to have loved and lost than never to have loved at all" (Tennyson), or "good riddance," or whether the parent feels lifeless, apathetic, and identifies with the dead partner, or shares denial of the loss with the child. This may profoundly influence the child's attitudes, fantasies, and defenses, including tendencies toward denial, isolation of affect, and splitting of the ego. The child will attempt to master the object loss and adapt to the reconstituted reality situation in which the caretaking parent and other siblings are themselves changing consequent to mourning and attempts at new adaptations. Denial, splitting of the ego, confusion of past and present, identity

disturbance, may be shared and convergent in parent-caretaker and child. The split that may ensue in the parental and self-images antecedent and subsequent to the loss, the split of the one-parent image from the bi-parental protective image of the dual parents (compare with the frightening image of the parents in the primal scene), and the tendency toward the splitting of representations are linked to extraordinary ambivalence and the inability to express aggression in the one-parent bereaved family. The fact that the other parent is no longer available to buffer the impulses of the surviving parent and child leads to a complex set of alterations, inconsistencies, and contradictions. For some parents and most children, depending on the level of ego maturity, regression, or arrest, the capacity for synthesis will be overtaxed. The child will not be able to fully discriminate all the many complex and confusing changes and will incompletely integrate the transformed psychic and external reality. In a sense, the split engendered by denial and isolation is between psychic and external reality, between primary- and secondary-process dominance.

Splitting of the ego in the process of defense will be reinforced by the confusion, defensive maneuvers, and the difficulties in reality adaptation of the transformed family. The denial in fantasy, word, and action, and the concomitant ego splitting oppose the integration of fantasy and reality, past and present, and comprehension of sequential experience, cause and effect. While the defensive process may provide a safe haven, there can also be permanent developmental damage and vulnerability to psychological disorder. Surviving objects, even if not models of denial, may rationalize withholding truths from the child to spare the child unnecessary suffering. In this connection, the surviving parent may foster pathology, e.g., lying or learning inhibitions, or support reality testing, clarification, and synthesis. The failure of internal communication with a split ego organization may also reflect the limits of object relation and lack of appropriate communication between parent and child due to the pathology of either or usually both partners in degree, and the past relationship between the parents.

Adults with persisting denial and ego splitting following childhood object loss lack a sense of wholeness and cohesion. There are many possible consequences and outcomes, for example, ambivalence tends to be poorly tolerated with wide mood swings or frozen affect; self-reliance often oscillates with clinging dependence, separation anxiety, and fear of change. Contradictory attitudes and incompatible beliefs may be associated with doubt, indecision, and lack of initiative. Self-deception may be concurrent with deception of and by others. Tendencies toward dissimulation, doubt, and distrust of perceived reality and parental authority may be associated with efforts to test the changing realities and synthesize the fragments of fact and fiction into a coherent pattern. Familial fabrication adds to the child's ego confusion and corrupts superego standards. The shared parent-child denial and distortion of other traumata such as intrafamilial assault or seduction may lead to some similar consequences (Shengold, 1979; Blum, 1983; Kramer, 1983).

The rifts and discontinuities, inconsistencies and contradictions within the personality will tend to persist unless the regressive tendencies and fixation to trauma can be reversed and integration can be achieved at a higher developmental level. Childhood parent loss fractures the experience of personal, object, and reality continuity, internally characterized by personality instability and by at least temporary impairments of ego integration, object relations, and identity. The inner disorganization and splitting lead to inconsistent ego subsystems with intrasystemic as well as intersystemic conflict. These changes will, in turn, further influence object relations and the perception of and response to external reality (Blum, 1980). While denial and splitting of the ego are associated with incomplete mourning and impaired reality testing, denial is simultaneously a delaying, self-comforting attempt to adapt to the lost, divided, and surviving object world. Temporary denial may "buy time" for the child to cope with shock and confusion. Denial of illness and death, in degree and under specific conditions, is adaptive. The child has to gradually learn to master

separation anxiety, sadness, and depression, and eventually without undue dependence on or recourse to denial and other defenses. Disappointment and depression may be denied along with full affective recognition of loss, but the spread of denial will lead to ego constriction and "splitting," while recognition and assimilation of reality and unpleasurable affect will tend to strengthen the ego. Where long-range adaptation is based on denial, it is likely to be precarious and at the expense of sectors of ego development and stability.

Anniversary depressions represent controlled, circumscribed forms of mourning and efforts at mastery. After childhood parent loss, the fracture of family life and parental function and the variable changes in the surviving parent and surround all contribute to the enormous developmental stress and confusion that burden the child's already overtaxed ego. These divisions parallel the internal tendencies toward splitting of the ego. Both external and internal reality are divided in various forms, and the child may not be able to bridge the internal, familial, and psychosocial gaps and alterations antecedent and subsequent to the loss. The splitting of the ego is linked to and influenced by the fractured object world. Opposing identifications, e.g., with the deserting parent and the caretaking parent, with the devalued and the idealized parent, are regularly discerned and coincide with a "divided self."

The repetition and tolerance of anniversary depression may be a significant effort at mastery of a traumatic era. This is not a single event, but the telescoping of a period of inner and outer turmoil in the past and in the brief anniversary recapitulation. The patient's present symptoms cannot be understood without recollection and reconstruction, and the past referents and determinants of the anniversary have to be elucidated. The temporal discontinuity and symptomatic periodicity will be related to the internal splitting and rifts within the ego, or in a larger sense, to the personality discontinuity which so often underlies the anniversary depression. In such cases, the anniversary reaction, such as the anniversary depression,

may only be symptomatic of ongoing efforts to restore personality continuity, to resolve the intensified intrapsychic conflicts
associated with the loss, and to repair the splitting and other
pathogenic sequelae of the childhood traumatic experience.
The anniversary may mark a great divide, psychological and
social, antecedent and subsequent to object loss.

Finally, it may be useful to question the value of the term
splitting which has so many theoretical, metaphorical, and descriptive meanings. The different meanings are linked to different domains of discourse, differences that have to be kept
in mind to avoid the same type of confusion that occurs with
failure of ego integration. Clinically, splitting invites technical
questions of interpretation and reconstruction. The concept of
splitting as a defense, as a consequence of defense, and as a
failure of defense or integration are simultaneously important
theoretical and technical issues. Splitting is related to the dissociation of incompatible self- and object representations, identifications, repression and isolation of ideas and affects, and the
disruption of logical and temporal sequence. It is illustrative of
the importance of denial in fantasy and the defensive, adaptive
functions of fantasy. The analysis of splitting should lead to
greater personality cohesion, greater ego stability and flexibility,
and the recovery of lost areas of ego dominance and restoration
of previously impaired ego functions. At the same time, the
concept of splitting of the ego, with "ego" used as a global
structure, may tend to obscure a careful delineation of other
defenses, of specific ego functions which are impaired or intact,
specific areas of vulnerability, the quality and stability of intrapsychic representations, and overall personality disturbance as
well as preferred modes of adaptation and conflict solution.
Splitting of the ego is not the only consequence of denial or the
consequence only of denial. It is also a consequence of what is
defended against—trauma and conflict. It will be associated
with other forms of defense, possible developmental disorder
and areas of ego disturbance. The "split" is not simply of the
ego, i.e., intrasystemic, but involves superego and id elements

(Schafer, 1968). The division within the ego results in differ-ential, often highly selective impairments (e.g., reality testing, perception, judgment, and synthesis), but also preserves an in-tact, realistic ego organization relatively outside the sphere of conflict.

Summary

Splitting of the ego as defined by Freud does not refer to the segregation of polarized affect states of affection and hostility, but to contradictory ego states in which reality is, on the one hand, acknowledged, and on the other hand, denied. In the case of parent loss, splitting of the ego refers to the simultaneous but dissociated belief that the parent is both alive and dead. This type of ego splitting has defensive and adaptive functions, initially giving the child time to assimilate shock.

The internal "splitting of the ego" becomes coordinated with and reinforced by the fracture of the child's object world and social surround. Inevitable developmental strain ensues, and depending on the child's developmental phase and per-sonality resources, there will be variable tendencies toward se-lective regression and arrest at the pre-loss level. The familial and social circumstances are inevitably altered following paren-tal death, and there are frequent changes in the child's sur-round. The denial in fantasy and attitudes toward the deceased and living parent are strongly influenced by the relation and identifications, not only with the deceased parent, but also with the surviving parent or caretakers. The earlier emphasis on identification with the lost object does not do justice to the child's continued development and identification with the sur-viving parent. The sharing of denial or of particular memories and attitudes toward the lost parent, especially the fantasies and reality presented by the surviving parent, will powerfully influ-ence the splitting tendencies and fantasies of the child. In ad-dition to the splitting of the ego due to denial and acceptance of the reality of parent loss (and the possible splitting of self-

and parent representations into idealized and denigrated), there is a temporal splitting of the ego. This is the splitting of the ego and object world antecedent and subsequent to the object loss, leaving a gap which is characterized by confusion, disorganization, and inability to integrate the inner and outer transformations that have occurred. The ego splitting that results from denial of reality is interwoven with the confusion and lack of synthesis of the personality before and after the loss. Anniversaries of parent loss can be understood from many dimensions, but always include attempts to complete mourning, master trauma, and restoration of the continuity of the personality and of reality disrupted in childhood.

Splitting of the ego is a metaphor with multiple meanings. It is a clinically and theoretically useful concept, but should not be misconstrued in a concrete or literal sense. Splitting of the ego is illustrative of denial in fantasy and of other forms and functions of defense and of fantasy. To avoid confusion, clinical, developmental, and theoretical dimensions of splitting should be delineated, recognizing, at the same time, that the many internal and external alterations, inconsistencies, and contradictions cannot be entirely encompassed within the splitting concepts. Splitting of the ego should not diminish awareness of the significance of other consequences of parent loss and of the child's further development.

REFERENCES

ALTSCHUL, S. (1968). Denial and ego arrest. *J. Amer. Psychoanal. Assn.*, 16:301-318.
BLUM, H. P. (1977). The prototype of preoedipal reconstruction. *J. Amer. Psychoanal. Assn.*, 25:757-786.
——— (1980). The value of reconstruction in adult psychoanalysis. *Int. J. Psychoanal.*, 61:39-54.
——— (1983). The psychoanalytic process and analytic inference: clinical study of a lie and loss. *Int. J. Psychoanal.*, in press.
DEUTSCH, H. (1966). Post-traumatic amnesias and their adoptive function. In *Psychoanalysis: A General Psychology*, ed. R. M. Loewenstein et al. New York: Int. Univ. Press, pp. 437-455.
ENGEL, G. (1961). Is grief a disease? *Psychosom. Med.*, 23:18-22.

FLEMING, J. & ALTSCHUL, S. (1963). Activation of mourning and growth by psychoanalysis. *Int. J. Psychoanal.,* 44:419-431.

FREUD, A. (1936). *The Ego and the Mechanisms of Defense. Writings,* 2. New York: Int. Univ. Press, 1966.

———— (1965). *Normality and Pathology in Childhood. Writings,* 6. New York: Int. Univ. Press, 1965.

———— (1967). About losing and being lost. *Psychoanal. Study Child,* 22:9-19.

FREUD, S. (1900). The interpretation of dreams. *S. E.,* 4 & 5.

———— (1923a). A seventeenth-century demonological neurosis. *S. E.,* 19.

———— (1923b). The ego and the id. *S. E.,* 19.

———— (1927). Fetishism. *S. E.,* 21.

———— (1933). New introductory lectures on psychoanalysis. *S. E.,* 22.

———— (1938). Splitting of the ego in the process of defense. *S. E.,* 23.

———— (1939). Moses and monotheism. *S. E.,* 23.

———— (1940). An outline of psychoanalysis. *S. E.,* 23.

FURMAN, E. (1974). *A Child's Parent Dies.* New Haven: Yale Univ. Press.

FURST, S. (1967). Psychic trauma: a survey. In *Psychic Trauma,* ed. S. Furst. New York: Basic Books, pp. 3-50.

JACOBSON, E. (1971). A special response to early object loss. In *Depression.* New York: Int. Univ. Press, pp. 185-203.

KANZER, M. (1953). Writers and the early loss of parents. *J. Hillside Hosp.,* 2:148-151.

KERNBERG, O. (1975). *Borderline Conditions and Pathological Narcissism.* New York: Aronson.

KRAMER, S. (1983). Object-coercive doubting: a pathological defensive response to maternal incest. *J. Amer. Psychoanal. Assn.,* 31 (Suppl.): 319-345.

LICHTENBERG, J. & SLAP, W. (1973). Notes on the concept of splitting and the defense mechanism of the splitting of representations. *J. Amer. Psychoanal. Assn.,* 21:772-787.

MAHLER, M. S. (1961). On sadness and grief in infancy and childhood: loss and restoration of the symbiotic love object. *Psychoanal. Study Child,* 16:332-351.

———— PINE, F. & BERGMAN, A. (1975). *The Psychological Birth of the Human Infant.* New York: Basic Books.

NEUBAUER, P. (1960). The one-parent child and his oedipal development. *Psychoanal. Study Child,* 15:286-309.

NUNBERG, H. (1932). *Principles of Psychoanalysis.* New York: Int. Univ. Press, 1955.

POLLOCK, G. (1970). Anniversary reactions, trauma, and mourning. *Psychoanal. Q.,* 39:347-371.

PRUYSER, P. (1975). What splits in "splitting"? a scrutiny of the concept of splitting in psychoanalysis and psychiatry. *Bull. Menninger Clin.,* 39:1-46.

RANGELL, L. (1982). The self in psychoanalytic theory. *J. Amer. Psychoanal. Assn.,* 30:863-891.

ROSS, J. & DUNN, P. (1980). Notes on the genesis of pathological splitting. *Int. J. Psychoanal.,* 61:335-349.

SCHAFER, R. (1968). *Aspects of Internalization.* New York: Int. Univ. Press.

SEGEL, M. (1981). Review of Otto Kernberg's books. *J. Amer. Psychoanal. Assn.,* 29:221-236.

SHENGOLD, L. (1979). Child abuse and deprivation: soul murder. *J. Amer. Psychoanal. Assn.*, 27:533-557.
WOLFENSTEIN, M. (1966). How is mourning possible? *Psychoanal. Study Child*, 21:93-126.

23 The Hemlocks
Roslyn Estates, New York 11576

OBJECT-COERCIVE DOUBTING: A PATHOLOGICAL DEFENSIVE RESPONSE TO MATERNAL INCEST

Selma Kramer, M.D.

I SHALL REPORT A DEFENSIVE constellation I encountered in patients who had experienced the trauma of prolonged and unremitting handling of the genitals by the mother. I call this treatment of the child by the mother "maternal incest"; I will give my reasons for doing so later in the paper. Here I wish only to call attention to the fact that it was concerning the ubiquitous reports of incestuous experiences with the father that Freud developed the concept of the Oedipus complex and furthered his understanding of defense. I shall not review the evolution of Freud's refinements of the concept of defense and resistance but will instead focus on this particular defense and its vicissitudes.

The early writings of Breuer and Freud (1883-1895) and Freud (1896) stressed the neurosogenesis of childhood inces-

---

Training and Supervising Analyst, Adult and Child, Philadelphia Psychoanalytic Institute; Professor and Head of Child Psychiatry Section, Medical College of Pennsylvania.

Earlier versions of this paper were presented to the Philadelphia Psychoanalytic Society, the Michigan Psychoanalytic Society, the Topeka Psychoanalytic Society, and the Metropolitan Society of Psychoanalytic Psychotherapists.

tuous experiences. Freud's continued work led to the landmark formulation of the Oedipus complex, as he concluded that most reports of incest were derived from ubiquitous fantasies of childhood. He amended this concept and later stated (1931) that actual seduction was common. He said, "When seduction intervenes it invariably disturbs the natural course of the developmental processes, and it often leaves behind extensive and lasting consequences" (p. 232). He added (1932), ". . . I was able to recognize in this phantasy of being seduced by the father the expression of the typical Oedipus complex in women. And now we find the phantasy of seduction once more in the pre-Oedipus prehistory of girls; but the seducer is regularly the mother. Here, however, the phantasy touches the ground of reality, for it was really the mother who by her activities over the child's bodily hygiene inevitably stimulated, and perhaps even roused for the first time, pleasurable sensations in her genitals" (p. 120). Many authors emphasize that sexual stimulation of a child may include exposure to the primal scene and parental nudity as well as the actual manipulation of the anus or genitals, and they describe the defenses they cause. Freud addressed the question of what happened when a child's wish becomes reality, in *Dostoevski and Parricide* (1928) when he stated, "The phantasy has become reality and all defensive measures are thereupon reinforced" (p. 186).

Greenacre (1973) describes what she calls, "a special form of denial," which is erected to keep the child from being overwhelmed by external stimuli as well as from being overcome by his own primitive aggressive and sexual drives in response to "overwhelming violence to the infant's own body." Among the forces she considers to be overwhelming in violence, Greenacre includes even the administration of repeated enemas; she feels that the strongest walls of denial are those that have been reinforced by operations on or painful manipulation of the genitals themselves, even when undertaken for therapeutic reasons. She also feels that inclusion in the primal scene may be the equivalent of an incestuous experience to the child.

Blum (1979) regards the primal scene as a phallic phase fantasy, but as a phase-specific or nonspecific traumatic experience. In speaking of preoedipal primal scene experience, he says, ". . . the possibility of contagion of excitement with traumatic overstimulation of the infant is significantly increased if the child's presence is important for the parents' excitement, and if the child's self-object differentiation is not fully consolidated and is vulnerable to regression. If ego boundaries are unstable, there is more likely to be primary identification and confusion fantasies. . . . The primal scene would then be a relatively nonspecific trauma impeding separation-individuation, but it could also predispose the infant to anal fixation and to heightened castration anxiety and narcissistic injury" (p. 38). In questioning the parents' need for nudity and for the child's presence in the bedroom or bathroom, he says that it appears primal scene exposure ". . . has become an umbrella concept for various forms of pathological object relations, insufficient parental auxiliary ego functioning, and the sexual and aggressive abuse of children and their narcissistic exploitation by immature or deviant parents. . . . Today . . . we are inclined to give much more weight to the organizing and disorganizing effects of *real trauma* (italics added) and to attempt to differentiate between incestuous fantasies and actual seduction and primal scene exposure" (pp. 39-40).

I feel that the "umbrella" of primal scene should be separated into the components mentioned, and not lumped together. My experience is that sexual and aggressive abuse of children and their narcissistic exploitation is not the same and does not have the same after-effects as does the exposure to the child of parental sexuality.

Greenacre (1952), Keiser (1962), Laufer (1968), Shengold (1967, 1974, 1979), Blum (1973, 1979), and Galenson et al. (1975), among others, have said that a specific factor contributing to pathological processes in children, adolescents, and adults is actual overstimulation by the parents. The remarkable thing is that when the stimulator happened to be the mother,

these acts were not usually regarded as or named incest. Inasmuch as I label deliberate maternal sexual stimulation as incest, I am at variance with many writers of today.

Maternal Incest

Just as incest by a male relative need not involve genital penetration, nor necessarily result in orgasm, but may consist of his overstimulation of the child's body, usually of the genitals, anus, or breasts, or of his demand that there be mutual sex stimulation, incest by a female relative should be, I feel, defined similarly as *deliberate and repetitive* overstimulation by her of genitals, anus, or breasts of a child of either sex, or as mutual sex play which the mother instigates.

Why are authors so loathe to label sexual stimulation by the mother as incest and relatively ready to acknowledge paternal incest? I suggest that:

1. There is a reluctance to attribute to the mother, who to so many must remain sexless, the deliberate pursuit of sexual excitement by stimulating her child's body or by seeking to have her child stimulate the mother's genitals. The resistance to the concept "maternal incest" is, I feel, related to the deep-seated, almost universal split between the mother as madonna and whore.

2. As Freud noted (1932), some sensual and sexual response inevitably arises in a child from the mother's bathing, diapering, or fondling.

I regard maternal incest to be more than inadvertence; it is the mother's repetitive, deliberate actions, aimed at stimulating the child to gratify herself. The child may be male or female.

My patients also experienced repeated primal scene exposure. While exposure to primal scene or to parental nudity may contribute to developmental pathology in children (Greenacre, 1952; Johnson, 1949), I find that children whose genitals have been deliberately stimulated by their mothers or who have

been invited to actually stimulate their mother's genitals have specific pathology which differs from that of children who are merely visually and auditorially overstimulated. (Stimulation of the child's anus or the mother's breast or anus is also "incestuous" in character, but is not identical to direct genital stimulation.)

The Mothers and the Meaning of the Child to Them

The mothers of my patients were very sick; two were schizophrenic, one of whom was floridly paranoid; the third mother was borderline, with an impairment of her ability to be logical and orderly in her thinking. The mothers had serious superego lacunae and were really polymorphous-perverse in that they stimulated and obviously derived pleasure from rubbing their child's genitals, rectal area, breasts, and general skin surfaces. Because these mothers were not analyzed, I can only speculate on their pathology, but I assume that they must have been acting out oedipal as well as preoedipal conflicts. However, in addition to the mother's mental problems, there are, I feel, special meanings to the mother of the particular child whom she stimulates sexually.

It appears that two factors exist in the mother-child relationship for maternal incest to occur:

First, the child is unwanted, unrewarding to the mother, not satisfying her narcissism, even from birth (Browning and Boatman, 1977). In addition, the mother-child symbiosis is parasitic and is not resolved, the mother unable to permit the child to individuate, much as the mother was stuck in the relationship with her own mother.

Litin et al. (1956) and Brandt Steele (personal communication) suggest a tight unresolved symbiosis exists (in cases which I call maternal incest) between the child and the mother who herself had problems in separating from her mother and also had sexual conflicts which interfered with her marriage. Steele says, "It is the adult using the unwitting, obedient child

to solve maternal needs, and exploitation and distortion of the normal, mutual interaction."

I found that where there was more than one child, the mother sexually stimulated only the one child who was unwanted and/or was perceived by her as inferior, a disappointment, so imperfect as to be dehumanized. She showed contempt by expressing most hurtful verbal hostility, derided (Kramer, 1974) and used the one child.

The sexual and psychological abuses of the "imperfect children" were overdetermined. As I learned in the course of my patients' treatment, the mothers had identified with both of their parents and had strong unconscious homosexuality. I speculate that they could not enjoy their own genitals for sexual pleasure, but masturbated the genitals of their incompletely separated and individuated children as dehumanized extensions of the maternal body. One mother called her child "my music box" when she invited her to bed. She started sex play by saying, "Your lid is up," and would end the play abruptly, saying, "Your lid is down. Get out of the room."

Ego pathology and superego lacunae permit the mothers to enact and at the same time to deny their masturbatory use of the child's genitals. The maternal superego is then selectively permissive, but at the same time it is excessively moralistic. The sexually abused child gets very confused messages: "I am a loving mother who is perfect, good, and clean; you are not allowed to think that I play with your genitals, for anyone who does that is bad and dirty, and I am your mother and I certainly am not bad." Litin et al. (1956, p. 40) say that, ". . . 'double talk' instead of a firm direct statement is employed by the parent."

In addition to ordering their children not to know what they did but to believe what they said, the mothers were harshly punitive when the child masturbated, so that masturbation, which had an early onset in these overstimulated children, was more guilt-ridden than in the average child. The children's masturbation would reveal that genital pleasure stemmed from the very actions the mothers used under the guise of cleaning,

cuddling, or medicating of that area. Patients may cease masturbating during latency and may develop genital anesthesia, or they may displace the masturbation conflict.

The child's expression of hostility also caused conflict. Overt hostility was forbidden; covert hostility was expressed by the child in many ways, including the doubting which paralyzed the mother or her substitute as well as the child. The children were often clinging and subtly manipulative. Ambivalence was a characteristic manifestation of my patients.

The Fathers

Just as the mothers of my patients had serious problems in the area of sexual identity, so did the fathers. My description of Donald's father (Kramer, 1974) is typical for all these fathers. They were successful in endeavors requiring considerable time away from their homes, and were passive men to the point of effeminacy in their marriages, who tolerated their wives' pathology and who suffered their wives' verbal abuse. The sexual relations were poor in each marriage.

The Nature of Doubting and Its Defensive Significance

My purpose in writing this paper is to describe a unique type of doubting which each of my patients manifested and which I feel resulted from the intrapsychic pathological effects of the maternal incest. I shall describe this in greater detail further on. Here I wish to emphasize that the *patients coerced the maternal object or her substitute to argue one of the opposing sides of the child's intrapsychic conflict* (or its derivative). The lack of adequate self-object differentiation (or the persistence of the self-object [Kernberg, 1976]), caused this type of doubting to be considerably different from the doubting of the obsessive-compulsive individual who has separated and individuated, who is troubled by conflict between components of his own psychic structure. My patients used the incompletely differentiated self and object

to express and to argue the conflict, a conflict which was usually, but not always, about knowing something; but there was almost never any closure to the conflict.

To portray and to formulate this type of defense I shall present vignettes of two female patients in whom it was encountered.[1]

Clinical Cases

Abby

Abby was brought for consultation when she was almost five years of age, after about six months of increasingly severe "panic states" which started with Abby expressing doubt about doing or knowing something. As her doubting accelerated, she would turn to her parents with questions "for which they could give no right answers." Her frustration would grow until she would have a "screaming fit," a temper tantrum in which she would hit or scratch herself or anyone nearby. For example, in going to the next room, Abby might be immobilized by anxiety and doubts about whether touching the doorknob would "give her germs and kill her." She could not relieve her doubts, nor could her parents' answers comfort her. Often she would touch the "dirty" surface in a quick, darting motion, and slyly suck her fingers. Many such episodes occurred daily.

Serious problems had long antedated the onset of the panic states. From age two, severe separation problems dictated that her parents no go out socially, and a related sleeping problem allowed her to demand that one of her siblings sleep in her room. At the same time, the relationship with her mother became very hostile and provocative. However, only her mother could put her to bed, for Mrs. S. had "a way, a ritual, you might say, which calmed Abby down." I could not elicit the nature of the ritual at this time.

---

[1] The case of a male patient, Donald, is presented elsewhere (Kramer, 1974).

Abby was the youngest of three daughters, each two years apart. The S.'s were open in telling of their disappointment in having a third daughter, especially one who was puny and not pretty. Abby's sisters were beautiful and talented, and gratified their parents by performing for guests.

Abby lost weight during the postnatal period. When she was three weeks old she developed severe diarrhea for which she was hospitalized for six weeks. Her parents visited her only once, for they "couldn't bear the sight of the intravenous tubes in that skinny body." After Abby returned home, her two-years-older sister complained of stomach aches. The pediatrician advised the S.'s to pay more attention to their middle child, whereupon Mrs. S.'s idiosyncratic logic, with which I became quite familiar, resulted in her ignoring Abby entirely (Mrs. S. was not at all contrite as she related this information, for she felt she did the right thing in following the letter of the law).

Treatment started off slowly. Abby's separation problem and distrust of people made it necessary for her mother to remain in the treatment room for many months. After Abby began to trust me and to believe that her mother would not abandon her with me, she revealed intense castration problems that coexisted with separation problems (Settlage, 1971). She looked at red finger paint with a mixture of terror and fascination, and soon began to show me "boo-boos," injuries that worried her, no matter how minute.

A panic reaction with transference implications occurred early in treatment when Abby stood transfixed, unable to enter the room because she had noticed a cracked floor tile and a broken doll. Her anxiety abated when I repetitively made quiet statements that I saw how upset Abby had become when she saw the broken things. I added that she seemed to be afraid she could get hurt in a place where I allowed things to be damaged. Abby began her doubting and questioning—"I don't know. Will I get hurt? I don't know anything. If I touch the crack in the doll, will I get hurt?" Half of this was directed at herself, the remainder to me. Her panic then escalated until I

said firmly, "This is a place where we must find out why you have such bad worries about getting hurt."

As if in response, Abby began to play with the parent dolls in such a way as to convince me that she had heard, and probably had witnessed, primal scene. She made the dolls roll on each other, do gymnastics, kiss and "go crazy"; erotic sighs accompanied the play which advanced to an orgastic crescendo. From time to time she masturbated, with a worried, distracted look on her face.

Soon, obvious sexual testing of me began. Abby sat on the floor, legs widely spread, and ordered me to do the same, so we could roll a ball hard at each other's perineum. Instead of doing what Abby ordered, I commented that the doll play made her want to see whether I *would* roll the ball against her bottom, adding that Abby must wonder whether I would like to have it rolled against *my* bottom. Abby was silent for a while, then asked, "If I whirl around, will I get dizzy and fall? Why won't you play ball with me?" I said to Abby that thinking of having her bottom touched by the ball made her think of being dizzy and losing control and of falling. Abby excitedly danced and twirled around, chanting songs about falling, and adding something about "falling to sleep." She then said, "Now shut up," and could not proceed further with this material.

At my next meeting with Abby's parents, I asked cautiously about primal scene exposure; Mrs. S. was surprised at my question for she was certain that Abby, whose room was directly opposite her parents', could have no inkling of parental intercourse because "we always leave the bedroom doors open during intercourse." Further questioning revealed more of the mother's illogical "logic." Since Mrs. S. always knew when her parents had intercourse because they *closed* their bedroom door, to be certain that her children did not know of the S.s' intercourse, Mrs. S. kept her door open. I decided to ask more about the bedtime ritual. Mrs. S. was somewhat embarrassed as she told me the ritual was to quiet Abby down so she could sleep, and to keep her from "getting sore down there." Every night

for about fifteen minutes, Mrs. S. rubbed Abby's vulva with a soothing ointment. As she described the process, Mrs. S. became flushed and noticeably excited. She repeated her certainty that if she rubbed her child's vulva, Abby would fall asleep quickly, would not get sore, and then added, "and she won't masturbate." She said with annoyance that her husband once said she "rubbed Abby too much." But when she told him she never wanted to hear him say such a foolish thing again, he complied. Mrs. S.'s thinking disorder allowed her to be more open than the other mothers in disclosing her erotic stimulation of her child, because of her pathological defenses.

One might suggest that Abby's questioning and pathological doubting arose in direct reaction to and in identification with her mother's thinking. The analysis revealed that this was not so, for in the course of treatment, the child gradually faced her mother's disturbed thinking in every area except that of the sexual stimulation. The doubting did not stop until the sexual stimulation was analyzed. I found this to be true in each of my patients.

For example, when Abby was about seven and a half years of age, she implored her mother to buy her a dog (since I had one). Her mother complied, buying a pedigreed female which they planned to breed. Abby could laughingly tell me of her mother's distorted thinking when Mrs. S. decided to have the dog bred at the office of the veterinarian. She transported the bitch in heat, together with a male dog, in the rear of her car where Abby and a friend were sitting. When the veterinarian informed Mrs. S. that the mating had been accomplished, Mrs. S. asked, puzzled, "How could that be? We hadn't reached your office yet."

An increasingly good relation with me, and the relief from anxiety her treatment provided, enabled Abby to use her superior intellect in the service of reality testing and to judge many aspects of Mrs. S.'s pathological thinking.

By the time material about her mother's sexual stimulation surfaced, Abby had improved in many areas. She was attending

school regularly, had begun to make friends, and no longer tyrannized her sisters. However, the doubting continued, as did her unending questioning of her parents, her teachers, and me. A teacher said that she had never had a pupil who questioned her so much, with such persistence, taking so much of her time, and with no relief from answers; the teacher said, "It's as if she or I are never right."

In the analysis, her doubting which involved questioning of me might start without much pressure, but it soon accelerated to a point where Abby was inconsolable, tearful, and she accused, "You never tell me anything right." She would then scream, "Tell me the truth!"

But for a long time I was unable to analyze her accusations that I was not telling her the truth, nor to analyze her *insistence that she did not know what she knew.* It appeared that verbal exploration of these conflicts in the transference was insufficient and that the play in which Abby increasingly reproduced with the dolls or my dog the erotic stimulation of her by her mother was too threatening and exciting, at the same time. Abby played with mother and baby dolls in "touching and getting dizzy" games, with increasing erotic excitement. She made furtive attempts to touch the genitals of my dog, pretending to use her mother's make-up, called "Touch and Glow." Abby said "glowing" was to "get red and warm," and she asked for hand cream to rub on my dog to "cool her off." It was obvious that she was attempting to act the role of the maternal sexual aggressor who always did the opposite of "cooling her off."

Abby began to play "hot and cool" games with her hands, running them under cold water and then holding them close to the warm radiator. The significance of the sequence of applying ointment to "cool down" the genitals, followed by the hot "glowing" and then by masturbation was increasingly clear in the analysis. However, although Abby repetitively played out this sequence, she could not talk nor let me talk about it. Her persistence in continuing the state of erotic excitement and her insistence that we not deal with it in analysis had multiple mo-

tives. First, there was a resistant need to enact the pleasure she derived from the sexual stimulation; and second, it represented Abby's identification with her mother who made her excited but denied having done so. The analyst and the analysis became both her exciters and at the same time forces that could cause the stimulation to stop against her will.

Finally, when Abby was eight and a half, the conflict could no longer be defensively contained and she could no longer hold back the flow of the material; she had to let me analyze the conflicts by expressing them in somatic terms. Mrs. S. phoned that Abby was writhing in pain and had to go to a nearby hospital for possible surgery. I asked her to stop at my office first. Abby was tiny and quite thin for her age. When she entered my office, I saw that her abdomen protruded considerably. After palpating her abdomen, I asked Abby when she had urinated last. Abby cried, "Not since yesterday. It hurts too much." I led Abby to the bathroom and told her that I imagined she had been afraid to wee-wee, and that I felt her "stomach ache" was really a pain caused by a very full bladder, and that after she let herself wee-wee, she'd feel better. Across the hall, in my office I heard her gasp with pain as she started to urinate. The stream of urine seemed to flow forever before Abby entered my office, smiling with relief.

I told Abby that I could guess what happened—that touching her bottom had made her so sore she had been afraid to wee-wee. Abby said, "Don't say a dirty thing like 'touch my bottom.'" When I persisted, quietly musing about the events, adding that I knew that Abby had problems in telling me that she and her mother rubbed her bottom, Abby listened and then blurted out, "I do it after *she* rubs me. Why doesn't she rub my sisters? Does she rub Daddy?" I said that Abby was so upset and puzzled about her mother rubbing her that she was afraid to clear up this matter in her analysis, and also that she felt naughty because of the way the rubbing made her feel, and after mommy rubbed her, she had to rub herself. Abby said, "It's to calm me down. That's what she says. I don't do it. She tells me not to."

I commented, "And you're puzzled because it stirs you up, and you have to rub your bottom, even though you are told not to." Abby sat on the floor with her head in her hands and said, "I don't know what to think."

She then proceeded to play once more with my dog, "tickling the dog's tummy" and slowly advancing to the dog's genitals. Abby and the dog became excited. I told Abby, as I limited this play, that she was doing to the dog what she knew had been done to her, and that she was showing me that the tickler got as excited as the person tickled. Abby said, "Shut up. You're not allowed to talk for five hours." But it was obvious that she knew what she and I meant.

Abby's questioning and the doubting abated as she now worked through in the transference her conflict about whether she could trust me to do what I said I was doing and whether I would allow her to perceive correctly what she and I were doing.

This material was interspersed with and followed by material focusing on whether Abby could really know what she perceived, even if her mother denied her permission to recognize reality. As with other patients reported in this paper, to accomplish this developmental task, Abby had to come to terms with her mother's psychopathology as it applied not only to her thinking disorder, but specifically to the sexual interaction between mother and child. Only after this could Abby confess to liking being rubbed, and angrily tell me it was my fault that the rubbing was stopped.

Casey

Casey (Kramer, 1980) manifested, during the early years of her analysis, splitting of both the self and the maternal object representations. The defensive purpose was to retain the intrapsychic representation of the mother as "good," relegating badness to the feared and hated teachers, who also wanted her to know things and to show it. The self was "good" and her peers

whom she envied but could not relate to, were bad. Slowly the two sides of self and object were fused, and only then could Casey tell me what she had known all along—that as far back as she could remember, and up to puberty, her mother had masturbated her. Even now, her mother would take every opportunity to touch Casey's breasts and genitals, using the excuse of tucking in Casey's sweater or straightening her slacks.

When Casey started treatment, at the age of twenty, she was regarded by her family and by herself as "dumb but nice," in contrast to her much more aggressive older sister who was the smart family success. It was known to Casey that her mother had not wanted to be pregnant with her, and had tried unsuccessfully to abort. When the mother realized that carrying the pregnancy to term was inevitable, she wished for a son. Instead, a daughter with a slight birth defect was born. A cast on her legs was required for one and a half to two years, necessitating more maternal attention to Casey's toileting and cleaning than for the average child. It is possible that the combination of the disappointment of the mother, who regarded Casey as an inferior child, and of the enforced passivity contributed to the extension of the early washing of the child's genitals to repetitive stimulation.

Casey's father manifested both detachment and poor sense of self. When Casey refused to let her mother knit for her, as she tried to establish boundaries between them, her father remained silent for a long time, then said, "You should let me, I mean mother, knit." Later, desperate because her father threatened to stop his support of treatment, Casey told him about her mother's sexual stimulation of her genitals. Her father's perplexed response was, "I never did that, did I?" Little or no differentiation seemed to exist between the parents. The significance of this is not clear, but it seems that both parents are driven to repeat their own incestuous pasts and have unconsciously sought each other out for that purpose.

In the analysis Casey's continuing pain and guilt because her mother's sexual play with her genitals was not entirely re-

pugnant to her, surfaced when she recognized that her new boyfriend was really critical and hostile, and used sex for his pleasure and not for hers.

Casey said with despair that she could see that what he did was like what her mother did to her. She then became upset and finally said, "It's one thing to say 'she did it to me' and I can be angry and can hate her, but it's another to say I wanted it and went out for it. Did I feel I was to blame? I know I got attention from her that way. I still feel guilty."

Later she showed the bind she was in. "If I want to get rid of mother as a judge, I have to see that she's so sick she can't be responsible. She has a basic flaw; she's so sadistic, it permeates every part of her life. It's in everything she does, but if I give her up, I won't have a mother."

I commented that we could see how Casey had felt and what she had known as a child when she perceived anger and confusion in her mother who would stimulate her; but Casey could not allow herself to stop it then although she too was angry, confused, and guilty. Casey repeated her plaintive statement, "But then I would have no one." She recognized, however, that although she was no longer the little helpless girl, she put herself in situations with mother and with others which reproduced her earliest mother-child relationships.

An example of the working through of the doubting comes from the fourth year of analysis of Casey, now 24, in a prestigious graduate program. Casey had a stimulating but disturbing dream about a hairy octopus which touched her but kept moving around, not staying in one place.

Associating to the dream, Casey said she recalled mother "touching her" when she was about ten. Mother did not stay a long time in one place. Casey then said she would not let her boyfriend "stay in one place," i.e., focus his touching on her genitals so as to lead to orgasm. Casey wondered whether her mother had ever done that (caused her to have an orgasm). Doubting immediately ensued with Casey attempting to make

me say whether mother had or had not caused an orgasm, until I stated that Casey and I knew that such doubting involved her concern about whether she could let herself know what she knew and what she felt, and that Casey wanted me to argue one side of her conflict about knowing or not knowing.

Casey said that when mother rubbed her all over, especially her genitals, she had complained that mother was an octopus and she threatened to leave mother's bed. Her mother would promise to not repeat it, but after a few minutes, she'd wrap her legs around Casey's and begin to rub Casey's genitals, meanwhile rubbing her own vulva against Casey's buttocks. Casey does not think she had an orgasm when mother stimulated her, but maybe she did; she wanted me to tell her whether or not she had one. Maybe that's behind her preoccupation with not wanting anyone to know she has had an orgasm, or to feel she has one. She can feel now her terror lest mother knew. Casey can now have orgasms by masturbation only.

She can remember in her dream and in waking life feeling immobilized (by mother) as if her *body* had been stung by a hairy spider but her head was awake.

"I couldn't stand it when we were in a public place and she held my hand. The guilty secret we shared, but she acted so good and pure. It's hard to get rid of my mother, to get rid of my paralyzed pleasure when she fondled my genitals. Why must I repeat this stuff? What I'm afraid to understand is this, 'Why didn't I stop it sooner?'"

Casey went on, guilty but less agitated, "I didn't want her to know how I felt. Sexy. She always said I shouldn't be dirty. I was afraid of her wrath (if I had dirty, pleasurable feelings); if I were dirty (sexy) with someone else, she'd be mad, and if I refused to do it with her because she and I were both being dirty, she'd be furious. I'm saying I kept on letting her play with me because I feared her anger. I'm trying to escape from something. It's that to say 'I like it' is the dirtiest thing of them all."

This material was followed by memories of her mother's alternations of interest and disdain, for Casey now knew that her mother was so ashamed of their sex play that when others were around, she acted as if Casey did not exist. Casey recognized that her return to her mother's bed had many purposes other than sexual. She also hoped but doubted that her mother could be a real mother, appropriately tuned in to Casey's development and to her appropriate needs, who would not stimulate Casey in response to her own sexual desires. So the return to her mother's bed represented a physical enactment of the doubting, as if to test whether or not the hated and sought-after experience would happen (see Freud, 1909).

Casey then pursued the emotional concomitants of the doubting. If Casey saw things clearly, without doubting, she would know her mother was crazy and really hated her, both when mother played with her genitals and when she ignored her. And she would have to face her mother's homosexuality. This, of course, brought Casey back to her need to deny her own pleasure, for pleasure could mean that Casey, too, was homosexual.

The doubting which involved me occurred very often in the analysis, with Casey demanding that I must answer her questions, although it was obvious that no answer could be correct. In the transference, I became the dirty object also, as was shown when Casey associated to a dream in which her study was untidy. Her study is the place where Casey tries to make sense out of her classroom notes and struggles against the hopeless confusion that even now overwhelms her. It was also my office, a place where she was gradually facing her "dark, messy self," her sexual awareness and excitement previously repressed.

In the transference, I was the dirty woman who made her feel that I was stimulating her when the analysis dealt with sexual material. And she fantasied that I would abandon her, since I might criticize her and walk out. I was, then, the stimulator and the abandoner, much as her mother had been.

Effects of Incestuous Mothering

The mother is the source of basic trust, the beacon of orientation in the world of reality (Mahler, 1958). As the maternal part of the symbiotic dual unity, her attitude toward the child forms the basis for his primitive concepts of self and the object; normal development separation-individuation eventually leads to the formation of separate intrapsychic self- and object representations, and thus to object and self-constancy. The mother's misuse of the child as a sexual object results in blurring of boundaries of mother and child, and fixates the child as a part-object and impairs self- and object constancy.

The analyses of my patients lead me to speculate that a mother's stimulation of her child's genitals produces its adverse effects early in the child's development, interfering with separation-individuation (Mahler, 1963). Mahler (1971) and Laufer (1968) address the vicissitudes of the inability of the child to take ownership of his body. Mahler (1971) says:

> If there was major failure of integration during the first three subphases of separation-individuation, particularly on the level of gender identity, the child might not have taken autonomous, representationally clearly separated possession of his or her own bodily self, this partly because he or she did not experience the mother's gradual relinquishment of her possession of the toddler's body. Such male and female patients alike will ever so often act out in the transference and in life . . . the unconscious role of a cherished or rejected part of the parent's hypothetical body-self ideal [pp. 416-417].

The relation between a somatic experience and representational schema, as formulated by Greenspan (1979) may help us understand the confusion, denial, and doubting my patients experienced. Greenspan follows maturational patterns and innate givens as they interact with the environment through somatic and then representational schemata involved in learning. He says:

Sensations in the somatic sphere are first experienced and organized in terms of somatic schemes. Later these sensations are perceived at the representational-structural level of learning. Depending on the dynamic relationship to the earlier somatic level of learning, the person may accurately perceive what is going on . . . or may "hyper-react" to it. If . . . during the stage of internalization, the youngster connects a pleasurable bodily experience to the withdrawal of the nurturing object, the pleasurable experience may take on a frightening meaning and foster the tendency to ignore certain sensations from the interior of the body [p. 335].

My patients not only ignored what they perceived from inside their bodies (the pleasure of being masturbated) but they struggled with whether they could know or must ignore what their minds had registered. They evidenced a mental state similar to that described by Mahler (1942) as "pseudo imbecility." Yet my patients did not function as pseudo imbeciles; they were plagued by a need to know, which was countered by the opposite need to placate the external and internalized maternal prohibition against knowing. They seemed to resolve their conflicts in the fashion described by Furman (1971) who said her patient's "terrible doubts were safer . . . than the more terrible truth" (pp. 282-283). Denial was not effective, for the possibility of recognizing the truth or, at least, that the mother lied, surfaced in spite of the prohibition against it.

Discussion

The pathological consequences of a mother's extended and repeated play with her child's genitals are significantly different from the outcome of the few reported cases of mother-son incest in which the act of sexual intercourse takes place between mother and an older son, as have been reported recently by Margolis (1977) and Shengold (1979). Their cases showed serious neurotic and characterological problems, yet both patients

seemed to lack the problems in dealing with reality which my patients showed.

My patients struggled with the fact that the parent in the flesh as well as the internalized parent denied them permission to recognize the seduction as such. Yet the mothers kept repeating the sexual acts and obviously derived pleasure from them. These striking facts of the sexual acts, the maternally enforced denial of the excited and usually unrelieved genital arousal, and the masturbatory prohibitions rendered the child unable to believe his own perceptions and intensified the child's need to seek answers by repetitively questioning himself and the adult world in what I call "object-coercive doubting."

I have called attention to this "object-coercive doubting" because I feel that it may be unique to patients who are incompletely separated from the maternal object. In contrast to the severe obsessional neurotic who is plagued by doubting derived from two opposing or divided feelings within his tormented self, my patients coerced the maternal object to take an opposite side of the child's intrapsychic argument, as if the object were still a part of the self-representation. This process has many determinants.

1. Adequate self-object boundaries have not been formed. Just as the mother acts as if she still possesses her child's body or mind, the patient, like a rapprochement subphase child, feels entitled to engage the mother in what is usually an intrapsychic phenomenon when the mother is seen as part of the self. The child engages the mother in endless arguments or ruminations, as a still acted-out defense both against the persistence and the disruption of the undifferentiated self-object (Kernberg, 1976).

2. The mother-child doubting often ends in orgasmlike fury for both, thus reenacting the sexual play between them.

3. The coercive doubting represents a hostile tormenting of the mother. Now the child can force his needs and wishes on her.

4. The child wants the still omniscient object to tell him the truth, to free him from the burden that her dishonesty and

guilt have imposed upon him and, conversely, to maintain the denial and repression.

My patients revealed more than ambivalence, more than indecision. They could not trust themselves to think, to know, nor could they trust adults to be honest. Their ultimate questions were, "Did I want it to happen? Was it pleasurable?" As Freud (1909, p. 245) said, "The thought-process itself becomes sexualized, for the sexual pleasure which is normally attached to the content of thought becomes shifted on to the act of thinking itself. . . ."

Ferenczi (1933) described patients with similar problems of doubting. He said, "I obtained . . . new corroborative evidence for my supposition that the trauma, especially the sexual trauma, as the pathogenic factor cannot be valued highly enough. Even children of very respectable, sincerely puritanical families, fall victim to real violence or rape much more often than one had dared to suppose. It is the parents who try to find a substitute gratification in this pathological way for their frustration, or it is people thought to be trustworthy . . . who misuse the ignorance and innocence of the child" (p. 161). He describes interferences with the child's thinking and reality testing as well as with his autonomy, and alludes to the formation of pathological defenses. "These children feel physically and morally helpless, their personalities are not sufficiently consolidated in order to be able to protest, *even if only in thought*, for the overpowering force and authority of the adult *makes them dumb and can rob them of their senses*" (p. 162, italics added). Ferenczi describes identification with the sexual aggressor and goes on to say:

> The most important change, produced in the mind of the child by the anxiety-fear-ridden identification with the adult parent, is the *introjection of the guilt feelings of the adult* which makes hitherto harmless play appear as a punishable offence.
>
> When the child recovers from such an attack, he feels enormously confused, in fact, split—innocent and culpable

at the same time—and *his confidence in the testimony of his own senses is broken* (italics added) . . . Not infrequently . . . the seducer becomes over-moralistic . . . [pp. 162-163].

The mothers I encountered had unconscious guilt in spite of their superego lacunae, their denial, and their distorted thinking. As Ferenczi said, this guilt was introjected by the child.

Shengold (1974, 1979) addresses himself to the effects of parental (usually maternal) sexual overstimulation. Shengold alludes to "vertical splitting." He refers to a female patient whose mother exhibited herself to the child and made sexual contact with her, yet did not acknowledge the child's existence during the mother's sexual excitement:

The confrontation in the bathtub had meant castration shock, overstimulation, and terrifying rage. This made for an overwhelming need to be rescued by a good mother. The rage was turned inward; the bad mother was taken in as "introject." *The good mother was preservable only at the expense of the compromise of reality testing by denial* [pp. 107-108; italics added].

Shengold (p. 112) describes, ". . . the confusion and cloudiness that denote an alteration of consciousness affecting the feeling of identity and inhibiting thinking." This is the state of confusion, inhibition and cloudiness I have seen in my patients. My patients coerced a parent or a teacher (a parent substitute) by demanding that the individual tell them what was right, as if to finally extract the truth. But no truth sufficed, for they could not trust the adult object who had so used them and lied to them. There was a similar use of the analyst in the transference, together with the aim of the patients' questioning of the analyst.

The child's sense of self and self-worth and his ability to test reality are so very tied up with those of the parent that the recognition of the extent of pathology of the parent is very difficult, but it is necessary. In fact, children tend to accept the mother's blame and to shoulder her guilt more readily than to

probe the depth of her pathology. It is my impression, that if we are open-minded to the possibility of maternal incest, we shall recognize and treat many more patients who have been victims of such seduction. It is technically and theoretically valuable to distinguish the fantasy from the reality of incest. Transference repetition, reconstruction of the childhood pattern of seduction and incestuous experience, and the delineation of pathological sequelae are clinically significant for analytic working through and full analytic comprehension.

Conclusion and Summary

Prolonged unremitting maternal incest stimulate the child's sexuality and aggressiveness to a grossly abnormal degree. The child cannot use massive denial which would be necessary to cope with the knowledge of the incest and with the excitement and rage it causes. At the same time, the child's ego cannot reconcile the contradictory demands put upon it by his own reality testing and memory as opposed to the mother's denial of reality and imposition of her guilt on the child. Constant tormenting doubting ensues. But the incomplete separation of self and object allows or possibly even forces the child to coerce the maternal object to take one of the contradictory sides in an argument that expresses his extreme conflict, which he cannot assimilate or handle in any way except by doubting. The child takes the other side of the argument, an argument for which there is no resolution.

A defense Freud described, which appears closest although not identical to that of my patients, is that of disavowal (Freud, 1940, pp. 204, 273, 275). Although Freud originally considered disavowal to have been used by the ego to fend off certain perceptions from the outside world which it found distressing, as when the boy must face the castration complex, Freud extended disavowal to other painful perceptions, defining disavowals as ". . . incomplete attempts at detachment from reality. The disavowal is always supplemented by an acknowledgement;

two contrary and independent attitudes always arise and result in the situation of there being a split in the ego" (p. 204). In my patients' attempts to resolve conflicts in which they could neither acknowledge nor deny the overstimulation by the mother or their response to it, they tried to make the not yet separate mother recognize and test reality for the child—a confused reality, for the maternal part of the self-object does not permit clarity. The fact that this defense is inadequate was demonstrated by the repetitiousness with which the children attempted to coerce the parent or the parent substitute and the anxiety and markedly heightened affect which accompanied the coercive doubting. Before the child's conflicts could be resolved, the meaning and function of the defensive object-coercive doubting had to be analyzed. In each case, side by side with the doubting, was the patient's memory of having been sexually stimulated by the mother, for repression and denial were not sufficient. The child was capable of some memory and reality testing independent of the mother; however, separateness and autonomy were only partial, and the child was driven in a frantic attempt to coerce the mother to resolve the doubting that basically involved both of them.

Postscript

Rachel Parens (personal communication) has pointed up repeated references in Sophocles' *Oedipus Rex* (Gould, 1970) to the doubting of Oedipus. Some of these doubts are in relation to his responsibility for the murder of Laius. Other doubting centers on whether his wife, Jocasta, is also his mother.

Jocasta tries to alleviate Oedipus' worries and doubts, saying, "How many times men in dreams, too, slept with their own mothers." Oedipus agrees, then doubts, replying, "Except that my mother is still living, so I must fear her, however well you argue" (verses 984-986).

Gradually Oedipus allows himself to know that he of "pierced feet" (imperfectly made) was "shown monstrous in my

birth, in marriage monstrous, a murderer monstrous in those I killed" (verses 1169-1185).

The Oedipus myth, as is so well known, has Jocasta hang herself, for she knows the truth in what Oedipus has said. Oedipus blinds himself.

I feel that there are interesting similarities between Oedipus and my patients: all were considered imperfect at birth (his pierced feet); all experienced doubting which served the purpose of knowing and not knowing. In the Oedipus myth the father who abandons his child to a danger which may destroy him is himself killed; in the case of my patients, he is rendered trivial by the child's knowledge of having been so important to the mother. The children have to bear the guilt for their parents' sexual behavior.

REFERENCES

BLUM, H. P. (1973). The concept of erotized transference. *J. Amer. Psychoanal. Assn.*, 21:61-76.
———— (1979). On the concept and consequence of the primal scene. *Psychoanal. Q.*, 48:27-47.
BREUER, J. & FREUD, S. (1883-1895). Studies on hysteria. *S. E.*, 2.
BROWNING, D. & BOATMAN, B. (1977). Incest: children at risk. *Amer. J. Psychiat.*, 134:69-72.
FERENCZI, S. (1933). Confusion of tongues between the adult and the child. *Selected Papers*, 3:156-167. New York: Basic Books, 1955.
FREUD, S. (1896). The Aetiology of Hysteria. *S. E.*, 2.
———— (1909). Notes on a case of obsessional neurosis. *S. E.*, 10.
———— (1928). Dostoevski and parricide. *S. E.*, 21.
———— (1931). Female sexuality. *S. E.*, 23.
———— (1932). Femininity. *S. E.*, 22.
———— (1940). An outline of psychoanalysis. *S. E.*, 23.
FURMAN, E. (1971). Reconstruction in child analysis. *Psychoanal. Study Child*, 26:372-385.
GALENSON, E., VOGEL, S., BLAU, S. & ROIPHE, H. (1975). Disturbances in sexual identity beginning at 18 months of age. *Int. Rev. Psychoanal.*, 2:389-397.
GOULD, T., Trans. (1970). Sophocles' *Oedipus the King*. Englewood, N.J.: Prentice Hall.
GREENACRE, P. (1952). *Trauma, Growth and Personality*. New York: Int. Univ. Press, 1971.
———— (1973). The primal scene and the sense of reality. *Psychoanal. Q.*, 42:10-41.

GREENSPAN, S. I. (1979). *Intelligence and Adaptation. Psychol. Issues*, Monogr. 47/48. New York: Int. Univ. Press.

JOHNSON, A. (1949). Sanctions for superego lacunae of adolescents. In *Searchlights on Delinquency*, ed. K. R. Eissler. New York: Int. Univ. Press.

KEISER, S. (1962). Disturbances of ego functions of speech and abstract thinking. *J. Amer. Psychoanal. Assn.*, 10:50-73.

KERNBERG, O. (1976). *Object Relations Theory and Clinical Psychoanalysis*. New York: Aronson.

KRAMER, S. (1974). Episodes of severe ego regression in the course of adolescent analysis. In *The Analyst and the Adolescent at Work*, ed. M. Harley. New York: Quadrangle.

———— (1980). Residues of Split-Object and Split-Self Dichotomies in Adolescence. In *Rapprochement*, ed. R. Lax et al. New York: Aronson, pp. 417-438.

LAUFER, M. (1968). The body image, the function of masturbation, and adolescence: problems of ownership of the body. *Psychoanal. Study Child*, 23:114-135.

LITIN, E., GRIFFIN, M. & JOHNSON, A. M. (1956). Parental influence in unusual sexual behavior in children. *Psychoanal. Q.*, 25:37-55.

MAHLER, M. S. (1942). Pseudo imbecility: a magic cap of invisibility. *Psychoanal. Q.*, 11:149-164.

———— (1958). Autism and symbiosis: two extreme disturbances of identity. *Int. J. Psychoanal.*, 39:77-83.

———— (1963). Thoughts about development and individuation. *Psychoanal. Study Child*, 18:307-324. New York: Int. Univ. Press.

———— (1971). A study of the separation-individuation process and its possible application to borderline phenomena in the psychoanalytic situation. *Psychoanal. Study Child*, 26:403-424.

MARGOLIS, M. (1977). A preliminary study of a case of consummated mother-son incest. *Ann. Psychoanal.*, 5:267-293.

SETTLAGE, C. F. (1971). On the libidinal aspect of early psychic development and the genesis of infantile neurosis. In *Separation-Individuation*, ed. J. B. McDevitt & C. F. Settlage. New York: Int. Univ. Press, pp. 131-154.

SHENGOLD, L. (1967). The effects of overstimulation: rat people. *Int. J. Psychoanal.*, 48:403-415.

———— (1974). The metaphor of the mirror. *J. Amer. Psychoanal. Assn.*, 22:97-115.

———— (1979). Child abuse and deprivation: soul murder. *J. Amer. Psychoanal. Assn.*, 27:533-557.

3902 Netherfield Road
Philadelphia, Pennsylvania 19129

WORKING THROUGH
AND RESISTANCE
TO CHANGE: Arthur F. Valenstein, m.d.
INSIGHT AND
THE ACTION SYSTEM

S OME YEARS AGO, AN EMINENT PSYCHOANALYST told me about a most intelligent, cooperative man whom he once had in analysis in Vienna. The analysis seemed to progress, a great deal was learned; the patient accepted the interpretations as genuine, and they seemed to be included into the analytic work, to the enhancement of the process. This went on for several years, but apparently nothing changed. Finally the patient himself complained about it. He said he had been coming faithfully for some time; a great deal seemed to have become clear and understandable; it was all very interesting, but he had not changed in any significant way.

His analyst at that point said, "What about your insights?" to which the patient replied, "Oh well, I have them—I have them alright." The analyst then asked, "Well, what about them, what do you do with them?" The patient replied, "I have them. They are on the top shelf of the closet. Someday I might need them."

Clinical Professor of Psychiatry, Harvard Medical School; Training and Supervising Analyst, Psychoanalytic Institute of New England, East.

A slightly different version of this paper was presented to the Chicago Psychoanalytic Society and the Institute for Psychoanalysis on the occasion of their 50th anniversary program, November 7, 1981, and to the Los Angeles Psychoanalytic Society, April 15, 1982.

Even so, insight remains the paramount aim of analysis in the classical tradition, notwithstanding that current shift in practice which assigns therapeutic priority to the experiential recapitulation in the transference of early object relations, with an emphasis on attachment to early objects and separation from them, and their further vicissitudes and normative significance for the emergent sense of self. However, if insight is not enough, if insight *in itself* does not quite do it, does not lead to definitive change, then we must consider other factors.

The familiar concept "working through" is broad and covers various aspects of the therapeutic process, including not only the progressive development of insight, but its significance for change, depending on whether it is used. The ultimate working through of insight is pivotally related to the function of action and to definitive changes in action patterns as they are consolidated into the "action system," this last term, one that I specified some twenty years ago.

It was at that time that I wrote a paper on "Affects, Emotional Reliving, and Insight in the Psycho-Analytic Process" (1962). I think I understand better now than then why I wrote it. Out of my own experience as a candidate and as a practicing analyst early in his career, I felt that affect and experience in the form of emotional reliving were possibly understated in the theory of psychoanalytic therapy, and in those descriptions and advices which, insofar as they suggested the ritualization of technique, gave a warped picture of the psychoanalytic situation and process. Also, it was not uncommon then to characterize psychoanalysts as being either warm and responsive, feelingful, and at least by implication, sympathetic and giving; or cold and intellectual, possibly bright but again, at least by implication, perhaps hard and withholding, and unempathic, although that was not the term of first choice at that time. As I look back, I think this was an oversimplification, and by no means always correct, but that was the trend then, and perhaps it is so, still. Affects and action responses were there—no question—but it was the so-called "warm and easy" analysts who were expected

to be more attentive to those modalities of expression and communication. Would it be correct to think of them as being of a "humanist persuasion," a partiality that has been in the ascendancy in recent years? But then, what of the others, the so-called "traditionalists" (although this polarization also is an oversimplification)? Really, are they nonhumanists?[1]

In 1962, I wanted to call attention to the role of affects and experiential reliving in the classical analytic situation and to emphasize that these modalities were there, that they had always been there, and that they were proportionally clinically interlocked, along with cognitive concomitants, in the psychoanalytic process. In fact, I stressed that the *erlebnis* phenomenon, i.e., the inner emotional experience, was instrumental to the emergence of veritable insight. I added a postscript addressed to "Insight and the Action System," for although it seemed that I had adequately dealt with the development of a "mutative" insight (borrowing the term "mutative" from Strachey [1934], to indicate that it combined both affective-conative and cognitive components) as it becomes established in the course of the psychoanalytic process, it followed that, "However vital and veritable it may become, there is nothing magical about insight; in and of itself, it is not equivalent to a change in behaviour, nor does it *directly* produce the relatively conflict-free readaptation which is the hoped-for outcome of a successful psychoanalysis. For there to be final adaptive change, alterations in behaviour, whether subtle or obvious, must somehow come about as a result of modifications of action patterns" (p. 323).

Recently there has been a considerable revival of interest, on the clinical front, in issues of neurosogenesis and nosology, and the nature of the therapeutic process and the basis of change;[2] while on the theoretical side, substantial criticism of

---

[1] Stone (1981) has discussed similar historical aspects at some length.

[2] The role of action in the psychoanalytic process and its significance for change was presaged, in principle, by Freud's (1914) paper on "Remembering, Repeating and Working Through." It was certainly a motif of Ferenczi's (1921) proposals for an "Active Therapy in Psycho-Analysis." Wheelis (1950) published a pivotal paper on "The Place of Action in Personality Change," and among recent contributions to the theory of change, Rangell (1981) discussed the "responsibility of insight," and "the executive functions of the ego, the patient himself directing his next moves in life" (p. 128).

psychoanalytic metapsychology has emerged. A series of thoughtful publications have appeared, particularly from former students and associates of David Rapaport, which vigorously question the operational validity and value of psychoanalytic metapsychology, with the concluding recommendation that it be discarded as distracting and extraneous to the main and operationally valid body of psychoanalytic clinical theory and practice.

Action Language and a Psychoanalytic Theory of Action

During the last decade, Schafer (1976) has written at length on the concept of "action" and "action language." He has done so, apparently, largely in order to establish this concept as the basis for a strictly phenomenological clinical theory of psychoanalysis. His thesis is that psychoanalysis has been historically encumbered by a mechanistic, anthropomorphic metapsychology which is both anachronistic and specious.

I am not alone[3] in concluding that Schafer, in his effort to avoid abstractionism and sterile theory, which for him apparently means all of psychoanalytic metapsychology, has gone the other extreme to an exclusive literalization of action. What is more, this concept of action is so reductionistic and sweeping that it loses its clinical value; everything is action.

It is important that a distinction be established between Schafer's concept of "action language," with its implications for psychoanalytic theory and the advised demise of metapsychology, and action and the "action system," with respect to the clinical theory of psychoanalysis and its practice which I find quite compatible with many metapsychological formulations. Metapsychology and the clinical theory of psychoanalysis are at different levels of discourse, except that metapsychology is not a tightly closed system with all propositions speculative and at the same level of abstraction. In many respects, particular

[3] See recent critiques by Calogeres & Alston (1980), Friedman (1976), and Meissner, (1979).

metapsychological constructs, even though they may tempt the "sin" of anthropomorphization, can be usefully related to evidential clinical observations and immediately related constructs of psychoanalysis, and to psychoanalysis as a treatment method. In the clinical situation, the action aspect or modality which is expressed motorially, but which includes the language of action in both the explicit articulate sense and in paraverbal accompaniments, is only one of a number of the operant modalities that bear upon the development of insight and the ultimate outcome of a psychoanalysis with respect to change.

Indeed, we need a theory of action in psychoanalysis just as much as a theory of cognition and a theory of affect—but it need not be an exclusive theory unto itself, outside of and replacing psychoanalysis or psychoanalytic metapsychology. Nor need we shy away from what I call with some hesitancy, behavioral considerations, for introducing behavioral considerations into a psychoanalytic theory of therapy and theory of cure does not require that we become behavior therapists or behaviorists.

Modal Functions: Cognition, Affection, Conation, and Action

I have found it convenient to use, for purposes of study and analysis of the therapeutic situation, a familiar coordinate system of constructs based on the traditional trichotomy of cognition, affection, and conation. This derives from the historical philosophic inquiry into consciousness and the analysis of it according to these three principal functions. To them, however, I have added a fourth, namely the function of action, as it fulfills and goes beyond conation,[4] which in itself refers to the experienced incipience of action, or the consciously known impulsion to act in a particularized way. If conation, by traditional

---

[4] Webster's *Third New International Dictionary* defines conation as "the conscious drive to perform apparently volitional acts with or without knowledge of the origin of the drive . . . striving that may appear in consciousness as volition or desire or in behavior as action tendencies."

definition and usage, refers to a voluntary activity, to the imminence of action, then perhaps "action" might refer to the actual carrying out of an (impelled and sensed) imminent activity.

Psychoanalytic "modernists" who argue that psychoanalysis should be made "scientifically" respectible and who are sweepingly critical of psychoanalytic metapsychology in this regard generally regard this trichotomy, which I have revised into a quaternary, as metaphysically Aristotelian and scientifically untenable.[5] Conceptually, these four modalities are logical abstract constructs. Clinically described, as they are identified in their referent functions, they are by no means independent of one another. As Rapaport (1951a) pointed out, they are merely aspects of a unitary process, and no one functional modality is conceivable without the others. However, for purposes of qualitative analysis and classification, this modality system is heuristic and clinically useful. Specifying phenomenological aspects of communicative and expressive mental activity in a succinct conceptual form enhances the study of the therapeutic process of psychoanalysis with respect to technique and the ultimate aim of change, namely the working through of new or changed ways of behaving.

We usually speak at a social and a more or less euphemistic level. However, as a psychoanalysis extends and deepens—through free association made possible by a lowering of censorship, through fantasy, dreams, and other data, and under the impact of the transference neurosis—patients regress in the service of the analytic process. Optimally, they become more comfortable in speaking of their private world and in their private language. Analysts, in turn, have their own linguistic predilections, which are more than stylistic. Yet it is important that they be flexibly able to share the personalized terms of their patients and be attentive to their developmental locus of origin. The opposite prevails also, in that the patient

[5] Gedo (1979) for example, prefers "a psychology based on the hierarchy of personal aims" (p. 12).

identifies with the analyst as the communicative empathic fit between analyst and patient develops. And as this communicative ambiance of the analytic situation becomes consensual, it becomes technically feasible to intuitively phrase interpretations so as to *predominantly* signify action potentials, or cognitive or emotive attributes.

My attention was originally drawn to the action system for technical reasons, and consequently to its significance for a comprehensive theory of psychotherapy, including psychoanalysis, as such, and a theory of change (formerly termed a theory of "cure").[6] I find it informative to listen closely to the language of therapeutic intervention and interpretation in particular, with special attention to verbal expressions and paraverbal constructions that not only signify cognitive realization, but, possibly more so, affective, or conative, or action correlates. These, depending on the hierarchy of attributes, might sometimes be more cognitive, sometimes more affective, and sometimes more action-oriented. Included might very well be psychomotor and visceral referents, i.e., body or "gut" language. Commonly, there is articulate movement from the *more* abstract and derivative language of the adult back toward the childhood concretistic, the personal literal language which is close to feeling (affection), close to the impulsion to act (conation), and to action itself. To be further sensed is the unique *lingua franca*, the private, even biographically pivotal language of the individual, within the conventions and the colloquialisms of his culture as he grew up in it—namely, the individual's predilection for his own personally underscored terms and communications within

---

[6] A theory of the mind and its operations and a theory of psychoanalytic technique are quite different. Formulations regarding each need be consistent with those distinctions that specify them as different, even though they finally may be related at the clinical level.

Although psychoanalytic theory adds immeasurably to clinical understanding, that does not mean that it is technically appropriate to interpret in the language of theory, much less to "talk metapsychology" in the psychoanalytic situation. Yet, putting forward "action language" as practically the sole basis for a clinical theory of psychoanalysis fails to do justice to metapsychology, or to psychoanalytic technique, and to the relation between the two.

this context. Pertinent in this respect is the implicit insight and vital potential for "working through" of appropriate metaphor and metonymy and of the onomatopoeia, in the form of expressions which might be relevant to the particular person.

Also to be contextually included are the personally originated or innovated language emanating from the earliest period of interaction between the infant or toddler and his surround, the primary objects, the mother and father. Relative to that is the importance of learning from the patient the origin of his experiences and associative data—from whom, how, and when; what external stresses, traumas, indulgences, deprivations, he was subjected to; the nature and source of paradigm intrapsychic conflicts, their current derivative expression in behavior, and in what form they are articulately expressed—in what modal language (cognitive, affective, conative, action), what hierarchy of modalities.

Assimilation of Insight and the Process of Reorientation and Change

To introduce another conceptual and methodological consideration, I propose the utilization of the successive therapeutic operations formulated by Bibring (1954). He conceptualized four major types of operations which he termed "processes and procedures" within the therapeutic process, namely: (a) the production of material; (b) the utilization of the produced material (mainly) by the therapist and/or by the patient; (c) the assimilation by the patient of the results of such utilization; and (d) the processes of reorientation and readjustment.

I shall consider the last two items in this sequence, namely, the processes of assimilation and of reorientation and readjustment toward therapeutically induced change. As Bibring specified:

> The process of *assimilation* refers to the patient's positive reaction to the activities of the therapist by which he

makes use of the material, to their absorbtion by the ego
and to those changes which we named "curative agents."
The processes of *reorientation and readjustment* are intimately linked up with the function of certain curative
agents, such as the two forms of insight. They may require
an additional, sometimes prolonged and repetitive process
of testing and learning [pp. 761-762].

For many years—save but for a few implied qualifications until
this current period of the "widened scope"—psychoanalysis was
a conflict psychology. Its theory of neurosogenesis was based
on a concept of infantile neurosis, with repression of predominantly oedipal but also preoedipal conflicts, the outcome being
symptom formation. The corresponding theory of "cure" was
that if the paradigm infantile conflicts were reactivated and
recapitulated in the transference neurosis, they could be
brought into consciousness and made accessible to insight and,
in this way, resolved. The neurotic symptoms would fade away,
as they had been no more than compromise expressions of the
now resolved conflicts. Psychic integration, enhanced in consequence, would further effective functioning. The implication
was that once infantile memories, fantasies, and conflicts had
become conscious, there would be an opportunity to compare
reliving the *past* in the present, with living the *present* in the
present, and for action consonant with the reality principle.

The oedipal phase and conflict are still pivotal features of
the so-called structural neuroses (formerly termed "transference neuroses"), and psychoanalysis is still a conflict psychology.
However, with the broadened scope of its application, conditions attributable to external conflict and traumatic and hap-
hazard events during the earlier, even preverbal, phases of
development have come within the sphere of psychoanalytic
practice. Such conditions are distinctly preoedipal and are developmental neuroses (formerly termed "narcissistic neuroses")
for the most part. The transference replications in such cases
are likely to be diadic, centering on security and nurturent
needs with misperceptions and misconstructions of self-object

discrimination. In consequence, at least through the initial and middle phases of treatment, the more interactive and experiential therapeutic features of necessity assume a temporal hierarchical priority over cognitive aspects, over the explanatory content of interpretive interventions.

Nonetheless, the qualitatively different neurosogenetic levels of the structural neuroses and the developmental neuroses are not mutually exclusive. Nowadays, we are aware that, for a middle group of patients, very early preoedipal developmental determinants and later preoedipal and oedipal conflict determinants are both pertinent, depending more or less on the particular patient. This correlates theoretically with contemporary psychoanalysis being both a conflict and a developmental psychology.

The processes of assimilation, reorientation, and readjustment depend on the working through of insight and its associated effects and potentialities. In that regard, Robert Waelder, in a discussion about 20 years ago, suggested that working through be called "suffering through," as it is often a painful and extendedly difficult process. Resistance in the form of defenses against painful affects and anxiety as well as resistance to the renunciation of neurotically gained gratification are involved, through which the patient must make his way. Change contingent on *assimilation* of insight, with concurrent reorientation finally entails new patterns of behavior. Taking chances and *acting*, and finally living[7] in a readapted way, contrary to the familiar, in themselves give rise to anxiety attributable to resistance from all the psychic agencies—id, ego, and superego—to an inertia against change conceptualized as the conservative principle of the repetition compulsion.

Behaving in significantly different ways comes under the rubric of learning in the broadest sense. To what extent is psychoanalysis a therapy implicitly related to learning, with the therapeutic outcome to be understood according to theories of

[7] Leo Berman (personal communication) stated: "Where does acting out end and living begin?"

learning (i.e., learning about oneself–insight–learning to use the insight–using it)? This extended frame of reference is entirely consistent with a theory of the unconscious and the therapeutic intention of resolving unconscious conflict by bringing it to consciousness, with the aim of eventually modifying behavior through the elective use of insight worked through into changes in action patterns.

Activity-Passivity: Ego Strength and the Will to Action and Change

Both in practice and in the theory of psychotherapies, I favor the making of a distinction (1979), between psychoanalysis as such, in the classical or standard sense, where insight and change through insight are the paramount goal, and the widened scope, widened variety of psychoanalytic psychotherapies which are predominantly interpersonal and mutually experiential in their intention and therapeutic effect. Not that the latter are second best (the copper rather than the pure gold of analysis [Freud, 1919]); indeed they may require just as much or more of the therapist in intuitively perceptive improvisation than analysis, but they are not paramountly insight-oriented, and perforce are more appropriate to different clinical circumstances and a different sector of conditions.

Current technical trends consequent to the widened scope of practice of the psychoanalyst blur this distinction. Furthermore, they incline toward more active interventionalism and an emphasis on the realistic aspects of the patient-therapist relationship. Therapies so modified resemble supportive, corrective, and even reparative transactional methods on the here-and-now level rather than the familiar interpretative approach of traditional Freudian psychoanalysis which, through the transference neurosis as it gradually evolves according to the patient's predilections, searches out unconscious sources of conflict at the paradigm genetic level. I am not proposing any substantive change in the setting and form of a psychoanalysis

as such; the technical considerations implied follow naturally from an appreciation of the communicative set that directs the quality of understanding and its relation to behavior and change. The predominant use, much less the overuse of any specific language of intervention or interpretation is not being advocated. Although the appropriate use of "action" referents is central to the main thesis of this paper, it is by no means suggested that this be to the detriment of the timely intended and yet *balanced* communicative utilization of all of the modality referents, i.e., cognitive, affective, conative, and action.

I shall now focus explicitly on what heretofore has been left mostly at an implicit level and essentially in the silent area of a psychoanalysis, namely the ultimate working through of a synthesis of insight into action and change.

The concept "Ego" in the structural sense is no more than the mental construct of a coherent agency of integrative functions. High in its hierarchy of psychological structures, in that regard, is the synthesizing function, which can be counted upon to exert a silent effect, reciprocating *pari passu* with the conflict-resolving and corrective influence of insight, as it becomes substantial and significant in the course of the analytic experience. Neubauer (1979) called attention to Nunberg's "synthetic function of the ego," and the fact that "insight depends upon those synthetic activities of the ego which bind together [i.e., integrate] various isolated parts into a new ego organization" (p. 32). However, particularly to the outsider and even to some analytic patients during the early phase of treatment, the psychoanalytic process might seem simplistically reductive—that is, an unraveling, a taking apart rather than a reconstructive putting together. It may be difficult, especially during the early phase of analysis, to appreciate that the analytic experience, the reduction of defenses used for resistance and the taking apart, is also very much a concomitant resynthesis of component aspects and functions of the ego made available for constructive integration into the self ("Where Id was, there ego shall be" [Freud, 1933, p. 80]), made possible by the successful analysis

of characterologic distortions and symptomatic disturbances. And a patient's misconstruction of analysis as being one-sided can usually be managed through timely interpretative interventions, short of the supportive and alliance-building maneuvers advocated by some analysts nowadays, as if a standard analytic position were stiltedly mechanistic and nonhumanistically intellectual and abstract.

No inquiry into the working-through process toward change would be complete without at least a brief consideration of the mental set that mobilizes the individual to chance necessary actions for change consistent with insight embedded into the variety of therapeutic effects sequential to a successful psychoanalytic inquiry into the developmental misadventures and unconscious conflicts with which the patient came. Germane to the utilization of assimilated insight and correlative experiential effects is the capacity (actively) to initiate and sustain (concomitantly) corresponding action, both with regard to the self and others (objects). Insofar as it is purposeful and at the level of the preconscious-conscious, it is action under the aegis of ego, and in that sense, active and in keeping with Rapaport's (1951b, p. 541) systematic metapsychological formulations concerning activity and passivity, the former being seen as "coterminous with the developing autonomy of the ego." Rapaport also specified as synonym to ego autonomy "the roots of the subjective experience of volition," the "ability to delay discharge" (drive tension and impulsion to action), and the ability "to undertake detour actions toward the drive object," all of which are closely related to activity.

Action, structured into activity patterns, according to this conception of the "activity" mode in contrast with its reciprocal, "passivity," coincides with certain aspects of the age-old concept of "will," an inexact, more philosophic than scientific concept. As an explicit matter it has been out of the mainstream of psychoanalysis, albeit that it became a feature of Otto Rank's technical proposals for psychoanalysis during the last period of his life.

Over the centuries, less so in modern times, the concept of will has been much the subject of discourse and debate in philosophy, particularly in the question of "free will or determinism," or in its theological equivalent, whether "man proposes and God disposes" or whether man has freedom of choice. While such a question seems philosophically dated and obscure and not scientifically psychological, for both humanistic and scientific reasons we cannot ignore its significance for change and the ultimate issue of personal responsibility for it, whether the term will is used explicitly or implied in some reformulation so as to be more acceptable scientifically. Leaving to the periphery the philosophical view, including its historical transcendental underpinnings, free will and determinism need not be antithetical. They can be complementary when it comes to human behavior, including changes in behavior that become possible as a consequence of psychoanalysis. There are determinants which are relatively external and impersonal, outside of individual choice, and those inner factors which when conscious may tip the balance and make for choice, given "the will" to act in accordance with achieved insight within the associated therapeutic aspects of a successful analysis. In the structural neuroses, for the so-called "good neurotic" with a strong ego who is motivated by suffering and disposed to change, the "will to act," for the most part, can be expected to exert an effect in a relatively silent, ego-syntonic way. For other patients, with so-called narcissistic neuroses, including borderline disturbances, the not-so-strong, ego-deficit patients anchored in a regressed position with a firmly entrenched passive orientation, it is quite different. It is not so silent a matter, this issue of the "lack of will" to change, to exert oneself toward action in keeping with insight and reality.

The term "will" immediately has the connotations of (a) self-determination, inner volition, and resolve which intends responsibility, and by means of which an individual consciously undertakes deliberate and purposeful action; (b) a testament, a legal declaration of wishes for posthumous action; (c) the

future tense of the verb "to be"; (d) a man's name—his full name being "Will Power."

Is it not interesting that all four of these connotations are related and that they imply something in common, even the fictional "Will Power," in the externally attributed sense? The intentionality is certainly in the verb "to be" and in the legal testament which is meant to guarantee a considered and decided set of posthumous actions. And when a patient complains initially, "I have no will power," we are not surprised to learn presently that he expects to get the so-called "will power" from his therapist, possibly in a symbolic concretistic form. His therapist is expected to assume the mantle and embody the essence, the power of "Mr. Will Power," who, in some magical way, should become available to him, perhaps for anaclitic fusion, as with the omnipotent parent, or less voraciously, perhaps by dependently exploiting the therapist as surrogate, as *Doppelgänger*. Therapeutically, it is pivotal that the patient presently become aware that he has externalized and attributed to his therapist an exaggerated version of the substance of strength and decisiveness which he has, for whatever mishappence, disavowed in the course of his own development, often secondary to anxiety and conflict over autonomy and aggression, and their adaptive transformation and modulated equivalence, assertiveness. We understand too little of the developmental aspects of what is conveyed by the term "will." Some facets are suggested by the autonomy given the individual from the beginning, including its subsequent transformations—corresponding to the familiar psychoanalytic modal *activity*, rather than *passive* compliance.

The active ego, which reflects the potential for effective executant assertiveness, has in the past been thought of as a "strong" ego—indicative of the strength of the ego versus the id (the drives) and the external world (reality)—and also the superego, although it may coincide with a strong superego, or even with an intransigently punitive superego unhappily enough

for the self and/or the external world of other people.[8] It is this very "strength," this relatively autonomous potential that connects with the essence of "will" and the so-called strong will, and its will power. When Freud (1918) set a definite termination date, an ending time for the analysis of the Wolf Man, an active intervention which appears to have been the only parameter to classical technique he introduced, he essentially manipulated[9] the ego (will) of the patient in the direction of personal responsibility and the reciprocation of active (ego activity) for passive. Do we not do something similar when we are confronted by a patient who passively, albeit with a certain (active) insistence, says to us: "So what! What are *you* going to do about it?"

I once pointed out to a patient whom I had in psychotherapy, the specifics of a certain piece of acting out. After I had interpreted its congruence with fantasy, with transference distortions from out of the past, not to mention its self-damaging and egocentric insensitive implications, the patient was quiet for a moment and then calmly replied, "You are right—but since when do I have to be realistic?" This attitude serves as a serious resistance to inner change and adaptive action. Considering the inherent limitations of psychoanalysis and the "imperfect" state of the art, there comes a time when it may be both reasonable and pragmatic to decide that an analysis has run its course. Not *always* is it germane to state, "Perhaps you should have further analyzed this or that aspect of the transference," or, "Did you continue long enough to reach this or that developmental phase or deficit?" Need analysis be necessarily "interminable" in practice, in order to be certain that it is "complete"? We may have analyzed, as best we can, the egocentric narcissism of an arrested or regressed position—and not uncommonly within it, the persistent maintenance of a passive

---

[8] alas—for there are those self-righteous moralists who act as if *they* were born with the book of rules in their hands.

[9] See Bibring's (1954) discussion of manipulation as a *therapeutic* principle (pp. 750-753).

stance, including the denial of personal responsibility. However, consistent passivity serves as both a gratification and a defense against activity and the active position which enhance ego autonomy and that component attribute of the self known as the sense of personal responsibility. All too often, especially when gratification exerts a prior claim over *unlust*, anxiety, or suffering of some sort, the patient holds to his denial of responsibility and resists chance-taking toward actions that might make for change. Do we not then in some way respond, possibly directly or at least in effect, "Well, what are *you* going to do about it?" or "Do you *really* want to live your life that way?" Is not the setting of a time for ending the analysis (or the psychotherapy) a step that may be resisted by the patient, a move that conveys that the inevitable "in due course" is now about to fall due, that the analysis is not to be a "cure" away from Lourdes or the analyst a mythical and omnipotent deliverer himself "reborn"?

To return briefly to Otto Rank, who left psychoanalysis for more active experiential and existential methods, he collaborated with Ferenczi in the latter's innovative proposals for an active technique, which culminated in their monograph, *The Development of Psychoanalysis* (Ferenczi and Rank, 1923). A few years later, however, he broke away from Ferenczi as well as Freud. About ten years before he died, Rank wrote three short volumes on psychoanalytic technique, subsequently published in English as *Will Therapy* (1936), in which he elaborated on the issue of personal responsibility as it becomes pivotal in the closing phase of a psychoanalysis. He proposed "end setting" into every analysis as an active intervention, since "it seemed certain that the ending of the analysis represents a will contest" (p. 14), and as a definite way of requiring the patient to resolve the "battle of wills" which he saw as the crux of the therapy. By actively setting a time for termination, chosen on the basis of criteria of the "inner conflict of will" (active assertiveness), Rank sought to avoid a "battle of wills" between patient and therapist and instead to turn it back to the patient who would then, in

the interest of recovery, have to resolve the inner conflict between his will and his "counter-will."

Does not this seem related to current dynamic *a priori* specified short-term time-limited therapies? And can we accept any aspect of Rank's formulation into our understanding of the outcome of an analysis for change, whether successfully or unsuccessfully? To a certain extent, is there not something of a struggle within the patient, if he is going to *actively use* his laboriously won insight and work it through into consistent and reliable action patterns, i.e., to structure insight intrapsychically and concurrently into behavior and adaptive living patterns? Blum (1979) emphasizes that "Insight promotes structural change and then reflects that change [p. 55] . . . [It] is related to the mastery of conflict and regression, but also to creative solutions and to the creation of new organization and structure" (p. 60). Consistent with intra- and intersystemic restructuralization of the ego, i.e., change intrapsychically, is the possibility of consonant change interpersonally. Rapaport (1951b) introduced his paper on "Ego Autonomy" with an intuitively insightful allegorical tale from the Talmud, which epitomizes the issue.

> There was an Eastern king who heard about Moses. He heard that Moses was a leader of men, a good man, a wise man, and he wished to meet him. But Moses, busy wandering 40 years in the desert, couldn't come. So the king sent his painters to Moses and they brought back a picture of him. The king called his phrenologists and astrologists and asked them, "What kind of man is this?" They went into a huddle and came out with a report which read: This is a cruel, greedy, self-seeking, dishonest man. The king was puzzled. He said, "Either my painters do not know how to paint or there is no such science as astrology or phrenology." When Moses heard this he was surprised and asked the king what he meant. The king explained, but Moses only shook his head and said, "No. Your phrenologists and astrologists are right. That's what I was made

of! I fought against it and that's how I became what I am" [p. 357].

It not only illustrates the autonomy of the ego, but it clearly implies the significance of this autonomy for change through action, insight driven home through consonant and consistent actions. We could call it insight in the service of action and behavioral change, or possibly analytically informed action (a phrase which might please psychoanalytic "modernists" and be acceptable to "traditionalists") which, through habitual use, becomes ego-syntonically patterned and relatively autonomous. It is worked through into the character structure and becomes a reliable part of the ego.

Summary

The concept working through is broad and covers various aspects of the psychoanalytic process, including not only the progressive development of insight, but its significance for change, depending on whether or not it is used. Ultimately, the working through of insight is pivotally related to the function of action and to definitive changes in action patterns as they are consolidated into the action system.

Added as a fourth modal function to the traditional trichotomy of cognition, affection, and conation, action refers to the actual carrying out of an (impelled and sensed) immanent activity, i.e., conation. Change that is contingent on the assimilation of insight, with concurrent reorientation, finally entails undertaking new patterns of behavior. Acting and behaving in significantly different ways consequent to the elective use of insight lead to personal and consonant interpersonal change, as the modified or new action patterns are worked through. In conclusion, action is considered with regard to the synthesizing function of the ego and activity-passivity modes. Activity is seen as "coterminous with the developing autonomy of the Ego," and as such, is related to the concept of will, which is also discussed.

REFERENCES

BERMAN, L. (1949). Countertransferences and attitudes of the analyst in the therapeutic process. *Psychiat.*, 12:159-166.

BIBRING, E. (1954). Psychoanalysis and the dynamic psychotherapies. *J. Amer. Psychoanal. Assn.*, 2:745-770.

BLUM, H. P. (1979). The curative and creative aspects of insight. *J. Amer. Psychoanal. Assn.*, 27 (Suppl.):41-69.

CALOGERES, R. & ALSTON, T. M. (1980). On "action language" in psychoanalysis. *Psychoanal. Q.*, 49:663-695.

ERIKSON, E. H. (1956). The problem of ego identity. *J. Amer. Psychoanal. Assn.*, 4:56-121.

FERENCZI, S. (1921). The further development of the active therapy in psychoanalysis. In *Further Contributions to the Theory and Technique of Psycho-Analysis*. New York: Basic Books, 1952, pp. 198-217.

———— & RANK, O. (1923). *The Development of Psychoanalysis*. New York: Dover, 1956.

FREUD, S. (1914). Remembering, repeating and working through. *S. E.*, 12.

———— (1918). From the history of an infantile neurosis. *S. E.*, 17.

———— (1919). Lines of advance in psychoanalytic therapy. *S. E.*, 17.

———— (1933). New introductory lectures on psycho-analysis. *S. E.*, 22.

FRIEDMAN, L. (1976). Difficulties of an action theory of the mind. *Int. Rev. Psychoanal.*, 3:129-138.

GEDO, J. E. (1979). *Beyond Interpretation*. New York: Int. Univ. Press.

MEISSNER, W. W. (1979). Critique of concepts and therapy in the action language approach to psychoanalysis. *Int. J. Psychoanal.*, 60:291-310.

NEUBAUER, P. B. (1979). The role of insight in psychoanalysis. *J. Amer. Psychoanal. Assn.*, 27 (Suppl.):29-40.

RANGELL, L. (1981). From insight to change. *J. Amer. Psychoanal. Assn.*, 29:119-141.

RANK, O. (1936). Will Therapy. New York: Norton.

RAPAPORT, D. (1951a). The conceptual model of psychoanalysis. In *Theoretical Models in Psychology*, ed. G. Klein & D. Krech. Durham, N.C.: Duke Univ. Press, 1952, pp. 56-81.

———— (1951b). The autonomy of the ego. In *The Collected Papers of David Rapaport*, ed. M. M. Gill. New York: Basic Books, 1967, pp. 357-367.

———— (1953). Some metapsychological considerations concerning activity and passivity. In *The Collected Papers of David Rapaport*, ed. M. M. Gill. New York: Basic Books, 1967, pp. 530-568.

SCHAFER, R. (1976). *A New Language for Psychoanalysis*. New Haven, Conn.: Yale Univ. Press.

STONE, L. (1981). Notes on the noninterpretive elements in the psychoanalytic situation and process. *J. Amer. Psychoanal. Assn.*, 29:89-118.

STRACHEY, J. (1934). The nature of the therapeutic action of psycho-analysis. *Int. J. Psychoanal.*, 15:127-159.

VALENSTEIN, A. F. (1962). Affects, emotional reliving, and insight in the psycho-analytic process. *Int. J. Psychoanal.*, 43:315-324.

———— (1979). The concept of "classical" psychoanalysis. *J. Amer. Psychoanal. Assn.*, 27 (Suppl.): 113-136.

WHEELIS, A. (1950). The place of action in personality change. *Psychiat.*, 13:135-148.

140 Foster Street
Cambridge, Massachusetts 02138

ID RESISTANCE AND THE STRENGTH OF THE INSTINCTS: A CLINICAL DEMONSTRATION

ALVIN FRANK, M.D.

T O THE END, FREUD'S DEFINITIVE formulations on the psychoanalytic process were clear statements of the indivisibility of quantitative, economic, instinctual drive, id forces and qualitative, structural, ego capacities in considering therapeutic results. In "The Question of Lay Analysis" (1926b) he discussed "the normal causes of neurotic illness." He cited:

> an innate strength and unruliness of the instinctual life in the id, which from the outset sets the ego tasks too hard for it. . . . Such factors must of course acquire an aetiologic importance, in some cases a transcending one. We have invariably to reckon with the instinctual strength of the id; if it is developed to excess, the prospects of our therapy are poor [p. 242].

In "Analysis Terminable and Interminable," Freud (1937) further elaborated this thesis. Here Freud first referred to the "constitutional" or "congenital" strengths of the instincts. Since the inference of presence since birth is contradicted by their strengthening at puberty or, in women, menopause, he modified his terminology to "the strength of the instincts *at the time*" (p. 224). The idea that it is possible to permanently dispose of instinctual demands as a result of analysis is quickly dismissed:

"No, we mean something else, something which may be roughly described as a 'taming' of the instinct. That is to say, the instinct is brought completely into the harmony of the ego . . ." (p. 225). The outcome is then obviously dependent on the *economic* factor, as critical to the relative strength of the instinct and the ego. In theory analysis should put an end to the dominance of the quantitative factor. Freud states, "repressions depend . . . entirely on the relative strength of the forces involved." Analytically an adult ego can revise old repressions formed at a time when they were "primitive defensive measures taken by the immature, feeble ego" (p. 227). In influencing quantitative factors analysis ideally effects a qualitative change. However, analytic experience could not invariably confirm this ideal expectation.

> In the past, the quantitative factor of instinctual strength opposed the ego's defensive efforts; for that reason we called in the work of analysis to help; and now that same factor sets a limit to the efficacy of this new effort. If the strength of the instinct is excessive, the mature ego, supported by analysis, fails in its task, just as the helpless ego failed formerly . . . the final upshot always depends on the relative strength of the psychical agencies which are struggling with one another [p. 230].

Yet "id resistance" and instinctual strength are rarely discussed definitively. There are a number of overlapping possible explanations for this neglect.

First, after an era of "id analysis," analytic attention has been focused for over three decades on issues of the ego. The limitations of the former approach led to appreciation of structural considerations. The impact of the seminal contributions of Anna Freud (1936) and the school of ego psychologists is reflected in attempts to formulate and apply their concepts and discoveries. This has led to a shifting of attention from the ego in conflict (with id and superego) to the supraordinate ego.

Inasmuch as we almost exclusively view any mental phe-

nomenon through its impact on the ego, observations of its functions and resistances have avoided troublesome problems and difficult judgments regarding what is observed. For example, and particularly relevant to the clinical data of this paper: when is a given observed disruptive psychological event to be explained as id eruption as opposed to ego weakness? Since our judgments regarding the id forces are necessarily more inferential, we are prone to choose the more certain option. Further, in viewing the ego one can advantageously simultaneously survey it as both the *seat* of all resistances and the *source* of its three specific variations, the resistances of repression, transference, and gain from illness. With time resistance has come to mean, in usual parlance, defense.

Schur (1966) states that Freud's association of id resistance with the repetition compulsion and death instinct to explain the incurable patient has led to undesirable consequences. "Assigning to this type of defense the term 'id resistance' and locating its source in the death instinct must create a fatalistic attitude in the analyst" (p. 187).

A number of important analytic thinkers object to the ordering and understanding of clinical observations as manifestations of instinctual forces on epistemological grounds. The inclusion of quantitative and energic dimensions or the substantive, "id," constitutes an affront to basic limitations consistent with their proposed theoretical systems and philosophies of science. Many of them would restrict psychoanalysis to "hermeneutics," the understanding of meaning. I have reviewed some of these proposals elsewhere (Frank, 1979).

The inevitable consequence of discouraging systematic consideration of instinctual forces is a narrowing base of relevant reported clinical data. A vicious cycle is set up; as less is reported, less is looked for and observed, and what is reported is discounted and explained in other ways. In turn, lacking explanatory data and concepts, there is a tendency to explain more and more in terms of what does not exist (i.e., nonspecific structural deficiency propositions) rather than what does. Gedo

and Goldberg (1973) criticize Johnson's theory of superego lacunae on this very basis, as explaining what does not happen rather than what does (p. 14).

In any event, the presentation of such considerations of id resistance and strength has been sorely neglected. Clinical examples are particularly lacking and we find only an occasional brief vignette and no convincing systematic clinical-theoretical expositions. I attempt here such a more ambitious undertaking in the hope of a reassessment with the advantages of perspectives resulting from the understandings derived from ego psychology. The analysis was conducted technically in this fashion; an appreciation of the ego as mechanism guided observational and interpretative efforts. In particular, I shall focus on id forces as resistance, the relevance of the strength of such forces, and the relations between aggressive and libidinal drives. But first, I shall briefly review the topic of id resistance.

The Resistance of the Id

When the concept of an id resistance was first postulated by Freud (1926a), his characterization was limited. It was the resistance necessitating "working through," the "resistance of the unconscious" (p. 160), and was attributed to the power of the repetition compulsion (p. 159): "there are likely to be difficulties if an instinctual process which has been going along a particular path for whole decades is suddenly expected to take a new path that has just been made open for it" (1926b, p. 224). After this initial delineation he had little to say about it. In "Analysis Terminable and Interminable" (1937) he stated, apparently parenthetically, that it was not to be confused with a hereditary "depletion of plasticity." He added the following remarks:

> We are, it is true, prepared to find in analysis a certain amount of psychical inertia. When the work of analysis has opened up new paths for an instinctual impulse, we almost invariably observe that the impulse does not enter upon them without marked hesitation. We have called this be-

haviour, *perhaps not quite correctly*, "resistance from the id". But with the patients I here have in mind, all the mental processes, relationships and distributions of force are unchangeable, fixed and rigid [pp. 241-242; italics added].

Freud did not consider much of the subject matter of "Analysis, Terminable and Interminable" to be properly subsumed under the id resistance category. This included the constitutional strength of the instincts, and the characterizations of "adhesiveness of the libido" and "depletion of plasticity." Here Freud was inconsistent (1915a, p. 272n), and in fact most analysts do in practice seem to so consider them. Stewart (1963) understood these same writings to indicate such an identity. Perhaps Freud was maintaining a differentiation between innate constitutional factors and experiential factors. In this paper I shall follow common usage and consider the strength of the instincts, i.e., the quantitative factor, in the category of id resistance. In treating resistance of the id heuristically in the following case study I hope to confirm the usefulness of this broader definition. I shall adhere to the broader definition of resistance: *"whatever interrupts the progress of analytic work is a resistance"* (Freud, 1900, p. 517).

The Strength of the Instincts

The following case study is of a young woman with symptoms of psychomotor epilepsy. Over the course of the analysis, I was impressed by evidence of the unusual impact of her drives on her symptomatic states, personality, resistances, and the treatment process and results. It is my belief that the excessive strength of her drives was related to the same factors responsible for her cerebral dysrythmia, but this speculation is incidental to this paper's central thesis. I also consider that the same etiologic elements led to general and specific ego impairments. In considering both drive and ego aspects of central nervous system disorders, I follow others (e.g., Weil, 1981) whose observations compel such a distinction.

I do not assume or propose here a general theory of the psychopathology of epilepsy, although I am not the first analyst to report evidence of overwhelming drive tensions associated with this syndrome (Kardiner, 1932; Schick, 1949; Heilbrunn, 1950). Unless otherwise stated, I limit my interpretations and conclusions to this single case. Accordingly I will restrict my inferences to observations from this analysis. I shall begin with indications of excessive or overwhelming drive (*Trieb*) strength. This included both aggressive and libidinal forces. I deduced their presence from the patient's direct statements and representations (including the manifest content of dreams), descriptions of her subjective states (including particularly features consistent with a "traumatic state" indicating instinctual overstimulation and "psychic helplessness"), and inferences explanatory of her symptomatology. Hence, I had respectively subjective, metaphoric, and phenomenologic indications of a specifically quantitative factor. The examples given have varying proportions of drive and defense. Classical symptomatic primary and secondary compromise formations are often simultaneously discernible and inferrable; demonstrating a quantitative drive factor is not meant to detract from or obviate other significance and meanings. Included in what I propose to demonstrate here is that such considerations of id strength were regularly relevant and useful in explaining interference with the analysis of defensive, fantastic, and symptomatic configurations.

From the beginning of work with this patient I was confronted with the necessity for an operational definition of "instinct" or "drive" which would be least prejudicial to the ordering of my observations. My first concern, implied above, was in maintaining some distinction between the manifestations of drive strength and ego weakness. Also, I did not wish to prejudice my psychological observations with judgments as to the "organic" or the "emotional" origin of their objects. I was working in a psychological field with reported psychological data. Such diagnoses quickly became phenomenologically irrelevant with the exception of unusual to rare distinct altera-

tions of consciousness. The critical issues involved psychological impact rather than some ultimate neurochemical versus psychological origin. The pragmatic solution was to dismiss the need for such distinctions and adopt a definition appropriate to the material, the mode of observation, and the aims of deduction. Therefore, following Freud (1915b), I considered an "instinct" or "drive" to be demonstrable "as the psychical representative of the stimuli originating from within the organism and reaching the mind, as *a measure of the demand made upon the mind for work* in consequence of its connection with the body" (p. 122; italics added).

Instinct Strength and the Fear and Experience of Being Overwhelmed: Case Illustration

The patient, an unmarried graduate student in the physical sciences, in her early thirties, began treatment on referral from her neurologist because of year-long complaints of depression. She had been diagnosed as epileptic ("psychomotor" but with a history of three grand mal seizures) since the age of thirteen. She was seen in a twice-weekly psychotherapy for seven months prior to the recommendation for analysis. By that time she had improved symptomatically sufficiently so that her original goals had been achieved. She considered stopping therapy or continuing to work on chronic symptoms of purposelessness, unhappiness, and unrewarding and painful patterns of personal and professional interpersonal relations and experiences. My own opinion was that little more could be accomplished with a limited supportive psychotherapy. Despite my reservations about that poorly definable attribute designated "ego strengths," I made a recommendation for analysis which she only eventually and very ambivalently accepted. I was unsure of her analyzability. My experience with her demonstrated the usefulness of considering analyzability as a question of "more or less" rather than "yes or no." I shall consider this issue in more detail below.

In my first interview with the patient, she had told a vignette of overwhelmed helplessness which at that time I was unable to fit into a context. In fact, she related it in some vague way to the onset of her symptoms. The previous summer she had worked as the horsemanship instructor at a girls' camp in Vermont. She was leading a group of perhaps twenty campers toward the end of a day ride through mountainous terrain. While she was not familiar with this particular trail, she did know the area and its landmarks so well that she had full confidence in her ability to find her way home. Suddenly the late afternoon sky darkened, clouds gathered ominously, and the mountains reverberated with thunder as the half-light was illuminated only by an awesome display of brilliant flashes of lightning. The campers were frightened, the horses difficult to control, and she felt totally overcome. The summer storm passed over quickly, but she had lost her bearings and her sense of sureness. Despite what she later recognized as familiar surroundings, she could not pull herself together and the party of riders wandered aimlessly for hours until a fortunate encounter with a searcher from the camp.

In the course of the ensuing psychotherapy, she told me another symptom, associated with nocturnal sleeplessness. It was not until much later that I appreciated the severity of the symptom. She even attempted a series of what superficially seemed to be obsessional rituals in attempts to induce seizures in the hope that they would lead to sleep. In time she told me this symptom was so unbearable that she seriously considered suicide. She described feeling as if she were falling into endless space while lying in bed. She then could not allow herself to fall asleep and would "go into a panic." She would awaken her father who joined her in the living room and participated with her in some activity, usually a card game. He might thus sit with her throughout the night. In time and with further description, I came to particularly appreciate her feeling of being overwhelmed and consequent helplessness. In particular, I appreciated the features that identified this syndrome with the

sleep disturbances appropriate to the second year of life. It coincided with Fraiberg's (1950) attribution of these problems generically to the ". . . traumatic situation, that of helplessness, the experience of being overwhelmed and indefensible" (p. 287).

Confirmatory of this formulation was elaboration of the phenomenon I had originally misunderstood as obsessional. It consisted of alternating accusations: "You're pregnant! No, you're homosexual! No, you're pregnant!" And so on. The content of the charges involved not only obvious sexual conflicts expressed as compromise formations of impulses and defenses, but issues of instinctual control. At issue in this context was that this sequence, together with conscious alterations of her breathing patterns, was an attempt to imitate and produce a pre-ictal state. Terrorized by the tensions which made sleep impossible and which were in turn augmented by the panic of her sleeplessness, she hoped to induce a seizure which could provide relief with loss of consciousness and the hope of awakening without tensions and at peace.

The patient was very aware of the strength of her feelings and carefully consciously controlled herself so as to avoid situations that might lead to control failure or overstimulation. She presented herself as overcontrolled, cautious, and inhibited. In an emergency she was the person who could always be counted on to keep her head. Logic and reason were her shibboleths. In this she emulated her father and repudiated the example of her "scatter-brained" mother (as detailed below). But under her invariably calm poised exterior, she was terrified of being swept away by tensions, impulses, hatreds, and passions.

She was a virgin; her sexual experiences were limited to infrequent heterosexual "necking" and some fleeting and unfulfilling homosexual experimentation in college. In the first months of the analysis she told of a date during which she began some affectionate physical exchanges. After a few kisses she abruptly pushed herself away, stating she had to stop herself

before losing control and consummating the relationship sexually: "If we don't stop right now I could become pregnant!" Of course, the relating of this experience was also an important statement of her fear, indeed aversion, of transference. Defense against transference became a hallmark and critical impediment of this analysis. For example, during this same period the patient arrived at my office at *exactly* the scheduled time of her appointment. To arrive early and wait, she said, involved insufferable tensions. What she did not explicitly state, but became clear, was that arriving late with consequent awareness of loss of something she expected and wanted was equally intolerable.

Another, of many, comparable expressions pertained to her curiosity about me. To permit it more than peripheral recognition would, she feared, lead to single-minded preoccupation and obsession with my personal life. Hence, the analysis of its origins was preempted by her fear of its perceived strength.

Even the patient's experience of her thinking processes, the classic epitomization of mental apparatus stability through "bound cathexes," verbal residues, and secondary-process mentation (Freud, 1911), involved the experience of extraordinary drive intensity. In an hour toward the beginning of the second year of analysis, she described what happened in her mind as she associated:

She got ideas too swiftly, so quickly she could not feel secure with most of them until she had a chance to think them over. She described again how the ideas went flashing by. She needed to reflect on them in order to even know what they were. I asked her about simply stating the ideas as they came up. She indicated she could not do this—that they were not in a form where they could be said. She had to wait until they "zoomed by" and then "grab a hold" of some of them, put them together, reflect on them; only then could she present them to the analyst. She compared her choosing an association to throwing a lasso into a corral filled with stampeding mustangs. When I ques-

tioned her, she said she experienced these things as neither words, impressions, nor feelings. It was impossible for her to describe them, but she could compare them to an experiment in the lab. At one point she had to wait 30 seconds. She counted to herself, "thousand one, thousand two, thousand three." Eventually she timed herself. She found it took her five seconds to count to 30 in this way.

The defensive usefulness of this phenomenon, comparable to what occurs in hypomanic states, was clear. Underlying unconscious fantasies were unavailable to detection. However, the endowed state which made this defensive utility possible and mitigated against its resolution with interpretation constituted an obstacle in its own right.

There was reasonable evidence of excesses in both the aggressive and libidinal endowments. Consistent with usual experience, the agency of aggressive forces was often the skeletal musculature, its aim—harm or destruction. This is consistent with Freud's (1924, p. 163) and Hartmann, Kris and Loewenstein's (1949, p. 72) propositions. In addition it coincided with a particular meaning of the patient's seizures to her, i.e., a shameful loss of control of her body's destructive force with dreaded injury to others. She had been told of an incident many years before when she had allegedly attacked a child during a seizure. The report had been elaborated into a frightening tale of awesome potential destructiveness. Aggression could also be represented with instruments of explosiveness or machines, or natural forces. The following example has some of both. The patient was subject and object, aims were both active and passive, the themes were phallic ejaculatory and masochistic incestuous vaginal intrusive fantasies.

It was strange—one of these deals where things go back and forth. Like I was in a circus tent, but it was the Muny Opera. My dad and I were talking about improving on something. A cannon was there on the platform. The platform was pointed up at a 45-degree angle; we're going to have a cannon shoot up in the air; I said you can't do that;

it will hit the top of the circus tent; just then we're in the Muny Opera, not the circus. Then Dad said, "it won't work anyway"; then it wasn't a cannon; it was a gorilla tied to the platform. He said, "don't you know that a gorilla can't roar unless it raises its arm; its arms are tied to the platform; I don't know. . . . Actually the cannon didn't shoot a ball. It shot a lot of junk; I know that because as I pictured it going through the circus tent there would be a lot of little holes.

Libidinal forces were often distinguishable. Here heat and cold were among the patient's favorite metaphors. The following excerpt from a dream to be reported later in full presents primarily the more libidinal aspect of the same analytic phase, reported five weeks later than the gorilla-cannon dream. Here she is consumed by overwhelming exciting fantasies and feelings toward her father associated with primal-scene memories:

. . . All of a sudden I was back in my bedroom. This source of . . . like a . . . flame thrower. It wouldn't hurt you. It was emanating from my father filling all the rooms that were locked from the hall. In the dream, the reason to lock the doors was to maintain control. It was my father. No doors unlocked meant no way of escape. It was a weird feeling, him filling up all this space. We don't close off the doors any more.

On occasions when both aggressive and libidinal drives were represented together their impact was often additive. I did not observe the phenomenon of libido and aggression offsetting each other.

There were continual signs that the patient perceived herself in the position of "Sorcerer's Apprentice," struggling to stem the tide of a constantly replenished flood of drives.[1] The manifest contents of two dreams, widely separated in time, convey the patient's experience.

[1] Cf. Freud's (1937) citation of a reinforcement of the instincts (p. 226).

Tenth month of analysis:] I had worms in my hair. They were ordinary worms, except that they were purple and green. I washed my hair. I thought it was alright. Then these worms would drop out at the dinner table, someplace where I didn't want them. Then I'd brush them out, but they'd come back. No matter what I did I couldn't get rid of them. I seemed to get rid of them, but they weren't gone.

[*Twenty-eighth month of analysis*:] There were stones. I was arranging them into different piles, each pile containing the same sorts of stones. It wasn't as if I had a big bunch of stones mixed up. The stones would sort of appear and then I'd put them into the right pile. I turned around and some of the stones had somehow moved into other piles. I went back and put it back into the right pile. This happened a number of times.

I was particularly interested in the interplay between endowment and experience, of the reciprocal impacts of the patient's innate drive intensity and the familial patterns of drive control and expression and the parental personalities. The analysis of specific developmental constellations often led to considerations of nonspecific (nonphasic) general drive regulation. Hence, it was important to reconstruct childhood familial influences on tension regulation and drive control. My ultimate conclusion was that the patient's environment contributed to the intensification, rather than regulation, of such forces. Further, I inferred that the controls internalized during childhood had been of an undiscriminating, even arbitrary all-or-nothing quality.

The patient's mother was characterized by her and her siblings as "scatter-brained," that is, incompetent. On examination it consistently seemed that she was unable to tolerate the responsibility and guilt or frustration, or even anticipating the frustration, of another. For example, the patient observed her mother caring for a group of children. She ran about frantically, trying to anticipate their wishes. She refused to discipline the

children, that would be "cruel" and "mean." As soon as her
mother learned that the patient had seen something she liked
in a store, she would run out and get one of each color for her.
Expensive and extraordinary gifts, particularly of the special
something which one could not even dream of having, were
important to both her immediate and extended families. The
implicit counterdemand was that the recipient respond effu-
sively as totally satisfied.

The mother's unwillingness to assume responsibility for
control meant that all restrictions and punishments were deferred until the father's return from work each day. He explicitly and verbally insisted on total self-control and presented
himself as totally controlled and rational. Control, rationality,
and logic were equated for him as for the patient. He stated
repeatedly that he was the final judge of reality: "If you're
smart, you won't believe the evidence of your eyes; you'll believe
me!"

The father spoke Latin at home because he considered it
more precise than English; with that precision, rational logic
and self-control through expression were attained. In an often
repeated vignette, the father led his dogs to their food, close
enough so that they saw and smelled it. With the first sign of
eagerness and impatience as they approached, he restrained
them with a "Stay!" They remained controlled by that single
word while he watched them closely for what seemed an eternity
to the patient. Only when he had satisfied himself that they
were well enough trained would he release them with another
command. The patient stated she often felt herself treated by
her father as if she were one of the dogs.

However, despite so many explicit statements of total self-
control and rationality, the father (unlike the patient) was capable of frightening explosiveness. For example, she told me
many times of how her father, enraged by another driver or
the inconveniences of traffic, jammed the accelerator to the
floor, careened wildly about at speeds 30 miles in excess of the
speed limit, and screamed obscenities and gestured threaten-

ingly at drivers who did not make way before him. His outbursts were ignored; there was an unwritten law within the family to the effect that they did not exist.

The collusion of the parents which facilitated overstimulation and loss of control in the names of self-determination and growth was exemplified by another familiar vignette. The children were taken to an expensive restaurant regularly for Sunday dinner. They were encouraged to order anything, it seemed everything, including any number of entrees or desserts. The mother excitedly described the attractions of the menu, the father boasted that his children were grown up enough to make up their own minds. However, they were compelled to eat everything they had ordered. For years dinner ended with the children running to the restroom vomiting or doubled over with pain in the car. Yet this practice was never altered.

The Course of Analysis and the Taming of the Instincts

From the onset this analysis was shaped by recognition and reaction to the quantitative aspects of drive manifestations at all libidinal and aggressive levels. They regularly constituted a complementary facet to the analysis of meaning and defense. A characteristic pattern began with the recognition of the symptoms and anxieties either in or outside the transference. There was usually concurrent appreciation of the fear of the strength of the implicated drive forces as reflected in the symptoms. Ideally, but hardly invariably, the patient would cooperate in the analysis of the defenses and associated conflicts. However, her fear of being overwhelmed at any step could result in the interruption or preemption of this process. If the meaning of the symptoms was analyzed, with understanding of the synthesis of drive and defense or opposing drives into symptomatic compromise formations, her fear of the impact of the drive forces often intervened. There was usually another period of reaction to this quantitative aspect. The underlying drives and their

consequent traumatic anxieties might then be understood to a greater or lesser degree.

The examination of the transference was limited to whatever degree the patient dictated, and the working through was done at whatever level and with whatever objects the patient chose. It was clear that she reserved the right and justification to tell me as much or as little as she felt she could tolerate, ignoring or consciously omitting what she "must." This was determined by how much tension she felt, or her trial and error indicated she could tolerate. Small wonder that the initial concept of me (i.e., defense transference) was of a computer! She would not feel nor want anything from a cold electronic gadget; similarly she need not fear the shamefulness, censure, or prohibition she would project onto a person. In controlling me through her reactions to my interpretation and controlling the transference, she hoped to control herself. To let loose, she stated, would mean to unleash boundless insatiable drive pressures and aggressions with loss of control, affective flooding, traumatic states, irrational behavior, shame, guilt, exhaustion, terror, and destruction of herself or others. Our experiences at those times when she did experiment, however cautiously, with relaxing her defenses too often supplied credence to her fears.

We carefully examined her defensive postures. Masochism meant that she could kill all hopes and aspirations through suffering. Submission to external authority, her boss or father or teachers, meant she could feel relief through control by external forces. She prayed for a rape which would alleviate her sexual tensions without participation or guilt. Idealizing others meant she could submit totally to them and dismiss her own aspirations. An almighty omnipotent father introduced security and surety to her chaotic world. At the same time she was perfect and needed no one and nothing. Inhibition meant self-control. She used time as a defense; by holding back her reactions she waited until her feelings had passed over before responding. For example, she deferred her responses to my

interventions for hours, days, weeks, months, or years. Token-
ism allowed her to satisfy others' demands and requirements,
including mine, without belief, commitment, desire, or fear.
She attempted to use logic, particularly through its representation in language (following her father's example and exhortations), to assure herself of objective reality's presence in the
face of immense forces lending feared power and credence to
her infantile wishes. It was as if she had read (she had not) and
was parodying "Formulations on the Two Principles of Mental
Functioning" (Freud, 1911). But she could not completely suppress her desires and aggressions. A world of carefully guarded
precious fantasy constituted her universe of love, lust, desire,
aggression, and hate. A casual college friend, in her mind, was
her true love. He awaited her a thousand miles away, unable
to communicate with her except for a rather formal annual
Christmas card, until his family's objections to her ethnic group
were overcome and they could marry. Financially strapped, she
regularly went to the area's most splendid stores and imagined
she could have anything, or again everything, if only she wished.
Her rivals, injurers, and frustrators all suffered their deserved
inevitable and terrible punishments in her imagination. No
matter how much she had endured, some facet of the experience was elaborated in fantasy so that she emerged the victor,
the benefactress, or the satisfied party.

With the aspect of drive intensity so critical to any area of
libidinal or aggressive development, fixation, regression, or
conflict, I hope to further illustrate the therapeutic process by
demonstration of the process of working through. In considering the limitations of the analysis, later I will focus more on
specific content. The major work of this analysis was the understanding and interpretation of the defensive postures and
object relations alluded to above in the context of understanding the patient's development within her unique family. The
degree to which this was accomplished via the dynamism of the
transference neurosis and its resolution was limited, as stated
above and elaborated in the following section. The most stable

positive transference configuration was to that constructive aspect of the father's personality which was evident in his remaining with her through the night during her desperate hours. Here, in the occasional sessions she would talk about it, she emphasized my perceived patience, steadfastness, and tolerance. She contrasted our experience with tales of other analysts or psychiatrists who had reputedly been dictatorial, provocative, critical, destructive, insensitive, and controlling. These disreputable colleagues, of course, were constituted through projections of her father's less therapeutic qualities.

Freud proposed that resistance of the id led to the process of working through (1926a, p. 160; Stewart, 1963). Its equivalent in "Analysis Terminable and Interminable" was what he called the "taming of the instincts" (Freud, 1937, p. 225). In order to illustrate these processes of taming of the instincts, I present here a sequence of dreams including horses in the manifest content. The patient had many other dreams which manifestly dealt with issues of instinctual strength, being overwhelmed, and control. They included a variety of symbols and representations of force including natural, animal, and mechanical sources. However, because of the unique importance and specific significance of horses to her and the coincidence of the metaphor of training with Freud's characterization of "taming" I have chosen this medium. I have in mind also Freud's (1923) comparison of horse and rider to id and ego. There were a sufficient number of such dreams to illustrate the sequential evolution of this process.

Horses were particularly important to the patient from childhood. She also dated the onset of her symptoms to a ride, as described above, and her first seizure occurred after mounting a horse. She had owned a horse until after her undergraduate years. She loved her horses deeply and felt that her adoration was returned by the unquestioning love and absorption only an animal can offer to its mistress. In addition, she was, from the beginning, very preoccupied with and intensely committed to the training of her horses. In training her horses

she practiced the curbing and directing of her own impulses. These observations were confirmed by her associations. The horses regularly represented herself as loving and hating, the objects of her love and hate, and the forces of the love and hate themselves.

All in all there were twelve dreams in the analysis involving horses, of which six are included here. Each dream is identified by the month in analysis of its occurrence. My comments will be largely confined to the demonstration of the vicissitudes of the involved forces.

[*Seventh month*:] I was standing in the middle of a race track. The horses all the way across the track were coming toward me. They were really pretty horses. First thing I thought was they're really pretty horses. Look how fast they're running. Right before they got to me I remembered they were going to trample me. I realized I was scared. When they got to me, I was on an island. They went by me. Then I thought I knew the island was going to be here, why was I so scared?

Comments. Here she characterized the immense and threatening power of her inner forces as well as her experience of a lack of capacities to handle the needs and impulses symbolized other than by getting out of their way. Both libidinal and aggressive impulses are implicated. Their impact is additive. She is not mounted on the horse and sidesteps its impact. This corresponded to her symptomatology and adaptive posture at this time, which included marked defensive shifts of attention, ignoring what was unpleasant, and even falling asleep narcoleptically.

[*Eighth month*:] I had a dream last night, it was really strange. I was riding a horse over kind of like meadows. We were cantering, slow, collected canters. I was counting. I wasn't counting in time to the horse's canters. It seems strange to me. We came to a ditch. The horse fell. I stayed on top of him. He got back up. He kept going. I kept counting but I had to count still faster. That was it.

Comments. She allows herself to get closer to her drives and is mounted. The drives are in charge. She tries to stay on top of them. She attempts to assert control by counting, a characteristic way for her of slowing down her feelings and ideas.

[*Twenty-first month:*] I was on a particular plateau on top of a mesa-type thing riding this horse going at a dead run, feeling free and open. All of a sudden I was back in my bedroom. This source of . . . like a . . . flame thrower. It wouldn't hurt you. It was emanating from my father filling all the rooms that were locked from the hall. In the dream, the reason to lock the doors was to maintain control. It was my father. No doors unlocked meant no way of escape. It was a weird feeling, him filling up all this space. We don't close off the doors anymore.

Comments. She experiments with letting go and is consumed by overwhelming "flame-thrower" feelings (exciting primal-scene memories and fantasies and sexual feelings toward her father which are latent in the transference).

[*Twenty-seventh month:*] I was on horseback, riding across a field. Everything was fine—horse stumbled, I fell off of it. The horse ran away. I was hurt; I can't remember exactly how. When the horse ran away my feeling was concern for the horse. I had to get somewhere—I didn't know how to get there without the horse. That wasn't the main thing; the main thing was whether the horse was hurt or not. That's all I remember. When he stumbled everything wasn't fine anymore. It seemed my reaction was wrong, that my concern should be about me and my being hurt. Getting there. Yet, on the other hand, if the horse hadn't been well he wouldn't have run away. So he must have been well enough.

Comments. She is now taking more chances with her feelings. The horse is now more representative of an object. She concurrently admits she can be hurt by a loved one's absence and wants to hurt in retaliation.

[*Thirty-third month:*] It was a familiar dream—lots of symbols—it had my favorite character. I was riding a horse. My fiancé was on the horse, bareback with me. We were on a long trip—we had to go through a series of towns. I had to get something in the towns, but I kept forgetting about it. I'd remember it only between the towns. Then suddenly my fiancé produced what I'd forgotten. It was reins. The reins on the horse were paper—they wouldn't stand my pulling back hard or if the horse broke away. He had stopped the horse and was starting to put on his reins. I wouldn't stand for it. I said no, it has to be my reins. He didn't understand. I was very upset and insisted that it had to be my reins.

Comments. She includes another person, the fiancé-analyst. She is anxious about my closeness and reliability. She insists on keeping control and mocks me as ineffective.

[*Forty-second month:*] It had to do with horses again. I was somewhere. Someone came in and said they wanted my help. A horse had escaped. I went out and looked in the corral. There were two horses there. I said, "They're there." This person said yes, but there used to be three. The rest of the dream consisted of my going around looking for the horse. I'd go to people—who had seen the horse, or had bought the horse, or just sold it—a whole bunch of them. Sometimes I'd feel that I was just about to find the horse—other times that I couldn't find the horse, and there was no sense in continuing to look. I'd run into a man, he'd say yes, but he had sold it, because he was such a pretty horse.

Comments. The quantitative factor has been superseded by a qualitative factor. The ego's control is established through the innovation of the danger situation, illustrating typical separation anxiety. It was the first of four such dreams.

The Resistance of the Id

In the preceding pages I hope I conveyed a sense of the resistances that characterized this analysis. Perhaps the last section, in its focus on a particular process, conveyed a feeling of greater movement and resolution than justified. Indeed, much did happen. The patient, after five years, declared herself eminently satisfied. She had come from desperation and the brink of suicide to success and fulfillment. The symptoms which led to her referral and treatment had been long since forgotten. She had moved from home but still maintained a warm and meaningful relationship with her parents. Her father no longer represented omnipotent divination; in fact, she was now able to look at him in his failing years with understanding and compassion. The intense rivalry and jealousy which had contaminated her relations with her siblings were no longer evident; she felt she could, and had demonstrated to her own satisfaction that she did, appreciate their worth and significance while accepting their shortcomings philosophically. She was no longer embroiled in the battles of her childhood. She regarded epilepsy as a tragic mischance; no longer did she feel it as an exemplification of inner shame, loss of control, or punishment for incredible childhood fantasies and actions. She accepted herself and her abilities reasonably, delighting in her new-found capacities and their appreciation by others. From an academic dead-end at beginning analysis, she had moved to another area of scholarship, successfully completed requirements for a graduate degree, and was well ensconced in a successful, remunerative career. Her terror of sexuality was a thing of the past; she was, in addition, securely married. Fantasy was an occasional safety valve. She was no longer a habitual victim; in fact, she exercised a number of leadership qualities which would have been unthinkable five years before.

However, the question of analyzability was best not answered with a simplistic "yes" or "no." A more penetrating and discerning examination had to take into consideration "how much," "why," and "why not." This involved both the patient's

capacity to function analytically and her ability to sustain momentum in the analysis. The fear and actual strength of the involved drive forces acted as a resistance to the analytic effort at all stages, as discussed earlier. Further, therapeutically evolving ego capacities regularly failed to keep pace with constantly reinforced drive pressures.

It is true that much of the initial defensive structure had been altered. But many areas of improvement represented a better level of adjustment and compensation rather than a resolution which brought the instincts into the full harmony of the ego. To give an example of the limitations of her improvement, her father's authority had been gradually transferentially given to me, as implied above. However, in the period of termination, without presentation in the analysis, the patient committed herself in an absolute and total sense to a religious conviction in a very personal God. She was never outside, she stated in the last week of analysis, the presence of an accepting "Heavenly Father" to whom she could turn as needed. Or, to further illustrate, in order to tolerate her anxieties about closeness and sexuality, she had chosen so profoundly passive a man that his sexual symptomatology, dependency, troublesome ties with his own family, irresponsibility, provocativeness, and masochistic propensities imposed a considerable painful burden on her life.

The absolute limit of analysis was ultimately quantitatively defined; she could not tolerate this or that feeling or wish because it was too strong, would lead to intolerable tension, being overwhelmed, mindless addictionlike subjugation to the wanted object, or loss of control. The decisive focus for the success or failure of the analysis of her fear of instinctual strength was the transference. The transference not only invoked the danger of repetition of childhood experiences which had been disproportionally strong in the past. It also threatened her with the consequences of contemporary, overwhelming, excessive, constantly reinforced drive power. Hers was an adult ego, but the balance of power in the ratio of ego strength to id impulse had not swung sufficiently for the optimal analytic curative opportunity.

Considering the profound resistance to transference, were there therapeutic factors other than the realignment of defenses cited above? And how had it, as well as a better level and adjustment and compensation, been achieved?

First, there was some, although far from desired, exposition, analysis, reconstruction, working through, and resolution within the context of a limited transference neurosis.

Second, her powers of logic and comprehension of reality had specifically been inordinately strengthened through the recognition and resolution of the identification with the irrational elements in the father's thinking processes. This was to a large degree the result of the most analytic aspects of our work, in my first category above.

Third, there was an element of "transference cure," involving shifts in feeling, investment, and discharge in contemporary objects, institutions, ideals, and activities. This was implied in the two examples given earlier in this section.

Finally, she was able to achieve some defensive shifts and realignments as the result of her own work with withheld transferences. In the final weeks of analysis she told me of this process. She had known somewhere, she said, even at the times of my transference interpretations, of their truth. She "could not" permit my observations to connect in her mind with the experiences that evoked them, and also wondered now about the fact that she disavowed (my term) their impact. For example, she was sometimes aware, as suspected, of intense jealousy of anyone she observed who might have preceded or followed her into my office. At a certain point in the latter part of the analysis she decided it was a repetition of childhood sibling rivalries and used this judgment to dismiss her curiosity. She was consciously aware of being physically very attracted to me, as she remembered being to her father, and was bemused by her conscious denial of what was so obvious. But her concern was erased when she reassured herself with the "realization" that these attractions were not sexual but only represented a wish for nurturant warmth and closeness.

I believe that these limited, defensive, partial explorations, insights, and reconstructions exerted an impact equivalent to Glover's "Inexact Interpretations" (1931). There was enough working through and expansion of ego capacities, in however limited a way, to achieve some change, with whatever pathological stigmata and regressive vulnerability were involved. To whatever degree the patient's reconstructions were closer approximations of realities than had existed previously, the ego was strengthened. As her "personal myth" (Kris, 1956) approached her real experiences and self, she was freed from burdensome defensive efforts. To whatever extent a new, more stable (albeit pathological), defensive organization resulted, a clinical improvement was reflected.

Discussion and Conclusions

In these preceding pages I hope that I have satisfactorily articulated and illustrated the clinical observations and reasoning which led to the propositions of this paper. First, it was possible to operationally identify and categorize phenomena consistent with a formulation of excessive and constantly reinforced drive strength as proposed by Freud (1937). There were evidences of excesses of both libidinal and aggressive drives and indications of an additive impact were noted. The interplay between presumed endowment and the patient's unique experiences and identifications was explored. It was possible to operationally distinguish between drive and structural (ego) characteristics. From the limited standpoint of this case, the question of the ultimate origin of these forces is irrelevant. It was sufficient to observe, evaluate, and illustrate their quantitative excess in a psychoanalytic observational field. An objection might be made that two distinct modes of observational discourse should be invoked, one psychological and the other neurological. I believe this objection to have been countered on phenomenologic grounds, considering the heuristic aim of this study. The observed impact of these assumedly distinct forces on the mental apparatus was regularly identical.

In ordinary practice, while paying lip service to the inevitability of variations in drive endowment, we rather automatically assume some sort of "average expectable" level pragmatically. While what seem to be extraordinary variations may be acknowledged parenthetically, there are few, if any, systematic accounts of the vicissitudes of such forces. The grounds for more carefully considering this variable are supported by observations in the idioms of child observational studies. There are repeated demonstrations of marked individual differences in drive endowment predisposition, however observed, conceived, or categorized. This has been observed neonatally (e.g., Richmond and Lustman, 1955), in terms of impact on development (e.g., Mahler et al., 1975), and temperamentally (Thomas and Chess, 1977). Such formulations do not imply an equation in terms of the origin or inherent nature of the observed and described forces. It refers to their impact on the manifestations of the mental apparatus (a psychological construct) which are observable as psychological variations whatever the means or modes of observations.

In the reported analysis this instinctual strength and reinforcement exerted an influence consistent in all particulars with Freud's construct of id resistance. It interfered with both the evolution of the analytic process and the therapeutic results. The associated processes of repetition and working through, with clear quantitative dimensions and vicissitudes, were also consistent with Freud's formulations. The process of supercession of the quantitative factor by the qualitative innovation of the danger situation of separation and anxiety in this context, even in a limited and tentative way, highlights and confirms these judgments.

I carefully examined the clinical data to ascertain indications of the presence or absence of other elements usually implicated, as cited in my introductory remarks, as "id resistance." The tendency to fixation referred to as "adhesiveness of the libido" and the "psychical inertia" (Freud, 1915a, p. 272n; 1937, pp. 241-242) inconstantly equated with it were not demon-

strated to my satisfaction. Perhaps I was not sensitive to its means of representation, phenomenologically or metaphorically. I believe the more likely factor is that considerations of exaggerated drive force so predominated the picture as to make its detection impossible if indeed it was present.

As implied, my material was not consistent with Freud's hypothesis of the unique and ultimate destructive and resistive power of the aggressive instinct (1937, pp. 242-243). Within the scope of these observations, interpretations, and deductions, the patient was as overwhelmed, impeded, and crippled by the excesses of libido as those of aggression. An additive rather than reductive factor was deduced regularly. Perhaps such an independent ruinous impact or algebraic vectors of love and hate could have been observed in the vicissitudes of such hypothesized phenomena as aggressivization, deaggressivization, fusion, defusion, and neutralization. But again, I did not feel certain enough regarding evidence of the phenomenology or representations of these processes to make such conjectures. To paraphrase and quote Freud (1937), within the scope and considering the inevitable limitations of this particular study, ". . . victory [was] in fact on the side of the big battalions" (p. 240).

In the years since analyzing this patient my experience has indicated that considerations of quantity and nature of drive forces have observational, technical, and therapeutic usefulness. I have not seen such consistently marked and inescapably powerful and predominant forces as in this woman again. But, in many patients I have found that formulations of more subtle variations of drive dimensions have added significantly to investigative and therapeutic results. It is not surprising that we learn from the extreme to appreciate the less marked. Further, I have found appreciation of these variations and vicissitudes invaluable in the understanding and analysis of resistance and working through. In my experience sensitivity to the issue of id resistance has repeatedly confirmed the validity and usefulness of this concept.

Summary

This paper reexamines, assesses, and expands the construct of id resistance. Clinical material has been presented which illustrates that phenomenon and its associated facets, repetition and working through. The process is quantitatively characterizable, and a clear distinction can be made between the latter and qualitative vicissitudes. The variable of the relative strength and nature of the involved drive forces is clinically demonstrated as integral to the analytic process. Other considerations of id resistance are considered.

Reconsidering the vicissitudes of instinctual forces from the vantage point of experience with ego psychology was also useful here in appreciating and understanding the complexity of the implicated structural phenomena. A particular facet of this application was attempting to understand the experience and issues of analyzability from this viewpoint. Approximations were made regarding the distinctions to be made between analytic and nonanalytic factors in clinical improvement in the patient described.

REFERENCES

FRAIBERG, S. (1950). On the sleep disturbances of early childhood. *Psychoanal. Study Child*, 5:285-309.

FRANK, A. (1979). Two theories or one? Or none? *J. Amer. Psychoanal. Assn.*, 27:169-207.

FREUD, A. (1936). *The Ego and the Mechanisms of Defense. Writings*, 2. New York: Int. Univ. Press, 1966.

FREUD, S. (1900). The interpretation of dreams. *S. E.*, 4 & 5.

——— (1911). Formulations on the two principles of mental functioning. *S. E.*, 12.

——— (1915a). A case of paranoia running counter to the psycho-analytic theory of the disease. *S. E.*, 14.

——— (1915b). Instincts and their vicissitudes. *S. E.*, 14.

——— (1923). The ego and the id. *S. E.*, 19.

———(1924). The economic problem of masochism. *S. E.*, 19.

——— (1926a). Inhibitions, symptoms and anxiety. *S. E.*, 20.

——— (1926b). The question of lay analysis. *S. E.*, 20.

——— (1937). Analysis terminable and interminable. *S. E.*, 23.

GEDO, J. & GOLDBERG, A. (1973). *Models of the Mind: A Psychoanalytic Theory*. Chicago: Univ. Chicago Press.

GLOVER, E. (1931). The therapeutic effect of inexact interpretation: a contribution to the theory of suggestion. *Int. J. Psychoanal.*, 12:397-411.

HARTMANN, H., KRIS, E. & LOEWENSTEIN, R. M. (1949). Notes on the theory of aggression. *Psychoanal. Study Child*, 3/4:9-36.

HEILBRUNN, G. (1950). Psychoanalytic aspects of epilepsy. *Psychoanal. Q.*, 19:145-157.

KARDINER, A. (1932). The bio-analysis of the epileptic. *Psychoanal. Q.*, 1:375-483.

KRIS, E. (1956). The personal myth: a problem in psychoanalytic technique. *J. Amer. Psychoanal. Assn.*, 4:653-681.

MAHLER, M., PINE, F. & BERGMAN, A. (1975). *The Psychological Birth of the Human Infant*. New York: Basic Books.

RICHMOND, J. & LUSTMAN, S. (1955). Autonomic function in the neonate: implications for psychosomatic theory. *Psychosom. Med.*, 17:269-275.

SCHICK, A. (1949). Psychopathology of genuine epilepsy. *Psychoanal. Rev.*, 36:217-239.

SCHUR, M. (1966). *The Id and the Regulatory Principles of Mental Functioning*. New York: Int. Univ. Press.

STEWART, W. (1963). An inquiry into the concept of working through. *J. Amer. Psychoanal. Assn.*, 11:474-499.

THOMAS, A. & CHESS, S. (1977). *Temperament and Development*. New York: Brunner/Mazel.

WEIL, A. (1981). Anxiety in childhood: developmental and psychopathological considerations. In *Three Further Clinical Faces of Childhood*, ed. E. J. Anthony & D. Gilpin. New York: Spectrum, pp. 135-149.

4524 Forest Park Boulevard
St. Louis, Missouri 63108

SUPPRESSION
AS A DEFENSE

DAVID S. WERMAN, M.D.

THE MENTAL PHENOMENON WE CALL SUPPRESSION has been relatively neglected in the psychoanalytic literature. Among the major defenses it is unique in being the only one which has been identified as volitional. By that single trait, it immediately throws into question the generally accepted notion that defenses are necessarily unconscious processes. Clinical observation leads one to believe that there is probably a continuum from fully conscious defensive phenomena to unconscious ones. This has been suggested, in regard to suppression and repression, by Brenner (1955). Additionally, suppression merits our attention because, as Laplanche and Pontalis (1973) observed, it remains poorly delineated in theoretical terms. Such confusion is comprehensible given the traditional insistence on the unconscious nature of defenses. Suppression operates in a wide variety of ways: in the daily life of an individual, pathologically and adaptively; and, more specifically, in psychoanalytic treatment, where it may be used as resistance by the analyzand, and as a means for the analyst to maintain an optimal analytic stance. For the moment it will suffice to loosely define suppression as the conscious attempt to "put something out of one's mind."

People have long known that they are often capable of expelling unpleasant thoughts and feelings from awareness. Samuel Johnson advised Boswell to deal with his bouts of "melancholy," by making it ". . . an uninvariable and obligatory law to yourself, never to mention your mental diseases; If you are never to speak of them, you will think on them little, and if you

405

think little of them, they will molest you rarely" (Bate, 1975, p. 552). Examples from literature and everyday language are legion.

The concept of suppression has had other related meanings and nuances. In the mid-nineteenth century, for example, "moral treatment" characteristically related to the exhortation of the psychiatric patient to ". . . (divert) his mind from morbid trains of thought," to "fix his attention," "direct his mind to new subjects" and to give a "new current to his thought" (Bockoven, 1956, pp. 299-303).

Throughout his earlier writings, especially those prior to 1915, Freud used the word repression (*Verdrängung*) synonymously with suppression (*Unterdrückung*). In the *Interpretation of Dreams* (1900) he observed that "Linguistic usage hits the mark in speaking of the 'suppression' [i.e. the 'pressing down'] of . . . impulses" (p. 235). The context clearly refers to what we today call repression. A few years later he again used suppression and repression interchangeably, with the implicit sense that the impulse or the idea being repressed is not evicted from consciousness but is being prevented from entering it (Freud, 1905, p. 134).

Freud's synonymous usage of suppression and repression is carried over into English where both words linguistically express virtually the same idea as in German. While suppression etymologically means to press down, repression expresses a checking, restraining or keeping under of an idea, desire, or feeling. The Oxford Universal Dictionary uses suppression as a synonym for repression (of a "painful or otherwise undesirable memory, desire, etc.") (Onions, 1955, p. 1708). This linguistic overlapping suggests that psychologically the two concepts lie on a continuum.

There are two additional accepted meanings of suppression that have psychological implications. One relates to the usage which describes the deliberate withholding or distortion of one's thoughts leading to a falsified communication. In this process, ideas or feelings *remain* conscious in contrast to the process of suppression being discussed here.

Another special meaning of suppression concerns the prohibition of certain behavior because of social standards; again, the wish to carry out such actions is not necessarily excluded from consciousness. For example, Hsu (1949) employs this usage specifically in contrast to repression. The crux of his point of view, based on an analysis of the cultures in China, Japan, Germany, and the United States, is that the first two nations "represent the cultures in which suppression [i.e. conscious constraint of some action] is the more important mechanism of socialization of the individual; America [sic] and Germany represent cultures in which repression is the more important mechanism of socialization . . ." (p. 241).

Anna Freud did not include suppression among the defenses she described in *The Ego and the Mechanisms of Defense* (1936), perhaps because she stressed the unconscious nature of defenses. However, over the ensuing years several writers have placed suppression among the major defense mechanisms and while there is a loose general agreement regarding its definition, there are some differences between authors. Hinsie and Campbell (1960) observed that suppression is: "The act of consciously inhibiting an impulse, affect, or idea, as in the deliberate attempt to forget something and think no more about it. Suppression is thus to be differentiated from *repression*, which is an unconscious process. It is probable that there is no sharp line of demarcation between suppression and repression, and it seems also likely that on occasion the unconscious defense of repression may be directed against material which the individual consciously suppresses. Nonetheless, it seems advisable in most instances to regard suppression and repression as distinctly different mechanisms" (Hinsie and Campbell, 1960, p. 708).

Brenner (1955) describes suppression as "a conscious activity which is somewhat analogous to repression . . . It is the familiar decision to forget about something and to think no more about it." He also suggests that there may be intermediate stages between suppression and repression but that when we

use the word repression, "we mean that the barring from consciousness and the erection of a durable countercathexis have taken place unconsciously" (p. 83).

Vaillant (1977) places suppression among the major "mature" defense mechanisms, together with anticipation, altruism, and humor, and he defines it as ". . . the conscious or semiconscious decision to postpone paying attention to a conscious impulse or conflict. The mechanism includes looking for silver linings, minimizing acknowledged discomfort, employing a stiff upper lip, and deliberately postponing but not avoiding. With suppression one says, 'I will think about it tomorrow'; and the next day one remembers to think about it" (p. 386).

This definition focuses on the delay of impulse gratification and decision-making, the maintenance of hope (which appears to range from careful testing of reality to something at the limits of denial), and stoicism. Vaillant seems to imply that the mental contents in question remain in awareness but do not press so urgently for discharge; hence the subject can plan on dealing with the problem "the next day." This is in contrast to the sense of suppression I am advancing here, in which the objectionable mental contents are put out of one's mind, even though they may be easily retrieved or, as is commonly the case, intrude back into awareness despite one's efforts to keep them out.

What the nature of the suppressed material is has been touched on by a few writers. Eidelberg (1960) regards suppression as "a preconscious and conscious psychical process in which *ideas and affects* [italics added] are eliminated from consciousness." He states that this material is recoverable from the preconscious, although ". . . in some cases the endopsychic censor may intervene between the preconscious and the conscious systems" (p. 424). It is possible that in such instances repression has set in instead of the force of the censor having been intensified. Eidelberg also notes that, characteristically, suppression may eliminate or subdue affects from consciousness while an associated idea is retained in awareness. This is suggestive of a volitional form of isolation.

Both Eidelberg and Rycroft (1968) use the term inhibition in connection with suppression; for the former there is conscious inhibition of *affect*, while for the latter inhibition bears on *activity*, although he does not clarify whether or not the desire for the action remains conscious. It would seem preferable to retain the original concept of inhibition, as described by Freud, which relates to the holding back of unconscious drive impulses and their derivatives.

Among the scanty contributions on the nature of suppression one finds no consideration of its precursors, either from child observation or from psychoanalytic reconstruction. However, some tentative and avowedly speculative ideas can be formulated. Thus, the child, as the adult, at times has the experience—at least after the fact—of realizing that the contents of consciousness have disappeared from awareness; this realization often comes about when what has been consciously forgotten is suddenly recalled, and the sense of relief which had been experienced after the psychological pain had disappeared, is lost and the original unpleasant feelings and thoughts return to awareness. Frequently, the unpleasant forgotten material is replaced by pleasurable, or at least neutral, mental contents. From such spontaneous occurrences, brought on by the wish to diminish pain and to experience pleasure, there is but a short step to the deliberate attempt to substitute pleasurable for unpleasurable thoughts and feelings.

Further, we may suppose that this process is supported by the effects of magical thinking—the belief that one can affect phenomena by means of one's thoughts. As one can affect the external world, so one can exert an influence on the inner, and the child attempts to cause unpleasant mental contents to vanish from his awareness. As every parent knows, this process is best carried out by the substitution of new perceptions and experiences for the old. What "was" is no longer experienced, and thus no longer exists. In economic terms, this suggests a shifting of cathexes.

Since the process of suppression occurs within a certain

lapse of time from the first experience of unpleasure to its elimination or reduction, that lapse probably represents the necessary quantum of time for the individual to hit upon a substitute for the frustrated wish.

It can be assumed that repetition of this process, with its learning effect, leads to a greater mastery and manipulation of suppression. While there are considerable differences from one individual to another in their ability to suppress, these differences do not seem to be limited to any dominant level of fixation or diagnostic category, but tend to depend on the flexibility and overall character of the defense organization. Here too, clinical experience tends to contradict traditional thinking on this subject.

Early spontaneous experiences of suppression are enhanced by the adults in the child's environment. They frequently tell the child—indeed their admonishments and exhortations may be accompanied by rewards or punishments—to "forget" something that is troubling him. This is often allied with powerful suggestions—powerful because of the parent-child relationship.

The child does feel better when his wound is kissed and "made better" by his mother, who bandages it and tells him to go out and play and to forget about the hurt. Throughout such processes parental suggestions would subsequently become integrated into a form of auto-suggestion.

Valliant (1977), as previously cited, and Meissner (1980), have characterized suppression as a "mature" defense and it may indeed be utilized in ways that indicate ego strength. However, the same can be said for many other defenses which, according to Hartmann's (1939) formulation, may undergo a change of function. In general terms, one might say that suppression is a "mature" defense when the subject is confronted by a reality situation—whether external, psychological, or somatic—about which no effective thinking or action can be taken. Typical situations are those in which one must wait for time to elapse, e.g., for the results of an examination or a lab-

oratory test; for a letter to arrive; or for an arduous trip to come to an end. In like manner one may have to "absorb" the anguish of a keen disappointment in love, a failure at work or in school, bad news about one's health or that of a family member, or a severe financial loss. Incidents of this nature are common, and beyond a purely stoical acceptance of the fact, suppressive techniques to handle them are most useful and seem to be related to the ability to tolerate frustration. Here too, one sees how defensive functions are not simple mechanisms but are intimately related to other psychological functions.

If a person is unable to expel, or at least temporarily modulate, the unpleasant thoughts or feelings from his mind, he may ruminate on them to such an extent that other areas of his life are seriously impaired. Or he may be called upon to carry out some action he finds distasteful or stressful; although the required behavior must be performed, the person repeatedly suppresses the thought that relates to action. Such ostrichlike behavior utilizes suppression in an obviously ill-adaptive manner which is in the service of conflict and is closely akin to denial, except that it is volitional. All suppression is thus not indicative of "mature" adaptation.

Suppression can also serve as a powerful resistance in analysis, and here I do not refer to the conscious *withholding* of what is in awareness, but rather the actual *removal* from awareness of unpleasant thoughts and feelings by the analysand. The following vignette represents what is probably an unusual example of such use of suppression:

A young widow entered analysis because of attacks of anxiety and guilt, a lack of confidence in herself, and difficulty in concentration. She reported that outside of her work, her life was filled with "trivia": mindless and unnecessary chores, games, movies, spectator sports, and a continuous round of late-night, informal get-togethers, with friends and neighbors. Consequently her life was a hectic hodge-podge of activity. She was afraid of "running out of things to do" and being at the

mercy of distressing feelings. As analysis proceeded certain memories emerged with associated painful emotions. Although the patient made some effort to work on this material in the hours in which it appeared, she afterwards went home to "grind up," as she described it, these thoughts and emotions. By the next hour she had managed to put the issue out of her mind and was no longer troubled by it. When the analyst identified her behavior as a resistance against the analytic work, the patient acknowledged that indeed this was so, and as far as she was concerned, if she was not reminded of her difficulties, she would just as well leave them in oblivion.

This patient was never able to satisfactorily explain the process by which she "ground up" unpleasant mental contents. It seemed to involve the fragmentation of, for example, a memory, into the smallest component parts possible, to the extent that each fragment became virtually meaningless for her. The process could last two or three hours and was associated with the insertion of substitutive thoughts, feelings, and behavior: "trivia," love affairs, acting out, and rather more than social drinking. After two years in analysis, the patient decided to leave treatment when her new and impulsively wedded husband insisted that she terminate.

In contrast to the preceding example, in which material from analysis was excluded by the patient, there is the necessity of the analyst to maintain his professional position by excluding from consciousness (or minimizing) any thoughts or feelings related to his extra-professional life that might interfere in his analytic work.

Winnicott (1960) discussed this matter in a paper on countertransference. He contrasted the analyst whose defenses are highly structured with one who remains "vulnerable" but can "yet retain his professional role in his actual working hours" (p. 18). He may suffer from a stomach ache or be aggressively or erotically stimulated by an idea given by the patient, but these events do not affect his interpretations. My understanding of this process is that the analyst consciously, albeit quasi-au-

tomatically, deals with these intrusions into his professional attitude by isolating them.

These examples, by no means exhaustive, are cited to illustrate the protean quality of suppression, how it can be used equally well in the service of neurotic and mature goal-oriented behavior. But having stated this, it must also be noted that the same can be said for many other, perhaps all, defense mechanisms.

The nature of defenses has been the subject of debate during the past quarter-century. The point of view elaborated by Anna Freud (1936), that defenses are unconscious mechanisms that protect the individual from the unpleasure of instinctual impulses and the affects associated with them, has been modified and expanded by several authors. This literature need not be reviewed here but may be epitomized by Brenner's view that defenses are mental "postures" defined by their function. "There are no special ego functions that are 'defenses,' functions that serve solely a defensive purpose and no other. Ego functions are all-purpose, as it were. They mediate instinctual gratification, they are used to oppose instinctual derivatives, they serve as means of enforcing or opposing superego prohibitions and demands, and they enable one to adapt in the psychological sense of the word to one's environment" (Brenner, 1976, p. 77). The description of suppression I have presented here seems, in part, to support the views of those who have broadened the definition of defenses.

In summary, suppression may be more fully defined as the volitional elimination or diminution from consciousness, by any means, of undesirable thoughts, feelings, or bodily sensations. Consequently, one may include as suppressive processes the use of self-hypnosis or intoxicants. It is also apparent that suppression may be the conscious equivalent of certain unconscious defense mechanisms such as isolation or reaction formation, which clinical observation suggests may be volitional as well as unconscious.

Conscious defenses, such as suppression, probably lie at

one end of a continuum, while those which are patently unconscious, such as repression, are at the other end, with a variety of intermediary, shifting phenomena inbetween. Some suppressed ideas or emotions may be all too readily recalled, whereas others may be repressed and not subject to recollection. Repressed ideas may emerge into consciousness only to be suppressed or re-repressed. Many such possibilities are common clinical observations.

The foregoing exploration of the nature of suppression is presented as a contribution to other current studies of defenses which increasingly perceive these phenomena in their rich-complexity and their wide range of functions.

Summary

Suppression, as a defensive process, has been relatively neglected in the psychoanalytic literature. This communication seeks to define and illustrate suppression in its protean manifestations. Suppression serves a variety of psychological functions that may relate to conflict, modulate affect, serve development, or adaptation.

It is also proposed that suppression, defined as a conscious, volitional process, actually lies on a continuum with defensive processes that are unconscious.

REFERENCES

BATE, W. J. (1975). *Samuel Johnson*. New York: Harcourt Brace, Jovanovich.
BOCKOVEN, J. S. (1956). Moral treatment in American psychiatry. *J. Nerv. Ment. Dis.*, 124:167-194, 292-321.
BRENNER, C. (1955). *Elementary Textbook of Psychoanalysis*. New York: Int. Univ. Press.
——— (1976). *Psychoanalytic Technique and Psychic Conflict*. New York: Int. Univ. Press.
FREUD, A. (1936). *The Ego and the Mechanisms of Defense*. Writings, 2. Int. Univ. Press, 1966.
FREUD, S. (1900). The Interpretation of Dreams. *S. E.*, 4 & 5.
——— (1905). Jokes and their relation to the unconscious. *S. E.*, 8.
EIDELBERG, L. (1960). *Encyclopedia of Psychoanalysis*. New York: Free Press.

HARTMANN, H. (1939). *Ego Psychology and the Problem of Adaptation*. New York: Int. Univ. Press, 1958.

HINSIE, L. E. & CAMPBELL, R. J. (1960). *Psychiatric Dictionary* (3rd ed.). New York: Oxford Univ. Press.

HSU, F. L. K. (1949). Suppression versus repression. *Psychiat.*, 12:223-242.

LAPLANCHE, G. & PONTALIS, J. B. (1973). *The Language of Psychoanalysis*. New York: Norton.

MEISSNER, W. W. (1980). Theories of personality and psychopathology: classical psychoanalysis. In *Comprehensive Textbook of Psychiatry* (3rd ed.), ed. H. I. Kaplan & A. M. Freedman. Baltimore: Williams & Wilkins.

ONIONS, C. T., Ed. (1955). *Oxford Universal Dictionary* (3rd ed.). Oxford: Clarendon Press.

RYCROFT, C. (1968). *A Critical Dictionary of Psychoanalysis*. Middlesex, Eng.: Penguin, 1977.

VAILLANT, G. E. (1977). *Adaptation to Life*. Boston: Little Brown.

WINNICOTT, D. W. (1960). Counter-transference. In *The Maturational Processes and the Facilitating Environment*. New York: Int. Univ. Press, 1965, pp. 158-165.

Department of Psychiatry
Box 3812
Duke University Medical Center
Durham, North Carolina 27710

SPECIAL OFFER
20% Discount

CUMULATIVE INDEX,
Volumes 1 through 22 (1953–1974),
Journal of the
American Psychoanalytic Association

This Index has been designed with two principal criteria in mind: comprehensiveness and convenience.

It consists of a Subject Index organized so that page references within each subject category are grouped chronologically and by author; a Tracings Abstracts section, intended primarily as a screening device, which lists, alphabetically by author, all the articles that have appeared in the *Journal* and, through subcategories, gives a picture of the essential contents of each article. Users will thereby be able to determine whether they wish to consult the article in question. A third section of the Index contains the Tables of Contents of each of the twenty-two volumes of the *Journal.*

For those who do not subscribe to the *Journal* as well as for those who do, this *Index* provides an invaluable survey of the contents of its twenty-two volumes.

	Individuals		Institutions	
	Reg. Price	20% Discount	Reg. Price	20% Discount
Soft cover	$40.00	$32.00	$50.00	$40.00
Hard cover	$55.00	$44.00	$62.50	$29.60

Please add $2.75 for postage and handling.

INTERNATIONAL UNIVERSITIES PRESS, INC.
315 Fifth Avenue • New York, N.Y. 10016

NAME INDEX

Abend, S. M. 185–186, 189, 192, 199
Abraham, K., 151, 171, 252, 271
Adler, 154
Aichhorn, 74, 87
Ainsworth, M. D. S., 277, 297
Alexander, R., 154, 171
Alston, T. M., 356, 372
Altschul, S., 307, 322, 323
Arlow, J. A., 12, 148, 171, 236, 243, 244, 293, 297

Bak, R., 180, 184, 190
Bate, W. J., 406, 414
Baudry, 231, 240, 241
Bell, S. M., 277, 297
Benjamin, J. D., 289, 297
Beres, D., 241
Berger, A., 19
Berger, M., 42, 50, 51, 57, 62, 66, 75, 81, 115–116, 139
Bergman, A., 273, 403
Berman, L., 362, 372
Bibring, E., 360, 368, 372
Bibring, G. L., 204, 205, 206, 212, 218–219, 224
Biven, L, 19
Blau, S., 350
Blum, H. P., 5–17, 156, 171, 265, 271, 301–322, 327, 350, 370, 372
Boatman, B., 329, 350
Bockoven, J. S., 406, 414
Boesky, D., 227–244
Bornstein, B., 287, 297
Brenner, C., 12, 149, 162, 163, 165, 171, 177, 179, 193, 196, 199, 212, 217–218, 219–220, 224, 234, 242, 243, 244, 293, 297, 405, 407, 413, 414
Breuer, J., 150, 171, 201, 224, 325, 350
Browning, D., 329, 350

Calef, V., 235, 243, 244

Calogeres, R., 356, 372
Campbell, D., 19
Campbell, R. J., 407, 415
Chess, S., 400, 403
Compton, A., 229, 244

Deutsch, H., 178, 306, 322
Dunn. P., 303, 323
Dwyer, T. F., 224

Edgecumbe, R., 19, 68–69
Eidelberg, L., 408, 409, 414
Eissler, K., 98
Elkan. I., 19, 92
Emde, R., 290, 291, 297
Engel, G., 306, 322
Erikson, E., 8, 17, 153, 171, 353–371, 372
Evans, R., 19, 55, 60

Fairbairn, W. R. D., 179, 199
Fenichel, O., 12, 74–75, 148, 163, 166, 171, 179, 199, 232–234, 244, 247, 248, 258–259, 266, 267, 270, 271
Ferenczi, S., 125, 151, 172, 264, 271, 346–347, 350, 355, 369, 372
Fine, B., 179, 195, 199
Fleming, J., 307, 323
Fraiberg, S., 277, 297, 383, 402
Frank, A., 375–402
Freedman, A. M., 415
French, T. M., 154, 171
Freud, A., 2, 6, 7, 8, 9, 10, 11, 12, 13, 15, 16, 17, 19–146, 152, 153, 154, 164, 165, 166, 172, 178–179, 183, 190, 199, 201, 203, 204, 221, 222, 224, 232, 235, 244, 278, 286, 291, 292, 293, 295, 297, 301, 302, 309, 323, 376, 402, 407, 414
Freud, S., 5, 6, 10, 11, 12, 13, 14, 15, 16, 17, 44, 46, 47, 71, 150, 151, 152, 154, 156, 158, 162, 163, 164,

SUBJECT INDEX

Acting out, 26–30
Action
  character and, 238–239
  language of, 356–357
  in psychoanalytic process, 354–360
Activity-passivity in working through, 363–371
Adaptations, 102
  aggression in separation-individuation, 291–292
  to parent loss, 311–312
Adaptive mechanisms, defense mechanisms vs, 219
Adjustment and id resistance, 398–399
Affection, 357–360
Affective dominance, 261–262
Affects
  defense against, 14, 21–22, 30–32
  internalization of prohibition against, 76–77
  isolation of, 60
  localization of, 166
  in psychoanalytic therapy, 354–355
  separation of, model for, 165ı
Aggression
  in separation-individuation, 273–297
  turned inward, against self, 73, 79–80, 105–112
Aggressive behavior, 292–295
  definition of, 274
Aggressive drive, 292–295
Aggressive instinct
  evidence inconsistent with Freud, 401
  evidence of excesses of, 385
Aggressive wishes, reaction formations against, 122–123
Agoraphobia, projection in, 69–70
Ambivalence, term, 105
Amnesias, childhood, 185
Anal child, 62
Analyst
  aim of, 19–20

use of own emotional reaction, 265
Analyzability, id resistance and, 396–397
Anger, 293–294
Anniversary depressions in parent loss, 319–320
Anxiety, 165–166
  defensive or adaptive value of, 119
  in parent loss, 313–314
  unconscious, 59
Arts and sublimation, 89, 90
Atrocities, 67
Avoidance, 115–121
Autonomy, 33

Beating fantasy, 15
Biting impulse, inhibition of, 125

Censorship, 134
Character; *see also* entries beginning Character
  analysis, 33–34, 235–238, 258–266
  ego and, 239–240
  definitions of, 228–233
  impulse-ridden, 96
  reaction formation and, 121–122
  repertory of defenses of, 242
  resistance, 21, 227–244
  self and, 239–240
  structure of, 243–244
  symptoms and, 242–243
  transference and, 34–35
Character traits, 227, 229, 240–242
  action and, 238–239
  ego-syntonic aspect of, 241–242
  of facetiousness, 237–238
  neurotic symptoms vs neurotic, 243
  pathological, 248–249, 268–269
  in transference, 259–266
childhood amnesias, 185
Children/child
  anal, 62
  analysis of, 21, 31, 93